GEOGRAPHIES OF MUSLIM WOMEN

Geographies of
MUSLIM WOMEN
Gender, Religion, and Space

Edited by
GHAZI-WALID FALAH
CAROLINE NAGEL

THE GUILFORD PRESS
New York   London

Last digit is print number: 9 8 7 6 5 4 3 2 1

Library of Congress Cataloging-in-Publication Data

Geographies of Muslim women : gender, religion, and space / edited by
Ghazi-Walid Falah & Caroline Nagel.
    p. cm.
  ISBN 1-57230-134-1 (pbk.) — ISBN 1-59385-183-9 (cloth)
  1. Muslim women. 2. Women—Legal status, laws, etc.—Islamic countries.
3. Human geography. I. Falah, Ghazi-Walid. II. Nagel, Caroline Rose.
  HQ1170.G44 2005
  305.48′697—dc22
                                                            2004028841

For Mohammad-Allam and Philippa

Contents

Part III. Discourse, Representation, and the Contestation of Space

GEOGRAPHIES OF MUSLIM WOMEN

Introduction

CAROLINE NAGEL

In January 2004 thousands of Muslim women took to the streets in Cairo, Tehran, Gaza, Amman, and Beirut to protest efforts by French authorities to ban the *hijab*, or Islamic headscarf, in state schools and other public institutions. A photograph published in the *Economist* shows a group of young veiled protestors in Beirut holding a French tricolor (which flew over that city for three decades after World War I) emblazoned with the words "*Le Voile: Droit et Liberté*" (The Veil: Right and Freedom). In France itself Muslim women protestors similarly waved the tricolor and sang the "Marseillaise" while carrying banners with slogans such as "The veil: my choice" and "Beloved France, where is my liberty?" ("Veil of Tears," 2004, p. 34).

The French government has maintained for several years now that its policies to restrict the wearing of religious attire in schools is not anti-Islamic, but rather that it reflects France's historical commitment to secularism in the public sphere. Indeed, the ban covers not just the *hijab*, but also Jewish skullcaps (or *yarmulkes*) and "large" Christian crosses. But many Muslims in France and beyond remain unconvinced by the French government's position, and French authorities have been compelled to defend the official line both to French Muslims and to Muslim leaders abroad.

The French authorities' sense of embattlement has been heightened by criticism of the French headscarf policy from politicians on the other side of the Atlantic. Seizing the opportunity to challenge French moral authority in the wake of the U.S. invasion of Iraq, which France vehemently opposed, U.S. officials have criticized France for not adhering to its own revolutionary principle of individual liberty. The Bush administration, having used

1

the imagery of women in *burqas* in 2001 to condemn the oppressiveness of the Taliban regime and to justify military action in Afghanistan, has more recently championed the Muslim headscarf, declaring publicly that such religious displays constitute "a basic right that should be protected" ("Chirac Backs Law . . . ," 2003, p. A17). The U.S. Department of Justice, in particular, which has been otherwise noted for the targeting and harassment of Muslim immigrants in the name of "antiterrorism," has emerged as the great advocate of Muslim women and their right to veil. In 2004, for instance, the U.S. Department of Justice filed a motion in a federal district court in support of a Muslim girl in Oklahoma who had been suspended from school for wearing her *hijab*. In the words of an assistant attorney general, "No student should be forced to choose between following her faith and enjoying the benefits of a public education. . . . Religious discrimination has no place in American schools" (U.S. Department of Justice, 2004).

Several observations can be made about this evolving controversy. First and foremost, the headscarf issue in France and the tremendous political response it has engendered worldwide, both among ordinary people and among powerful politicians, is indicative of the centrality of women in long-standing cultural politics that span and link together the Muslim world and the West (Abu-Lughod, 2002). Clearly, the headscarf debate in France is not simply about what French Muslim girls wear in French state schools. Instead, Muslim girls and their attire have become a flashpoint in wider debates about the relative worth of Western and Muslim culture that have taken place since the era of European colonialism (Ahmed, 1992; Fleuhr-Lobban, 1993). The gender discourses of European colonialism, which assumed the inferiority of Arab and Muslim societies and which attributed the colonial subjugation of these societies to the supposedly lowly, cloistered status of Muslim women, generated a great deal of soul searching and debate in the colonized Muslim world. For some religious scholars and social reformers, the emancipation and revival of Muslim societies required the transformation of women's roles in society through education, legislative reform, and, perhaps more symbolically, the abolition of the veil. For others, the rebirth of Muslim societies and freedom from Western domination required the achievement of greater cultural authenticity and stricter adherence to gender roles prescribed by Islam (see Baron, 1994). In the postcolonial era, these gender-centered debates continued and indeed intensified as newly independent states struggled to set forth a new path of economic, political, and social development (Haddad, 1998; Hatem, 1995; Hijab, 1998). At the same time, the growth of Muslim populations in Europe through labor migration and subsequent family reunification brought the "woman question" to the West itself. Today issues relating to women and gender—for instance, headscarves, sex segregation in schools, and arranged marriages—remain intertwined with discussions about the assimilability of Muslims and Islam in Western societies.

In the post-September 11 geopolitical context, these cultural politics appear ever more complex. While some commentators—Muslim and non-Muslim—speak in dualistic terms of a "clash of civilizations" between Islam and the West, the actual political engagement between Muslims and non-Muslims reveals a multitude of contradictions and ambiguities. Thus, as we see with the recent headscarf controversies in France and elsewhere, Muslim women are using the language of religious freedom, citizenship, and universal human rights to defend practices like veiling, which some see as inimical to Western secularism and liberalism (Soysal, 1997). At the same time, the United States asserts its commitment to liberal democratic values and defends its military intervention in Muslim regions by championing Muslim women's cultural practices.

Another observation that emerges from the recent headscarf controversy is that while women have typically been objectified in the cultural politics of Islam and the West, they are also increasingly visible and active in shaping gender discourses or practices. One important set of voices to emerge in recent years has been that of Islamic feminists who have sought to reclaim the emancipatory message of the Qur'an and to recover the rights bestowed upon them in the earliest Muslim communities. Islamic feminist viewpoints have often defied Western conceptions of feminist politics by contesting male-dominated interpretations of Islam and the subjugation of women while at the same time embracing gender divisions as natural and desirable (Hatem, 1998; Poya, 1999). To be sure, many of those women involved in the protests to support the headscarf might not think of themselves as "Islamic feminists," as Islamist, or even as participants in a political movement. Yet they are intent upon publicly reclaiming Islam on their own terms, and in a manner, as described above, that draws upon a variety of political discourses.

But despite the growing visibility of veiling practices in the Muslim world and the West, it must be emphasized that not all Muslim women advocate the incorporation of Islam into public life. In fact, while the controversy at hand has been portrayed as one pitting Muslims against a secular (and anti-Islamic) French state, a recent survey reported by the *Economist* ("Veil of Tears," 2004) suggests that more French Muslim women support the headscarf ban than oppose it. It also appears that the debate has led to conflicts within major Muslim organizations in France, as Muslim groups grapple in different ways with competing imperatives of secularism and religious freedoms and obligations. This leads us to a final observation that the voices and viewpoints of Muslim women and Muslims more generally need to be understood as highly differentiated and not easily reducible to notions of "religion" or "culture." There is no single perspective among

Muslims on any political or social issue, just as there is no single perspective among Christians or any other group.

ABOUT THIS VOLUME

By highlighting the centrality of Muslim women's position in the gendered cultural politics taking place within and between the West and Muslim countries, their complex and often ambiguous roles within these cultural politics, and the diversity of their voices and viewpoints, the French headscarf controversy underscores our motivation for putting together this collection of writings on Muslim women. The contributions to this volume reflect the important efforts by feminist scholars in various disciplines to elucidate the contentious position of women and gender relations in the Muslim world and in the geopolitical engagement between Western and Muslim societies. This scholarship has taken the category of "Muslim woman," so often invoked in public debate and discourse, and has sought to destabilize it by revealing the ways in which women's lives are complicated by economic inequalities and class relations, distinctive regional cultural practices, and ideologies of race and ethnicity (Kandiyoti, 1996; Khan, 2000). As such, this scholarship has emphasized that Muslim women's experiences are not definable solely in religious terms, and that Islam itself serves as a repertoire of social practices and ideals articulated in different historical and geographical contexts, rather than as a monolithic belief system with causal power (Moghadam, 1993). Muslim women's experiences, we have been urged to recognize, are, like all women's experiences, ambiguous and highly variable, marked by subordination and opportunity, mobility and immobility, security and insecurity.

This book attempts to build upon this scholarship by presenting specifically geographical perspectives on the experiences of Muslim women. The discipline of geography, as many geographers concede, is rather difficult to define, as it encompasses a multitude of subfields that, to many outside observers, seem to bear no relation to one another. The contributions to this volume represent a wide range of disciplinary subfields and perspectives— cultural geography, political geography, development studies, migration studies, and historical geography—each with its own set of debates and methodologies. But what is common to geography scholars is a concern with space and place, and, more specifically, with (1) the way in which social relationships are inscribed in and organized through space—be it the space of a home, a village, a nation-state, or the globe; (2) the way in which specific places become imbued with particular social meanings; and (3) the way in which the meanings and representations associated with certain places are contested, negotiated, and transformed through individual and collective action. Geographical themes have emerged in a great deal of recent literature about Muslim women—most clearly in discussions about women's use of various veiling practices to negotiate and to transform the nature of public space (e.g., El Guindi, 1999; also see Ask & Tjomsland, 1998; Macleod, 1991). But, for the most part, the spatiality of gender relations, identities, and practices has seldom been explicitly theorized or made the focus of attention. The aim of this book therefore is to bring issues of space and place to the forefront of accounts of Muslim women's lived experience in a variety of regional contexts.

While the purpose of compiling this volume is to explore the complex spatiality of women's lives, it must be recognized that this venture carries the risk of validating the very category of "Muslim women" that it seeks to unhinge. There are few social categories today that generate as much interest, attention, and scrutiny as that of "Muslim women." To illustrate, in 2001, an informal book search I conducted on Amazon.com generated a list of 292 publications on Muslim women. In contrast, a search on Hindu women generated only 47 books (Nagel, 2001). In 2004, in the wake of the "War on Terrorism," I repeated this exercise and found that the number of publications on Muslim women had increased to 383, while the publications on Hindu women had increased more modestly, to 58. If the public's fascination with Muslim women seems boundless, so too is the capacity for scholars and popular commentators to analyze their lives and experiences, largely for the benefit of non-Muslims.

So while I have relished the opportunity to coedit a book about the geographies of Muslim women, I have also been acutely aware that this volume may further reify the category of "Muslim woman," thereby reducing the identities and experiences of these women to their religious affiliation. Yet, as with many contentious social categories, the social currency of the "Muslim woman" category—not least of all in the eyes of many Muslim women for whom Islam serves as a moral code and a source of identity—requires that it be addressed as such, even as it is shown to be highly problematic. In the present political climate, in which Muslim women more than ever are subject to stereotypes, negative representations, and constant scrutiny within their own societies and by others, it becomes important to present more complicated readings of the Muslim woman category, even if this means, in a sense, legitimating the category itself.

A final issue to be raised is that only a few of the contributors to this volume are themselves Muslim women, reflecting the underrepresentation of Muslim women in geography and other social science disciplines. The limited presence of Muslim women in this volume and in the academy more generally is highly problematic given the amount of literature generated about them, and it raises troubling questions about the accuracy and representativeness of accounts given of Muslim women's lives. At the heart of the matter is who controls the production of knowledge—that is, the formulation of research questions, the gathering and interpretation of data, and the validation and publication of findings—about Muslim women. *How* is knowledge being produced, *who* is producing it, and for *whose* consumption?

Such issues have been the subject of intensive discussion at least since the 1980s, when feminist scholars began to challenge notions of objectivity and scholarly detachment found in mainstream social science approaches (Haraway, 1988; Harding, 1991). As a result of such critiques, many feminists have adopted a reflexive approach to research that considers the ways in which the researcher's position in various social categories and hierarchies (e.g., class, "race," and gender) affects research encounters (e.g., McDowell, 1992; Moss, 2002). While embracing reflexivity in research, however, feminists have also questioned their own ability to truly elucidate the complex relationships involved in the research process. Some have suggested that being an "insider" in a particular group gives one greater insight and authority to speak about that group (Collins, 1991). But others argue that identities and human interactions are so complex and contingent on different circumstances that the impact of the researcher's social position can never fully be elucidated or understood (Rose, 1997). So while they have not abandoned reflexivity, feminist researchers have increasingly suggested that one is never fully an insider or fully an outsider, but usually some combination therein, giving the researcher access and insight in some respects but only a very partial understanding of a particular research subject in other respects (Mullings, 1999).

What this means is that the outcome of any research encounter is inevitably incomplete, regardless of the authorship. Each contributor to this volume, whether male or female, Muslim or non-Muslim, has brought to his or her research different viewpoints, experiences, and identities that have shaped the knowledge presented in the chapters. While we maintain that the lack of visibility of Muslim women in this volume is highly problematic and indicative of wider inequalities in the production of knowledge about Islam and women, we also reject the notion that having a particular identity gives any scholar privileged access to knowledge or total authority to speak on behalf of others. I would therefore urge readers (as have several of the contributors) to approach these accounts not as the definitive expert "truth" about Muslim women, but as limited, unfinished accounts that are subject to multiple interpretations, including your own.

THE CONTRIBUTIONS

This collection has been divided into three main sections addressing different geographical themes. These divisions are somewhat arbitrary, in that there are many common themes *across* sections and many differences *within* them in terms of the contexts, issues, and experiences being described. But each section reflects a particular cluster of research in geography and is intended to expose readers to some of the different theoretical approaches and empirical concerns that have been brought to bear on this topic.

Gender, Development, and Religion

The first set of chapters considers the intersections between gender, development, and religion. Geographers have played an important role in critiquing mainstream models of "Third World" development and uncovering the unequal power relations inherent in the development programs often imposed on the global South (Routledge, 1995; Slater, 1995). Feminist geographers, in particular, have been instrumental in illustrating the gendered character of development policies in terms of their formulation, implementation, and outcomes (see, e.g., Chant & Gutmann, 2002; Lawson, 1998; Radcliffe, 1999). Such concerns have often led feminist geographers to explore local experience and the ways in which policies, often generated at a national or a global scale, are mediated and transformed by, as well as transformative of, gender divisions of labor and women's access to resources at more localized scales (e.g., Rocheleau, 1995).

The authors of the four chapters in this section examine the intersections between gender relations and development processes as they are mediated by Islamic practices and discourses. Sarah J. Halvorson's study of Gilgit, a community in northern Pakistan, for instance, uncovers the different life options made available to boys and girls as households face more intensive marketization. In her conversations with Gilgit's mothers, Halvorson finds that girls are becoming increasingly important to household and farm management as families become more dependent on local and external cash economies and markets. But the increasing value placed on girls' labor does not necessarily translate into expanded opportunities for them. While some girls are able to take advantage of new educational and employment opportunities, it is usually boys who are given familial resources to gain the education necessary to secure off-farm employment. Indeed, the region's growing religious conservativism—reflecting ideological influences from Iran and Saudi Arabia—has, in some instances, placed girls' behavior under greater scrutiny, thereby increasing constraints on their spatial mobility.

The ambivalences of development processes described by Halvorson are also highlighted in Naheed Gina Aaftaab's chapter on girls' education in post-Taliban Afghanistan. The overthrow of the Taliban was widely viewed, especially in the West, as a victory for Afghanistan's oppressed women, and many anticipated an improving "quality of life" for women as a result of their expanding educational opportunities. Yet in Afghanistan, Aaftaab suggests, new institutions for women's education appear to be reinforcing culturally and religiously sanctioned roles for women rather than freeing them from such constraints. Insofar as rural communities look favorably upon female education, it is to improve girls' marriageability and domestic competency in the private sphere rather than their employability in the public sphere. The main change engendered by the education system, from Aaftaab's perspective, is not "freedom" and mobility in a Western sense, but rather women's enhanced ability to navigate existing social systems and spaces in ways not imagined by liberal development discourses.

Diana K. Davis's chapter also deals with Afghanistan, and, like Aaftaab's chapter, reveals the limitations of mainstream development discourses and the unintended consequences of Western-led policies. Revisiting research on livestock management programs in rural, nomadic communities conducted prior to the rise of the Taliban, Davis argues that such programs tended to disempower women, as they operated under the assumption that Muslim women are not significantly involved with the raising of livestock. In post-Taliban Afghanistan, the Western-led development agenda, which is focused on privatization and commercialization, is more likely to hurt rural women by eroding their basis of subsistence than to free them from oppression. Moreover, the growing control over rural areas by so-called warlords, many of whom uphold deeply conservative interpretations of Islam and women's roles in society, is likely to further curtail women's productive spaces and capacities. Socially just development programs, Davis concludes, need to consider the ways in which gender divisions of labor and attitudes toward women and their work in particular communities may differ markedly from the views espoused by either conservative Islamic leaders or Western development agencies.

Susanne H. Steinmann's research on sedentarized pastoralist communities in eastern Morocco reiterates Davis's point that standard discourses about gender roles and gender segregation in Muslim society—discourses propounded both in the West and in the Muslim world—fail to capture the ways in which gender divisions of labor and gendered spaces are constantly negotiated in particular contexts. Steinmann's study of the sedentarization of the Beni Guil people in two towns uncovers distinctive land-use patterns and gender divisions of labor. In one town Steinmann notes the increasing importance of agricultural—rather than pastoral—livelihoods and of women's work in household gardens, while in the other town she observes the growing reliance on men's labor migration and women's investments in livestock. In both instances, gender roles and identities have been negotiated in different ways that simultaneously challenge and uphold established patterns and discourses of Islamic gender relations.

Geographies of Mobility

The second section of this volume deals with issues of mobility and migration, which in the present era invariably include transnational identities and linkages. The first two chapters engage with new theoretical approaches to migration that complicate the view of migrants as individual, rational, economic actors by focusing on the ways in which gender relations, political structures, cultural ideologies, and economic processes intersect to shape migration flows and experiences (e.g., Lawson, 1998, 2000). The third chapter in this section examines the labor market experiences of "second-generation" women living in the diaspora—in this case, the Pakistani diaspora in Britain. For the authors of these chapters, as for other feminist migration researchers, the use of migrants' personal narratives becomes crucial to understanding how everyday decision making takes place at the intersection between gender, culture, and political–economic processes (e.g., Dwyer, 2000; Yeoh & Khoo, 1998).

Rachel Silvey's chapter, to begin, examines the growing number of low-income Indonesian women—most from rural areas of Java—migrating to Saudi Arabia as domestic servants. Silvey's research focuses on the ways in which religious beliefs and practices, which intersect with gender roles and ideologies, inform and shape every aspect of the mobility experience. She notes, for instance, that the recruitment of Indonesian women often takes place in girls' Islamic boarding schools, where strict religious observance and the teaching of Arabic are viewed as producing ideal workers for the Saudi labor force. That Saudi Arabia is strictly Muslim—unlike other potential destinations in Asia—and that working there brings the possibility of making the pilgrimage to Mecca, serve as selling points for recruiters, who must counteract frequent testimonies of hardship and abuse in the Gulf. At the same time, the Indonesian state has built on the moral authority of Islam to encourage the migration of these young women. Specifically, it has recast the ideal of the domestically located Muslim wife and mother to include the migratory income-earning woman, who is portrayed as sacrificing her own interests for the sake of national economic development. The migration of Indonesian women, then, is not simply a matter of pure economic calculation on the part of individual migrants. Instead, it reflects the confluence of economic need, religious identity, gender discourses, and state development aims.

Amy Freeman's chapter similarly critiques traditional economistic analyses of migration and examines how Moroccan women's mobility—both transnational and more localized—is both constrained and enabled by cultural and religious practices and discourses, and by one's material circumstances. Freeman is particularly interested in the idea of "freedom," and she notes that in the Muslim world—as in the West—anxieties about women's freedom have been related to the desire to control, socially and spatially, women's sexuality to ensure their purity. But she, like other contributors to this volume, cautions against rigid views of gender segregation and public/private dichotomies, arguing that the "moral geographies" in which Muslim women are situated are, in some ways, fluid and open to interpretation. Thus, she shows that women, particularly those in migratory and transnational situations, constantly move in and out of geographies where "freedom" takes on different meanings and where they must adjust their behavior to accommodate different norms. For the most part, Freeman's interviewees express a desire for greater freedom to control their own lives and mobility, but they also reject notions of freedom that imply disregard for community norms and religious beliefs.

The construction and negotiation of transnational moral geographies is also a key theme of Robina Mohammad's chapter on Pakistani-origin women in Great Britain. For Mohammad, the continuous interchange between Pakistani communities in Great Britain and the homeland has reinforced a conservative interpretation of Islam among British Pakistanis that posits women as guardians of collective identity and that requires the regulation of women's spatiality. For young British Muslim women, the emphasis on female purity has a profound influence on educational outcomes and labor force participation. Mohammad finds that women from less educated backgrounds seem to face much tighter spatial constraints than those from better educated backgrounds, who may be permitted to pursue higher education away from home. In general, though, the types of jobs that young British Pakistani women perform are circumscribed by community imperatives to control women's presence in public spaces, and women's ability to pursue and to advance in particular careers requires their careful negotiation of parental and communal strictures.

Discourse, Representation, and the Contestation of Space

While all of the chapters discussed thus far deal in some way with the production and circulation of discourse, the final set of chapters focuses more directly on the representation of Islam, gender, and Muslim women by the media, government officials, novelists, and Muslim women themselves. Discourse and representation, of course, are not simply about imagery and descriptive language. Instead, these concepts make reference to systems of power that operate to shape knowledge of other people and places and, in many cases, to justify political domination and social inequalities (Said, 1978). While certain discourses and representations can be thought of as hegemonic or dominant in any given context, these are always subject to the challenge of alternative ways of seeing and knowing. Geographers have been especially keen to explore the ways in which dominant discourses and representations are enacted by—and contested through—spatial practices (e.g., Anderson, 1991; Cresswell, 1996; Nagar, 2000), and the authors of the following chapters examine different kinds of spatial conflicts that emerge from competing articulations of Islam and gender relations.

Anna Secor's chapter, for instance, explains the intense debate over the wearing of the headscarf in public spaces in Turkey. For those sympathizing with Islamist movements, the Turkish state's restriction on the wearing of the veil in certain public spaces in the name of state secularism calls into question the state's commitment to democratic freedoms. As with the women protestors described at the beginning of this Introduction, Secor's interviewees speak of veiling not so much as a religious imperative, but as a basic human right that cannot be denied by the state. Yet the articulation of the headscarf as a human right belies complicated ideas about democracy at the heart of Islamist discourse. For the advocacy of the right to wear the headscarf in public is not necessarily accompanied by a more general desire to abolish regulatory regimes of public dress and behavior. Instead, for many of those participating in Secor's study, the state's views on headscarves becomes proof of the need to Islamicize the public sphere—precisely what the Turkish state and many secularists are seeking to avoid by exercising rigid control over public space.

Abdi Ismail Samatar's account of the formation of a women's mosque in the Somali town of Gabiley presents a very different instance of the contestation of Islamic space. In the early 1960s, Samatar shows, the education of girls had become a topic of intense debate in Gabiley, as government efforts to promote girls' education clashed with local discourses about girls' natural role as future housewives. Into this fray in the 1970s stepped Sheikh Marian, a female Islamic scholar who brought religious education to local women—a prerequisite for entry into state schools. A women's mosque was built under her leadership, but it continued to lack the support of local townsmen, even after it was damaged in the civil unrest of the 1980s. At the heart of the controversy over the women's mosque, Samatar argues, has been a conflict over views of women's rightful geographical place and their place within Islam. As Samatar notes, the women who built the mosque were not informed by Western feminist ideology or by anti-Islamic sentiment. Rather, "they felt that Islamic practice in this society unduly restricted women's opportunities to learn and interpret Islamic texts and traditions," and the radicalism of this project lay in its questioning of the marginalization of women in local Islamic practice.

Like other contributions in this collection, Malek Abisaab's chapter questions dichotomous conceptions of public–private space that dominate the literature on women in Arab/Muslim societies. Contrary to many accounts that situate Arab and Muslim women squarely in the private domestic sphere, Abisaab explores the urban factory as "women's space" and as a site of gendered struggles. His account focuses on the 1970 strike involving female tobacco factory workers in Lebanon and the ways in which Arab women in Lebanon—both Muslim and Christian—resisted public–private dichotomies in their demands to be included in societal conceptions of factory as well as home. The particular shape their activism took, Abisaab shows, reflected the integration of their factory labor with their roles and experiences outside the industrial workplace, thus calling into question the division of space in Arab and Muslim societies into discrete male and female realms.

Marc Brosseau and Leila Ayari's chapter is distinctive in its use of fiction—specifically, novels written by Tunisian women—to explore representations of Muslim women and their geographies. Brosseau and Ayari note the ambivalence with which Tunisian women writers view practices of gender segregation experienced by many middle-class Arab/Muslim women. The female characters often view their childhood homes with great nostalgia and tenderness, and yet, as adult women, bristle against their own sense of isolation in the home and the feeling that their presence on the street is an intrusion on men's space. The novels also speak to women's ability to transgress spaces by describing instances in which female characters covertly or openly defy gender boundaries. In doing so, their work resonates with Malek Abisaab's critical approach to understanding public and private space. Paralleling Amy Freeman's analysis of transnational Moroccan women and Abdi Ismail Samatar's interpretation of the Somali women's mosque, the authors caution against reading these novels as radically feminist accounts of Muslim women's lives, and suggest that the authors desire a middle ground "which accommodates respect for tradition as well as a woman's need for empowerment and equality."

The final chapter in the collection is Ghazi-Walid Falah's analysis of the visual representation of Muslim women in American newspapers between September 11, 2001, and the start of the U.S. attack on Iraq in the spring of 2003. Falah's main concern is the way in which supposedly objective reporting may in fact serve to promote particular geopolitical discourses and agendas. Falah's survey of scores of newspaper photographs reveals that images of women and girls tend to revolve around a few key themes—for instance, women's victimization at the hands of "terrorists" or the slavish adulation of corrupt leaders. Significantly, editors seem inclined to insert such images into articles that have little or nothing to do with gender or women's issues. The common deployment of these images, Falah suggests, projects a view of Arab and Muslim societies as foreign, irrational, and in need of Western civilization and enlightenment. Even where editors are critical of U.S. military intervention in various Muslim contexts, these images, in a sense, validate such intervention, while at the same time hiding from view the root causes of conflict in Arab and Muslim states.

IN CLOSING

The diversity of topics, themes, regional contexts, and research approaches covered by the contributions to this volume provide some indication of the myriad challenges, dilemmas, and opportunities faced by Muslim women today. In presenting such a diversity of accounts our aim has been to complicate understandings of Muslim women and to reveal the different ways Islamic discourse and practice intersect with gender relations and wider political and economic processes to shape women's geographies.

As indicated in the title, this volume makes a special attempt to explore the ways in which religious beliefs, institutions, practices, and discourses shape women's spatiality. Religion has taken center stage in many popular accounts of global cultural change and conflict (e.g., Samuel Huntington's *Clash of Civilizations* [1996] and Benjamin Barber's *Jihad versus McWorld* [1996]). Yet religion remains curiously absent from many academic accounts of cultural transformation, especially in the discipline of geography. It is our hope that this volume helps to remedy this situation by making religion a more explicit factor in analyses of human experience and spatiality, while at the same time countering views of religion as a monolithic entity or "civilizational" force. The significance of Islam—and indeed, any belief system—varies a great deal between and within societies, and should not be treated as a causal force in and of itself, a point that seems to be lost on many contemporary social commentators both in the West and in predominantly Muslim societies. Our intention is that this volume, against the tide of current events and contemporary discourse, enables and encourages dialogue between Muslims and non-Muslims, men and women, and helps them to identify commonalities in their experiences rather than only difference and otherness.

REFERENCES

Abu-Lughod, L. (2002). Do Muslim women really need saving?: Anthropological reflections on cultural relativism and its others. *American Anthropologist, 104*(3), 783–790.

Ahmed, L. (1992). *Women and gender in Islam: Historical roots of a modern debate.* New Haven, CT: Yale University Press.

Anderson, K. (1991). *Vancouver's Chinatown: Racial discourse in Canada, 1875–1980.* Montreal and Kingston, Canada: McGill–Queen's University Press.

Ask, K., & Tjomsland, M. (Eds.). (1998). *Women and Islamization: Contemporary dimensions of discourse on gender relations.* Oxford, UK, and New York: Berg.

Barber, B. (1996). *Jihad vs. McWorld: How globalism and tribalism are reshaping the world.* New York: Ballantine Books.

Baron, B. (1994). *The women's awakening in Egypt: Culture, society, and the press.* New Haven, CT: Yale University Press.

Chant, S., & Gutmann, M. C. (2002). 'Men-streaming' gender?: Questions for gender and development policy in the 21st century. *Progress in Development Studies, 2*(4), 269–282.

Chirac backs law to keep signs of faith out of school. (2003, December 18, p. A17.). *The New York Times.*

Collins, P. H. (1991). Learning from the outsider within: The sociological significance of black feminist thought. In M. M. Fonow & J. Cook (Eds.), *Beyond methodology: Feminist scholarship as lived research* (pp. 35–59). Bloomington: Indiana University Press.

Cresswell, T. (1996). *In place/out of place: Geography, ideology, and transgression.* Minneapolis: University of Minnesota Press.

Dwyer, C. (2000). Negotiating diasporic identities: Young British South Asian Muslim women. *Women's Studies International Forum, 23,* 475–486.

El Guindi, F. (1999). *Veil: Modesty, privacy, and resistance.* Oxford, UK, and New York: Berg.

Fleuhr-Lobban, C. (1993). Toward a theory of Arab-Muslim women as activists in secular and religious movements. *Arab Studies Quarterly, 15,* 87–106.

Haddad, Y. Y. (1998). Islam and gender: Dilemmas in the changing Arab world. In Y. Y. Haddad & J. L. Esposito (Eds.), *Islam, gender and social change* (pp. 3–29). Oxford, UK: Oxford University Press.

Haraway, D. (1988). Situated knowledges: The science question in feminism and the privilege of the partial perspective. *Feminist Studies, 14,* 575–595.

Harding, S. (1991). *Whose science? Whose knowledge?* Ithaca, NY: Cornell University Press.

Hatem, M. (1995). Women in the post-modern Arab world. *Development, 2,* 26–29.

Hatem, M. (1998). Secularist and Islamist discourses on modernity in Egypt and the evolution of the post-colonial nation-state. In Y. Y. Haddad & J. L. Esposito (Eds.), *Islam, gender and social change* (pp. 85–99). Oxford, UK: Oxford University Press.

Hijab, N. (1998). Islam, social change, and the reality of Arab women's lives. In Y. Y. Haddad & J. L. Esposito (Eds.), *Islam, gender and social change* (pp. 45–55). Oxford, UK: Oxford University Press.

Huntington, S. (1996). *The clash of civilizations and the remaking of the world order.* New York: Simon & Schuster.

Kandiyoti, D. (Ed.) (1996). *Gendering the Middle East: Emerging perspectives.* Syracuse, NY: Syracuse University Press.

Khan, S. (2000). *Muslim women: Crafting a North American identity.* Gainesville: University Press of Florida.

Lawson, V. (1998). Hierarchical households and gendered migration: A research agenda. *Progress in Human Geography, 22,* 32–53.

Lawson, V. (2000). Arguments within geographies of movement: The theoretical potential of migrants' stories. *Progress in Human Geography, 24*(2), 173–189.

Macleod, A. E. (1991). *Accommodating protest: Working women, the new veiling, and change in Cairo.* New York: Columbia University Press.

McDowell, L. (1992). Doing gender: Feminism and feminist research methods in human geography. *Transactions of the Institute of British Geographers, 17,* 399–416.

Moghadam, V. (1993). *Modernizing women: Gender and social change in the Middle East.* Boulder, CO: Lynne Rienner.

Moss, P. (Ed.). (2002). *Feminist geography in practice.* Oxford, UK, and Malden, MA: Blackwell.

Mullings, B. (1999). Insider or outsider, both or neither: Some dilemmas of interviewing in a cross-cultural setting. *Geoforum, 30*(4), 337–350.

Nagar, R. (2000). I'd rather be rude than ruled: Gender, place, and communal politics among South Asian communities in Dar Es Salaam. *Women's Studies International Forum, 23*(5), 571–585.

Nagel, C. (2001). Contemporary scholarship and demystification—and remystification—of "Muslim women." *Arab World Geographer, 4*, 63–72.

Poya, M. (1999). *Women, work, and Islamism*. London and New York: Zed Books.

Radcliffe, S. A. (1999). Rethinking development. In P. Cloke, P. Crang, & M. Goodwin (Eds.), *Introducing human geographies* (pp. 84–92). London: Arnold.

Rocheleau, D. (1995). Maps, numbers, text, and context: Mixing methods in feminist political ecology. *Professional Geographer, 47*, 458–466.

Rose, G. (1997). Situating knowledges: Positionality, reflexivities, and other tactics. *Progress in Human Geography, 21*, 305–320.

Routledge, P. (1995). Resisting and reshaping the modern: Social movements and the development process. In R. J. Johnston, P. J. Taylor, & M. J. Watts (Eds.), *Geographies of global change: Remapping the world in the late twentieth century* (pp. 263–279). Oxford, UK: Blackwell.

Said, E. (1978). *Orientalism*. New York: Pantheon Books.

Slater, D. (1995). Trajectories of development theory: Capitalism, socialism and beyond. In R. J. Johnston, P. J. Taylor, & M. J. Watts (Eds.), *Geographies of global change: Remapping the world in the late twentieth century* (pp. 63–76). Oxford, UK: Blackwell.

Soysal, Y. N. (1997). Changing parameters of citizenship and claims-making: Organized Islam in European public spheres. *Theory and Society, 26*, 509–527.

U.S. Department of Justice (2004, March 30). *Justice Department files complaint against Oklahoma school district seeking to protect student's right to wear headscarf to public school* [press release]. Washington, DC: Author. Accessed online: *www.usdoj.gov/opa/pr/2004/March/04_crt_195.htm*

Veil of tears. (2004, January 17). *The Economist*, p. 34.

Yeoh, B., & Khoo, L. M. (1998). Home, work and community: Skilled international migration and expatriate women in Singapore. *International Migration, 36*(2), 159–186.

Part I

Gender, Development, and Religion

1 Growing Up in Gilgit

Exploring the Nature of Girlhood
in Northern Pakistan

SARAH J. HALVORSON

The geography of girlhood remains understudied in much of the so-called Islamic world. My aim in this chapter is to consider the relationship between Muslim girlhood and rural livelihood in a mountain community in the Islamic Republic of Pakistan. In recent decades this relationship has undergone a dramatic transformation as the mountainous northern part of the country has transitioned from a subsistence-based to a market-oriented economy. This transformation is acutely manifested in the deepening integration of the lives of rural girls into market and civil society relations of the global economy and the increasingly arduous and impoverished circumstances under which they work and contribute to their families' survival. One challenge presented by the unprecedented social transformation in mountain communities of northern Pakistan has to do with the complexities of "growing up" as the specific meanings of Muslim girlhood are (re)interpreted by families, secular and religious development actors, and the state.

The body of knowledge addressing the geographies of Muslim girls is fragmented and parallels the incomplete nature of evidence on Muslim women in the region (see, e.g., Kandiyoti, 1991; Papanek & Minault, 1982). In Pakistan relatively little has been written about girlhood or the role of female children in the history of the country's development trajectory. Additionally, very little scholarship has given attention to the role that religious discourse plays in shaping constructions of gendered childhoods and gendered spatial ranges at the local scale. While true of the historiography of development in Muslim societies in general, this lacuna presents special problems in a nation like Pakistan where Islam has long been the predominant social framework of a culturally and ethnically diverse population.

In this chapter different aspects of girls' lives are examined, including, first, the highly spatialized constructions of girlhood in a Muslim community, and second, the changing nature of girls' social relationships in the everyday spaces of the home, field, school, and community at large. The research described here took place between 1996 and 1998 in a mountain village near Gilgit, the regional capital of the Federally Administered Northern Areas, which is located near the northeastern border with China.[1] To explore the concept of girlhood, I carried out life histories of 30 women, all mothers of at least two children at the time, from a range of socioeconomic and religioethnic backgrounds. In all cases they were married and bearing children by their early or midteens, during which time their mobility within public spaces was sharply curtailed. The women belonged to one of two prominent sects among the Shiite Muslims who have settled in this region and who identify themselves as Shia or Ismaili. I conducted the interviews in respondents' homes while carrying out semiparticipant observation. Each life history interview was conducted either in Urdu or in one of two local languages—Shina or Burushaski—with the assistance of two local field assistants. Translations of the 4- to 6-hour taped interviews were done with the help of a professional translator. The life histories were supplemented with five focus-group interviews with community women, and shorter interviews and conversations with village elders, shopkeepers, community activists, religious leaders, teachers, development workers, and community health workers. I also analyzed policy documents and reports of state agencies and nongovernmental organizations (NGOs) working in the region.

The intent of the life history approach employed in this research is not to create a "representative" experience of girlhood in northern Pakistan. Rather, the narratives are intended to impart vital information about social and economic context, personal conceptualizations of childhood, and community values, thereby challenging dominant development paradigms, which tend to mask the very textured local-scale experience (Nagar, 1997; Personal Narratives Group, 1989). While this research is directed at exploring experiences that have been "out of sight" historically and geographically, the process of conveying these experiences raises complex questions about interpretation and representation. For example, some of the richness of individuals' expressions, language, and imagery is inevitably lost in translation. Furthermore, my retelling of these narratives within an academic framework represents another level of translation to make these narratives fit within a particular analytical framework. In spite of these shortcomings, it is out of these life histories that a local discourse connecting the meanings of childhood, Islamic ideals, gendered spatial ideology, and rural change emerges.

The discussion that follows draws on a discursive analysis of study participants' personal narratives to examine the embedding of girlhood in local and global processes over time. The associations between gender norms and expectations and the broader concerns about moral uprightness and the maintenance of codes of family honor have practical and ideological consequences for girls' geographies, including their use of space, the demands placed on their labor, and the opportunities they face as they grow older. Here I argue that an analytical focus on social change and its interactions with religious discourse can enable us to develop a nuanced perspective on girls' geographical experiences. This focus demonstrates how girls' lives are defined by the specific contexts of livelihood, gender relations, and religion, and how girlhood is constructed in relation to shifting views and visions of girls' place in rural mountain society.

The majority of the people in the Northern Areas of Pakistan face extreme isolation, limited income-generating opportunities, and deprivation in basic needs such as a proper diet and potable water (Streefland, Khan, & van Lieshout, 1995; World Bank, 1996). In spite of their marginal position geographically relative to the center, girls living in the relatively remote Northern Areas are integrally connected to processes of change within the country, particularly as they affect household livelihood systems, gender relations, and current religious transformations such as the rise of Islamism. The region as a whole is being increasingly integrated into the national economy, yet for the most part it remains on the periphery of national development initiatives. The manner in which girls in this mountainous area have been impacted by these forces and the ways in which these impacts are tied to current religious discourse and gender politics is less clear.

The argument in this chapter is that an adequate analysis of the position of girls in Muslim societies must be grounded in a detailed examination of socioeconomic and historical transformations. I propose that the operation of Islam in relation to discourses of girlhood is of central relevance to an understanding of the roles and position of girls in Pakistani society. The representation of children in national and local discourses, the modalities of children's participation in economic life, and the nature of the childrearing practices that lead to their socialization into adult roles are intimately linked to the conditions of Pakistan's current economic crisis and are responsive to the religiocultural context.

The chapter begins with a discussion of the theoretical framework of the research, which argues that a focus on gender and Islamic influences is critical for shedding light on the social construction of childhood in Muslim societies today. This section is followed by an overview of the national discourse regarding the relationship between "the girl child" and the state of Pakistan. Since girls also belong to families, neighborhoods, and communities, it is necessary to examine how adults, and in this case their mothers, conceptualize and influence their daughters' lives. Hence, the following section presents an analysis of women's narratives concerning their daughters' childhoods to shed light on what it means to be a Muslim girl and how this articulates with other discourses of work, mobility, religion, family, and future. In looking at the case of northern Pakistan I hope to broaden our thinking about child–society relations in an Islamic context as well as the shifts in girls' geographies as they become, and as their families and communities become, inserted into the global economy.

THEORETICAL FRAMEWORK: ENGENDERING MUSLIM CHILDHOOD

"In Islam a child belongs to everyone. A child does not just belong to one family. Everyone is responsible for looking after that child."

The above statement by an elderly man in the District of Gilgit recorded in the spring of 1998 serves as a starting point for theorizing connections between Islam and childhood that may help to account for the variations encountered in girls' circumstances within Pakistani society. Specific concepts of girls' and boys' roles have long-standing bases in Muslim cultural norms. Muslim children are trained early and at length in the tenets of Islam and the roles of Muslim men and women. In the case of Pakistan, Muslim norms have historically placed extensive restrictions on the lifeworlds of girls. As Sathar (2003, p. 41) puts it:

> For adolescent males, school, waged work, and recreation are likely to take up most of the day, while females are most likely to be involved in household chores with less time for going to school and little potential for recreation. Clearly, young females in Pakistan lack the opportunities of schooling, work, and recreation afforded to males. While males in urban and rural areas across socioeconomic groups have uneven opportunities as well, it is the gender differences that are most striking.

The idealized girl stays close to home, helps her mother, serves the boys and men in her family, takes care of her younger siblings, contributes to the family livelihood, and upholds the honor and reputation of the family. The "everyone" (i.e., the extended family and even neighbors) to whom the village elder refers in the quotation above is involved in socializing girls to adhere to these norms. Importantly, a girl is expected to emulate the behavior and attitude of adult Muslim women in conformance with *purdah*: the practice of modest behavior and seclusion from the view of men outside the family, described by Weiss (1998, p. 125) as "the practical as well as figurative curtain separating the everyday worlds of women and men." In many parts of Pakistan it is practiced through the use of veiling in public or through limited access to public space and limited mobility outside the home (Mumtaz & Shaheed, 1987).

The relationship between girls' status and *purdah* is highly complex and varied depending upon the sociocultural context within the country (Ibraz, 1993; Mumtaz & Fatima, 1992; Weiss, 2002). For the most part, this powerful ideology of seclusion begins to strictly define the parameters of girls' access to geographical spaces even before puberty. In rural parts of the country, it underpins many public-sector decisions that ultimately disenfranchise girls from access to education, healthcare, and economic opportunities. For example, various local and regional governments have suggested a need for separate girls' schools, but many girls in rural areas of the country will never go to school because of the nonavailability of such schools (Sathar et al., 2003). The socioeconomic transformations taking place within households and livelihood systems in rural parts of Pakistan have given rise to reinterpretations of *purdah*, gender roles, and expectations of girls. As *purdah* bolsters gender discrimination within the community at large, it helps to institutionalize and to reinforce girls' low secondary status and dependency within the household. Conflicts emerge over the roles girls are encountering in society and the ways in which their families and communities accommodate these roles. Indeed, parental and state interpretations of religious and social values regarding girls' marriage, education, seclusion, veiling, and mobility intersect with broader debates about the compatibility of Islam, modernity, and globalization.

Recent feminist writings on Pakistan have begun to trace the manner and extent to which the spatial experiences of girls are shaped by the influences and intersections of gender discourses, ideals of Islamic practice, and development policies adopted in different parts of the country (Alam, 1995; Durrand, 2000; Hafeez, 1993). Some questions remain: How do these factors affect, for instance, girls' experiences, the nature and meaning of their livelihood work and responsibilities, their control and access to space, and their visions of their futures? If the predominant notions of gender are inextricably linked to religious discourse in Pakistan, how do processes of globalization and development inform and complicate Muslim girls' current relations to household struggles for survival? One place to begin answering these questions is to draw upon academic theories of childhood and youth, especially the theoretical developments coming out of the "new social studies of childhood" (see Holloway & Valentine, 2000).

In recent years our theoretical understanding of girlhood has been enriched by scholarship that has recognized the multiple and contested assumptions and realities of childhood (Boyden, 1990; Mayall, 1994; Stephens, 1995). A major achievement of this scholarship over the last two decades is the recognition that the organization and meanings of childhood are not simply a given, but are in fact historically and socially constructed in accordance with local realities (Scheper-Hughes & Sargent, 1998). Indeed, every society has a certain way of thinking about childhood. Recent feminist scholarship has brought to the fore the idea that the historical, geographical, and social variability of childhood should be seen as part of complex social and economic processes that are crosscut by relations of gender, class, religion, region, ethnicity, and other forms of difference (Holloway & Valentine, 2000; Nieuwenhys, 1994). A number of empirical studies have found that gender norms are a key part of early socialization and education in childhood (Holloway & Valentine, 2000). Furthermore, it has been recognized that girls and boys themselves participate in the (re)construction of childhood and the (re)production of their place in society (Woodhead, 1998).

Relatively few empirical studies, however, examine the specifics of children's geographies in Muslim societies. A notable exception is Katz's (1993) research on children in rural Sudan. Katz argues that children's everyday lives are produced through particular institutions, ranging from global political–economic structures to families and communities. Katz's ground-breaking study of children's access to and control of space in the Muslim context of rural Sudan suggests that shifts in the configuration of households that have been brought about by socioeconomic and cultural–ecological changes can have profoundly different impacts on girls' and boys' spatial ranges. Another example of work on specifically Muslim childhood is Fernea's (1995) look at children's lives in the Middle East. This work supports the idea that gender relations and globalization have implications for shifting societal attitudes toward Muslim girls and boys, their labor, and their livelihood contributions. Furthermore, this research foregrounds the ways in which an Islamic framework influences the moral, cultural, political, and gendered contexts and assumptions about children. This is also the case in Pakistan, where approximately one-half of the population (49% of 140 million people) is under 18 years of age (UNICEF, 2003).

THE GIRL CHILD, ISLAM, AND THE STATE IN PAKISTAN

Since the International Year of the Child (1979) and the World Summit for Children, held in New York in 1990, the international children and development and child rights lobbies have put pressure on national governments such as Pakistan's to implement programs and policies to promote and improve the situation of children, especially that of girls (UNICEF, 1990, 1996). Governments have been encouraged to eliminate all forms of economic, social, and legal discrimination based on the sex of the child. The

United Nations Convention on the Rights of the Child, for example, explicitly states in Article 2:

> State Parties shall respect and ensure the rights set forth in the present Convention to each child within their jurisdiction without discrimination of any kind, irrespective of the child's . . . race, color, sex, language, religion, political or other opinion, national, ethnic or social origin, property, disability, birth or other status.

This declaration has helped to place children's concerns, and the plight of girls in particular, on the broad policy agenda of the Pakistani government. In 1990 Pakistan became a State Party to the United Nations Convention on the Rights of the Child. Since that time, the Children's Division, a part of the Education and Social Welfare Division of the Government of Pakistan, has been charged with the explicit responsibility of implementing the goals of the Declaration of the 1990 World Summit for Children and the UN Convention on the Rights of the Child within the binding strictures of the Holy Qur'an and the Sunnah. In response to international discussion, Pakistan launched the Girl Child Project (UNICEF, 2001). In addition, a number of documents, such as the *National Programme of Action for the Goals of Children and Development in the 1990s* (Inter-Ministry Task Force, 1992) and the *Islamabad Declaration on the Survival, Protection, and Development of the Child* (Government of Pakistan, 1991), were put forth to outline the roles of girls and boys in perpetuating Islamic social values and in actively participating in the promotion of economic and social development. Central to the policies regarding children and development, as spelled out in these documents, is the idea of "[assuring] every Pakistani child a bright and better future." This aim includes

> [highlighting] the rights of the child, especially the Girl Child, within the framework of the Islamic social order in Pakistan and the need to promote greater awareness of the important role that the Girl Child has to play in nation building after adulthood. (Government of Pakistan, 1991, p. 40)

Statements such as this one assert the centrality of Islam in the lives of children as well as the centrality of children, and "the girl child," in the development, national identity, and progress of a Muslim nation. In a country where 98% of the population is Muslim, the girl child is constructed as playing an integral role in engendering Muslim civil society. Assumed to be future wives and mothers, girls are placed at the very heart of upholding Islamic values, a Muslim religiocultural identity, and notions of family and nation that are seen as crucial to the maintenance of social order and the resolution of wider socioeconomic dilemmas.

Before going further in broadening our understanding of the situation of girls in northern Pakistan, I think it is important to not obscure the processes through which Islamic traditions and Islamisms are invented and transformed in Pakistan. Just as gender and childhood are socially constructed and reconstructed, Islam undergoes change and is reinvented to meet new needs and challenges (see Ahmed, 1992; Bernal, 1994; Haddad & Esposito, 1998). Islam, in the context of development in Pakistan, is recognized as pivotal to modernity. However, competing notions of modernity crosscut Islamic discourse and practice, scripturalist interpretations, and vernacular understandings, and have resulted in tremendous political tensions between the two predominant sects in the country, the Sunni and the Shia (Ahmad, 1992; Zaman, 1998). These tensions, in part, have been shaped by national-level dialogue that has politicized Islam, issues of gender, and the roles and places of girls and women in society (Jalal, 1991; Mumtaz & Shaheed, 1987).

While pressure has come from the international arena to improve the conditions confronting Pakistani girls, Pakistan continues to search for a workable way to implement its goals and directives regarding the girl child. This is in part related to the issue of women's rights, which has become a focal point in national political discourse (Government of Pakistan, Ministry of Women's Development, Social Welfare, and Special Education, 1998; Jilani, 1998; Weiss, 2003). Since 1979, when General Zia ul-Haq and his military government announced its intentions to create an Islamic state, conservative Islamic laws have limited girls' and women's roles in the public sphere (Haq, 1996). This "Islamization" campaign resulted in many negative ramifications for women's legal status, participation in the political process, and protections against gender-based discrimination and violence. Significantly, this program issued a set of legislative policies that effectively supported and justified state-sanctioned discrimination against girls and women in the name of Islam (Commission of Inquiry for Women, 1997). Today the issue of girls' and women's rights and position within the larger social order remains highly contentious. Gender disparities in the legal, economic, and political realms continue to constrain girls' choices and opportunities in many aspects of life. Moreover, some segments of society have adopted strict regulation of girls' lives and bodies.

When we review the economic and social indicators for Pakistan, it is evident that girls' marginalized status is in part a result of the state's gender ideology manifested in development policies and draconian laws. Nearly every social and economic indicator for the country describes significant differences in opportunities for girls and boys and for women and men (Government of Pakistan & UNICEF, 1992; UNICEF, 2003). The gender bias at a state level significantly impacts policies regarding education, maternal and child health, and social and political organizing. According to UNICEF (2003),

Nearly one third of the country's 140 million people live in poverty. The girl child faces greater risks to survival, is more subject to violence and abuse, and has less access to education, proper nutrition and health services. The low status of children and women is a manifestation of low literacy levels, wide gaps between legislation and enforcement, and limited participation in civil society.

The gender bias is also evident in the inverse sex ratio of 91 women for every 100 men, the reverse of a global norm where females typically outnumber males. As one of the lowest in the world, the sex ratio in Pakistan suggests unequal access to healthcare, proper nutrition, and a nurturing environment. Access to education is also strikingly limited for girls and women in the country. The basic literacy rate for females over the age of 15 is 28%, compared to a literacy rate among males of 51% (United Nations Development Program [UNDP], 2002). A 1995 study of the situation of girls in especially difficult circumstances concluded that girls "are poorly fed, do not get health care, are married early, get beaten, face sexual harassment, are overworked, have no recreation, and are in short, deprived of childhood to which they have an inherent right" (Alam, 1995, p. 10). In spite of the growing recognition of the ways in which Pakistani girls' experiences have been influenced by gender-based discrimination perpetuated by the state, many questions remain regarding some of the most egregious problems of poverty and changes in family structure faced by girls today.

The points raised in this section about gender disparities embodied in state policies and their implications for Pakistani girls' experiences apply to the local context. Several social, economic, and political trends that have emerged in the District of Gilgit are critical to shaping girls' lives today. These trends are integrally linked to the opening up of this mountainous region since the late 1970s through the development of transportation networks, including the Karkoram Highway. The expansion of government infrastructure, and the subsequent movement of goods and people, have been integral to a program of mountain development that has been pursued since the late 1970s and early 1980s—a program motivated by the strategic and economic importance of the Northern Areas for Pakistan. These sociospatial shifts have gender and livelihood implications for girls and their families in rural, predominantly farming, communities of the District of Gilgit, in northern Pakistan.

ON AND BEYOND THE FARM: VIEWS ON GIRLS' GEOGRAPHIES

In northern Pakistan the interpretations of how girls and boys should be raised are conveyed among mothers around the hearth, in the garden or field, and so on. While carrying out this research, it became apparent to me that these types of social interactions between mothers play a key role in establishing local norms about the acceptable behavior of girls, the types of work they should do, and the places they can and cannot go. These spatial constructions of girlhood are undergoing a profound alteration as a result of changing social attitudes toward girls and new and emerging market relations. Until recently, the mothers in the study site seem to have had few reservations about childrearing goals or their aims as parents. Similar to patterns observed elsewhere in the Muslim world (Fernea, 1995), widely accepted notions about the structure of the family and the functions of family members of all ages influenced the concept of childhood and childrearing practices in the past. However, as women themselves respond to the social and economic changes going on around them, their views on the place and roles of girls are being (re)interpreted and negotiated.

The Value of Girls

A major factor shaping girls' life experiences is a strong gender preference for sons rather than daughters. These attitudes are similar to those documented elsewhere in the region (Das Gupta, 1987; Filmer, King, & Pritchett, 1998; Sathar, 1987). Attitudes toward girls affect their ability to control their lives and, since their status is typically interpreted as lower than boys, they have little influence over decisions about their own education or marriage. Many consider a daughter to be a financial liability, someone who will, in the end, take away part of her family's wealth.

In spite of the pervasive gender preference for boys, mothers' narratives suggest that attitudes toward girls are slowly changing. Over half of the mothers interviewed said that girls are just as important to them personally as boys because of the significant contributions girls make to easing their work burdens. Girls are generally seen as being useful doing traditionally ascribed tasks such as helping with food preparation, taking care of younger siblings, and working in the garden and fields. Two women expressed their perception of the value of girls as follows:

> "They are equal. In the olden days they liked boys more. Now we treat them the same because the girl can also have a job. Before there was no education or employment for girls. Now there are many differences. If some parents do not have a son, the daughter will be able to take care of her parents."

> "Before I had a son, I thought to myself that a boy would be good. Now that I have a son, I realize that girls are good. The boy does not help me with work around the house. The son does not work, and the husband does not work. This is why the girls seem more important to me now."

The mothers' narratives I heard highlighted the clear advantages of having girls that have changed over time. Women emphasized their reliance on the labor and assistance of their older daughters in the management of their households. This reliance is related, in part, to substantive changes in rural livelihoods. Cash incomes have attained a new degree of importance to household economies, thereby delimiting new measures of wealth and differentiating patterns of resource use and access within households and communities (Azhar-Hewitt, 1998). Even though some transactions continue to be based on bartering, especially those conducted between women, cash assumes a key role in people's lives. Residents offer a range of reasons to explain the growing need for cash: change in local dietary habits; population growth; limited farm size; the need to purchase seeds, pesticides, and chemical fertilizers; and home construction. Overall, increasing interest in acquiring the growing array of *jadeed* (modern) products, coupled with the need to supplement household production, have added to families' growing dependence on local and external markets. This growing importance of and dependency on cash for survival, as well as new cultural orientations toward large weddings, gift exchanges, and dowries,[2] have heightened the need for incomes (Halvorson, 2003).

To satisfy these needs, men and boys have been taking advantage of off-farm employment and educational opportunities outside their villages, thereby widening the divisions between boys'/men's and girls'/women's contributions to farm maintenance. Given widespread unemployment in the Northern Areas, many men and teenage boys migrate to the urban centers of Rawalpindi, Lahore, or Karachi. Some even find work in the Persian Gulf states of Saudi Arabia and Oman and send remittances back to their families. The decision to work off-farm is usually made out of necessity and is dependent upon family dynamics and access to financial or social resources to facilitate a move away from the family. Furthermore, gender is an important factor playing into the trend since men have the social mobility to take advantage of wage-earning opportunities in distant urban areas. Some educated women have also found off-farm employment, primarily in the areas of health and education; for the most part, however, cultural and structural exclusions preclude rural women from working outside the home.

The extent of men's participation in wage labor, either domestically or internationally, has perforce reshaped the quality of life and the workloads of those remaining in the household (Halvorson, 2002). This pattern has been observed elsewhere in Pakistan and South Asia (Azhar-Hewitt, 1989, 1999; Carpenter, 1991; Government of Pakistan, 1990; Joekes, 1995; Mumtaz & Shaheed, 1987; Raju & Bagchi, 1993; Sathar & Desai, 1996). These changes have brought about important implications for the lives of women and girls. My observations suggest that regardless of their households' wealth category (i.e., poor, middle income, or wealthy), girls face incredibly demanding on-farm workloads and responsibilities as male family members become increasingly engaged in off-farm capacities. Reconfigurations in family structures are apparent. For example, there is evidence of increasing numbers of women becoming the de facto heads of households while their husbands are working in down-country cities. Women circumvent some of the time limitations on the essential tasks of the day by relying on their daughters. For women who rarely participate in tasks that take them outside the realms of the farmstead, the contributions of girls to household reproduction and to enabling the practice of *purdah* are invaluable.

Spatialized Constructions of Girlhood

The gendering of space in northern Pakistan has resulted in spatial and social boundaries marked in accordance to gender norms. Girls are rarely encouraged to go beyond the realms of house, garden, and field except when accompanied by a parent, an older relative, or a brother. The roads, bazaars, bus stations, and schoolyards are coded as male spaces of social interaction. On holidays and weekends these spaces are dominated by men and boys passing time by drinking tea, gossiping, or playing cricket and soccer. Girls do frequent the bazaars, but they are usually accompanied by elderly women, women in groups of three or more, siblings or neighborhood children, or other male relatives. Other spaces of distinctly male interaction include hotels (restaurants) where men gather to watch satellite TV, drink tea, and exchange ideas about news and politics. Girls and women never frequent these places, and come together instead in women's spaces such as homes, gardens, and fields. The gendered nature of these spaces has important implications for girls' access to transportation services and health facilities. A routine visit to the health center or school located in the middle of town requires crossing these invisible boundaries into the male domain. This experience of walking through the bazaar can be an incredibly uncomfortable one for even young girls, and attempts are made to avoid it altogether by taking back alleys through neighbors' gardens and fields.

An important theme that emerges from mothers' narratives is the ways in which girlhood is spatially organized around the household economy. The contributions daughters make to livelihood and childcare represent a critical strategy for mothers who are occupied during the course of the day with livestock management, food production, fuelwood collection, food processing, and other domestic tasks. The use of girl's labor at the household level reflects gender-differentiated notions of entitlement that suggest two significant patterns. One pattern similar to other rural contexts in the developing world is that daughters are expected to perform a number of gender-defined tasks around the farm and house. By 8 or 9 years of age, girls are engaged in a routine variety of tasks around the household domain. For daughters, the list includes a range of what the women who participated in this study call *chota kam*, "the small work" of daily domestic chores and errands, such as sweeping, cooking, making *roti* (flatbread), food preparation, washing clothes, tending the garden, and feeding and milking cows. Adolescent daughters are expected to accompany the women to the fields to assist with weeding and harvesting. They are called upon to assist with the collection of firewood and fruit, tasks they often carry out with girlfriends. Education and training in these tasks begins at an early age. Four-year-old Safina,[4] for instance, already has been taught to rid the ears of the family's goats of ticks and to collect fallen leaves for fodder. Even at a young age the work girls are expected to do becomes routinized for them, a process confirmed by Bano's daughter when she said, "I started making *roti* when I was 8."

Daughters are particularly important because they assist their mothers in the care of babies and younger siblings. From the age of 5, girls and, to some extent, boys are socialized to hold, watch over, and play with small children. Girls are also expected to develop other domestic skills such as sewing, knitting, and making clothes for family members. For Khadija, the labor contributions of her oldest daughter were so vital to her that she decided not to send her daughter to school, thereby reserving other activities such as playing and school attendance for the younger children. This work is rationalized in the context of how best to prepare girls for their roles as wives, mothers, and daughters-in-law after they are married. Mothers' reliance on their daughters for help around the house is reflected in their comments about the necessity for girls to gain certain types of knowledge and skills by the time they reach 12 years old:

"From early on the girl should learn how to do all of the work the women do."

"Right now my daughter is too small to help me, but when she grows up she will lend a hand with everything. She will look after the young ones if I am away from the house. She will bring the harvest from the fields. . . . Girls should help their mothers in all the routine work."

Recently, with the advent of education, girls are leaving the spatial range of the household and neighborhood to attend school. The education of girls has implied that mothers are losing the option of depending on their daughters during the morning school hours. However, girls are still expected to resume their work upon returning home from school and are not at liberty to explore the surroundings beyond the purview of their parents and relatives. These types of cultural entitlements to girls' labor are also reflected in the way that parents periodically keep girls home from school or withdraw them from school at an early age because of the necessity of their labor for the family. Families with scarce financial resources, in particular, tend to view the education of girls as a less viable long-term investment than the education of sons. For most families in the community, it is a recent experience to send their children, both boys and girls, to school.

By the time girls reach the middle- and secondary-school levels—that is, if they are provided the opportunity and resources to pursue their education to this level—they experience a "triple day," with school in the morning, farm and household labor in the afternoon and evening, and homework at some point during the evening (or not at all). Zenab, for instance, explains that after school her daughters "make *roti*, sweep, clean, take care of the younger siblings, and wash the clothes of the adults and children." To Zenab, girls today should be expected "to work in the kitchen, clean the house, learn how to take care of children, keep children clean . . . and to study." Training in the mandatory skills of housecleaning and childcare makes for a specific experience that is crucial for girlhood among the social classes of Pakistani society. Early introduction in the female domain and the sharing of the responsibility for the well-being of the family is fundamental to the socialization process of girls.

In contrast to girls' work, the livelihood work of boys is constructed as *bara kam*, or "the big work," that frequently takes them outside the household compound or neighborhood. This work includes irrigation, chopping fuelwood, harvesting crops, collecting branches and leaves for livestock fodder, and clearing fields of rocks. Boys frequently leave the community to assist their fathers or grandfathers in selling produce in the market or doing errands. It is notable, however, that while these livelihood tasks are constructed as part of the domain of men and boys, women and girls regularly perform these tasks as well. Tasks that require a monetary exchange or social interactions outside the house—making purchases in the bazaar, borrowing a tractor from the neighbors, or sending messages to people in the community—are viewed as indispensable for enhancing the life skills of boys.

The rationale for sending boys outside of the home at a young age for various errands underscores parental concerns about preparing sons to responsibly navigate new market relations and their social roles beyond the home range. Frequently, people say, "A son should think about helping his clan" or "Boys should learn to speak well and use *accha zaban* [good or proper language]." These concerns are iterated by the following quotations regarding what boys should be expected to know when they reach the age of 12:

"They need to learn everything. To study their lessons, to learn to *salaam* [greet] all neighbors, and to have manners with guests."

"He needs to learn about his education, to learn to do some kind of work, to do a business or a job after he has studied further."

"A son needs to learn respect for his parents. He needs to learn about his social environment and to think about his education."

As these quotations suggest, local discourses on childrearing underscore the necessity of education in preparing boys for their future roles as providers and breadwinners. Here a second pattern in the relationship between mothers and their children emerges. As sons are increasingly removed from their menial labor roles because of the emphasis parents place on their schooling, the social expectations of boys have concomitantly shifted in this rural setting. For boys, this shift has meant a relaxation of their fieldwork and obligations around the household and an elevation of their status within the household. This patriarchal view of the superiority of boys raises a key issue of gender inequity at the intrahousehold level. After school, boys are granted the freedom to study, to meet with tutors, to play sports, and to visit with their friends. Mumtaz, the mother of eight children and the primary caregiver for her two elderly parents, continues to rely extensively on her daughters rather than her sons to help her around the house even though both her daughters and her sons are going to school. She stated:

"The daughters help no doubt. They wash clothes. They wash the utensils. They sometimes prepare the food and make tea for us. . . . The sons are all going to school. They are unable to help us. Sometimes the oldest son fetches a bucket of water from the nearby well. Nothing else. They spend their time in schoolwork. They go to the public school as well as to the *deeni* [religious] school at the mosque."

Dil expressed a similar experience as Mumtaz, adding jokingly, "My son does nothing, what can I do?" Most mothers feel that the loss of sons' labor from livelihood work is a reasonable and minor sacrifice for the contributions they will make to family survival in the future. Dil explained:

". . . I get help from those in the house, mainly my daughters. My husband helps with the harvesting of the wheat. The son does not help me with this work. He himself does no farmwork. We cannot force him to do farmwork. Instead, we should be happy to have him work with us. We are happy to leave him alone because he is the only son in the family. When he marries and has children, then he will be responsible for working."

The engagement of boys with education and employment outside the household is facilitated and sustained by the work and responsibilities of girls within the household. The communication of these gender norms takes place between mothers and daughters in everyday spaces. For example, the training of girls in what it means to be an *accha ami* (good mother) is constructed locally and within the household, and the interactions between mothers and daughters plays a key part in this process. Bibi emphasized the importance of the transfer of knowledge between mother and daughter:

> "She should . . . learn the good manner which our religion tells us. A girl will be a mother in the future. She has to control the house in the future. She must learn what her mother teaches her."

As the above quotation suggests, Islamic belief and practice are key components in the construction and negotiation of gender images and expectations, and they mediate the way mothers view the relationship between children and the community context. The construction of Muslim ideals of "good" boys and "good" girls and their roles in upholding these ideals are reflected in expressions of Muslim identity. For example, in her view of girls' domestic education, Bibi emphasized not only the skills necessary for the conduct of mothering, but also the social role Islam ascribes to girls and women. Shara iterated a similar view as Bibi:

> "According to our religious teachings, a girl is supposed to learn her religious responsibilities such as *namaz* [prayer] and *roza* [fast]. Then, she must learn home management. . . . Education is very important for her since she has to take over the responsibilities in the future. If she is educated she will become a responsible mother."

In this quotation education and Islam are linked in the construction of girls' preparations for adulthood. Taken as a whole, Islamic teachings represent a moral discourse on roles and responsibilities that prescribes what girls should know and be prepared to do when they become adults. In this way there is an association between Islamic ideals, socially constructed responsibilities, and the conduct of mothering that underlies the informal education and training of daughters. Information about hygiene, childcare, gardening, food preparation, and morality is transmitted in an ad hoc fashion and occurs whenever mothers observe the need to provide instruction to their daughters. The importance of this knowledge transfer should not be overlooked in a consideration of the response to environmental and health problems because it is this knowledge that permits girls to mediate the risk environment for family members (Halvorson, 2002).

Visions of Girls' Futures

The incorporation of the District of Gilgit into the global economy has led many mothers to expand their vision of their daughters' futures. What is remarkable about much of what the women discussed is the strong statement made about how girls' lives are and will be radically different than in the past. Mothers made very strong statements about how their children's lives will be vastly different from their own, in part because employment will take them out of the community setting. One mother's statement that "my son could go to the moon" reflected tremendous optimism about her son's future. Many mothers were hopeful that in spite of high rates of unemployment in the country, their sons will find employment opportunities, especially if they are prepared to migrate out of the community.

The visions of girls' futures, I would argue, are much more complex and reflected two contrasting shifts in thinking about girls' mobility. One shift is the notion that mobility for girls is increasing. The idea that "my daughter might be a teacher" represents in some ways a radically new idea. Only recently have employment opportunities as teachers or government health workers opened up to permit women to earn wages. Women's wage earning is a topic of great debate locally and is a source of conflict within households. Such conflicts reflect fears that the loosening of control over girls' and women's bodies and spatial boundaries will result in a moral tarnishing of the family and the community.

Another more recently introduced component of raising girls is formal education. The main reasons given in support of girls' education were so that they are marriageable, could get a job, be able to educate children, to be able to properly provide good care of children, and to learn about the world:

> ". . . If she is uneducated then she cannot learn anything. These days everyone is educated. An uneducated girl cannot get married. If she is educated she will be able to say something and learn something. The relatives who come by who are interested in our daughter ask how far she has studied in school."

> ". . . She will learn about caregiving. When she is educated and goes to someone else's house, she will learn all work in their house. She can teach her children something."

> ". . . An uneducated girl does not learn how to respect her parents. When she becomes educated she will be able to learn everything, how to respect her relatives and parents."

> "[A girl's] future will be good if she has been educated. If she is uneducated her mother-in-law, her father-in-law, and husband will not respect her, and they will scold her."

These quotations reflect an important transformation in attitudes toward girl children that is slowing taking place in the region. The new educational trends can be seen as enhancing the roles and responsibilities of the family in the preparation of Muslim girls. Most concede that education for girls is a worthwhile pursuit if it supports their roles within the natal and the marital family. Education could potentially have an impact on the status of girls within families. Younger mothers feel strongly that being educated provides more power within the home, and perhaps more control over time and work.

Religiously affiliated NGOs are playing an increasing role in expanding the range of development and modernization options in the District of Gilgit. NGOs (namely, the Aga Khan Rural Support Program,[3] the Aga Khan Health Service, Pakistan, and the Aga Khan Education Service, Pakistan), community-based self-help groups, and religiously affiliated committees play important roles in creating health, education, and livelihood options for girls and their families. The development "solutions" put forth by these groups are often cast in Islamic idiom. For northern Pakistanis, Iran, Saudi Arabia, and the Ismaili community are three different sources of ideological and cultural influence on approaches to development. Their influence is transmitted through the funding of schools, mosques, health centers, agricultural extension offices, and microcredit and finance programs. These forms of development interventions are associated with particular religious identities, and, for community members, with a vision of prosperity and progress that may or may not be compatible with their own identities and religiocultural perspectives.

It should also be stressed that while respondents' statements express a vision of their children's future, they mask the desperate need felt by most parents to have their children go to school and to enter the skilled labor market. This desperation is an integral component of the articulations of raising children and is a result of the major movement on the part of the World Bank, UNICEF, and the Aga Khan Education Services, Pakistan, to create educational opportunities in the region. Many parents feel that school fees are an additional pressure on top of their struggles to deal with poverty, unemployment, and inflation, as well as complicated local religious politics. While girls are used to symbolize the aspirations of cultural authenticity expressed in Islamic terms, they are also caught in contentious negotiations as they are integrated into a new set of labor market relations outside the home.

The question of the extent to which reforms such as literacy projects and education will challenge gender relations remains to be answered in light of restrictions on girls' mobility. Communal controls over girls continue to flourish and in some instances have been intensified. This has taken place in a context riddled with contradictions over what girls should and should not be allowed to do. The reorganization of the social structure has intensified tensions that are expressed in gender, religious, and ethnic terms. Some mothers commented that today girls are expected to stay close to home, should no longer play with boys, and should begin learning *purdah* at an early age. According to one mother named Lal, there have been major changes in rural expectations regarding the mobility and dress of girls. In describing what seems to be an increasing pattern of segregation between girls and boys, she commented:

> "When I was growing up boys and girls played together. No one minded at all if we did not wear a *chaddor* [head scarf]. This *zamana* [era] is bad. The tradition has changed. Back then, men and women worked together and no one cared. Now they have to be separated. In the past we did not have to hide our faces."

Here, she expressed her sense that the social expectations placed on rural girls and women have changed over time. The quotation also indicates a sense of the tightening of social controls on girls' and women's bodies and space. Similar impressions were revealed by Zara, a mother of two small children. In describing her childhood, Zara drew comparisons with what her mother had recounted about her experiences growing up, saying:

> "When she was younger, our mother went to the mountains to collect wood, to the pastures to graze the animals, and she used to play with boys and girls together. People did not mind when the boys and girls were together. We do not go to the mountains, or to the pastures, or play with anyone. . . . The situation today for us is not good. The boys are very naughty, and this is why no one lets their girls out of the house."

This excerpt from Zara's life-history narrative demonstrates a concern that many rural women experience regarding controls on their spatial mobility in the face of religious conservatism and rapid social change. The tensions existing between generational views on women's mobility (especially girls' and young mothers' mobility) within and outside the community have been critical to day-to-day decisions for Zara and the other rural women I interviewed. Since the various development interventions in the region have been undertaken, women's experiences have been increasingly influenced by gender and intergenerational struggles to define the appropriate codes of *izzat* (honor) and respect in the context of shifting gender norms associated with socioeconomic development. Even young men from both Shia and Ismaili sects have become active participants in recent local struggles centered on conceptualizations of *purdah* and girls' and women's access to public space. Some of the most vivid examples of intense contestations between the two groups surround the painting and effacing of graffiti portraying certain ideals of female piety and behavior (see Halvorson, 2002).

Sectarian relations and tensions have become a salient force in precipitating changes in social relations and interactions between religious communities at the local scale. Conflict and rivalries sometimes of a violent and militant nature between Muslim sects have a long and bitter history in Pakistan (Zaman, 1998). One of the most noticeable areas in which sectarian differences play out is in the context of women and development programs. Opposing visions of women's roles and participation in development processes have emerged as a powerful divisive force within and between communities. For example, the activities of the Aga Khan Rural Support Program (AKRSP), especially the women's microcredit services and participatory model, have come under opposition from a segment of the Shia population. Claims have been vociferously raised that local women are being corrupted by "outsiders" and female staff who are not upholding *purdah*. The dilemma within the Northern Areas that has come to light is that there is no one interpretation of girls'/women's roles in society that is embraced by the full range of sects living in the region. Rather, there are multiple and oftentimes competing interpretations of development, notions of the family and community, and gender relations manifest in the development policies.

CONCLUDING REMARKS: BLURRING THE SPACES BETWEEN MUSLIM GIRLHOOD AND WOMANHOOD

As this chapter reveals, girls in the District of Gilgit are now facing new challenges stemming from the region's participation in a cash-based economy and in the complex processes of rural development. Islam is one of a set of powerful ideologies that influences the geographical experiences and options of girls in the region. Children in this part of the Hindu Kush–Karakoram–Himalaya have long participated in the sustenance, maintenance, and religious lives of their families. However, the shifting livelihood practices combined with development discourses are spurring yet another realm of gender politics that shapes Muslim children's lives and the different ways in which parents and children exercise their agency in response to these forces.

While the cultural and economic changes in the Northern Areas have increased the spatial ranges for some girls, for others the changes affecting gender relations have actually resulted in the reduction of girls' access to the social and physical environment beyond the household. As religious ideology has continued to be associated with the promotion of various development patterns, the residents of the Northern Areas have faced intensified sectarian tensions. Tensions surrounding the meaning and practice of *purdah* have intensified both within the household and the community scales, placing heightened social pressure on some women and girls to stay within the *char diwar*. Boys, on the other hand, have experienced a stretching out of their ranges to even include distant urban centers.

There are practical consequences of these processes for girlhood and for gendered spatial ideology. For most girls, their day-to-day activities are spatially structured around the maintenance of the household. As a result,

gendered notions of work and skill are reinforced. This also serves to reinforce Islamic notions of *purdah*. The continuing trend toward increases in
girls' and women's subsistence and nonsubsistence farm activities in northern Pakistan further highlights the complex features of girlhood at the local
level. Traditionally domestic and farm responsibilities were ascribed to
men/boys and women/girls in fairly equal proportions. Today, girls' roles in
feeding families, managing agricultural resources, and maintaining the economic and physical health of households has become even more visible and
salient. Increasing pressure for cash has led some girls to take up additional
income-generating activities that are viewed as socially acceptable (e.g., tai-
loring or assisting at the health clinic). Similarly, many girls assist their
mothers in the cultivation of cash crops such as potatoes, onions, and fruit
to sell in regional markets. Overall, girls' labor has intensified due to the
expansion of the cash economy, their mothers' reliance on their daughters
to share the work burden, and the partial to complete release of men and
boys from the work on the farms. For sons who were once highly engaged
in farm tasks, these changes have meant a lightening of their responsibilities
as their parents place a heavy emphasis on their educational advancement.

The evidence in this chapter suggests that contemporary children's experiences of rural development are very different from the experiences of
their parents when they were growing up. In exploring reasons for why patterns of girls' mobility have changed between generations, two distinct areas can be identified. First, the assessments of the women, as well as others
with whom I spoke, suggest that changes in the relations between sects
have resulted in a reinterpretation of girls/women's access to space. As sectarian violence has deepened throughout the country and in the Northern
Areas, the possibilities for involvement and participation open to these girls
have changed, as have the ways that women conceive of and negotiate their
own daughters' geographies.

Second, the ideological stance toward the seclusion of women in many
of the study households further legitimized girls' lower status and dependency within the boundary of their households. The limitations on girls' mobility depend on the norms of the religious community to which they belong and to the particularities of their respective families. Within these
limits girls were expected to help meet livelihood needs. The significance of
their lack of control over their workloads, so evident during planting and
harvesting seasons when mothers decide the work schedules of their daughters, cannot be overemphasized.

Finally, the process of religious change at least in Pakistan does coin-
cide in often ambiguous and multifaceted ways with the integration into
capitalist relations of production and exchange. There is tremendous diversity of responses to the modalities of children's participation in economic
life. The emergence of new secular and religious notions of gender difference as they affect childhoods in this Muslim setting are direct results and

responses to economic, political, and ideological conditions of globalization. In this respect, it is important not to overlook the ways in which local discourses also help to shape Islam as an important context for the articulation of girlhood and girl–society relations under conditions of change.

ACKNOWLEDGMENTS

My very deepest thanks go to all of the individuals and families who participated in the research and who shared aspects of their lives with me. I would especially like to thank James L. Wescoat, Jr., who has been and continues to be an inspiration. I would also like to thank Rachel Silvey and Richa Nagar for their constructive and insightful comments on an earlier draft of this chapter. Thanks to Zeba Rasmussen who introduced me to my field site and many individuals who played a role in seeing this research to fruition. I would also like to express my appreciation to Caroline Nagel and Ghazi-Walid Falah as editors for their patience, encouragement, and good humor. This research was supported by grants from the University of Colorado Graduate School, Fulbright Foundation, the Social Science Research Council, and the Woodrow Wilson National Fellowship Foundation.

NOTES

1. The territory that is today the Federally Administered Northern Areas is officially disputed territory with India. The region came under the control of Pakistan at the time of Partition in 1947. I have used the name "Northern Areas" in accordance with the contemporary use of this term in Pakistan. Because it is not an official province within the nation-state of Pakistan, the Northern Areas lack representation in national legislative bodies and the residents of the Northern Areas do not have the right to vote in federal elections. Since 1972, elections for local government in the Northern Areas have been held. Only recently, in 1995, did a legislative body, the Northern Areas Council, come into existence to represent regional interests at the national level of policymaking in Islamabad.

2. Spending money on large, elaborate weddings, formal gift exchanges during engagements, and dowry requirements are symbolic of social change and the infusion of Punjabi and Sindhi culture into rural, mountain society. With the introduction of Hindi films and exposure to Punjabi culture through magazines and TV, these traditions are growing in importance. Dowry is now seen as a way to enhance family status and represents a new form of social contract between families.

3. The most ambitious program addressing poverty and underdevelopment in the Northern Areas has been spearheaded by the Aga Khan Rural Support Program (AKRSP), an NGO with bilateral and multilateral support. Through a bottom-up participatory approach to defining local problems, priorities, and interventions, AKRSP's initiatives introduced new possibilities for addressing livelihood concerns. AKRSP began working in northern Pakistan in 1982. Following a model of participatory development, AKRSP introduced the idea of village orga-

nizations (VOs) to function as institutional arrangements through which com munities could address their development needs and priorities. In addition to village organizations, women's organizations (WOs) were formed in the mid-1980s.
4. To preserve anonymity, names of research participants have been changed.

REFERENCES

Aga Khan Education Services, Pakistan. (1996). *Northern Areas and Chitral programme proposal: 1997–2001*. Gilgit, Northern Areas: Author.

Ahmad, A. D. (1992, July 21) Organized sectarianism in Pakistan. *The Nation*.

Ahmed, L. (1992). *Women and gender in Islam: Historical roots of a modern debate*. New Haven, CT, and London: Yale University Press.

Alam, S. (1995). *Summary of the report on girl child in especially difficult circumstances in Pakistan*. Islamabad, Pakistan: UNICEF.

Azhar-Hewitt, F. (1989). Women's work, women's place: The gendered life-world of a high mountain community in northern Pakistan. *Mountain Research and Development, 9*, 335–352.

Azhar-Hewitt, F. (1998). All paths lead to the hot spring: Conviviality, the code of honor, and capitalism in a Karakorum village, Pakistan. *Mountain Research and Development, 18*, 265–272.

Azhar-Hewitt, F. (1999). Women of the high pastures and the global economy: Reflections on the impacts of modernization in the Hushe Valley of the Karakorum, Northern Pakistan. *Mountain Research and Development, 19*, 141–151.

Bernal, V. (1994). Gender, culture, and capitalism: Women and the remaking of Islamic "tradition" in a Sudanese village. *Comparative Studies in Society and History, 36*, 36–67.

Boyden, J. (2001). Childhood and the policy makers: A comparative perspective on the globalization of childhood. In A. James & A. Prout (Eds.), *Constructing and Reconstructing childhood: Contemporary issues in the sociological study of childhood* (4th ed., pp. 190–215). London: Falmer Press.

Carpenter, C. (1991). Women and livestock, fodder, and uncultivated land in Pakistan: A summary of role responsibilities. *Society and Natural Resources, 4*, 65–79.

Commission of Inquiry for Women. (1997). *Report of the Commission of Inquiry for women in Pakistan*. Islamabad, Pakistan: Ministry for Women's Development, Social Welfare and Special Education, Government of Pakistan.

Das Gupta, M. (1987). Selective discrimination against female children in rural Punjab, India. *Population and Development Review, 13*, 77–100.

Durrand, V. (2000). *Adolescent girls and boys in Pakistan: Opportunities and constraints in the transition to adulthood*. Islamabad, Pakistan: Population Council.

Fernea, E. W. (Ed.). (1995). *Children in the Muslim Middle East*. Austin: University of Texas Press.

Filmer, D., King, E. M., & Pritchett, L. (1998). *Gender disparity in South Asia: Comparisons between and within countries* (Policy Research Working Paper 1867). Washington, DC: World Bank, Development Research Group, Poverty and Human Resources.

Government of Pakistan. (1991). *Islamabad declaration on the survival, protection and development of the child*. Islamabad, Pakistan: Government of Pakistan.

Government of Pakistan, Ministry of Women's Development, Social Welfare and Special Education. (1998). *National plan of action (NPA)*. Islamabad: Author.

Government of Pakistan & UNICEF (1992). *Situation analysis of children and women in Pakistan*. Islamabad, Pakistan: UNICEF and Pictorial Printers Ltd.

Haddad, Y. Y., & Esposito, J. L. (Eds.). (1998). *Islam, gender, and social change*. New York: Oxford University Press.

Hafeez, S. (1993). *The girl child in Pakistan: Priority concerns*. Islamabad, Pakistan: UNICEF.

Halvorson, S. J. (2002). Environmental health risks and gender in the Karakoram–Himalaya, Northern Pakistan. *Geographical Review, 92*, 257–281.

Halvorson, S. J. (2003). "Placing" health risks in the Karakoram: Local perceptions of disease, dependency, and social change in northern Pakistan. *Mountain Research and Development, 23*, 271–277.

Haq, F. (1996). Women, Islam, and the state in Pakistan. *Muslim World, 86*, 158–175.

Holloway, S. L., & Valentine, G. (Eds.). (2000). *Children's geographies: Playing, living, learning*. London and New York: Routledge.

Ibraz, T. S. (1993). Cultural context of women's productive invisibility: A case study of a Pakistani village. *Pakistan Development Review, 32*, 101–125.

Inter-Ministry Task Force. (1992). *National programme of action for the goals for children and development in the 1990s*. Islamabad, Pakistan: Government of Pakistan.

Jalal, A. (1991). The convenience of subservience: Women and the state of Pakistan. In D. Kandiyoti (Ed.), *Women, Islam and the state* (pp. 77–114). Philadelphia: Temple University Press.

Jilani, H. (1998). *Human rights and democratic development in Pakistan*. Lahore: Human Rights Commission of Pakistan.

Joekes, S. (1995). Gender and livelihoods in northern Pakistan. *IDS Bulletin, 26*, 66–74.

Kabeer, N. (2000). Inter-generational contracts, demographic transitions and the "quantity–quality" tradeoff: Parents, children, and investing in the future. *Journal of International Development, 12*, 463–482.

Kandiyoti, D. (Ed.). (1991). *Women, Islam and the state*. Philadelphia: Temple University Press.

Katz, C. (1993). Growing girls/closing circles: Limits on the spaces of knowing in rural Sudan and US cities. In C. Katz & J. Monk (Eds.), *Full circles: Geographies of women over the life course* (pp. 88–106). New York: Routledge.

Mayall, B. (Ed.). (1994). *Children's childhoods: Observed and experienced*. London: Falmer Press.

Mumtaz, K., & Shaheed, F. (1987). *Women of Pakistan: Two steps forward, one step back?* London and Karachi, Pakistan: Zed Press/Vanguard Books.

Mumtaz, S., & Fatima, A. (1992). Cultural conception and structural perpetuation of female subordination: An examination of gender relations among the populations of the Chalt-Chaprote community in the Nagar Valley of northern Pakistan. *Pakistan Development Review, 31*, 621–632.

Nagar, R. (1997). Exploring methodological borderlands through oral narratives. In J. P. Jones, H. Nast, & S. Roberts (Eds.), *Thresholds in feminist geography: Difference, methodology, representation* (pp. 203–224). Landham, MD: Rowman & Littlefield.

Nieuwenhys, O. (1994). *Children's lifeworlds: Gender, welfare and labour in the developing world.* New York: Routledge.

Papanek, H. & Minault, G. (1982). *Separate worlds: Studies in purdah in South Asia.* Columbia, MO: South Asia Books.

Personal Narratives Group. (1989). *Interpreting women's lives: Feminist theory and personal narratives.* Bloomington: Indiana University Press.

Raju, S., & Bagchi, D. (1993). *Women and work in South Asia.* New York: Routledge.

Sathar, Z. A. (1987). Sex differentials in mortality: A corollary of son preference? *Pakistan Development Review, 26,* 555–565.

Sathar, Z. A., & Desai, S. (1996). *Work patterns in rural Pakistan: Intersections between gender, family, and class* (Research Division Working Papers No. 90). New York: Population Council.

Sathar, Z. A., Lloyd, C. B., ul Haque, M., Diers, J. A., Faizunnissa, A., Grant, M., & Sultana, M. (2003). *Adolescents and youths in Pakistan 2001–2002: A nationally representative survey.* Islamabad, Pakistan: Population Council.

Scheper-Hughes, N., & Sargent, C. (1998). *Small wars: The cultural politics of childhood.* Berkeley and Los Angeles: University of California Press.

Stephens, S. (Ed.). (1995). *Children and the politics of culture.* Princeton, NJ: Princeton University Press.

Streefland, P., Khan, S., & van Lieshout, O. (1995). *A contextual study of Northern Areas and Chitral.* Gilgit, Northern Areas: Aga Khan Rural Support Program.

UNICEF. (1990). *World declaration on survival, protection and development of children.* New York: UNICEF.

UNICEF. (1996). *Fifty years for children.* Accessed November 5, 2002, from *www.unicef.org/sowc96/50years.htm*

UNICEF. (2001). *The girl child project: Country evaluation.* Accessed November 15, 2003, from *www.unicef.org/reseval/evaldb/b3e.html*

UNICEF. (2003). *At a glance: Pakistan.* Retrieved October 15, 2003, from *www.unicef.org/infobycountry/pakistan.html*

United Nations Development Program. (2002). *Human development report 2002.* New York: Oxford University Press.

Weiss, A. (1998). The gendered division of space and access in working class areas of Lahore. *Contemporary South Asia, 7,* 71–89.

Weiss, A. (2002). *Walls within walls: Life histories of working women in the old city of Lahore* (2nd ed.). Oxford, UK: Oxford University Press.

Weiss, A. (2003). Interpreting Islam and women's rights: Implementing CEDAW in Pakistan. *International Sociology, 18,* 581–601.

Weiss, A., & Gilani, S. Z. (Eds.). (2001). *Power and civil society in Pakistan.* Oxford, UK: Oxford University Press.

Woodhead, M. (1998). *Children's perspectives on their working lives: A participatory study in Bangladesh, Ethiopia, the Philippines, Guatemala, El Salvador and Nicaragua.* Stockholm, Sweden: Rädda Barnen.

World Bank. (1996). *The Aga Khan Rural Support Program in Pakistan: A third evaluation.* Washington, DC: Author.

Zaman, M. Q. (1998). Sectarianism in Pakistan: The radicalization of Shi'a and Sunni identities. *Modern Asian Studies, 32,* 689–716.

2 (Re)Defining Public Spaces through Developmental Education for Afghan Women

NAHEED GINA AAFTAAB

Education is the pathway to progress, particularly for women. Nations where women are educated are more competitive, more prosperous and more advanced than nations where the education of women is forbidden or ignored.[1]

Both political activists and academics,[2] whether proponents or opponents of the attacks on Afghanistan after September 11, 2001, justified their arguments similarly by pointing to Afghan women as "mass victims." What struck me was how a diverse and multivariant group such as Afghan women was able to acquire a uniform and universal symbolic depiction. When I would suggest that representing Afghan women solely as victims is limited, the overwhelming and often emotional response was, "Then what are they if they are not victims?" How could one possibly ignore the atrocities that have been committed against them? The figure of Afghan women was thus constructed as a flattened trope that overlooks the contradictions and complexities in global power relations, and it was used to justify a masculine narrative that shows the United States to be the savior of the powerless women under the Taliban. Rather than discounting these representations of "victim," I will approach them critically and examine the power relations inherent in this view. I do not wish to deny the atrocities committed in Afghanistan, nor do I want to reinterpret them through a process of reidentification of the "Afghan woman." My goal is to challenge the inadequacies of the theoretical processes that support the representation of Afghan women as victims, and thus legitimized their violent salvation by the U.S. military.

The "plight of Afghan women" during the Taliban regime was used in the propaganda of the Bush administration to justify the "War on Terrorism" that led to the U.S. military invasion of Afghanistan on October 7, 2001. There is not enough space in this chapter to examine the Bush administration's representation of Afghan women at length, but a couple of examples will serve as a demonstration. On November 11, 2001, First Lady Laura Bush delivered the first ever radio address to the people of Afghanistan by a woman, expounding the atrocities against women done by terrorists. The following is an excerpt from that speech:

> Afghan women know, through hard experience, what the rest of the world is discovering: The brutal oppression of women is a central goal of the terrorists. Long before the current war began, the Taliban and its terrorist allies were making the lives of children and women in Afghanistan miserable. . . . Only the terrorists and the Taliban forbid education to women. . . . Because of our recent military gains in much of Afghanistan, women are no longer imprisoned in their homes. (L. Bush, 2001)

As President Bush himself expressed in the following press release, the U.S. military was not only bringing humanity and freedom to Afghan women, it also was directly linked to humanitarian and development efforts:

> Our soldiers wear the uniforms of warriors, but they are also compassionate people. And the Afghan people are really beginning to see the true strength of our country. I mean, routing out the Taliban was important, but building a school is equally important. (G. Bush, 2002)

The Bush administration drew on an established understanding of Afghan women[3] and women's role in development. While it is easy to critique the Bush administration's violent military actions and the propaganda that supported them, I want to draw attention to the gender development theories that support and strengthen the justifications of violence. As authors of these concepts, theorists need to continually stay critically engaged about their own work.

My thesis is a critique of development theories as they are applied to the education of "developing" women,[4] I contextualize this thesis with a case study of Afghan women in the process of nation building, social development, and empowerment. In order to construct a universal understanding of gender in development, some influential development theories do not account for the ambiguities and multiplicities of gendered education processes within various contexts. As an example of gendered development theories, I will focus on the influential work of Martha Nussbaum (e.g., Nussbaum & Glover, 1995) and her philosophical contributions to the Human Development Report's (HDR) discussion of "capabilities." While development theories posit education as necessary for incorporation into mainstream development (Moser, 1993), for improved health conditions (Bandarage, 1999), and integration in economic structures (ul Haq, 1995; Nussbaum & Glover, 1995), education's role in shaping "individual liberal" subjects is seldom theorized. Theoretical examination of the intersections between education, the state, and international development illuminates a number of power relations at multiple scales. By grounding my theoretical critique on fieldwork in Afghanistan, I am adhering to feminist thinking about critical development which advocates an examination of interscaler relations informed by ethnographic fieldwork (Nagar, Lawson, McDowell, & Hanson, 2002; Katz, 2001; Mohanty, 1991). By adding the perspective of the case study, I want both to initiate alternative discussions in response to the metanarratives that influence Afghan women and also to think critically about the space of education in development.

BEGINNING WITH CRITICAL DEVELOPMENT

Development discourse assumes a priori that a segment of the world is in need of improvement. These improvements are prescriptive and are intended for specific results; it is a process that Crush (1995) describes as "fundamentally about mapping and making, about the spatial reach of power and the control and management of peoples, territories, environments and places" (pp. 6–7). Development's control and management are manifested through material relations, ideological shifts, and cultural and political prescriptions. Increasingly, the result has led to militaristic measures. As Ferguson (1990) demonstrates, in postcolonial development one of the unintended "outcomes of planned social interventions" (p. 19) is the discursive construction (and privileging) of nation-state institutions in order to enable the implementation of development projects. More simply, development theories and institutions assume a strong state role. Moghadam (1993, 1999) underscores Afghanistan's weak institutionalized state to explain the government's inability to modernize its society, which is demonstrated by the contests over mandatory education and land reform. I argue that part of the reason for Afghanistan's institutional inefficacy resulted from a lack of domestic political representation as well as from its powerless geopolitical position in comparison to the outside influences of the Soviet Union, the United States, Pakistan, and others. Afghanistan's development process has been highly influenced by shifts in global development practices and their incorporation into international political agendas, which in Afghanistan's case have compromised the position of the state in relation to its nation(s).

Nussbaum's Human Development:
Teach a (Wo)man to Fish . . .

Critiques of economic development have advanced a shift toward the incorporation of social interests in development planning and implementation (Weaver, Rock, & Kusterer, 1997; Korton, 1995; Chambers, 1997). In 1995, Mahbub ul Haq, an advisor to the United Nations Development Programme (UNDP) and the chief architect of the UNDP's *Human Development Report* (HDR), stated:

> The human dimension of development is not just another addition to the development dialogue, it is an *entirely new perspective*, a *revolutionary* way to recast our conventional approach to development . . . Rather than the residual of development, human beings could finally become its principal objects and subject—not a forgotten economic abstraction. (pp. 11–12, emphasis added)

The *revolution* in development is concerned with increasing individual "choices" (ul Haq, 1995, p. 14); "Fundamental to enlarging these choices is building human capabilities" (UNDP, 2002, p. 27). The indexes of the HDR are statistical measures of "quality of life" (Sen, 1999; ul Haq, 1995; Nussbaum & Sen, 1993). The Human Development Index (HDI) is composed of indexes on health (life expectancy, infant and maternal mortality), education (literacy, enrollment rates), and economic measures (ul Haq, 1995, p. 62). Adjusting for gender disparity generates a lower HDI score; the centrality of gender attests to the importance of this framework's connection to liberal feminist issues.

Martha Nussbaum's (Nussbaum & Glover, 1995) work as a feminist philosopher with the UNDP at the World Institute for Development Economics Research (WIDER) has been identified as one of the philosophical underpinnings of the quantified measures of the HDI. In place of relativist assertions of difference, Nussbaum offers a list of universal functions that enable development to improve the quality of life. In examining the gender aspects of the HDR—as expanded by Nussbaum's theorization of capabilities and common humanity—I hope to instigate a dialogue about the seductiveness of gender development in UNDP's HDR and its implications on current development practices. Discourses drawing on liberal development, democratic governance, and capitalist individualisms have formed a powerful trinity that support current power structures, though through dynamic methods. Within this structure, the role of Muslim women as individual symbols used for nationalist interests in an international development context becomes an important focal point.

Nussbaum (Nussbaum & Glover, 1995) bases universal feminism on a definition of common humanity that incorporates the capacity and needs of all human beings through which the end goal is to address gender equity issues by enhancing the capabilities of all people to improve their lives

(p. 63). This does not ignore developmental context insofar as programs for enhancing capabilities are applied and developed according to the experience of specific contexts. But the aim is to create a common end goal of benefits, a uniform environment in which specific capabilities, as defined by Nussbaum, provide the highest return. She identifies indisputable universal commonalities and capabilities such as needs of the body, mobility, imagination, and practical reason (pp. 72–78). Her basic claim is that development's "central goal of public planning should be the *capabilities* of citizens to perform various functions," thereby overcoming other adversities and expanding their choices (p. 87, emphasis added). And while societies are required to develop their members' capabilities, the choice of performing the functions is left to the individual (p. 97).[5]

If the concept of capabilities is to be applied universally, then it must be based on an understanding of humanity that is universally applicable. Rather than differentiating individuals as members of a culture (Nussbaum & Glover, 1995, p. 72), Nussbaum proceeds to define human life according to capabilities that function to enhance all individual lives and are based on a universal ethic—as opposed to nature or biology (p. 74). The first level of functions concerns mainly physical needs such as mortality, nutrition, shelter, sexuality, and mobility (pp. 76–80). The second level concerns the capability to, or "being able to", meet identified physical needs (e.g., good health, use senses, form attachments, etc.); a lack of ability to meet these needs means the lack of a "good life" (pp. 83–85). Thus, a "good life" is not the assurance of resources, but the *capability* to compete for and secure resources. The ability to compete is measured by the HDI through the examination of income, political participation, education, and health.

In addressing development and the HDR specifically, Nussbaum (Nussbaum & Glover, 1995) takes the nation-state as the basic unit of analysis and views the role of public policy to be one that *enables* the citizenry to practice functionalities that would make a good life possible (pp. 86–87). Governments can ensure active participation leading to these capabilities through education. "Good governments, especially through education, facilitate the formation of good capabilities, remove impediments to their exercise, and provide means for their use" (Crocker, in Nussbaum & Glover, 1995, p. 184). According to Nussbaum, the state enables citizens with capabilities through education and employment; yet it must also provide certain freedoms (from cultural coercion) in order to promote these capabilities (pp. 94–95). The neutral state and its public policy become especially important since Nussbaum's gender framework depends on the efficiency and power gained from education leading to well-paid employment for women in the development process (pp. 92–93).[6]

Nussbaum asserts that the quantitative measurements of HDI focusing on capabilities and functionalities provide an assessment of one's quality of life that is not available through simple economic measurements such as the gross national product (GNP) (p. 90). According to Nussbaum, another possible way of measuring quality of life is by "polling people concerning the satisfaction of their preferences," but this approach misses "the obvious fact that desires and subjective preferences are not always reliable indicators of what a *person really needs*" (p. 91, emphasis added). Furthermore, reliance on local preferences or utility often "support the *status quo* and oppose radical change" (p. 91, emphasis in text). Thus the HDI provides a matrix wherein different contexts can be measured according to how much they deviate from an ideal environment that would provide a good life. An assessment of needs according to set criteria and the disregard for local preference sidesteps the structural realities and histories of diverse groups of women, and such a procedure relegates their views to something akin to a "false consciousness," excluding them from and suppressing their ability to decide how to define their own "good life."[7]

I have focused on Nussbaum's contribution to human development discourse and her work on a universal understanding of the "good life" as it relates to women. Thus my critique of Nussbaum is also limited to this construction of universalism and common humanity in development, which is informed by Benhabib (1995), a political theorist who joined Nussbaum in the conversation regarding human development's focus on women. For Benhabib, claims to a "common humanity" have always been a regulative method, a tool for prescription, not a descriptive one (p. 242).[8] Identifying a group as "like" or "unlike" us by providing a list of commonalities is simplistic (p. 244) when it gives one group the right to identify who is a human.[9] For Nussbaum, being human depends on the active practice of capabilities, and so she concludes that "being a woman is indeed not yet a way of being a human being"(1995, p. 104), given that women lack the support to achieve that potentiality in many parts of the world.[10] This creates a victimized figure that is in need of development's intervention.

Drawing from Habermas's (1985) communicative action model, Benhabib (1995) advocates for a communicative process of identifying the common goal of development and change. What enables communities to work together is the ability to communicate and make sense of each other's reality (p. 245). This relationship comes only through communication with and strong self-evaluation (p. 250) relating to the "Other(s)."

> We recognize this common humanity not because we share some belief in some philosophical concept of essence; but because we can understand her language, her actions, her emotions, her needs, and because we can communicate with her and see the world, more or less, maybe never wholly but adequately enough, as she sees it. (p. 251)

Of course, questions such as who decides what is "adequately enough" and the role of interpretation come into play. But what I'm interested in is the process of dialogue and communication in Benhabib's critique. Nussbaum's assurance that the "capabilities model" is not another form of imposed mo-

dernity or colonialism is dependent on the assumption that dialogue is taking place between the providers of development and their beneficiaries.
Though her empirical examples are often drawn from research that privi-
leges beneficiary participation and input (Nussbaum, 1995, p. 94), she requires that assessments be based on the measurements of the HDI and *not*
on local preference or utility (Nussbaum, 1995, p. 91). This is far from the
form of communication that Benhabib advocates: to form common understanding of needs through dialogue and respect for differences and multiculturalism. As Feldman and Gellert (in press) point out, a more representative list of capabilities, interests, and commonalities are formed through
deliberation, collaboration, and contestation.

Liberal feminist development theories privilege mobility and visibility
as a necessary precursor to access public education and employment, making the veil and the *burqa* a symbol of power and submission in the public
realm. The homogenized view of the veil as submissive is a disempowering
process because it ignores the variations of meaning behind the *burqa*
(Feldman, 2001). The ubiquitous images of Afghan women invisible in
their *burqas* post-September 11 attested to their powerless positions as activists, and politicians justified the use of violence to free these women. The
images were supported by descriptions of the denial of education, healthcare and mobility—all factors that provide the capabilities that lead to a
"good life." The veil and access to public resources in this case opens a
space of dialogue about gender and development; the veil represents an
icon of traditional hegemony and exclusionary power. The importance of
the *burqa* and mobility was also reflected in my conversations with participants in Afghanistan. As I discuss below, the *burqa* played a significant
though ambiguous role; it allowed women to be mobile in the public realm
while protecting their privacy from the public gaze. At the same time, it reflects the reality that they are not full participants in the public realm and
must negotiate a secondary role in the public. Given lack of space, I will
only focus on the experiences of education for Afghan women as part of
the public sphere in order to complicate universal assertions of developmental education's benefits.

EDUCATION IN DEVELOPMENT

The links between education, the state, and economy have been theorized
in a number of ways both as a site of reproduction and of emancipation.
First, schools are the institutions that facilitate the link between nation-
state and individuals through public policy (Anderson, 1983; Ramirez &
Ventresca 1992, p. 50; Torres, 1998). This link reinforces a specific process
of identity formation in a collective culture or system. Willis (1981) and
Bowles and Gintis (1977), provide examples of how public education "re-
produce(s)" class hierarchies within capitalist state structures. Second, and

in contrast to "reproduction," education also contributes to the creation of a public sphere, which is *potentially* a critical site of political discussion and action that keeps (hegemonic) powers in check (Torres, 1998, p. 23).[11]

Third, education in the developmental state is viewed to be a form of human capital investment that benefits the nation-state in the process of economic growth (Fägerlind & Saha, 1989; Easterly, 2001). According to current development theories, mass education and literacy provide a number of benefits to women: greater economic activity (Bandarage, 1999, p. 27; UNDP, 2002; Nussbaum, 1995; Chen, 1995); better knowledge of health, hygiene, and lower fertility rates (Hynes, 1999, p. 55); and empowerment within their communities, social structure, and state institutions (Tax, 1999, p. 121; for a critique, also see Kabeer, 1994, pp. 32, 219). This has become central to the HDR, which attempts to incorporate social indicators such as education in development, measured through enrollment and literacy, and also is used as an index of gender disparity.

Finally, and I would argue most importantly for the case of Afghanistan, women's education can also play an ambiguous role as a tool of nationalism. Postcolonial studies of women's education in South Asia suggest a melding of modern and traditional that would train women how to be both better mothers and good citizens (Gupta, 2002, pp. 166–167; see also Fägerlind & Saha, 1989). Thus, a specific form of education can be constructed for women, which is distinct from Western, male education (Gupta, 2002, pp. 168–169). Despite their prescriptions and limitations, educational institutions can provide alternative spaces for women's activities and identities. For example, reading can be a way of bringing the public into the private, and thus it can challenge the control of the private male (Gupta, 2002, pp. 172–174). Chatterjee (1989) emphasizes that in colonial Bengal education allocated an autonomous interest to women, even with debates over a "feminine curriculum," to preserve their role within the home. "Indeed, the nationalist constructs of the new woman derived its ideological strength from making the goal of cultural refinement through education a personal challenge for every woman, thus opening up a domain where woman was an autonomous subject" (Chatterjee, 1989, p. 246). In Afghanistan, as my field research indicates, new institutions for women's education reinforce culturally and religiously sanctioned roles for women, though the institutionalization process itself has impacts on cultural and religious interpretations.

AFGHANISTAN AND ITS WOMEN

The U.S. attack on Afghanistan was a pivotal moment in the complex historical relationship of the two states, especially in the last 30 years (for further readings on Afghanistan's political history, see Goodson, 2001; Rashid, 2001; Shahrani, 1990; Dupree, 1990; and Marsden, 1998). Issues surrounding women's education in Afghanistan are not new; contests over mandatory education took place in the 1970s between local religious leaders and the socialist government. And recently the denial of education for Afghan women was a major focal point of the representations of Afghan women in the United States. My fieldwork also demonstrates that there is a great deal of attention and work put into women's education in Afghanistan by both local and international actors. I will briefly review some major political and historical aspects of women's struggles and education policy in Afghanistan before discussing my fieldwork and the actual experience of Afghan women regarding education in the current context.

For Afghan women, issues of gender rights have not improved since the 1970s, when major activities and contests for women's liberation took place.[12] Women in Afghanistan live in a highly unequal society, perpetuated by and propagating numerous other hardships in their daily experience. The oft-changing political leadership and governmental structure has also meant unstable, and at times contradictory, policies concerning women's rights. It is important to note that while women were legally allotted equality under the 1931 constitution and its subsequent amendments, the practiced rights and provision of services have been far from equal and repeatedly contested. In the mid-1950s, separate schools were established for girls in urban centers such as Kabul, and women were admitted into the University of Kabul in 1959. By this time women were appearing in public without full veils. They were entering the workforce, joining government ministries, and voting. Civil laws and legislation were put forward in the 1960s and 1970s protecting women with respect to child marriage, dowry, and inheritance. But these civil laws were voluntary, and many of the changes did not affect the primarily rural population (Skaine, 2002).

It was not until the late 1970s when the communist government of the People's Democratic Party of Afghanistan (PDPA) came to power that penalties were enforced for the civil laws, and mandatory education was implemented in rural areas despite limited popular support. Gender policies became a major point of contention between the traditionalists and the reformists, at times taking extreme and violent forms. Moghadam (1999) states that "in the summer of 1978 refugees began pouring into Pakistan, giving as their major reason the forceful implementation of the literacy program among their women" (pp. 178–179). As the feminist wing of the PDPA, the Democratic Organization of Afghan Women, demanded gender rights, the rural population of Afghanistan turned away from these reforms, especially mandatory education for women, given the mistrust and hostility toward the government (Moghadam, 1999).[13] An examination of the uprisings previous to the Soviet invasion of 1979 also points to education being a major reason for the violent revolts against the government, which in many cases targeted teachers and schools, with Herat being one of the only areas indicating an organized and planned revolt (Roy, 1986, pp. 107–108). With the departure of communism in 1992, these laws became invalid or unenforceable. The legal situation of Afghan women under the rule of the Taliban, who began to consolidate their power in 1994, was one of the harshest experiences, especially for urban women. With fluctuating political institutions, other social structuring such as religious or cultural codification became more prevalent in legitimizing the use of power by the Taliban.[14]

One should not view women outside of this political spectrum and practice; Afghan women's guerilla activities with the mujahideen against the Soviet Union signify the importance of cultural identification by these Afghan women, despite the chauvinistic or extremist views of the mujahideen. Interviews with such activists reveal that they viewed the communist form of "gender rights" as foreign and oppressive in that it did not afford them the freedom to practice what they viewed as their religious and cultural rights (Skaine, 2002, pp. 18–19). Nancy Dupree's (1990) work in the Pakistan refugee camps points to a similar trend in women's social activism. These activities can be viewed as a part of public, civic action, reflecting the needs of citizens to challenge collectively what they view as an oppressive political system throughout Afghanistan's modern history. For example, women publicly demonstrated against parliamentary decisions regarding their education in 1968 during the monarchy (Skaine, 2002, p. 16) and against the Taliban's decision in 1996 not to accept small bank notes (Skaine, 2002, p. 21). My research points to women being highly active in education during the Taliban rule, and their activities were not limited to their economic needs.

With these ideas in mind, the following section briefly examines the public–private spatial designation of education, in which the use of the *burqa* simultaneously becomes a tool of access and subordination. While many Afghan women recognize and identify with the social values of institutional participation and unrestricted access, the *burqa*'s restriction reflects a spatial construction where the public is an unsafe arena to be negotiated between various powers of influence and control. In the case of restructuring the education system, the space of education is being constructed as a hybrid space of public and private representing the multiplicity and precariousness of the Afghan woman's position. All of these characteristics add to an understanding of education as a process of development and as an indicator of "quality of life," and they are aspects that cannot be measured through the HDI or other quantitative tools.

FIELDWORK

For Nussbaum (1995), "customs" that hinder "functionalities" in achieving a "good life" must be abolished for "human capabilities" to be effective, and this requires a certain political and legal environment. In the international view, any trace of the Taliban had to be removed from the politics of Afghanistan before policies of human development of education and labor could be implemented—thus justifying the use of violence for the sake of the well-being of women. My research points to a more flexible and hybrid form of dialogue that takes place at the local level, leading Afghan women to negotiate between their Muslim communities and international liberal enforcement (not always in opposition). They are active in negotiating their spaces within their communities and through how they impact social transformation. In studying education, I want to examine a partial component of this dialogue, influenced by Minault's (1998) work that suggests educational reform is more a symptom of larger social reforms, rather than the cause thereof.

The Context

I conducted preliminary fieldwork on women's education in Herat, Afghanistan, and in surrounding areas in the summer of 2002. The qualitative research consisted of informal conversations, participant observation, and site visits to public and private schools. After I presented an explanation about the project and its intended purposes, I asked the participants to discuss their background and understanding of education in Afghanistan at the time; my questions were only a guide for the conversation. As a native Farsi speaker, I was able to communicate in the local language, which gave me access to forms of interpretations that are nuanced and unique, though I did need explanation of some historical and cultural references. I did not tape-record the interviews for reasons of security and in order to keep the atmosphere casual and informal.[15] Thus, the study is based on detailed field notes. Given the lack of recording, I will not be quoting what the participants said. At this point there are many layers of interpretations, from the conversation to notes to the multiple stages of writing. This an exploratory project to raise relevant questions about the context as well as the theoretical insights that are applied through development. For the sake of brevity, I will not go into detail about the dire conditions of education in Afghanistan. A brief examination of organizations active in Afghanistan, especially UNICEF, will be illustrative; my own experiences did not contradict these more popular descriptions.

Though the scope of the research is limited, I examined schools in both rural and urban areas, the results and analysis of which are presented below. The participants were teachers and one principal at a rural school. All of the teachers were women who were married and who had children; the principal was male and viewed as a leader in the community. All the teachers explained that economic hardships required them to work. Teaching income provided enough benefits to outweigh the added hours of work to their usual busy schedules at home as well as the often serious reprimands from community and family members for jeopardizing the honor of the family by working outside of the home. In Herat hierarchies of power reflect status and prestige within the community and are a main point of contention concerning access to natural and social resources. Within these power structures, the role of political participation, through formal and informal debates and dialogues, was seen as an important form of practicing in the power structures. Political involvement was clearly linked to economic activity so that wages, employment sectors, and the role of education are clearly associated with social and political status, though more so for men than for women—as is discussed below. Thus, education and teaching is considered to be a political and potentially destabilizing force.

Afghanistan as a nation has gone through a number of transitions. Research participants often expressed that it has been the experimental ground for different methods of governance and development by outside interests, as discussed above. Though their "history" does not mirror the detail and critique of historians, it is part of their living social memory.[16] Importantly, education is not spoken of as a primary concern, at least not in the same way as access to food, water, healthcare, work, and consumer goods.[17] As women become more prevalent in development as symbols for "liberation" (especially as "development" is contrasted with the "Islamic world"), the question arises: How does this in turn influence development discourse and practice? What is the impact of this shift on the lives of women in Afghanistan, their needs and their coping mechanisms, despite the changes? And how do they shape their changing environment as agents? During my fieldwork, it was difficult to separate the discussion and beliefs positing development as anything other than modernization; the link between the two has been normalized, given the experience of many Afghans. Accepting Naila Kabeer's (1994) premise about modernization, development as modernization is presumed to be gender-neutral and thus produces gender equality in societies with large gender disparities. But, as Kabeer points out, the gendered processes of modernization itself are not considered, assuming that whatever the transformation, it is progressive and preferred (Kabeer, 1994, p. 18).

Findings on Education

Qalai-e Kemal (pseudonym), about 40 kilometers southwest of the city of Herat, is mainly a self-sustaining village of agriculturalists who have few opportunities for a cash economy outside of migrant labor to Iran. Though no vocational training existed for women at the time of my research, limited training does exist for health practices such as giving injections and midwifery. Such training does allow possible participation in the cash economy for women. Beyond this, teaching is the only opportunity for a formal salary. But there is much attention paid to the education of girls and how the process of their education should take place in their village.

During a site visit to a rural girl's school, I was able to speak with the principal, Kasem (pseudonym), and subsequently held group discussions with the teachers. About 35 girls of various ages walk from Qalai-e Kemal with two teachers to join the neighboring village's school for grades one through six; there are no opportunities for schooling beyond sixth grade for girls. Alternative forms of literacy also exist in the mosques, where girls can learn to read the Qur'an in Arabic, and to pursue religious studies—though the value of the education provided by the mullahs was continuously questioned. Nonetheless, many of the teachers in the school depend on their students having attained some degree of literacy in the mosque. The general feeling is that by the age of 6 or 7 everyone should at least be able to read and preferably write. How that skill is used and how much it is retained is more individualized.

Older girls (i.e., postpuberty) are not encouraged to go to school, given the distance, lack of safety, and early marriage. Education is not viewed as a worthwhile investment of their time and energy. But there are exceptions: a 14-year-old girl who was recently engaged will not continue with school, unlike her 16-year-old cousin, who is also engaged. At the time of the interview she was the oldest student at the school. According to the teachers, given the possibility, maybe 20% of the students would go on to finish high school. The reason behind the current low numbers is the restrictions posed by families, husbands, and fathers. Often girls are engaged once they are literate, when the family realizes that some benefit is met and assumes that the husband's family will oppose their daughter's education.[18] These obstacles are important when examining the teacher's views on the value and benefits of education: to achieve the ability to read and write letters, signs, instructions, and so on, but not necessarily to gain employment. Thus, at least publicly or in familial settings, there is ample enthusiasm about education, or at least the skills of reading and writing (literacy), and a frustration with the lack of education quality in the village as compared to the city.

Repeatedly the teachers and the principal expressed frustration with the shortage of teachers and the lack of training for current teachers. None of the six teachers in this case attended college, and only one had graduated from high school. Legally, those with a minimum of a sixth-grade education can teach in rural areas, whereas in the cities they are required to have a high-school diploma. This shortage makes literacy a sufficient qualification for some to teach, given the lack of official documentation and the widespread prevalence of migration, limited state involvement, and flexible regulation. Currently, there are no educators to take up the responsibility of training more teachers. The only qualified person is Principal Kasem, but given gender differences, it is socially prohibited for him to do so.

Principal Kasem, viewed as a leader of education in the community, expressed the importance of keeping with Islamic ways when teaching. According to him, there is a need to gain the trust of the people in order to be able to provide services—and the only way to do so is through Islam. Mosques provide an important service and high benefits in terms of teaching theology, so that doesn't have to be done so much in secular schools. But the secular schools must run parallel to the functions of the mosques. His discussion of religion was not unique; the benefits of women's education are supported by religious dictates and are required for the advancement of society as a whole, and, in this case, for the advancement of Muslim society. Principal Kasem expressed the idea that the literate are different people—they are more knowledgeable, especially in terms of religion. Women must participate in education, of course, as long as there is gender segregation. Every woman must be in Islamic dress, and since the dress is part of the environment here, it is needed. Afghanistan's underdevelopment, ethnic conflict, and political contestations are a direct result of the lack of education. Beyond economic security for both students and teachers, there needs to be freedom from fear through security and peace, which will provide an environment more conducive to learning. This points to a flexible understanding of custom, religion, and transformative education, in that education's specific characteristics must reflect social conditions to be viable.

In my discussions with teachers, I asked about the "value of education." If there was a tangible economic or legal benefit, then a quantitative measurement would be possible; but it was clear that such opportunities do not exist in the foreseeable future for these students. My interpretation of the value of education is that it will benefit students in terms of social standing, an expansion of the mind, and another *skill* to have. When asked what the goal of education is for the girls in the village, a number of the women noted that they wanted students to continue and finish high school. I further pushed the question of "why" and what the value of such an education will be. The response was that they can see their uneducated mothers— in comparison, they believe that the lives of the educated are bound to be better. Further questioning of what is a "better life" spurred no discussion. Thus the values of education are measured in a comparative manner and based on an assumption that changes within society and culture are taking place.

Principal Kasem said that just going to school is enough to change a person, in terms of discipline and behavior. In school there is greater exposure to children of other families, with differing ethical codes, and also a freedom in not having to be supervised by members of the family. That adds to any changes that might come from literacy. As Principal Kasem and a number of other teachers pointed out, an institution allows for a different kind of socialization: one highly structured and influenced by teachers, an institutionalized behaviorism, especially for women, who will directly shape their children's lives as mothers. Maybe this is the "benefit" of education: a more uniform, institutionalized socialization of young children outside of the environment of an almost closed family system and beyond ethnic and tribal divisions. For girls, it is justified through the potential of motherhood, the disciplining of their family along religious lines. Thus, in this context, the position of the public woman as mother is codified and it legitimizes the process of the public education system. This may be the only way that education can be implemented in Afghanistan at this moment, given the state's inability to influence the process.

The situation within Herat brings up a number of different concerns, though similar hardships and shortage of teachers apply to both contexts.[19] I was able to conduct site visits to public and private schools and to have discussions with teachers about education and its gendered aspects. When walking into a public school, one is struck by the numbers of white tents in the courtyard that house the large number of first-grade students. There are more than 20 first-grade classes, with an average of 60 students in each classroom. In comparison, there are only two 12th-grade classes, with about 20 students in each class. Three main reasons contribute to the high number of first-grade students. First, there is an absolute increase in the population of children in general; second, there has been a lack of education for the last 6 years under the Taliban, so that any girl between the age of 6 and 14 is eligible to attend first through fourth grade. And third, there is a more accepting social code for young girls to attend school, expressed as "the need for development," though this is not universally felt. Participation by older students is limited for the reasons discussed above, though with lesser impact than in the village.

The effectiveness of education can be furthered by a number of means in Afghanistan—at least in the urban setting. First, if women had access to other forms of publicity, such as television and newspapers, to bring the "outside public" into their homes, education could be made more meaningful. Also, opportunity for other forms of employment could be a great encouragement. One of the reasons why there is a lack of employment for women is that there is a lack of women in the public government sector beyond some figureheads. If jobs were legally opened, many women would participate given their economic needs, especially those who have fewer restrictions at home and who are willing to accept social admonition. Often in these cases, the lack of any opportunity to use education for economic needs is a determining factor in school enrollment. Education's benefits are not simply influenced by an outside developer or through a change in the political regime; more importantly, they are an integral part of local culture, politics, and economics.

As socially and religiously sanctioned institutions, schools in Afghanistan are strictly gender-segregated. Disciplinary aspects are important for both men and women, but the power consequences are different. Girls' schools will teach them to adhere to socially sanctioned gendered identities of women; thus it should be continually questioned whether a woman's education will produce the results desired by liberal developmental feminism. In this context, schools are an amalgam space where the rules of society are taught to future members, and the continual (re)constructions of private spaces emerge in which the private honor and role of women are ensured while accepting some (controlled) influences of the public. The role of teachers and administrators is crucial in making certain that this characteristic is kept. In the discussion of spaces, designations such as public, private, far, controllable, or insecure become important, but are shallow and symptomatic of other designated meanings.[20] In the same way, sites of education for women must be constructed to reflect the integrities of private spaces in order to be socially acceptable.

This does not negate the possibility that schools can provide a space that fosters change—as many of the women teachers pointed out. This reading has two implications when examined with the work of Nussbaum. First, a public institution, such as state education, does not mean a liberation of women from custom; rather it comes closer to Willis's (1981) understanding of education as creating a socially sanctioned individual. And second, the change that does take place within the education system is not through the possibility of employment (Nussbaum, 1995, p. 90) or the ability to defy and resist custom, but rather it is a navigation within the existing systems. In this case, identity and interests are a coproduction by the state and religion-sanctioned customary trends and the individual subjects because they are not mere subjects of the system, but are able to negotiate between powers and their own utility. The relevance of "personal utility" *is* important, and is something that the HDI is not able to measure.[21]

In addition to gender segregation, the role of the *burqa* is telling in the contest over the public and private body of Afghan women. The majority of women still wear the *burqa* with ever-increasing sales supported by purchases as young girls reach maturation.[22] There was a general view that the *burqa* is constricting but necessary for security as a symbol of privacy and in providing the ability to travel in public while keeping *purdah*. But *purdah* can also be applied to other women who are not part of the kinship system. One of the oppositions for women's education or employment is that they will not be able to keep *purdah* from other women so that those that do not want their daughters to participate may also bring up the issue that they don't want to associate with strangers, or *begoneh*, who are outside of the kinship system. Despite disagreements that this form of seclusion is anti-Islamic, the practice is generally justified by drawing on Islam.

In different discussions, participants mentioned that removing the *burqa* would have to be a collective act. Shortly before my visit to the school, in another public school in Herat, some of the students had gone through the *burqa* hangers and had cut large slits in the *burqas*, making them impossible to be worn again. Of course, this was not appreciated by other students, who decided to walk home in torn *burqas* and bought new ones soon after. Here again, participation within the education sector can collectively, though not uniformly, self-define the connotation of the *burqa*, but this can only happen if outside conditions are also conducive to change. I would question the assumption that schools act as catalysts of change following the induction of liberating desires; on the contrary, education systems must reflect social changes. The collective actions of Afghan women may depend on feelings of social and physical security before they take off the *burqa*. A sense of ethical or moral security is created through gender segregation, including strict control over appearance and continued use of the *burqa*. The enforcement of these rules allows for education to be socially supported and accepted. But one must ask what the long-term effects of such enforcement will be. The support for education is expressed through comments such as "we know the price of illiteracy" and through the idea that education has value beyond economics not met by other means.

This is above and beyond the framework of values set up by Nussbaum, where education plays a transformative role within a developing community. My research supports Feldman and Gelleret's (in press) discussion that education lacks viability without institutional shifts, especially in terms of the possibilities for employment. As Feldman and Gelleret point out, Nussbaum's support for education is also a support for indirect shaping of desires in a predetermined manner fitting UNDP's standardized measurements which are assumed to be neutral. But as this case shows, education for Afghan women is shaping myriads of desires including local customs and preferences. Nussbaum's understanding of not taking into account local preferences is not only an imposition of her own norms about the values of life, but it also has major drawbacks with respect to how education policies can be implemented. Even if localized preferences and utility do not fit the projected requirements of the UNDP's human development, it is and must be a central consideration of development planning and implementation process.

CONCLUSION

I began my discussion with observations of how theories of development and feminisms can be used to legitimize a form of dominance and even violence. My argument is not that these models of development have led to violence; indeed, such an assertion would give too much power to these discourses. These theories demonstrate and emphasize the "ends" of society, the *result* of what progress would look like. The desired goal becomes the construction of a society that is welcoming of "individual capabilities" provided by development and constructing a society by eradicating existing systems through multiple forms of violence. There is little in these universal models that can argue against violence. In formulating the universal goal, they lose sight of the "means" by which they are to achieve development. Thus communities experiencing violence are left to decide the means of constructing a society that is sanctioned internationally, since not meeting the requirements could mean, at best, a lack of funds to continue the provision of services, and, at worse, military action. Critical, nuanced studies must go beyond pointing out the contradictions in universalistic development, and must examine how this form of violence fits within development, and, in turn, how development legitimizes the use of violence.

In my case study, I have shown that understandings of women's development and education at the local level are formed within an understanding of history and power relations locally and at a larger scale. These historical and scaler concepts cannot be ignored in development projects. The popular use of human development and supporting theories of universalisms such as those of Martha Nussbaum do not allow for the multivariant and multilevel inclusion of context. A fuller understanding of context, then, depends on deliberative communication with the beneficiaries of development, which demands a reconsideration of power relations both within development and feminism to include views that represent more than just "victims" and are incorporated more fully into the system of knowledge production about development policy.

My critique of education, development, and feminism is not one of dismissal, but rather a call for increased engagement. The lack of funding and infrastructure capacity for the rebuilding of the education system in Afghanistan hinders many of the enthusiastic participants, reestablishing existing inequalities. At the same time, limited local resources are utilized to achieve the goals of education as defined by the community, often those already in influential positions, which has both positive and negative impacts on women. This points further to the inapplicability of the universalist criteria and casts doubt on the usefulness of uniform development criteria such as the HDI and its gender indexes. In the end, human development and a higher quality of life cannot be achieved without a more inclusive development agenda that also takes into account local utility and preferences.

As mentioned above, this was a preparatory project for further research. The goal was to find important questions and relevant theoretical bodies that are applicable in this situation. The next few years will be important as education becomes more accepted (or possibly contested, as the recent Taliban targeting of schools is demonstrating) and in considering how education may shift social structures and individuals in the long term. Questions of literacy, curriculum, pedagogy, and administrative quality in education must be coupled with investigations of the social, political, and economic role of education in designating an individual's place in society.

From this preliminary research, I find that schools are a "constructed social space"; the process of that construction and its social signifier points to interesting understandings of power relations. As development and the use of military power are joined in international relations, theorists and activists must stay actively engaged in the use and implementations of ideals of development and human rights. After all, we must be ready to consider whether Afghan women's lives and security should be exchanged for education, and we must be ready to inquire of them what their choices and ideals are.

NOTES

1. This statement was made in March 2002 after the United States sent textbooks to Afghanistan to promote education. Much of the argument by the Bush administration was centered upon the importance of education for Afghanistan.
2. For example, see numerous articles in *Signs* (Autumn 2002, Vol. 28, No. 1).
3. For examples, refer to Feminist Majority's Campaign against Gender Apartheid, the leadership of Mevis Leno (Feminist Majority Campaign Against Gender Apartheid *www.feminist.com/activism/take_genderap_dec00.html; www.feminist. org/afghan/facts.html)*, and popular documentaries such as CNN's Beneath the Veil by Saira Shah (*www.cnn.com/CNN/Programs/presents/index. veil.html*).
4. While I am aware of the important and nuanced critique of terms such as "underdeveloped," "less developed," and "developing," I will not go into a discussion of these terms in detail. I will use the term "developing" to reflect the dominant language within development institutions and their discourses.
5. Tradition and culture become important parts of examining societies and the capabilities of their members when examining subjugation and unequal power relations. In introducing the "capabilities model," Nussbaum (1995) points out that poverty alone does not determine the disadvantage in women's lives:

   > Custom decrees who gets access to the education that would open job opportunities and make political rights meaningful. Custom decrees who can go where in what clothing and with whom. Custom decrees who gets to make what sorts of protests against ill-treatment both inside and outside the family, and whose voice of protest is likely to be heard. (p. 3)

   Sweeping statements such as "a preference-based approach that gives priority to the preference of traditional culture is likely to be especially subversive of the quality of life of women who have been on the whole badly treated by prevailing traditional norms" (Nussbaum, 1995, p. 92) beg the question of what is traditional culture as well as whether Nussbaum's dependence on classical Western theories are not themselves a preference within a tradition.
6. Thus, since employment is linked to preservation of life in terms of healthcare and life expectancy, then formal employment is part of basic capabilities, without which a good human life will not be possible (Chen, 1995, pp. 53, 55, 90).
7. During my field study, the participants were quite knowledgeable about their

needs and obstacles. The changes they expected were not always in opposition to those put forward by Nussbaum; but their proposals were often sophisticated enough to take into account their reality and context. As postcolonial critiques of liberal universalisms and "false consciousness" point out, these theories are primarily formed to support liberalism's power in an international framework rather than describing the local context (Spivak, 1999; Mohanty, 1991; Mehta, 1999; Bhabha, 1999).

8. This is partly due to the impossibility of fully identifying and describing "tradition" as founded on a commonality. Traditions and customs are always changing and negotiated (Benhabib, 1995, p. 239), so that the vantage point of scale and time becomes an important determinant of how we understand these concepts.

9. As Nussbaum asserts, those who have lost or were born without the capacity of sensory, imagination, creativity, love, or autonomy cannot be identified as humans, although that does not negate our (human) moral responsibility toward them (Nussbaum, 1995, pp. 81–82).

10. Here Nussbaum deems it necessary to mention that women are different from "rocks and plants and even dogs and horses", and thus are human (Nussbaum, 1995, p. 104).

11. This is especially true in feminist struggles, as personal, private issues have been brought into the public and political for legal and institutional accountability and transformation (see Mies, 1986; Landes, 1998; Fraser, 1997).

12. Valentine M. Moghadam credits the socialist/communist governments of 1977 with starting the liberation of women in Afghanistan (Moghadam, 1999, p. 863). In contrast, William Maley (1996) argues that the monarchy of Zahir Shah began the advancement of women's rights by allowing the women to appear unveiled in public in 1959. Both views agree that the government was central in implementing women's rights, but government policies of neither regime affected the cultural and social role of the average Afghan woman as planned.

13. Communist development projects and legal policies were viewed to be an interference with the domestic sphere of the Afghan cultural life (Skaine, 2002, p. 18); my own research points to similar resentments toward the Taliban administration, often expressing that these political interests do not represent the interests of the population and reflect outside norms.

14. Denying the role of Islam, the Muslim Women's League states: "Taliban's stand on the seclusion of women is not derived from Islam, but, rather, from a cultural bias found in suppressive movements throughout the region" (in Skaine, 2002, p. 5). Former Afghan diplomats and officials have argued that the Taliban's activities were not based on cultural bias and point to the abovementioned political trends to demonstrate the (legal) progressiveness of Afghanistan (i.e., Haron Amin, in Skaine, 2002, p. 13).

15. There is often an apprehension about matters that seem public and official especially when they seem to contest the sanctity of the private, which includes any topic that incorporates women.

16. Socialism and communism were processes that begun during and ended with the interests of the Cold War. The purism of an (attempted) Islamic state reflects a shift in those interests; and democracy, with the attempt to establish an equal society, is yet another development project, or U.S. experiment. What is aston-

ishing is that all three processes of social change are part of the living memory of the majority of the population as this all has taken place in the last 30 years.

17. The explicit need for education is clearest in the case of men who can use it to get better jobs and thus economic security; for women, these benefits or opportunities do not present themselves as readily, or at all, except in the education sector.

18. It was expressed that mothers have little say in the marriage of their daughters, though this is a stereotypical norm that has repeatedly been contested by various women.

19. Despite the shortage of teachers, women have dominated the education sector in Afghanistan, and now the area of education seems to be the only sector for job opportunities often celebrated by local politicians and media along feminine gender-specific characteristics.

20. A more nuanced reading of the characterization of space in this case would be to examine the contest over the space of the self in terms of body politics. A woman under *burqa* or under *purdah*, invisible to nonfamilial or stranger's eyes, is equivalent to being in a private space while participating in a public act. Her protection is the duty of family members, male and female, even if their roles are defined differently.

21. Nussbaum brings up the discussion of utility when addressing the internalization of subordination and lack of knowledge for better opportunities. "The poor and deprived frequently adjust their expectation and aspiration to the low level of life they have known. Thus they may not demand more education, better health care" (Nussbaum, 1995, p. 91). In this case, the subordinate's view of utility is false, and a reliance on that shows "results that support the status quo and oppose radical change," not actual quality of life (Nussbaum, 1995, p. 91). She presents this after pointing to the quantified measurements of the HDR as a representation of measuring quality of life while objecting to the quantified "commensurability of values in utilitarianism" (Nussbaum, 1995, p. 91, fn. 71).

22. Though prevalent in the rural setting in Herat, the *burqa* was uncommon in Herat until the Taliban takeover. Today, the majority of women above the age of 12 wear a *burqa* when leaving home; many expressed that this is their own choice rather than the choice of male family members.

REFERENCES

Al-Hibri, A. (1982). A study of Islamic herstory; Or, how did we ever get into this mess? In *Women and Islam* (pp. 207–220). Oxford, UK: Pergamon Press.

Anderson, B. (1983). *Imagined communities.* New York: Verso.

Bandarage, A. (1999). Population and development: toward a social justice agenda. In R. Silliman & Y. King (Eds.), *Dangerous intersections: Feminist perspectives on population, environment, and development* (pp. 24–38). Cambridge, MA: South End Press.

Baranzangi, N. (1997). Muslim women's Islamic higher learning as a human right:

The action plan. M. Afkhami & E. Friedl (Eds.), *Muslim women and the politics of participation* (pp. 43–57). Syracuse, NY: Syracuse University Press.

BBC News. (2002). Bush sends books to Afghanistan. Retrieved March 16, 2002, from *news.bbc.co.uk/1/hi/world/americas/1876663.stm*

Benhabib, S. (1995). Cultural complexity, moral interdependence, and the global dialogical community. In M. Nussbaum & J. Glover (Eds.), *Women, culture, and development: A study of human capabilities* (pp. 234–255). New Delhi, India: Oxford University Press.

Bhabha, H. (1999). Liberalism's sacred cow. In J. Cohen, M. Howard, & M. C. Nussbaum (Eds.), *Is multiculturalism bad for women?* (pp. 79–84). Princeton, NJ: Princeton University Press.

Bowles, S., & Gintis, H. (1977). *Schooling in capitalist America: Educational reform and the contradictions of economic life.* New York: Basic Books.

Bush, G. (2002). President highlights humanitarian efforts in Afghanistan: Remarks by the president on U.S. humanitarian aid to Afghanistan. Office of the Press Secretary, October 11, 2002. Retrieved November 25, 2003, from *www.whitehouse.gov/news/releases/2002/10/20021011-3.html*

Bush, L. (2002). Radio address by Lady Laura Bush to the nation. Office of Mrs. Bush, November 17, 2001. Retrieved November 25, 2003, from *www.whitehouse. gov/news/releases/2001/11/20011117.html*

Chambers, R. (1997). *Whose reality counts?: Putting the first last.* London: Intermediate Technology.

Chatterjee, P. (1989). The nationalist resolution of the women's question. In K. V. Sangari & S. Vaid (Eds.), *Recasting women: Essays in colonial history* (pp. 233–253). New Delhi, India: Kali for Women.

Chen, M. (1995) A matter of survival: Women's right to employment in India and Bangladesh. In M. Nussbaum & J. Glover (Eds.), *Women, culture, and development: A study of human capabilities.* New Delhi, India: Oxford University Press.

Cheriet, B. (1997). Fundamentalism and women's rights: Lessons from the city of women. In M. Afkhami & E. Friedl (Eds.), *Muslim women and the politics of participation* (pp. 11–17). Syracuse, NY: Syracuse University Press.

Crocker, D. (1995). Functioning and capability: The foundations of Sen's and Nussbaum's development ethic. In M. Nussbaum & J. Glover (Eds.), *Women, culture, and development: A study of human capabilities* (pp. 153–198). New Delhi, India: Oxford University Press.

Crush, J. E. (1995). *Power of development.* London and New York: Routledge.

Dupree, N. H. (1990). A socio-cultural dimension: Afghan women refugees in Pakistan. In E. W. Anderson & N. H. Dupree (Eds.), *The cultural basis of Afghan nationalism* (pp. 121–133). London and New York: Pinter.

Easterly, W. (2001). *The elusive quest for growth: Economists' adventures and misadventures in the tropics.* Cambridge, MA: MIT Press.

Fägerlind, I. S., & Saha, L. J. (1989). *Education and national development: A comparative perspective.* Oxford, UK: Pergamon Press.

Feldman, S. (2001). Exploring theories of patriarchy: A perspective from contemporary Bangladesh. *Signs, 26*(4), 1097.

Feldman, S., & Gellert, P. (in press). The seductive quality of central human capabilities: Rethinking Nussbaum's liberal approach to development.

Ferguson, J. (1990). *The anti-politics machine: "Development," depoliticization, and bureaucratic power in Lesotho*. Cambridge, UK, and New York: Cambridge University Press.

Fraser, N. (1997). *Justice interruptus: Critical reflections on the "post socialist" condition*. New York: Routledge.

Freire, P. (1968). *Pedagogy of the oppressed*. New York: Seabury Press.

Goodson, L. P. (2001). *Afghanistan's endless war: State failure, regional politics, and the rise of the Taliban*. Seattle: University of Washington Press.

Gupta, C. (2002). *Sexuality, obscenity, community: Women, Muslims, and the Hindu public in colonial India*. New York: Palgrave.

Habermas, J. (1985). *The theory of communicative Action: Vol. 2, Lifeworld and system. A critique of functionalist reason* T. McCarthy, (Trans.) Boston, MA: Beacon Press.

Hynes, P. (1999). Taking population out of the equation: Reformulating I = PAT. In J. Silliman & Y. King (Eds.), *Dangerous intersections: Feminist perspectives on population, environment, and development* (pp. 39–73). Cambridge, MA: South End Press.

Kabeer, N. (1994). *Reversed realities: Gender hierarchies in development thought*. London and New York: Verso.

Katz, C. (2001). On the grounds of globalization: A topography for feminist political engagement. *Signs, 26*(4), 1213–1234.

Korten, D. (1995) *When corporations rule the world*. West Hartford, CT: Kumarian Press.

Landes, J. (Ed.). (1998). *Feminism: the public and the private*. Oxford, UK: Oxford University Press.

Maley, W. (1996). Women and public policy in Afghanistan: A comment. *World Development, 24*(1), 203.

Marsden, P. (2002). *The Taliban: War and religion in Afghanistan*. London: Zed Books.

Mehta, U. S. (1999). *Liberalism and empire: A study in nineteenth-century British liberal thought*. Chicago: University of Chicago Press.

Mies, M. (1986). *Patriarchy and accumulation on a world scale: Women in the international division of labour*. London: Zed Books.

Minault, G. (1998). *Secluded scholars: Women's education and Muslim social reform in colonial India*. New Delhi, India, and New York: Oxford University Press.

Moallem, M. (1999). Transnationalism, feminism, and fundamentalism. In C. Kaplan, N. Alarcon, & M. Moallem (Eds.), *Between women and nation: Nationalism, transnational feminism, and the state* (pp. 320–348). Durham, NC: Duke University Press.

Moghadam, V. M. (1993). *Modernizing women: Gender and social Change in the Middle East*. Boulder, CO: Lynne Rienner.

Moghadam, V. M. (1999). Revolution, religion, and gender politics: Iran and Afghanistan compared. *Journal of Women's History, 10*(4), 172–195.

Mohanty, C. T. (1991). Under Western eyes: Feminist scholarship and colonial discourses. In C. T. Mohanty, A. Russo, & L. Torres (Eds.), *Third world women and the politics of feminism* (pp. 51–80). Bloomington: Indiana University Press.

Moser, C. O. N. (1993). *Gender planning and development: Theory, practice and training*. London, NY: Routledge.

Nagar, R. L., Lawson, V., McDowell, L., & Hanson, S. (2002). Locating globalization: Feminist (re)readings of the subjects and spaces of globalization. *Economic Geography, 78*(3), 257–284.

Nussbaum, M. (1995). Human capabilities, female human beings. In M. Nussbaum & J. Glover (Eds.), *Women, culture, and development: A study of human capabilities* (pp. 61–104). New Delhi, India: Oxford University Press.

Nussbaum, M., & Sen, A. (Eds.) (1993). *The quality of life.* Oxford,UK: Clarendon Press.

Okin, S. M. (1995). Inequalities between the sexes in different cultural contexts. In M.C. Nussbaum & J. Glover (Eds.), *Women, culture, and development: A study of human capabilities* (pp. 274–297). New Delhi, India: Oxford University Press.

Ramirez, F., and Ventresca, M. (1992). Building the institution of mass schooling. In B. Fuller & R. Rubinson (Eds.), *Political construction of education* (pp. 47–59). New York: Preager.

Rashid, A. (2001). *Taliban: Militant Islam, oil, and fundamentalism in Central Asia.* New Haven, CT: Yale University Press.

Roy, O. (1986). *Islam and resistance in Afghanistan.* Cambridge, UK: Cambridge University Press.

Sen, A. K. (1999). *Development as freedom.* New York: Knopf.

Shahrani, N. (1990). Afghanistan: State and society in retrospect. In. E. Anderson & N. H. Dupree (Eds.), *The cultural basis of Afghan nationalism* (pp. 41–49). New York: Pinter.

Skaine, R. (2002). *The women of Afghanistan under the Taliban.* Jefferson, NC: McFarland.

Spivak, G. C. (1999). *A critique of postcolonial reason.* Cambridge, MA: Harvard University Press.

Tax, M. (1999). Power of the word: Culture, censorship, and voice. In J. Silliman & Y. King (Eds.), *Dangerous intersections: Feminist perspectives on population, environment, and development* (pp. 108–132). Cambridge, MA: South End Press.

Torres, C. A. (1998). *Democracy, education, and multiculturalism: Dilemmas of citizenship in a global world.* Lanham, MD: Rowman & Littlefield.

ul Haq, M. (1995). *Reflections on human development.* Delhi, India: Oxford University Press.

United Nations Development Programme. (2002). *Human development report 2002.* New York: Oxford University Press.

United Nations Development Programme. (2003). What is human development. *Human development report.* Retrieved November 2003 from *hdr.undp.org/hd/*

Weaver, J., Rock, M., & Kusterer, K. (1997). *Achieving broad-based sustainable development.* West Hartford, CT: Kumarian Press.

Willis, P. (1981). *Learning to labor: How working class kids get working class jobs.* New York: Columbia University Press.

3　A Space of Her Own

Women, Work, and Desire in an Afghan Nomad Community

Diana K. Davis

Although Afghanistan is often portrayed in the Western media as a predominately "male" country, so many men have died during the decades of war there that an estimated 60–70% of the population is now composed of women (Khanna, 2002). These women survived nearly a decade under Mujahideen and Taliban rule that placed great restrictions on their lives and livelihoods in multiple ways. These same women now face a male-dominated, Western development industry that brings many notions and stereotypes about women in general and about Muslim women in particular with its plans and projects for "development." The opportunities for women's participation in the development and rebuilding of their country are constrained due to the preconceived notions accompanying these overwhelmingly male spaces of development. This chapter presents research from an Afghan nomad community that reveals that, despite common beliefs to the contrary, these women have a sophisticated knowledge of livestock health and management, significant responsibilities for care of livestock, and a serious desire not only to continue working with livestock but also to expand their knowledge and their work with livestock in their community. These women have the knowledge, roles in society, and desire to define their own spaces of development if their voices can be heard.

Beginning with an overview of the myriad debates about women, Islam and development, and the status of women in Afghanistan, this chapter next introduces the Afghan nomads known as the Koochi[1] and provides a summary of their history and way of life. Women's work and knowledge within this pastoral society are subsequently detailed, accompanied by a description of men's work and knowledge. This is followed by a presentation of the results of a survey conducted to assess women's ability and desire to be trained and work as "basic veterinary workers" (BVWs) and an analysis of the survey results. As this research was conducted just prior to the rise of the Taliban, the results offer suggestions for development alternatives, most of which have not been possible in the intervening decade.[2] The implications of the research and the potential alternatives it suggests for present and future development programs in Afghanistan are discussed in the final section.

GENDER, ISLAM, AND DEVELOPMENT IN AFGHANISTAN

Any discussion of women and development in Muslim societies is necessarily situated within multiple debates concerning gender and Islam, as well as broader global debates over gender and development. The case of Afghanistan, however, stands out as an anomaly for several reasons. First, the literature on Afghanistan over the last quarter century has been dominated by discussions of geopolitics and suffers from a relative dearth of research on general development and/or gender issues. Second, Afghanistan was already one of the least developed of the Islamic countries before the most recent 25-year period of war and disruption began, and it is now one of the poorest and least developed countries in the world. Third, Afghanistan is widely regarded as an "extreme case" of classical patriarchy, the institutions of which dominate, to varying degrees, social, economic, and political life throughout the Muslim world today (Moghadam, 1999; Suad & Slyomovics, 2001). As a result, very little discussion of Afghanistan and its women has been included in the recent swell of academic writing on gender and Islam or gender and development in the Middle East.[3]

Although stereotypes of Muslim women still abound, a substantial literature has appeared that provides carefully researched and thoughtfully contextualized discussions of the multiplicity of experiences of these women (Ask & Tjomsland, 1998; Haddad & Esposito, 1998; Meriwether & Tucker, 1999; Shukri, 1999; Suad & Slyomovics, 2001). The majority of these discussions have moved far beyond earlier essentialized writings about the "typical Muslim woman" and instead argue for a reality richly differentiated by historical and geographical specificity that considers the social, economic, and political contexts of women's lives in addition to any religious dimensions.[4] Moreover, most of these authors understand gender as a system of social relations between women and men, and not simply as "gender equals women." Many of these researchers agree that although patriarchy is the dominant institution in most Islamic societies, women's experiences of it vary both by country and within individual countries. Furthermore, women in many contexts have negotiated these traditionally male spaces in successful ways, in some instances appropriating them and creating "new" female Islamic spaces that at times defy classical patriarchy (Ask & Tjomsland, 1998). The case of Iran since the Islamic revolution two decades ago is particularly interesting. Approximately 70% of Iranian women are now literate, their educational levels are high, and they have a growing presence in government and the workforce, despite the overt gender bias and inequality instituted during the early years of the revolution (Ansari & Martin, 2002; Moghadam, 1999).

In Afghanistan, however, the condition and status of women is nearly uniformly judged a disaster. Life expectancy for women is only 43 years; maternal mortality is the second worst in the world, with an estimated 16,000 women dying each year from pregnancy-related causes (that is more than double the rate of maternal mortality in 1985 [Moghadam, 1994]); and female literacy is estimated to be between 5 and 20% (United Nations Development Programme [UNDP], 2003; United Nations Development Fund for Women [UNIFEM], 2002; United Nations Office for the Coordination of Humanitarian Affairs [UNOCHA], 2003a). Seventy percent of the population is estimated to be malnourished, and women and children are likely to bear the brunt of this hunger (UNDP, 2003). War and severe social disruption have had significant influence on these indicators of women's well-being, but half a decade of Taliban rule played an equal or greater role.[5] Under Taliban rule access to education, opportunity to work outside the home, access to medical care, and basic mobility were all highly circumscribed for women and girls (Moghadam, 1999).[6] Because so many Afghan families were headed by females, all of these restrictions greatly impeded women's abilities to provide the basic necessities for survival to themselves or their children. Few, if any, women were able to negotiate a productive space for themselves under the severe Taliban patriarchy.

The Taliban, and many factions of the Mujahideen before them, held notions of Islam and gender relations/gender roles that were particularly conservative, even within the norms of other conservative Islamic states in the Middle East. Views of women and their proper roles in society do vary with the different interpretations of Islam dominant in each society. Women not infrequently become markers of cultural/religious identity, especially during periods of social disruption. Moghadam (1999) has shown that in Afghanistan under the Taliban, "women's reproductive roles [were] fetishized in the context of a kinship-ordered patriarchal structure . . . it [was] difficult to see women in other roles, such as students, citizens, or income-earning employees" (p. 173). That is to say, women's spaces were restricted to an unusual degree. When international aid workers and nongovernmental organizations (NGOs) gained greater access to development work in Afghanistan in 1992, they worked, to varying degrees, in cooperation with first the Mujahideen and then with the Taliban. Most of these aid workers were men and a majority of them accepted the Mujahideen's, and later the Taliban's, views on women with little question (Moghadam, 1994). As a result, most development programs were and are targeted toward men, with little if any analysis of gender roles/gender relations or of how such projects would impact women and their well-being.[7]

This is not surprising given that development theory and practice around the world have been dominated throughout the 20th century by Western men and are permeated with Western male bias (Elson, 1995; Hartwick, 1999). This is the case despite a profusion of theoretical work grounded in detailed field studies that has demonstrated the imperative of incorporating gender (the complex social relations between women and men) into development. Many of these feminist critiques of mainstream development are motivated by the facts revealed in an important United Nations (UN) report that "women are half the word's people . . . perform two-thirds of the world's working hours . . . receive one-tenth of the world's income . . . [and] own only one-hundredth of the world's property" (Hartwick, 1999, p. 164). This large body of critical research covers many different perspectives on gender and on development. Some of the primary theoretical approaches to gender issues in development are "women in development" (WID), "women and development" (WAD), "gender and development" (GAD), "women, environment, and development" (WED), and "postmodernism and development" (PAD).[8] All of these approaches are informed by different theories—for example, WID is grounded in modernization theory and neoliberalism, whereas WAD is often characterized as a socialist approach. Although each of these bodies of research is supported with convincing case studies of development projects and their often adverse affects on women around the globe, the WID, and, to a growing degree, the GAD approaches remain dominant in practice.

WID was one of the earliest approaches to consider women's issues and development, appearing in the 1970s. Although critical of mainstream development in a limited way, it accepted the modernization theory dominant at the time and has since accepted neoliberalism.[9] WID has become the primary way that powerful international institutions such as the United States Agency for International Development (USAID), the World Bank, the International Monetary Fund (IMF), and several UN agencies, among others, operationalize issues concerning women and development. WID has, however, received a large amount of criticism for "its exclusive focus on women and its avoidance of gender relations [and] for a shallow analysis" (Hartwick, 1999, p. 182). Furthermore, it has been documented that many WID projects have acted to mobilize women's labor for environment and development projects without remuneration, to increase women's overall workloads, and not infrequently to worsen women's economic and social situations (Elson, 1995).[10] Even microcredit projects specifically targeted to help women have been shown, on thorough analysis, to have left women with the debt and the responsibility for repayment, while the actual benefits (credit) have been appropriated by men (Goetz & Gupta, 1996). Although some progress has been made in incorporating other approaches, particularly GAD, at the international institutional level, the neoliberal paradigm and its attendant views and assumptions about women (WID) remain dominant in development practice today.

In the livestock development sector, the WID approach and the frequent exclusion of women have been particularly damaging. The dominant neoliberal development paradigm has strongly encouraged commercialization of pastoral production all over the world. It has further assumed that most women do not work with livestock in significant ways. These ideas have led to the disempowerment of women on several fronts. Subsistence dairy production is often the domain of women in numerous societies around the globe, especially in Africa and Asia. Women milk the animals, especially the small stock; not only do they feed the family with the milk and milk products, but they also barter or sell any surplus.[11] The income thus gained is frequently the woman's to dispose of as she likes.

Western-led development projects, however, usually promote commercialization of dairy production and/or the conversion of dairy to commercial meat production. The effects of such projects are complex and vary from one location to another. All too often, though, they transfer responsibility for and income from dairy production from women to men, thus eroding women's economic situation and social status (Ensminger, 1984; Waters-Bayer, 1994). In other cases, pastoral development projects have failed outright because they ignored women and women's work in the society. For example, one project that aimed to increase fodder production failed because "women had been excluded from the instruction process on feeding, . . . men . . . were the ones instructed on the new recommendations. But, in fact, it is women who gather forage and feed the animals" (Norem, Yoder, & Martin, 1989, p. 94). In these instances, not even a WID approach was implemented because of the planners' assumptions about women and their roles in the society. These examples, among many others, highlight some of the problematic patriarchal assumptions inherent in much of Western-led development.

The spaces of development in Afghanistan today, then, are overwhelmingly male, being dominated by conservative religious leaders and Western-led development and reconstruction efforts. Although the geopolitics have changed over the last decade, the spaces for women's participation are in many ways as limited as they were in the early 1990s, despite rhetoric to the contrary. This may be especially true in remote rural areas. Because women constitute the majority of the population in Afghanistan today, gender issues and the future of development in this impoverished country are particularly acute. The case study presented here, that of the pastoral no-mads known as the Koochi, explores some of the misperceptions of women and their roles, work, and desires that are inscribed in these male spaces of development. In doing so, a primary goal of this chapter is to try to answer two questions: What spaces of development do Afghan nomad women define/desire for themselves? And how might they begin to attain their desires?

THE KOOCHI: BACKGROUND AND HISTORY OF NOMADS IN AFGHANISTAN

In the late 1970s, before the war, nomads in Afghanistan were estimated to number 2,500,000, which constituted approximately 15% of the country's total population (Nyrop, 1986). Their numbers are estimated to be only 10% of the total population of approximately 25 million today, thus prob ably still numbering about 2,500,000 people (UNOCHA, 2001; UNOCHA, 2003b). Although likely more numerous in the previous decades and centu-ries, nomads played a significant role in the country's prewar economy be-cause they owned roughly 80% of the sheep and goat flocks in Afghanistan (Nyrop, 1986). The raising, selling, and trading of livestock (mainly fat-tailed sheep and goats) and livestock products (milk products and wool) formed the basis of their economy.

The Koochi are Pashtun nomadic pastoralists.[12] The Pashtun comprise the largest ethnic group in Afghanistan, their religion is Islam (the majority are Sunni), and their language is Pashto. In Pashto, *Koochi* means "no-mad." The Koochi are the largest group of nomads in Afghanistan, al-though there are nomads from other ethnic groups such as the Baloch and the Kirghiz (Dupree, 1980). As is the case with most nomads, the Koochi live in areas of low rainfall that also have very unpredictable rainfall pat-terns and frequent droughts. The regions in which they live and migrate re-ceive approximately 150–200 millimeters average annual rainfall or less (Nyrop, 1986). Since about 30–40 million hectares of Afghanistan's total area of 63 million hectares is arid and semiarid rangeland (47–63%), the nomadic raising of livestock in these difficult regions is important economi-cally because this land can be used for little else (Nyrop, 1986; Thomson, Barker, & Miller, 2003). Only about 8–13% of land in Afghanistan is arable.

Historically, the Koochi migrated twice a year with their livestock via camel caravans from the foothills of the Hindu Kush and other mountains in central Afghanistan to the plains of the Indus River Valley or the deserts of southern Afghanistan or Balochistan (see Figure 3.1). They grazed their flocks during the summer in mountain pastures and during winter in warmer lowland pastures. During the spring and autumn, the Koochi mi-

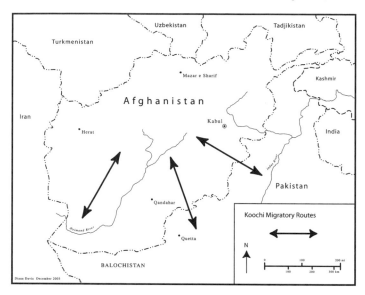

FIGURE 3.1. Map of Koochi migratory routes.

grated between these sites in large family groups. Significant numbers of Koochi have maintained their way of life over the last quarter century. They still migrate in large numbers and the people living near Quetta, Balochistan, still say, "The hills turn black with Koochi tents in the spring and the fall."

The year 1978 marked the beginning of 25 years of war and social disruption in Afghanistan. The war began with the Soviet invasion of Afghanistan, but war conditions continued even after the Soviets withdrew, during the Afghan civil war. Although the Taliban brought some stabilization to some areas, the U.S. bombing of Afghanistan in the fall of 2001 further worsened conditions for average Afghans and the situation has not improved much, if at all, since then. During the worst of the disruption, in the early 1990s, an estimated seven million Afghans were forced to become refugees, making them the world's largest refugee population at that time. At least two million Afghans have been killed during these conflicts and at least two million more have been displaced inside the country (UNOCHA, 2003b). An estimated four and a half million refugees remain today, concentrated in Pakistan and Iran. Currently, life expectancy in Afghanistan is 43 years, one of the lowest in the world; 25% of children die before reaching their fifth birthday; and an estimated 35% of children are severely malnourished (UNOCHA, 2003a). In the fall of 2002, the international community declared a "health emergency" for the country due to the terrible conditions.

One of the worst droughts in living memory gripped the country from 1999 to 2003.[13] Causing many problems throughout the country, it hit the livestock sector particularly hard. Livestock deaths among the nomadic groups have been astonishingly high, with losses estimated at 75–90% of nomadic livestock in many regions (Nekzad, 2003; Thomson et al., 2003). This has only increased the hardships faced by the Koochi, already suffering from the high number of land mines left by years of war often found in their migratory paths. At least 100,000 Koochi have been forced into refugee-like aid camps near Kandahar due to the unusually harsh conditions (Caritas, 2002).[14]

Part of the international community's response to these appalling conditions over the years has been the implementation, when and where possible, of development and rehabilitation projects in different sectors of the country. Many of these projects have focused on the agricultural sector, and some particularly on the livestock sector. One of these projects in the early 1990s was the Basic Veterinary Worker (BVW) Program funded by USAID. The NGO Mercy Corps International (MCI) managed the program as part of a larger development program for health and agriculture in Afghanistan. Tufts University School of Veterinary Medicine consulted on veterinary issues for the project. The project was designed to train male Afghan farmers and herders in basic animal healthcare, vaccine administration, and simple veterinary treatments with the aim of making them not only able to treat their own animals, but also able to treat the livestock of others and to charge for their services (Jespersen & Sherman, 1992).[15] Although the project explored involving Koochi women as BVWs, these plans were never realized. The research presented here was gathered while the author was a short-term consultant on veterinary and gender issues for this project.[16]

WORK AND KNOWLEDGE IN KOOCHI SOCIETY

Life in Koochi society is focused on animals: sheep, goats, camels, donkeys, dogs, and even cats. Most aspects of daily life are linked in some way to the lives of the animals. Nomads in Afghanistan have been studied by scholars during the 20th century and their work and roles in the society have been well documented. Most of what these authors have written about nomads in Afghanistan, as with writing in general about nomads in the Middle East, stresses that the roles of women are confined to domestic duties such as packing and unpacking the tent, sewing, washing, cooking, and taking care of children. With respect to animals, the literature generally agrees that women's work is limited to milking livestock, processing milk products, spinning (see Figure 3.2), weaving, and rug/tent production (Balikci, 1990; Barth, 1961; Glatzer & Casimir, 1983; Nyrop, 1986; Tapper, 1977).[17] All

FIGURE 3.2. Photo of a Koochi nomad woman, with two of her children, spinning wool and telling stories. Photo by author.

of these authors indicate that herding and the care of livestock are nearly exclusively the domain of men. The implication is that women have little or no knowledge of animal health and disease, nor a role in providing animal healthcare. As a result, most livestock development projects in Afghanistan have excluded women, especially those focusing on veterinary care in nomadic areas.

My research, however, reveals that women work with animals in significant ways and that they have a sophisticated knowledge of animal health and disease. One of the few things that Koochi women don't (often) do is herd animals far from the family tent. This is nearly exclusively the job of men. In addition to all the tasks described as women's work above, these women care for newborn and young animals at the tent until they are old enough to go out to pasture with the main herd. Ill animals are often isolated from the herd, to prevent spread of infection, by keeping them near the tent where women care for them and provide healthcare. Women are preferred to help with difficult births in livestock and often do so. When livestock are kept in pens near the tent, it is women who clean out the pens. Women are also responsible for feeding and watering animals kept at the tent. Despite the fact that only men slaughter livestock for food in this Islamic society, women clean the internal organs and prepare the carcass for cooking.[18] Additional duties performed by women include the removal of ectoparasites such as ticks from livestock, collecting manure (often used as fuel), and holding/restraining animals when necessary (e.g., at shearing time).

Perhaps not surprisingly, given their work with animals, these women have a good understanding of a wide range of livestock diseases, and moreover a good knowledge of how to treat these diseases with locally available treatments. They know, as do many of the men, how to employ and administer these local treatments by making use of indigenous plants, minerals, and animal tissues. Local plants and minerals are often used to treat parasites, both externally and internally, as well as other livestock diseases. Animal products such as lung tissue from a diseased animal are used in the indigenous "ear slit" vaccine.[19] In some areas, however, Koochi women have more detailed and sophisticated knowledge of livestock diseases and their treatment than Koochi men. These areas of women's superior knowledge correlate with the work that is most often women's work.

Women know significantly more than do men about mastitis (infections of the udder), about dystocias (difficult births), and about the care of newborn livestock. During this research, for example, 90% of the women were able to name at least one disease that causes mastitis, whereas 70% of the men explained that God or the Devil was the cause. Only women reported mastitis to be infectious, which it usually is, and mentioned the importance of hand washing (when possible) after milking each animal. Alternatively, infected animals are milked last by women to try to minimize infection. Nearly 20% more women than men understood the importance of newborns drinking colostrum (the first milk, high in antibodies) to protect them from disease. Furthermore, women knew more about internal parasites than did men. When asked to name which diseases or parasites might be found inside a dead animal, women listed four parasites as well as two other diseases (including anthrax). Men only listed two of the most common parasites. Importantly, 10% more women than men reported that intestinal worms can cause diarrhea in livestock. All of the women were able to list at least one other cause of diarrhea in livestock, while only 83% of men were able to do so, a difference of nearly 20%. Thirty-three percent of women knew that diarrhea can be contagious, but only 20% of men understood this. Many Koochi women editorialized about the men's limited knowledge in these areas. One woman explained that "men are usually ignorant of these things, they don't care if an animal is ill. Besides, men are usually not at home."

Even in areas outside the normal purview of women's work, women's knowledge of animal health and disease was at least as good as and sometimes better than that of men. Included in this research was a standardized survey of animal health and disease knowledge based on the most common diseases encountered in Afghan livestock in this region. This survey revealed that women have a marginally superior knowledge of livestock health and disease, although not "statistically significant."[20] Notably, the four highest "scores" in the survey all were obtained by women, with the highest woman's score being 10% higher than any of the men's scores. This survey was constructed based on the existing BVW project's training program and covered a majority of the most important diseases and animal healthcare issues targeted by this development project. The results of this research, then, are significant also in an applied context since, based on these results, women might well make better BVWs than men due to their extensive knowledge base. If only men had been asked about women's knowledge of animal disease and their care of livestock, a very different picture would have been obtained. When asked what work women do with animals, 94% of Koochi men listed milking and processing milk products. Ninety-four percent of these men also explained that women do not know anything about animals that men do not know.

Built into this Western-led development project, however, as in similar projects in Afghanistan and the Middle East in general, was the presumption that women do not work in significant ways with animals. Koochi men's responses suggest that men may foster this presumption (wittingly or not). In addition, it was assumed by project leaders that Afghan women's mobility and ability to work are severely restricted for religious/cultural reasons, so that they were not considered good "targets" for this project. These assumptions about women are an integral part of a wider set of essentialized assumptions about Muslim societies held by many Western organizations and individuals. It was only later, halfway through the project, that involving women in some way was explored. As mentioned earlier, though, involving women in this project was never realized despite evidence that refuted many of the assumptions outlined above.

WORK AND DESIRE AMONG KOOCHI WOMEN

Koochi women believe that they would make good BVWs. Koochi men agree. By asking detailed questions perhaps not often included by other researchers, my results suggest strongly that Koochi women have the knowledge, the skills, and the desire to be effective animal healthcare workers. Furthermore, it highlights the fact that most Koochi men agree that women can and should perform this kind of work. What conditions Koochi women and men place on how women might carry out this work are significantly less restrictive than international development organizations and other "outsiders" generally believe.

Koochi women know how to catch, handle, and restrain livestock. In fact, 40% of Koochi men who were asked reported that women can handle and restrain animals better than men. Koochi women also know how to administer healthcare to livestock, such as using the *shkur* (a hollowed-out cattle horn used to administer pills and other treatments), and to do so when necessary. Women say that they often know when animals are sick before men notice. This is likely because women work closely with the livestock, clean out animal pens, and feed and water the animals, which gives them frequent opportunities to notice disease symptoms like diarrhea. Women also displayed a better understanding of the correlations between internal parasites, diseases, and symptoms than did men, probably because they also clean the carcasses after slaughter and see any parasites or diseases present.

Despite the common Western misperception that nearly all Muslim women are kept as secluded as possible from men outside the immediate family, a practice called *purdah* in Afghanistan, Koochi women do not commonly practice *purdah*. In fact, few nomad or village women in the Muslim world do routinely keep *purdah* or wear a veil (Dupree, 1980). The practice does vary across the Muslim world, though, with many variations in custom. Nearly two-thirds of Koochi women said that they only observe *purdah* for the first 2 or 3 years after marriage. Seventy-two percent of these women explained that they did not observe *purdah*, even outside the customary boundaries of their own tribe. In stark contrast to this, however, 100% of the men who were asked stated that Koochi women observe *purdah* from those outside the tribe.

A unanimous desire for training in animal healthcare was expressed by Koochi women. All the women and 83% of the men said that women would like to be trained in animal healthcare. Although the men made it clear that they prefer men to receive such training first, both men and women agreed that training for women was desirable because it would be easy for them to learn, good for the livestock, good for other women, and a good way to earn income. Three-quarters of both women and men said that women would be successful in providing animal healthcare if they were properly trained. Approximately 85% of both men and women agreed that women could provide healthcare to animals belonging to any man in their tribe. For animals belonging to a man outside the tribe, 69% of women said they could provide healthcare for them; however, only 27% of men agreed. One woman elaborated, stating that she could give healthcare to animals belonging to anyone (male or female) as long as they were Muslim. Eighty-one percent of the women stated that they could receive money from those whose livestock they might treat, even from men. On the other hand, 80% of the men said that women could not accept payment in cash from men.

Just as the majority of Koochi women and men agreed that women want training in animal healthcare, the vast majority (100% of women and 90% of men) also agreed that training would have to be from other women, even from foreign women. Ninety-four percent of women and men further agreed that training would have to be in the family tent or in the tent of a friend in the tribe, not in a city. Three-quarters of the men stated that 2 weeks would be the maximum time period that women could be away from their normal work to receive training, and 40% of women agreed. A larger number of women, though, 46%, explained that up to 3 months might be needed for such training and that they could leave their work for that length of time. Nearly 80% of women chose winter as the best time for training, perhaps reflecting the boredom experienced during this season, when there is little for them to do.

Within the boundaries of their tribe, then, it is clear that both women and men agree that women want training in animal healthcare, that they would be successful treating livestock, and that they could treat nearly any animal owned by anyone in the tribe. The issue of payment for these basic veterinary services, however, provoked very different responses that would need to be addressed if such a project were ever implemented. This issue might be as easily addressed, though, as the issue of procuring veterinary supplies. Approximately three-quarters of both women and men stated that women could not go into the bazaar to buy veterinary supplies when needed. Twelve percent of both men and women said that old women could go to the bazaar. As a logistical solution, however, 100% of the women and 90% of the men explained that men or boys could be sent to buy veterinary supplies in the bazaar when needed. Neither the men nor the women saw the purchase of veterinary supplies as an impediment to women being trained in animal healthcare. With respect to the question of women receiving payment for services rendered to animals, the possibility exists for a woman to be found to give payment to a female animal healthcare worker.

DISCUSSION

As detailed above, Koochi women's real productive spaces (and their potential productive spaces) are larger and more complex than previously recognized. These women play an important role in caring for livestock in this pastoral society. They have the primary responsibility in caring for sick livestock, a task they perform with extensive knowledge and skill, being more knowledgable and performing more work than men in several key areas of livestock disease. Women's work, knowledge, and role in the production, processing, and distribution of milk is particularly complex and comprehensive, entailing a vital knowledge of the udder and its diseases and treatments, the value of the "first milk" in protecting newborns from disease, milking and processing milk products, and care of milking animals. Some of these women also sell surplus milk when they can, and several said that they kept money thus earned and could spend it how they liked—for example, to buy embroidery thread.[21]

These women are proud of what they know and the skills that they have. Most would, moreover, like to extend their knowledge of and skills for treating livestock. That is, they would like to define their own spaces of development and would choose to learn more about livestock health and disease if given the chance. Many of these Koochi women also explained that they would like to learn to read and write, and that they would like more and better religious education. Importantly, the majority of Koochi men support these desires, particularly in the area of training women to treat livestock diseases. These men listed few restrictions to women treating livestock within their tribal group. Within their own society, then, there are few limitations seen to women defining and attaining their own spaces of development. Even in areas that were potentially problematic, such as women transgressing the male spaces of the bazaar to buy needed livestock medicines, a solution was proffered by women and men: that of a boy or man being sent to buy medicines ordered by the woman.

Are Koochi women's productive spaces, their sophisticated knowledge, their extensive work, and their future spaces of development being eroded by patriarchal, Western-led development projects operating within a severely conservative religious ideological climate? This is a crucial question facing the country and the international community as the effort is made for "the reconstruction of Afghanistan." This case study of the BVW Project suggests that women's work and knowledge may be eroded by Western development projects in several ways. The current geopolitically defined development situation in Afghanistan unfortunately suggests that contemporary reconstruction activities may further disenfranchise women in the future.

The BVW Project trained men in the treatment and prevention of many livestock diseases. Treatment of several of these diseases is under the purview of women in Koochi society. Men were trained, for example, to recognize and treat udder infections with antibiotic udder infusions. Antibiotic udder infusions were included in the BVW treatment kit provided to each BVW trained. But milking as well as the care and treatment of the udder is a female productive space in Koochi society. By training men to treat udder infections, the possibility is created for men to appropriate not only the treatment of udder infections, but also for men to appropriate milk, the distribution (sale) of milk, and milking. This may be especially likely if the use of udder infusions becomes widespread, and many men are encouraged to treat their own livestock in this way. By making an economic investment in the udder infusion, men may begin to see the milk as their property. Combined with livestock development that encourages the commercialization of milk production and/or the conversion to commercial meat production, the disenfranchisement of Koochi women from one of their most significant productive spaces becomes even more likely. If this happens, the results will probably be very similar to the disenfranchisement of pastoral women in other societies when subsistence dairy production is commercialized (Ensminger, 1984; Waters-Bayer, 1994). Not only will

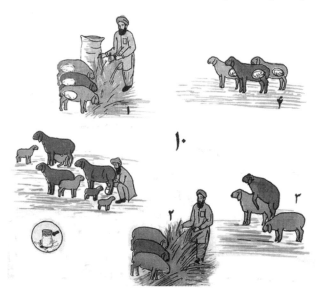

FIGURE 3.3. A page from the flip chart used for training BVWs showing men performing women's tasks.

these women lose work that they value, they may lose the power to control milk distribution in the family, and thus the women's and their children's health status may also suffer from loss of milk and loss of income.[22] Women's overall status in the community is also lowered in these cases, further disadvantaging them in their daily lives.

The BVW training process itself had many erroneous assumptions about women and gender roles built into it.[23] The teaching materials utilized for training the BVWs contained the depiction of men in many of Koochi women's roles in caring for livestock, suggesting that men should be performing such work (see Figure 3.3). All the visual material used for training only showed men performing the various tasks under discussion. In several of these scenes men were shown milking and working with milk. Such visual education will reinforce the possibility of men beginning to view milk as their responsibility or property. Other parts of the training materials showed men performing "female" tasks such as feeding corralled animals and cleaning out livestock pens. Furthermore, the treatment of diarrhea and parasites were ascribed to men during the training process although these are often the domain of women in Koochi society and women are generally more knowledgeable about these conditions. The BVW Project, then, trained men to work with livestock in several areas that are the domain of women in Koochi society, setting in place the possibility for men to disenfranchise women and their work.[24] Future development projects in any sector (agriculture, healthcare, etc.) that do not incorporate thorough gender analyses are likely to do the same.

The contemporary geopolitical reality of Afghanistan, in which development and reconstruction are led by Western powers, and influenced very strongly by neoliberal goals of privatization and commercialization, is likely either to ignore gender or to encourage WID-type development projects that too often erode the subsistence base of rural women.[25] The initiation of development projects without appropriate analysis of gender relations and the roles of women and men in society are nearly certainly going to repeat the mistakes of the past. Although some major urban areas of Afghanistan are controlled by the "moderate" government of President Karzai, a growing number of remote and rural areas are coming under the control of so-called warlords, many of whom hold deeply conservative notions of Islam and the roles of women in society. These men are as likely to misunderstand women's roles in rural life, and to curtail their productive spaces, as did the Taliban. In this doubly patriarchal reality, it is essential that women are allowed to speak for themselves and that they are heard.[26] Average women and men from the many different groups, ethnicities, and classes of Afghanistan must be given a voice and a stake in the development and reconstruction of Afghanistan. If the Western powers continue to operate within a quasi-orientalist interpretation of the limited role of women in an essentialized Islam, this is very unlikely to happen.

Fortunately, there are alternatives available. Both the GAD (gender and development) and WED (women, environment, and development) approaches, for example, stress that development projects must consider gender relations and analyze how all proposed development projects might impact these relations, and thus both men's and women's daily lives. This is a fundamentally different approach to adding women's programs to the primary development plans, as is so often the case with WID. If either of the GAD or the WED approaches to development were considered in the reconstruction of Afghanistan, they would entail detailed gender analyses throughout the country within the many different ethnic groups present, as well as in urban and rural areas. Detailed analyses and studies of this type take time, money, and levels of language and interviewing expertise that may be underestimated if not taken seriously. Only with such detailed context, however, can socially just and sustainable development projects be planned and operationalized.

The results of this research with Koochi women and men suggest some development alternatives that may not have been previously considered and were almost certainly not able to be operationalized under Taliban rule. Clearly, women play a large role in the care of livestock, women would like to be trained in livestock healthcare, and both women and men agree that women can be trained in this area. Any new BVW-type projects for nomads in Afghanistan should incorporate gender analysis from the very beginning and include women as an integral part of the project and not as an "add-on." A mobile training program, with female trainers, which could operate to address the constraints to training revealed here (namely, that women need to be trained within the nomad community and not in towns or villages) would be particularly effective. Moreover, this research suggests that both men and women could work as BVWs and that perhaps they could focus on different but complementary aspects of livestock health. For example, women could build on their strength of knowledge and practice with newborn animals, with udder infections, with feeding regimens, and with internal parasites. Not only would this build on preexisting strengths within Koochi society, it might preclude any deleterious effects of men appropriating women's labor and/or productive spaces (especially in the area of udder health and control of milk).

An encouraging development occurred in the late 1990s under the aegis of the U.N. Food and Agriculture Organization. While working on a project for livestock health and food security among sedentary farmers in Afghanistan, it was noted that women performed significant work with livestock. This came as part of an effort to incorporate farmer participation in the project by conducting local needs assessments and trying to incorporate locally defined needs into the project. As a result of these experiences, a program was started to train women in livestock healthcare.[27] Unfortunately, under Taliban rule, work was largely restricted to women treating other women's livestock and comprehensive incorporation of gender considerations into the project was not achieved. Although approximately 50 BVWs were trained, and approximately 2,500 farmwomen received some training in animal healthcare, the program collapsed for lack of funding in 2000–2001.[28] The lessons learned from this project, however, support the results from my research with the Koochi and highlight some of the alternatives for development projects in the future that could be more sustainable, inclusive, and socially just.

CONCLUSION

This chapter has argued that many Afghan women have been denied their own spaces of development by a male-dominated, Western development industry operating within an unusually conservative Islamic ideological climate. Using the specific case study of a group of Afghan nomads, the Koochi, we have seen that the complex and significant veterinary work that women perform with livestock has been invisible to or ignored by both Western-led development projects and by conservative Islamic leaders. By detailing the gender roles, gender attitudes, and gender-based division of labor in Koochi society, this chapter has shown that women and men in this society view women and their work very differently than either the conservative Islamic leaders or the Western development industry. These Koochi women and men would like to see women trained as basic veterinary workers (BVWs), and they believe women would be successful as BVWs. Indeed, Koochi women have superior knowledge of and perform more work in several key areas of livestock healthcare and management than do Koochi men. Women might, then, even make better BVWs than would men in this society. Assumptions about Muslim women ingrained in much of Western development thinking, and espoused by groups such as the Taliban, combine to curtail women's spaces of development in ways that are alien to Koochi society. In a country now populated by significantly more women than men, it is imperative that women's work and women's desires be given a voice in development efforts.

What, then, do Koochi women say that they desire? Nearly all of the women interviewed for this study expressed strongly that they want to return to Afghanistan. "May God bring the day when there is peace and we can return to our country," proclaimed one woman. All of them explained that they had left their country due to war. They are tired of living the refugee life.[29] They are tired of going hungry and having little or no clean water. They are tired of not being able to clean themselves, their children, or their few belongings. Many of these women expressed a poignant sadness for the loss of their animals; for the loss of "the open air, open spaces, and the wind"; and for not "being able to go where they want." One woman lamented, "I have no animals now. I miss my animals." "How can we be Koochi without our animals?" asks another woman. They are tired of having to break rocks for road construction all day only to be paid the equivalent of a few pennies. They are tired of being sick and not being able to obtain healthcare for their children. They want to learn to read and write, and they want better religious training. They would all like the chance to learn new skills and work, for example, as BVWs.

It is perhaps telling, though, that if given the choice of land or of animals, a majority of these women said that they would prefer to have some farmland rather than return to a completely nomadic way of life. Most would like to have both. Many of them are afraid of the estimated 10–50 million land mines strewn across the country. Some complained that they are tired of the nomadic life. One woman explained, "I am tired of moving and tired of camels. Just like you, we want an easy life." Others said that it would be impossible to be Koochi again without any animals and they did not know where or how to obtain new livestock. Programs designed to help the Koochi and other nomads to restock their sheep, goats, and camels would be very beneficial, as would accelerating the demining efforts already slowly underway.[30] These are starkly real concerns that must be addressed for the development and reconstruction of Afghanistan to be successful, sustainable, and equitable for both women and men.

ACKNOWLEDGMENTS

Partial funding for this research was generously provided by the Tufts University School of Veterinary Medicine. I would like to thank David Hooson, James Housefield, Karim Quraishi, Myron Jespersen, Sheila Moffett, James Ross, David Sherman, Al Sollod, and Chip Stem for their help and encouragement with various aspects of this project. I am grateful for the constructive comments on this chapter by an anonymous reviewer and the editors.

NOTES

1. Koochi is also spelled "Kuchi" in the various literatures.
2. The data presented here are the results of research with 35 nomad families (tents) over a 3-month period during the summer of 1992. All research was conducted in southern Balochistan (Pakistan), near Quetta, with refugees from Afghanistan while the author was a consultant on the BVW Project. Interviews were conducted with the help of a Pashto-speaking interpreter and generally lasted 2–3 hours. Interviews included a formal questionnaire as well as open-ended questions and discussion. The research reflects the knowledge and sentiments of these nomads before the Taliban rose to power in 1994, and thus is particularly relevant in the current post-Taliban context.
3. The primary exception to this is the work of Valentine Moghadam, who has written numerous excellent articles on Afghanistan's women over many years (Moghadam, 1994, 1996, 1999, 2002). Of course, the difficulty of access for researchers due to 25 years of war and severe social disruption has also had a negative effect on the quantity, if not the quality, of scholarship on Afghanistan.
4. Much of this has taken place at roughly the same time that debates over global feminism(s) were undergoing profound criticism and change, with the western model(s) coming under intense scrutiny and criticism from non-western scholars. See Mohanty (1991) for a particularly good discussion.
5. The Taliban ruled most of Afghanistan for approximately 5 years, although in some parts of the country, especially the south, their influence was felt as early as 1994. Coming out of the refugee camps, poor and largely illiterate, their interpretation of Islam was particularly conservative, influenced in part by Wahhabism (Moghadam, 1999). This group of former religious students won power from the Mujahideen in 1996. The Mujahideen had been ruling Afghanistan, with much infighting, since the Soviets withdrew in 1992. See Cramer and Goodhand (2002) for a good summary discussion of the history of governance in Afghanistan during the 19th and 20th centuries.
6. For example, the Taliban decreed that only the few female physicians were allowed to treat female patients and that women had to be accompanied by a male to leave the house (Moghadam, 1999, pp. 177–178).
7. Maternal and child health programs were a major exception to the exclusion of women from development projects.

8. See Hartwick (1999) for a particularly good overview of these different forms of feminist development theory.
9. See Peet (1999) for an excellent discussion of these and other development theories.
10. See, for example, Schroeder (1999) for an excellent case study of the ways in which women's labor has been appropriated, with the benefits often accruing to men.
11. In certain cultures, milking cattle and camels is strictly the domain of men.
12. Sometimes the Balochi nomads are also called Koochi.
13. Meteorological data for Quetta show that the period 1998–2001 was the worst period of drought since 1891 (Thomson, Barker, & Miller, 2003, p. 6).
14. A U.N. Food and Agriculture Organization (FAO) project has recently provided aid in the form of livestock feed for 5,000 Koochi families in southwestern Afghanistan which has helped to preserve some of the Koochi's livestock (FAO, 2003).
15. The original plan was to train 400 BVWs, but only 219 were actually trained. Of those, 75% were still working as BVWs a year after the program finished (Mercy Corps International and Tufts University School of Veterinary Medicine, 1994).
16. The portion of my work as a consultant on gender issues was conducted as a "WID consultant" for the existing BVW project, which was considering adding a WID component. The primary task for this part of my work was "to determine the feasibility and modality of training women as BVWs." Importantly, my task was not to conduct a gender analysis of Koochi work with livestock or of the existing male BVW project; nor was it to make suggestions to improve the gender equity of the existing project. The entire project was funded by USAID.
17. An exception to this trend is Dawn Chatty's work, which describes nomad women in Oman and details their ownership and control of livestock to a degree rarely found in the literature (Chatty, 1996). Care of poultry, usually the domain of women in Afghanistan, is not included in this discussion. Nor are poultry considered livestock in this chapter.
18. The practice of animal slaughter falling within the domain of male labor is quite common in Islamic societies and is largely based on religious grounds.
19. See Davis, Quraishi, Sherman, Sollod, and Stern (1995) for a discussion of the wide range of these indigenous veterinary treatments in Afghanistan.
20. See Davis (1995) for a detailed discussion of this survey.
21. Koochi women also sell surplus eggs, sometimes chickens, and surplus wool and goat hair when they can. All of those asked stated that they kept this money and could spend it on whatever they chose.
22. It has been shown in several case studies that women spend more money more frequently for necessities for their children and family first, whereas men tend to spend less on the family and more on personal items for themselves, to buy cigarettes, for example (Elson, 1995). Thus when women lose control over family spending, the health and well-being of the children and women tend to decline in many instances.
23. The project was designed at the outset without any studies to determine actual gender roles and gender-based division of labor among the Koochi or among

villagers. The flip chart shown in Figure 3.3. is still being used in Afghanistan (personal communication from Dr. David Sherman, country program director for the Dutch Committee for Afghanistan, December 2004).

24. I would like to make clear that the BVW Project was a well-intentioned project, and all of the people working on it with whom I had contact were working hard to do what they thought was helpful. Neither the project nor the staff wanted to make the lives of women worse in any way. The problems arose out of unrecognized but deeply rooted assumptions about women in this society and the complete lack of gender analysis.

25. Recent developments have made the WID approach in Afghanistan even more likely. The U.S. Congress recently approved $60 million (20% of the entire budget for the reconstruction of Afghanistan) for women's programs. All of these funds "will be administered by [USAID] and fed into existing women's programs" (Brun-Rovet, 2003). USAID is still dominated by the WID approach to development (Hartwick, 1999).

26. Patriarchy, of course, oppresses not only women but also men and children in innumerable ways and in a wide variety of societies around the globe. It is often ingrained not only in Western development thinking but in non-Western development thinking as well.

27. For details on these projects, see FAO (1997, 2002).

28. Personal communication from Dr. Terence Barker, former director of the program (November 2003).

29. Although the number of Afghan refugees was down in 1999 from a high of seven million to only about two and a half million, since the U.S. bombing of Afghanistan in 2001 refugee numbers have climbed back to nearly five million. See the United Nations annual survey of refugees for the last several years for detailed refugee numbers, online at *www.unhcr.ch*. The number of Koochi to have returned to Afghanistan is not currently known. Importantly, even among returnees, many former refugees are currently living in refugee-like conditions and/or as internally displaced persons within Afghanistan.

30. Restocking livestock for Afghanistan is being considered and tentatively planned (Thomson et al., 2003). Experts are concerned, though, about the long-term viability of restocking in general and reconstituting nomadic pastoralists and their traditional livelihoods in particular.

REFERENCES

Ansari, S., & Martin, V. (Eds.) (2002). *Women, religion and culture in Iran*. Richmond, Surrey, UK: Curzon Press.

Ask, K., & Tjomsland, M. (Eds.) (1998). *Women and Islamization: Contemporary dimensions of discourse on gender relations*. Oxford, UK: Berg.

Balikci, A. (1990). Tenure and transhumance: Stratification and pastoralism among the Lakenkhel. In J. G. Galaty & D. L. Johnson (Eds.), *The world of pastoralism: Herding systems in comparative perspective* (pp. 301–322). New York: Guilford Press.

Barth, F. (1961). *Nomads of south Persia*. Boston: Little, Brown.

Brun-Rovet, M. (2003, November). Congress does battle on Afghan women's rights. *Financial Times*, p. 3.

Caritas. (2002). *Caritas helps 30,000 nomads in their fight for survival.* ReliefWeb. Retrieved May 19, 2002, from *www.reliefweb.int/w/rwb.nsf*

Chatty, D. (1996). *Mobile pastoralists: Development planning and social change in Oman.* New York: Columbia University Press.

Cramer, C., & Goodhand, J. (2002). Try again, fail again, fail better? War, the state, and the "post-conflict" challenge in Afghanistan. *Development and Change, 33*(5), 885–909.

Davis, D. K. (1995). Gender-based differences in the ethnoveterinary knowledge of Afghan nomadic pastoralists. *Indigenous Knowledge and Development Monitor, 3*(1), 3–5.

Davis, D. K., Quraishi, K., Sherman, D., Sollod, A., & Stem, C. (1995). Ethnoveterinary medicine in Afghanistan: An overview of indigenous animal health care among Pashtun Koochi nomads. *Journal of Arid Environments, 31*(4), 483–500.

Dupree, L. (1980). *Afghanistan.* Princeton, NJ: Princeton University Press.

Elson, D. (1995). *Male bias in the development process.* Manchester, UK: Manchester University Press.

Ensminger, J. (1984). Theoretical perspectives on pastoral women: Feminist critique. *Nomadic Peoples, 16,* 59–71.

Food and Agriculture Organization (1997). *Gender and participation in agricultural development planning: Lessons from Afghanistan.* Islamabad: FAO Women in Development Services.

Food and Agriculture Organization (2002). *Afghanistan's women: The hidden strength of a war-torn land.* In *FAO News and Highlights.* Retrieved July 15, 2003, from *www.fao.org/News/2002/020105-e.htm*

Food and Agriculture Organization (2003). The Kuchi herders helped in the survival of their breeding flocks. *Activities Update in Afghanistan, 3,* 1.

Glatzer, B., & Casimir, M. J. (1983). Herds and households among pastoral nomads: Limits of growth. *Ethnology, 22*(4), 307–325.

Goetz, A.-M., & Gupta, R. S. (1996). Who takes the credit?: Gender, power and control over loan use in rural credit programmes in Bangladesh. *World Development, 24*(1), 45–63.

Haddad, Y. Y., & Esposito, J. L., (Eds.) (1998). *Islam, gender and social change.* New York: Oxford University Press.

Hartwick, E. (1999). Feminist theories of development. In R. Peet & E. Hartwick (Eds.), *Theories of development* (pp. 163–194). New York: Guilford Press.

Jespersen, M., & Sherman, D. (1992). *Private sector animal health initiative: A joint venture proposal request for continuation of funding for year 2.* Quetta, Pakistan: Mercy Corps International.

Khanna, R. (2002). Taking a stand for Afghanistan: Women and the left. *Signs, 28*(1), 464–465.

Mercy Corps International and Tufts University School of Veterinary Medicine. (1994). *Basic veterinary worker program for southwest Afghanistan.* North Grafton, MA: Authors.

Meriwether, M. L., & Tucker, J. E. (Eds.) (1999). *Social history of women and gender in the modern Middle East.* Boulder, CO: Westview Press.

Moghadam, V. M. (1994). Building human resources and women's capabilities in Afghanistan: A retrospect and prospects. *World Development, 22*(6), 859–875.

Moghadam, V. M. (1996). A reply to Maley. *World Development, 24*(1), 207–211.

Moghadam, V. M. (1999). Revolution, religion, and gender politics: Iran and Afghanistan compared. *Journal of Women's History, 10*(4), 172–185.

Moghadam, V. M. (2002). Patriarchy, the Taleban, and the politics of public space in Afghanistan. *Women's Studies International Forum, 25*(1), 19–31.

Mohanty, C. (1991). Under Western eyes. In C. Mohanty, A. Russo, & L. Torres (Eds.), *Third world women and the politics of feminism* (pp. 51–80). Bloomington: Indiana University Press.

Nekzad, F. (2003, 5 March). Snow brings drought relief to Afghanistan. *Environmental News Network.* Retrieved March 6, 2003, from *ens-news.com/ens/mar2003/2003-03-05.asp*

Norem, R.H., Yoder, R., and Martin, Y. (1989). Indigenous agricultural knowledge and gender issues in third world agricultural development. In D. M. Warren, L. J. Slikkerveer, & S. O. Titilola (Eds.), *Indigenous knowledge systems: Implications for agriculture and international development* (pp. 91–100). Ames: Iowa State University Research Foundation.

Nyrop, R. (Ed.). (1986). *Afghanistan: A country study.* Washington, DC: American University.

Peet, R. (1999). *Theories of development.* New York: Guilford Press.

Schroeder, R. (1999) *Shady practices: Agroforestry and gender politics in the Gambia.* Berkeley and Los Angeles: University of California Press.

Shukri, S. J. (1999). *Social change and women in the Middle East.* Aldershot, UK: Ashgate.

Suad, J., & Slyomovics, S. (Eds.) (2001). *Women and power in the Middle East.* Philadelphia: University of Pennsylvania Press.

Tapper, N. (1977). Pashtun nomad women in Afghanistan. *Asian Affairs, 8,* 163–170.

Thomson, E., Barker, T., & Mueller, J. (2003). *Drought, livestock losses and the potential for feed production from arable land in Afghanistan.* Aleppo: International Center for Agricultural Research in the Dry Areas.

United Nations Development Programme. (2003) *Human development report 2003.* New York: Oxford University Press.

United Nations Development Fund for Women. (2002). *Women's leadership role in the reconstruction of Afghanistan.* New York: Author. Retrieved August 28, 2003, from *www.undp.org/unifem/afghanistan*

U.N. Office for the Coordination of Humanitarian Affairs. (2001). *Afghanistan: FAO launches appeal for agricultural rehabilitation.* Islamabad: Author. Retrieved May 19, 2003, from *www.cidi.org/humanitarian/hsr/01b/ix193.html*

U.N. Office for the Coordination of Humanitarian Affairs. (2003a). *Afghanistan: Health profile one of the worst in the world.* Kabul: Author. Retrieved April 15, 2003, from *www.irrinews.org/print.asp?ReportID=33315*

U.N. Office for the Coordination of Humanitarian Affairs. (2003b). *Afghanistan: Heavy toll on civilians in years of war.* Kabul: Author. Retrieved April 15, 2003, from *www.irinnews.org/print.asp?ReportID-33369*

Waters-Bayer, A. (1994). Studying pastoral women's knowledge in milk processing and marketing—For whose empowerment? *Agriculture and Human Values, 11*(2–3), 85–95.

4 Changing Identities and Changing Spaces in Village Landscapes of Settled Pastoralists in Eastern Morocco

SUSANNE H. STEINMANN

Agricultural landscapes in the Middle East and North Africa have evolved continuously through natural and human activity. Over the last 50 years, one dramatic change in these rural spaces has been the shift from extensive nomadic pastoralism to more intensive agropastoral production and sedentarization. Geographers have long explored the connections between cultural change, social relations, and their imprints on the landscape. But few geographic studies in the Middle East and North Africa have demonstrated how changing gender relations affect household production strategies, which lead to transformations of agricultural spaces in livestock-raising regions (Davis, 1996; Steinmann, 1998a, 1998b, 2001).

This chapter illustrates how changing gender roles and shifting identities affect landscape patterns in two settlements of the Beni Guil pastoralists of eastern Morocco. The data analyzes primarily tangible, material evidence of diverse gender-based resource management practices. But the findings also point to the importance of broader humanistic interpretations of how identities and discourses of "pastoralists" and "farmers" as well as "males" and "females" converge with daily activities to create distinct spaces in these rural villages.

Perhaps the most celebrated work concerned with the meaning of male and female spaces in the Middle East is Bourdieu's (1973, 1977) analysis of the Kabyle Berber society in Algeria. In his study of the Kabyle house, Bourdieu (1973) shows how social and economic relations within the domestic unit create sets of contrasts that organize the production and meaning of spatial domains in the Berber world. He argues that space comes to have meaning through practice, which is dynamic rather than static. Several social theorists in geography have drawn from Bourdieu (1977) and emphasized that space is constructed through social systems, social practices, and everyday activities (Giddens, 1984; Pred, 1990; Soja, 1989). Giddens (1991) later elaborated on these themes, adding the formation of identity as central to daily activities and the creation of space.

Despite these acknowledgments of the dynamic nature of space, cultural norms and standard Islamic discourses about distinct and static male–female spaces persist in the Middle Eastern cultural context (Ask & Tjomsland, 1998). In the region's conservative pastoral societies, men are the purported managers of all productive resources for their households. Their activities, such as herding and selling livestock, generally occur in the external and public space. Women's responsibilities and spaces of production are supposed to be confined to the private, domestic space of reproductive and productive activity. This religious and cultural discourse about appropriate male and female spaces from within Arab Bedouin culture is reified in Western descriptions of these cultures (Said, 1978, 1993).

The implications of these discourses about women's roles and spaces in Middle Eastern society is particularly powerful in the social context of pastoral societies in eastern Morocco, where cultural norms of female seclusion and gender segregation discourage "outsider" researchers from gathering information among women in the domestic space. Yet it is in *this* "private" space that men and women negotiate gender-based livelihood strategies and identities, which articulate with broader cultural and economic processes to transform place.

Feminist geography offers a powerful analytical lens for explaining the production of distinct landscapes because it directs attention toward changing gender roles and identities at the household scale. This approach emphasizes how gender roles and ethnic identities, as well as discourses about them, create distinct spaces and places (Blunt & Rose, 1994; McDowell, 1999; Mills, 1994; Smith, 1993). Feminist geography builds on traditional geographic explanations of the human dimensions of landscape change by incorporating gender-based analysis from feminism and a discourse-sensitive perspective from the humanistic social sciences.

This chapter acknowledges the importance of discourse in shaping power relations, gender roles, identities, and spaces, but not to the exclusion of social, economic, and ecological realities experienced by local actors (Abu-Lughod, 2001). The Beni Guil case study, therefore, analyzes how gender roles and identities converge with larger political, economic, and cultural variables to produce material evidence of distinct land-use and land-cover patterns in two ecologically similar Beni Guil settlements in eastern Morocco.

THEORETICAL PERSPECTIVES ON GENDER, PASTORALISM, AND SPACES OF PRODUCTION

Understanding the transformation of place requires an analysis of power relations within the household and community and how these are linked to cultural identities and economic processes at broader regional scales. Feminist geographers have begun to explore these material and humanistic connections in different cultural contexts (Massey, 1991; McDowell & Sharp, 1997; Rocheleau, 2002). Yet few geographers have analyzed the process of landscape change in the Middle East and North Africa (MENA) through an analysis of gender relations and identity formation.

All cultures create distinct gender-based rights and roles within the household that evolve from a culturally specific division of labor for productive and reproductive activities. In the MENA, however, religious ideologies strengthen the cultural norm of segregating these activities into distinct and fixed public/productive and private/reproductive spaces.

According to cultural tradition and Islamic laws, men but not women are granted formal rights to public institutions of political power and resources management, which represent important gateways to a host of livelihood strategies. This accepted norm that segregates productive and reproductive space obscures informal gender-based negotiations about daily activities within the household and hides the fact that women actively participate in the productive realm of local livelihood systems.

The relative paucity of geographic work on women's involvement in the creation of productive spaces in rural environments of the MENA is explained by the difficulty of (1) transcending the spatial barrier into the domestic, female realm in these societies; and (2) measuring landscape change in livestock-raising environments that are prone to cyclical drought cycles. There have also been conceptual gaps in the distinct approaches of geography and feminist studies as they pertain to pastoral settlement, changing gender roles, and their expression in land-cover patterns.

Most of the geographic analyses of pastoral sedentarization and the conversion of public rangeland spaces to private agricultural use in the region generally, and in Morocco specifically, have focused on proximate causes such as population pressure (Bencherifa & Johnson, 1991), colonial legacies (Davis, 2000; Herpin, 1956; Paskoff, 1957), and changes in formal regulatory systems (Artz, Norton, & O'Rourke, 1986; Bedrani, 1991; Tozy, 1994). The analyses at regional and communal scales, particularly with respect to land and water management institutions in pastoral societies, privilege the public, formal, and male spaces of power. Research that emphasizes the *de jure* rights of citizenship in these formal institutions ignores women's spaces of power and obscures the negotiation between men and women that occur in private spaces but affect public spaces (Horowitz & Jowkar, 1992; Moore, 1996).

These private/public divisions of space are both imagined and real. Since the early works by Nancy Chodorow (1974) and Michelle Rosaldo (Rosaldo & Lamphere, 1974), a broad range of feminist work in social sciences had described the division of private and public space as central to masculinist power and feminist resistance (see Ardener, 1981). Unequal power relations at various spatial scales produce, maintain, and alter places in a very real material as well as a metaphorical level (Harvey, 1989; Moore, 1996; Okley, 1996).

In the Middle Eastern context, Cynthia Nelson's seminal work (1973) broke down the dualism of the public/private spatial divide. She pointed out the complimentary nature of gender roles and the flexibility of space within pastoral households. Her observations drew attention to the domestic realm, where men and women continually negotiate private and public boundaries and where women can influence the male-dominated "public" realm of livelihood production.

Many feminist scholars working in the Middle East have elaborated on Nelson's work by incorporating themes from postmodern deconstruction into their analyses of public and private spaces. El Guindi (1999), for example, notes that women in the Middle East often control public (male) spaces through temporary occupancy and modification of their behavior and dress. Others have demonstrated the cultural relativity of feminine power and the possibility of a feminine power within the domestic space (e.g., Abu-Lughod, 1986; Ahmed, 1992; Mernissi, 1989; Nelson, 1974) or under the veil in public (El Guindi, 1999; MacLeod, 1991; Mir-Hosseini, 1996). A common theme in this literature is that women's efficacy to extend power from the private into the public male-dominated realm depends on ascribed variables such as age and marital status.

Many of these gender-based analyses have pointed out that the ratio of men to women in the household is a key indicator of women's control over productive spaces. This is particularly true in rural communities where men frequently leave the household for extended periods of time to work as labor migrants in regional cities or abroad. Most pastoral households depend on diverse livelihood strategies that usually involve male labor migration for shorter or longer periods of time.

The destabilization of gendered demographics at the local scale has unleashed both new opportunities and new constraints for gender-based renegotiation of productive space. Since Nelson's (1973) pivotal work, many studies in the MENA have analyzed how social and cultural change (commercialization, male out-migration, and settlement) among pastoralists affects women's status, their use of space, and their power to influence the direction of new livelihood strategies (see Horowitz & Jowkar, 1992).

Meir's (1997) research among the Bedouin of the Negev suggests that settlement and migration decrease women's status because, with men as sole wage earners, women lose direct involvement in the productive resources of the household. On the other hand, Michael's (1991) study of Baggara pastoralists in Sudan found that male labor migration to oil-wealthy Gulf States confined women to the home, but led to social status gains because of the increased household wealth and cultural and religious value of female seclusion. Her findings challenge Western assumptions that seclusion to the domestic space necessarily reduces women's power vis-à-vis public male spaces of production.

In a recent study in Oman, Dawn Chatty (2000) found that settled pastoral women initially became more confined to the domestic space and dependent on male income earners. Over time, however, women reclaimed their interests within the public realm of male decisions and production. For example, they utilized truck transportation to access financial resources in larger commercial centers and developed small business enterprises of their own (Chatty, 2000). Lois Beck (1998) describes how pastoral women in Iran have supported the adoption of irrigation technologies, which has led to the construction of permanent settlements and converted overgrazed public rangeland spaces managed jointly by men into smaller, productive green spaces managed by men and women.

Despite these advances in the feminist literature concerned with exposing the subtle forms of female power in Middle Eastern societies, only a few recent geographic studies in the MENA have specifically linked changing gender-based resources management to environmental outcomes at the local (Alaoui El Mdaghri, 1995; Steinmann, 2001; Terranciano, 1994) and regional scales (Turner, 1999).

A subset of feminist geography, feminist political ecology (Rocheleau, Thomas-Slayter, & Wangari, 1996), provides a useful synthesis of the afore-mentioned geographic analyses of landscape change and feminist analyses of gender and space within the household. The rationale for a gender analysis at the household level is that women and men have different vested sets of interests in the natural resources they manage, depending on their responsibilities for maintaining the household (Rocheleau, 1991). This analytical framework investigates how decisions within the household are expressed by collective action at the community scale and thereby transform place (Rocheleau, 2002). Feminist political ecology also draws on poststructural theories to emphasize discursive dimensions of power (Foucault, 1980). This synthesis opens the conceptual lens to entertain how humanistic geographic sensibilities of sense of self and sense of place become visible through agricultural practices and landscape patterns.

Donna Haraway (1991) has addressed this idea of behavioral change by illustrating how a sense of self rests on diverse axes of identity that are never stable but are continually transformed through dynamic gender relations in a given time and location. This analytical perspective exposes often-hidden gendered environmental knowledges, resource management responsibilities, and power relations that affect the creation or destruction of cultural and ecological spaces.

This perspective is particularly relevant to the Beni Guil case where different labor migration patterns from the two villages reconfigure local identities, household spaces of production, and village landscapes. The process of settlement and male labor migration among pastoral nomads in Morocco ruptures deeply embedded cultural norms about gender-based activities and identities. And the consequent reformulation of sense of self and place occurs quietly, subtly, within the domestic realm rather than at the broader cultural scale of the tribe and the community.

The conceptual and methodological tools of feminist political ecology guided my research among the Beni Guil pastoralists and helped me identify how contemporary local identities and places are shaped by the broader cultural, economic, and historical context. The adaptation strategies available to individual households, however, depend on economic and labor resources within that small production unit. At this scale, culturally defined gender roles create opportunities and set limits on the transformation of resource management practices. The successes of livelihood adaptations at this scale depend on the ability of men and women to renegotiate appropriate gender roles within the private spaces of the household unit that do not overtly offend the parameters of culturally accepted "public" norms that evolve at a slower pace.

The following discussion of the traditional pastoral livelihood system, and the historical events that have encouraged sedentarization, provides the background for this case study, which analyzes the transformation of gender roles, identities, and spaces in two settled villages in eastern Morocco.

HISTORICAL BACKGROUND OF PASTORAL SEDENTARIZATION IN EASTERN MOROCCO

Traditional Nomadic Pastoralism

The Beni Guil are a large tribal community of approximately 54,000 people whose livelihoods have shifted from extensive large-scale herding of sheep and goats to more sedentary agropastoral or agricultural activities (Bencherifa, 1996). The diversity and limitations of the semiarid environment in which they live has always provided the physical and cultural framework for the Beni Guil's pastoral production, which until 50 years ago depended exclusively on herding flocks of sheep and goats to seasonally available grazing and water resources. These were found in various

FIGURE 4.1. Map of the Beni Guil landscape in eastern Morocco. Reproduced with permission from *The Arab World Geographer*, Vol. 1, No. 2 (1998), and the *Bulletin Series of the Yale School of Forestry and Environmental Studies*, No. 103 (1998).

ecological niches of their vast territory, which covers 25,000 square kilometers of the semiarid steppe of Morocco's eastern high plateau region.

Traditional seasonal migrations extended up to 250 kilometers and spanned two dominant environments that define their landscape: the northern high plateau (the *Dahara)* and the more arid southern pre-Saharan environment (the *Sahara)* (see Figure 4.1). Rainfall diminishes from north to south with a maximum of 450 millimeters in the Dahara and 150 millimeters in the Sahara. Cold temperatures and snow in the Dahara prompted the Beni Guil tribes to move their families and household camps in the early winter to warmer climates in the Sahara. In the spring, increasing temperatures and diminishing grazing resources drove the Beni Guil back north toward spring pastures in the Dahara. Using camel traction, the Beni Guil also ploughed and cultivated small barley fields in the moister depressions locally called *dayas* or *madders.* Barley harvested in June supplied pastoral households with bread and flour, and postharvest stubble helped sustain livestock through the dry summer months.

During the last century, the Beni Guil have decreased their mobility and use of rangeland pastures through increased cultivation of cereals, irrigating fodder resources, and supplementing livestock with commercial feed inputs. Land-use intensification and sedentarization occurred, in part, because of demographic change. The Beni Guil population rose from 10,000 in 1940 to 30,000 in 1982, and up to 54,000 in 1994 (Morocco, 1994; Raynal, 1949). These endogenous variables combined with French colonial policies and accelerated the shift away from the traditional nomadic pastoral system toward a more intensive and sedentary agricultural production system.

Winds of Change and the Trend toward Settlement

In 1908 the French arrived in eastern Morocco from Algeria with the goal of securing the region for French farmers and administrators. The French Protectorate (1912–1956) imposed a development vision that redirected rural economies toward national rather than local needs. In eastern Morocco the French developed metal or mining industries, halfa grass export for paper production, and increasing livestock and agricultural production (Dresch, 1959; Lauriac, 1940). An infrastructure of roads and railroads spread throughout the region to connect this hinterland and its resources to larger commercial markets in Europe. The French provided veterinary services, dug wells to access groundwater, and irrigated pastures to increase livestock production for the market (Müller-Hohenstein, 1979). These development initiatives reduced access to critical dry-season pastures (now under irrigation) and converted collective-use rights to private-use rights.

Many individual Beni Guil households benefited from more intensive and privatized land-use practices, which allowed them to produce surplus livestock for national or European markets. But growing competition for water and desirable locations for cereal cultivation forced many households out of the pastoral production system and into settlement.

The discourse of the postcolonial Moroccan government mirrored the French development model and justified national policies that encouraged greater agricultural output, which led to the collapse of highly mobile pastoral systems throughout the country (Davis, 2000). These policies arose from the dire need to feed a rapidly growing and increasingly urban population (Bencherifa, 1996). In order to ensure these national goals, the government passed the law (*Dahir*) of 1969, which nationalized all rangeland resources, thereby ensuring greater state control of livestock and agricultural production in these areas.

In eastern Morocco the 1969 *Dahir* effectively subjugated Beni Guil tribal political power, and their control of resources, to state authority. Without local Beni Guil leadership managing communal resources, respected codes of access to land and water became unclear (Tozy, 1994). Pastoralists' lack of confidence in new state-level land tenure "codes" encouraged more of them to cultivate or irrigate land (where possible), which secures quasi-exclusive rights to formerly communal tribal lands. This rush to secure land rights encouraged permanent settlement near the fields.

The trend toward settlement accelerated in eastern Morocco during the severe droughts in the 1970s and mid-1980s. These droughts caused widespread human suffering, led to substantial livestock losses, and increased permanent settlement in towns and villages. Settled pastoral households had to diversify their livelihood strategies.

Since the mid-1990s, 80% of the Beni Guil households have based their livelihoods on a mix of herding, farming, labor migration, and other commercial activities. Twenty percent of the Beni Guil have settled and found wage employment in larger commercial towns like Bouarfa and Tendrara (with populations of approximately 20,000 and 7,000, respectively). Thirty-five percent of the households have settled permanently in villages where they combine farming, herding, and labor migration. These trends suggest the demise of nomadic pastoralism as a cultural identity and economic way of life.

Nevertheless, the Beni Guil remain among Morocco's largest livestock producers: they raise as many as 600,000 sheep, 200,000 goats, and 11,000 cattle in an average-yield year (Direction Provinciale de l'Agriculture de Figuig [DPA], 2001). The continuation of a pastoral economy and a sustainable yield for urban markets therefore represents a top concern of the Moroccan government.

In 1990 the Moroccan government established an extensive economic development and rangeland conservation project (PDPEO) in eastern Morocco in order to address the concern of pastoral settlement and increasing agricultural production on fragile rangelands.[1] The PDPEO project focused primarily on improving pasture management and minimizing soil and wind erosion in heavily denuded areas around pastoral settlements. With the hope of minimizing overgrazing around pastoral villages such as Maatarka and Mengoub Gare, the project established several official policies intended to reverse the trend toward permanent settlement (DPA, 1997).

These project goals have sustained the pastoral economy. But their efforts have minimized the attention given to livelihoods and resource management within settled villages. Despite the hope that settled pastoralists will "remobilize" and reengage in pastoral production, the Beni Guil continue to trade in their woolen tents for mud-brick homes and settle more or less permanently in villages, notably Maatarka and Mengoub Gare.

In response to the project regulations that ban the construction of fixed homes, individual households—rather than collective tribes—engage in the process of establishing permanent homes in the villages. As discussed above, the relationship between insecure land-tenure policies and pastoral settlement is well documented at the regional scale in eastern Morocco (Bencherifa, 1996; Hammoudi, Hammoudi, Rachik, & Tozy, 1992; Tozy, 1994). This case suggests that similar strategies are replicated within the village context and driven by gender-based interests at the household scale.

Unfortunately, the PDPEO project staff has worked primarily with men and with formal, political organizations at the community scale. This approach, common throughout the MENA, ignores women and their interests, which are strongest at the household level (see Horowitz & Jowkar, 1992). And gender-based resource interests and consequent land-use practices are clearly visible in the settled villages.

Gendered Division of Labor and Spaces of Production

The Beni Guil production system at the household scale has always operated autonomously in terms of specific labor allocation, herd management practices, and decisions about specific labor allocations. These responsibilities are based on a culturally defined division of labor and on age and gender characteristics (Bourqia, 1989). Men and boys are almost exclusively responsible for herding and selling sheep, goats, and, more recently, cattle. Women and girls engage in activities that are also central to the pastoral household economy, but are generally carried out in spaces close to the home camp (Müller-Hohenstein, 1978). In these private spaces, women and girls care for sick and young animals and process a variety of animal by-products including milk, butter, wool, and hides. The private domestic space is also a site of negotiation between men and women. And contrary to public discourses, women are central to the decision-making process about which animals to sell, how much grain fodder to buy, and when to move animals to greener pastures (Steinmann, 2001).

Nevertheless, the cultural value placed in female seclusion (*purdah*) among the Arab Bedouin, including the Beni Guil, discourages social interaction among women from different family units. Consequently, women have developed informal arrangements through which they share information, labor, and surplus milk products. These informal social relationships allow them to establish economic networks outside the individual household. But the economic links between individual households are publicly recognized only through the formal male-dominated cooperative political system at the tribal level.

This culture of economic independence at the household scale is disrupted in settled villages, where most households cannot afford this degree of economic independence. Men and women therefore develop new alliances within the household unit and outside their tribal or ethnic communities. Some of these associations are cooperative, and some are not, depending on the gender dynamics at the household scale. The meaning of these alliances and the spaces within which they occur reflect social categories and systems of social organization (Moore, 1996). Since these meanings are related to a larger cultural order, they are theoretically described as stable.

But alliances and spaces of production at the household scale are contextual and necessarily reflect the dynamic patterns of the larger regional economy. The rapid changes ubiquitous in the global commercial economy demand more flexible production systems at local and household scales.

In Mengoub Gare, men encourage women to engage in farming and gardening activities, which is highly unusual in this cultural context and suggests a shift in the cultural identities associated with traditional pastoral production systems. At the same time, men and women uphold a public discourse that claims only men as household gardeners. In Maatarka, on the other hand, the high rate of male migration has discouraged household-level negotiations and women have not established gardens. Instead, women choose to invest time and cash remittances into livestock, but they are considering the creation of a multiple-household dairy cooperative, which challenges cultural norms at the community scale. These shifting cultural ideologies and gender dynamics in the two villages are expressed in distinct daily land-use practices and result in distinct household and village spaces.

RESEARCH METHODS

Gender analysis, as an entry point of research, sheds light on male–female power dynamics that create productive spaces. This analytical perspective uncovers complexities of land-use decisions at the household scale and helps explain emerging land-cover patterns in recently settled pastoral villages. I used both quantitative and qualitative research methods to examine three interrelated questions: First, how do gendered roles and responsibilities for managing household resources change in response to settlement and male out-migration? Second, how do gendered land-use strategies articulate with regional cultural and political themes? And, third, how do emerging and shifting identities affect landscape patterns in the villages?

Preliminary Research

I collected primary data while living and working with the Beni Guil from 1996 through 1997. This research built on previous fieldwork for my master's thesis and provided the empirical foundation for the larger project of writing my doctoral dissertation. I spent the first few months of this fieldwork period engaged in participant observation in order to establish a rapport with the various Beni Guil communities, specifically those in Maatarka and Mengoub Gare. I gained access to these communities through the formal Moroccan political structure and its local representatives (*sheiks* and *mukkadems*).[2] These community leaders introduced me to their respective tribes in the villages. They also helped with *wealth-ranking*

activities, a methodological approach that provided me with locally relevant economic class parameters (Grandin, 1988). I subsequently lived with
host families in the villages for 3-week rotations every 4 months throughout the year.

Quantitative Methods

I carried out 220 formal survey questionnaires in 159 Beni Guil households. One-third of these pastoral households were settled permanently in
the villages of Maatarka and Mengoub Gare. I interviewed both men and
women in order to identify gender- and age-specific perceptions of livestock
management and farming activities in the villages. The questionnaire elicited information about household demographics, income sources, labor relations, ownership and management of livestock, and farming activities.

Data generated from the survey questionnaire was analyzed using the
SPSS statistical program. Chi-square tests were used to analyze categorical
variables, and t-tests and multivariate regression tests were employed for
interval data. The rigor of the analysis, however, was only as accurate as
the honesty of the answers given on the survey.

As mentioned previously in this chapter, the formal (usually male) responses about appropriate male–female spaces often reified gender stereotypes, particularly when talking to outsiders. These formal responses often
revealed gender-specific perceptions and culturally prescribed *gender myths*,
rather than realities, about resource uses (see Slocum, 1995). Women and
men often answered questions in ways that matched culturally accepted
norms (Women and Geography Specialty Group, 1997) rather than the
daily practices that I confirmed through participant observation and informal, qualitative research methods. As Lila Abu-Lughod says, "to be a feminist entails being sensitive to domination; for the enthographer that means
being sensitive to that domination in the society being described" (1993, p.
5). A variety of research techniques, particularly qualitative and participatory methods, are necessary to uncover the various forms of domination,
which are expressed both formally and informally in diverse cultural contexts.

Qualitative and Participatory Methods

Qualitative and participatory methods verified that gender roles and identities were more flexible than revealed by the formal survey. Spending uninterrupted days and nights with families allowed me to observe and record
daily activities such as gardening and tending to livestock. As a foreign
woman, I had access to discussions with men and women in the villages,
which helped me to distinguish between myth and reality. I used space–time
allocation tables (see Kwan, 1999, 2000) and percentage of labor input

(daily and seasonally) to determine the relative importance of diverse productive activities and spaces for men and women in the villages.

I led focus-group discussions (Thomas-Slayter, Esser, & Shields, 1993; Barbour & Kitzinger, 1999) with several sets of 10–15 men and women. The participants discussed their perceptions of new land-use practices in the villages, including the establishment of small, irrigated household gardens. Men, women, boys, and girls also participated in *resource-mapping* activities in order to elicit input about diverse natural resources and their respective uses by villagers (Rocheleau, 1995).

Villagers helped identify the diversity and uses of medicinal herbs in the gardens and documented the water use, fertilizer inputs, and square-meter sizes of their irrigated garden spaces. These participatory (Chambers 1983, 1997) and feminist (Moss, 2002; Wolf, 1996; Women and Geography Specialty Group, 1997) research methods ensured that information I collected would also expand local and gendered awareness of landscape change and thus empower people, especially women, at the research site.

GENDER RATIOS AND THE PRODUCTION OF SPACE IN TWO BENI GUIL VILLAGES

Maatarka and Mengoub Gare (with populations of 620 and 310, respectively) are small villages settled by formerly fully mobile pastoral nomads. The villages appear on the landscape as isolated clusters of square mud-brick houses grouped closely along a grid-like maze of narrow footpaths. Neither village has electricity or running water. The groundwater table is at least 20 meters below the surface in both villages. Despite ecological similarities, settled pastoralists (now villagers) have adapted to their more sedentary livelihood system in distinct ways. In Mengoub Gare, villagers irrigate and cultivate small plots of land, while those in Maatarka have chosen to invest in the traditional livestock sector. The consequent spatial patterns evolving in the two villages are explained by variations in household demographics, shifting identities, local politics, and proximity to other settlements.

Men and women in each rural site have created new daily land-use practices and identities that share male–female spaces. These new spaces are produced through strategic intentions of the actors (Moore, 1996) and are grounded in daily livelihood needs within a specific historical and economic context (Rocheleau, 2002) and within the accepted community context of each village.

Mengoub Gare, as the name suggests, was originally a stop for refueling trains on the rail line that connected small mining towns located along the Algerian–Moroccan border. The French built the station in the 1920s and also used it as a military outpost in the Beni Guil's southern Sahara ter-

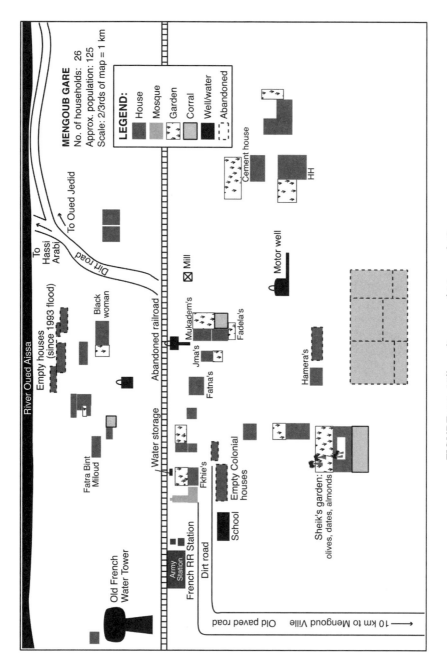

FIGURE 4.2. Village diagram of Mengoub Gare.

ritories. During the severe droughts of the 1940s, 1970s, and 1980s pastoralists of the Oulad Hammema tribe settled in Mengoub Gare because of its proximity to their *wolufs* (summer pastures) located in the *madders* (shallow, moisture-retaining depressions) just north of the village. Most villagers today still practice transhumance in the spring, herding their sheep and goats to pastures and water sources in the highlands located just south of the village. Their livestock also rely heavily on postharvest stubble from cultivated fields in their tribal *wolufs*.

As shown in Figure 4.2, the village today is still not much more than an abandoned railroad stop with a one-room elementary school, a mosque, and a small grocery store. The grocery is dormant most of the time since villagers prefer to shop for food and household items in the larger town of Bouarfa, which is located 35 kilometers northeast of the village.

Mengoub Gare is home to 25 households. Several pastoral households moved away from the village because of flooding in the early 1990s and because nearby towns like Bouarfa offer many more economic, social, and educational opportunities. The government, operating through the PDPEO project, also banned all home construction in Mengoub Gare in 1992. This policy was created in order to discourage permanent settlement, which was perceived as the cause of overgrazing and rangeland degradation around the village.

The government's efforts to promote pastoralism and mobility have not, however, prevented those already living in the village from irrigating land, a process that denotes private ownership of land and permanent settlement. Sixty-eight percent of the households have established lush, irrigated vegetable gardens hidden behind the mud-brick walls of their houses (see Figure 4.3). The creation of these gardens is unique, especially compared to other pastoral settlements in eastern Morocco.

What sets Mengoub Gare apart is its proximity to Mengoub Lakbab, which is located just 5 kilometers farther west. The water table in Mengoub Lakbab is only 5 meters from the surface and was settled originally by Berber farmers from the Figuig oasis, located 150 kilometers farther east. The Figuig Berbers, an ethnically distinct community, have drawn on their knowledge of oasis farming to establish rich irrigated fields of potatoes, onions, carrots, alfalfa, olive trees, and date palms.

By contrast, Mengoub Gare hardly resembles an oasis. And pastoralists settled in the village still rely on livestock as a central component of their livelihoods. Their identities also remain intimately connected to the daily practice of raising livestock. Yet neither cultural nor ecological deterrents (such as groundwater at 22 meters below the surface) have prevented the pastoralists in the village from establishing small irrigated gardens.

The men in Mengoub Gare have pooled their resources to maintain one communal motor pump. The pump operates periodically to raise water from the oldest and deepest well in the village. Rubber tubes are used to transport the water to small gardens in the nearby households. Those who cannot afford the tubing collect water manually from the two other wells in the village in order to water their gardens.

This system of pooling labor and capital expenses for the collective water pump, which is then used to generate water for independent household gardens, reflects the traditional pastoral political and economic ideology of communal organization at lineage or tribal scale and independent production at the household scale. Men in the village work cooperatively to secure communal water resources for individual use, while men and women manage the work in independent, secluded household gardens.

The cultural and pastoral system of individual household production within a formal tribal cooperative has been adapted to support settled agropastoral production in the village. This shift in land use and land cover and the daily chores associated with vegetable gardening have produced a new identity for men and women. This identity does not reject a pastoral heritage, but is open to a new sense of place and identity that is rooted to the daily practice of cultivation. As Giddens (1991) pointed out, identities are necessarily geographic since they are formed through the daily practice of livelihood production.

The gradual transformation of the pastoral identity and the village landscape in Mengoub Gare was spearheaded by the tribal sheik, Sidi Ben Amrane, who encouraged a cooperative water management system in the village. He established the first garden in the village 20 years ago, with wages earned in France during the 1960s and 1970s. Sheik Ben Amrane has since encouraged other village men to work as seasonal agricultural laborers in the Berber farming village of Mengoub Lakbab. Many of these Beni Guil laborers now participate in the water irrigation cooperative in Mengoub Gare and have established small subsistence gardens for their households.

Sheik Ben Amrane told me that the village men who started gardens in the early 1990s hoped to generate some income from them by selling the produce at the markets in Bouarfa. It became clear after a few years, however, that small vegetable growers from Mengoub Gare could not compete commercially with larger, more experienced producers in Mengoub Lakbab. Consequently, men have given up gardening in most households in Mengoub Gare. But garden spaces continue to flourish because women have developed the skills and interests in maintaining these household resources.

GARDENS, GENDER RELATIONS, AND STATE POLICIES

In Mengoub Gare, women in 68% of the households actively maintain small subsistence gardens. The fact that women are gardeners in Mengoub Gare is highly unusual because these practices directly challenge many of the Beni Guil's cultural norms and political institutions, which discourage the privatization of communal resources. Private ownership of land is not clearly articulated in any tribal laws among pastoral nomads. As a result of ambiguous laws, irrigation and permanent cultivation has proven to be the best method for establishing private-use rights on communal lands. Nevertheless, conflict and disagreements about land tenure are ongoing in the region. Under these circumstances, the Beni Guil and other Bedouin societies in Morocco support customary practices and cultural taboos that discourage anyone who is politically weak (especially women) from plowing, irrigating, and cultivating land (Maher, 1974).

In Mengoub Gare, however, women hoe, irrigate, and cultivate land because men are often away during the day herding livestock or working as day laborers in Mengoub Lakbab or in Bouarfa. The men who work with Berber farmers in Mengoub Lakbab have taught women in their households how to grow vegetables, fruits, and herbs. Figure 4.3 is a photograph of women in their gardens in Mengoub Gare.

Survey results from households with gardens in Mengoub Gare show that women work and have control of the produce in 40% of the households. In 8% of the households only men work the gardens, while in 52% of the households both men and women share garden work. The garden represents a shared endeavor and is not clearly designated as a male or a female space, at least vis-à-vis the public realm in the community.

FIGURE 4.3. Women in their garden in Mengoub Gare.

The ambiguity about whether gardens are exclusively male or female spaces has created a new opportunity for the renegotiation of productive roles within the private household space, which men and women use to their advantage. In households where men are present (except for daily work outside the village), women garden and distribute its produce within the household unit. This system is an adaptation of their pastoral cultural and economic system. Men and women negotiate the internal labor dynamics and production decisions at the household scale, but men are the key links to the broader communal structure that provides water resources to the individual production units.

Men in the village also claim proprietary rights to the gardens if social or political pressure requires it. Beni Guil men have always dealt with the "external" authorities from the Department of Agriculture or the PDPEO project staff. These government officials usually come to the village to ensure that no more houses or fence walls are constructed in the village. In these interactions men always identified themselves as the gardeners, thus protecting women from the "public" assumption that they cultivate land. Men and women in the village of Mengoub Gare convey to outsiders the impression that men, not women, are gardeners. This united front vis-à-vis outsiders is possible because 80% of the village men are absent only during the day, returning to the village in the evening or whenever necessary.

In households where men are absent for longer durations (weeks or months at a time), women do not have gardens. Of the five formally female-headed households, only two maintained gardens after their husbands left. Women gave the following reasons for abandoning their gardens, listed in order of importance: (1) "I could not afford fencing to protect the garden from grazing animals"; (2) "I could not afford to buy irrigation tubes to transport water from the well"; and (3) "Men in the village forced me to give up the garden."

Poverty is acute in all but one of these female-headed households. Yet village men pressured these women (all either widowed or divorced) to give up their subsistence gardens because of the perceived social and political threat generated by independent women cultivating land.

Land-use practices in Mengoub Gare are clearly explained through a close analysis of how gender roles in the private space of the household articulate with broader cultural, political, and economic systems. On a personal level, men and women in the village joke about their new "farming" activities, and they accept and project strong identities as farmers, despite their continuation of pastoral activities. These new land-use practices and identities are formed through social practices, which are not simple mechanical reactions to livelihood systems, but also operate out of "generative principles" infused with social and cultural meaning that inform action (Bourdieu, 1977, p. 72).

At the scale of community discourse and conscience, villagers in

Mengoub Gare support the cultural and political norms of pastoral societies, which discourage women from cultivating and owning land. Men actively prevent women from establishing gardens in those households where a man cannot claim public responsibility and participate in the communal aspects of water management. On the other hand, men encourage women to garden—a benefit to the whole family—in households where women can operate behind a high mud-brick wall and are concealed by the camouflage of a man's presence in the household. In this way beneficial but unorthodox land-use practices do not directly challenge broader cultural and political rules governing gendered ownership of land.

The focus of feminist geography combines analyses of the symbolic meaning of new identities as well as their material expression through new land-use practices. These new identities and their expression in the village spaces of production vary significantly depending on gender relations in the village context, as is clear from the second case study in eastern Morocco.

OBSTACLES TO IRRIGATED
LAND-USE PRACTICES IN MAATARKA

In the second village research site, Maatarka, relatively few (13% compared to 68% in Mengoub Gare) of the households have established individual household gardens. What explains these differences in place? There are several reasons, including high tensions about land tenure around the village of Maatarka, a high rate of male migration for long periods of time, and the fact that the PDPEO project established one communal garden in the village.

Maatarka is located in the Dahara, 70 kilometers west of the town of Tendrara (its closest neighbor). A very rough, unpaved road connects the two settlements. The road is often impassible during the rainy season in the winter and early spring. When the road is dry, a one-way trip takes 3–4 hours by truck or Land Rover. As illustrated in Figure 4.4, Maatarka is very isolated, hence villagers have very little contact with other ethnic and farming communities. Nor do they have daily access to larger commercial towns such as Tendrara or Bouarfa.

The village is located at the crossroads of migration routes between grazing pastures on the Dahara and important livestock markets in Ain Beni Mathar and Tendrara to the east and Taourirt to the north. Maatarka was founded as a French military outpost in 1911 because of its strategic location. And, like Mengoub Gare, the village population grew when demographic pressures and political constraints on their mobility forced pastoralists to become more sedentary. Many villagers also lost their livestock and settled in Maatarka, either permanently or temporarily, during severe droughts in the 1940s, 1970s, and 1980s.

FIGURE 4.4. Photo of Maatarka.

Today the village is home to 60 permanent households and 20 seasonal ones. The temporary households move tents and livestock to seasonal grazing sites in the hinterlands of the village. Approximately one-third of the permanent villagers are wealthy enough to maintain two full-time households: one in the village and one that moves with the tent and livestock. The majority of the permanent village residents, however, have not been able to rebuild their herds after drought losses. These households are poor, with 70% of them headed by women.

Divorced or widowed women formally head 25% of households in Maatarka. But an additional 45% of the households are informally headed by women, whose husbands, brothers, or fathers work as herders for wealthy pastoralists or as wage laborers in faraway cities like Oujda, Taza, and Fez (all located more than 200 kilometers to the northeast or northwest of Maatarka). These men are usually away from the village for several weeks or months at a time, leaving the women as de facto decision makers for the household.

The high degree of male absenteeism in the village explains why few households cultivate gardens. If women established gardens in households without men present most of the time, they would directly challenge customary and normative rights, which suggest that land belongs to men. Furthermore, cultural identities in Maatarka remain centered on pastoral activities, and men from the village most often find employment as herders for wealthy pastoralists in the area. They also migrate seasonally to aforementioned cities to work in construction or service industries. The men from this village rarely work in agricultural sectors elsewhere, so they do not teach nor encourage women to establish small vegetable gardens. These daily activities reify a pastoral sense of identity, which is expressed in the physical landscape of the village that lacks the creation of individual household gardens.

I surveyed women who did not have gardens in both Maatarka and Mengoub Gare in order to understand what factors prevent villagers in Maatarka from cultivating small gardens. The surveys suggest that pastoral identities, land tenure uncertainties, lack of access to water and information about farming, and male absenteeism discouraged irrigated agriculture in both villages. But, as noted in Table 4.1, twice as many women in Maatarka cited male absenteeism as the reason for not keeping a garden. Women in Maatarka frequently explained that "we are nomads, we don't farm." These cultural explanations of household land-use practices are also embedded in broader political contexts.

Conflict over rights to land is prevalent throughout the Beni Guil territories, but tensions are especially high around Maatarka. This situation discourages villagers from cultivating land. As discussed earlier in this chapter, plowing and planting land converts collective rights into private-use rights. Many pastoralists cultivate fields in order to enclose good pastures for private use. Conflicts often erupt over the private appropriation of communal land. These conflicts are much more severe in cases where land is irrigated, since this practice represents a more permanent claim to the land.

Several villagers in Maatarka told me that people had died fighting over access to land around Oglat Sedra, an area just 50 kilometers northeast of Maatarka. According to Mr. Zakaraya, the director of the Department of Agriculture in Tendrara, pastoralists have been fighting over the use of the area because of its irrigation potential. Several years ago those

TABLE 4.1. Women's Explanations for Not Establishing an Irrigated Garden

Reason why no garden	Women in Maatarka (%)	Women in Mengoub Gare (%)
We're nomads and don't know how to farm	24	21
No rights to land	24	13
No water	31	33
It's men's work, none at this house	21	11
Buy produce in Bouarfa	0	22
Total	100	100

Note. Source: Data collected by the author.

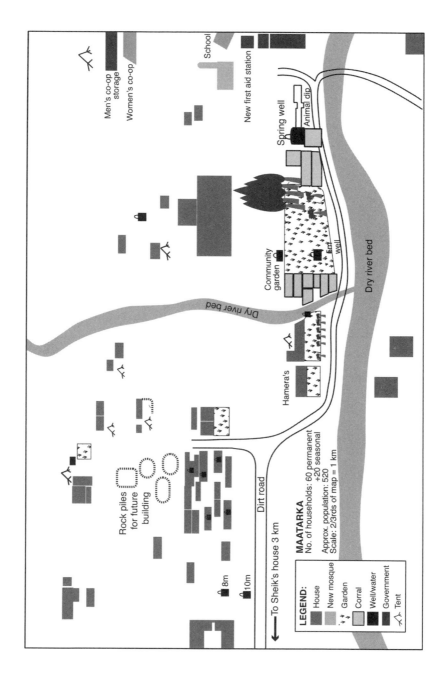

FIGURE 4.5. Village diagram of Maatarka.

112

families whose traditional summer pastures (*wolufs*) straddle the Oglat Sedra began irrigating fields. They soon abandoned their efforts because disputes with other Beni Guil tribes became so severe.

The land disputes around Maatarka have discouraged villagers, especially women, from irrigating land and growing individual household gardens. And, as articulated by feminist political ecologists, gender-based livelihood strategies at the household scale always operate in relation to broader sociopolitical, economic, and ecological contexts. In Maatarka, only eight households cultivate their own gardens. Of these, only three gardens are large enough to be visible on the landscape outside the home. These gardens belong to the wealthiest and most politically powerful families in the village. Resident men in these households work and manage the gardens. Two of the gardens are a half-hectare in size, the third about one-quarter of a hectare. The two larger gardens are located in the northeastern corner of the village, where groundwater is only 2.5 meters below the surface. One shared motor pump irrigates both gardens, which produce a few olive trees, vegetables, and alfalfa. These gardens were established and worked by men whose families have lived in Maatarka for more than 50 years. Both families are members of the Oulad Jenfi lineage within the Oulad Jaber tribe. Their traditional summer grazing pastures are all within a few kilometers of the village. These families have had rights to the land by tribal affiliation and their long history as permanent settlers in Maatarka.

The third private garden belongs to one of the wealthiest families of the politically and economically powerful Labyed lineage. A mud-brick wall surrounds this smaller garden (25 square meters) and attaches it to the household compound located at the southwestern edge of the village. The ground water is 15 meters below the surface in this location, but the family transports water to the garden with a relative's truck. Safia, the eldest woman in the house, grows olive trees, herbs, and vegetables in the garden. She has learned these skills from her son, who works with her and who learned these skills as a migrant laborer in France.

As noted in Figure 4.5, there is also a community garden in the village, which reduces the need for villagers to establish private home gardens. The PDPEO project staff established this garden in order to improve and diversify the diet for settled villagers, especially the poor (BenJelloun, 1996). The village garden occupies about 1 hectare of land located near the Jenfi gardens in the northeastern corner of the village. A mule-powered wheel raises water for irrigation from an on-site well. The water is just 3 meters below the surface. A mud-brick wall surrounds the garden and protects the produce from grazing livestock and thieves.

Although members of poor households, especially women and children, are the intended beneficiaries of the project, few women participate in managing the garden. The project staff and men in the village hoe the land and plant this green space. Men make all decisions about planting, harvesting, and distributing the produce. They water the garden and survey it at night. Occasionally, women are called upon to weed the garden.

This project has not empowered women, nor has it created an opportunity to improve their livelihoods. Instead, they have become more dependent on remittances from absentee male wage laborers. But most men in the village, and the project staff, consider the community garden project a "success" because it has given a few men part-time jobs and has kept the number of private gardens in the village to a minimum, and therefore has reduced disputes over land in the community.

In public, men and women both adhere to a discourse that is positive about the community garden, primarily because the garden was initiated by the PDPEO, which acts as the representative of the state. Ever since the *Dahir* of 1969, which transferred all rights over communal lands from tribes to the national government, local disagreements about land-use decisions initiated by the government are kept out of the public discourse.

As mentioned earlier in the chapter, the *Dahir* of 1969 disenfranchised Beni Guil tribes from their rights to communal land. Similarly, the men in Maatarka and the PDPEO staff have disenfranchised women from the community garden and discourses about it. As a result of their marginalization from the gardening project, women in Maatarka continue to identify themselves as pastoralists, not as farmers, and make investment choices accordingly, namely, by buying livestock. Maatarka's location along traditional and still active pastoral migration routes also sustains a continued cultural identity with pastoral rather than agricultural livelihoods.

The strong social and cultural construction and retention of a pastoral identity is expressed in the village landscape of Maatarka. Feminist geography points to the relevance of gender relations as a key component for explaining the form of the built environment in rural and urban settings (McDowell, 1999). Village landscapes in eastern Morocco are a reflection of specific types of productive investments.

As illustrated in Table 4.2, patterns of productive investments clearly reflect pastoral culture in both village communities, but the preference for

TABLE 4.2. Village Site and Livestock Investment Preferences

Livestock investment preferences (*n* = 69)	Village site	
	Maatarka (%)	Mengoub (%)
Sheep	48	45
Goats	2	14
Cows	40	24
Chickens	10	17
Total	100	100

TABLE 4.3. Gender and Livestock Investment Preferences

Livestock Investment preferences (n = 185)	Sex of interviewee	
	Male	Female
Sheep	76	42
Goats	0	7
Cows	22	37
Chickens	2	14
Total	100	100

buying cows in Maatarka also suggests an alternative and gender-based adaptation to village life. The data in Table 4.2 show that sheep remain the backbone of the pastoral economy. Goats have always been less commercially valuable, but are more resilient in drier climates. For this reason, significantly more villagers in Mengoub Gare (14%) would invest in goats compared to villagers in Maatarka (2%). Goats survive well in the arid Saharan environment, where Mengoub Gare is located, and are therefore still a desirable investment for villagers there. By contrast, the more humid environment in the Dahara lends itself more to raising cattle. Twice as many villagers in Maatarka (40%), compared to Mengoub (24%), would invest in cows.

Based on a Pearson's chi-square of .001, the data in Table 4.3 also indicate that gender interests affect preferences for particular livestock species. The data in Table 4.3 reveal that men, more than women, prefer to invest in sheep, primarily because men are responsible for herding sheep. Men also control most of the income generated from these livestock resources. Goats have always been a compliment to the larger sheep herds because they are more drought-tolerant, though less commercially valuable. Women, however, value goats (see Table 4.3) for their by-products such as hair, hides, and milk. These resources are important for domestic use in the pastoral household. Table 4.3 also shows that cows, rather than goats, are the second most desirable investment for men and women. This shift away from the traditional herd mix of sheep and goats represents a shift away from a nomadic pastoral culture toward more sedentary agropastoral livelihoods.

LIVESTOCK RATHER THAN GARDEN PREFERENCES IN MAATARKA

The persistence of pastoral identities, male out-migration, and intense land tenure conflict in the area has encouraged women in Maatarka to invest in livestock rather than to establish household gardens. Women said they want to buy cows because, relative to sheep and goats, they provide better commercial returns, larger manure by-products (used as fuel resources), and greater dairying potential. Women also said they prefer to work with cows because they can be kept close to home and needn't be herded by a male relative. Without both men and women present in the household on a daily basis, the renegotiation of productive activities and gender-based roles and responsibilities are stunted. Instead, women in Maatarka seek out new livelihood options that persist within the cultural constraints of female seclusion and the production norms of pastoral societies. Women's preference for keeping dairy cows represents a suitable economic adaptation to village life that does not demand the reformulation of pastoral identities and practices.

Feminist political ecology approaches direct attention to the synthesis of gender-based adaptations as local livelihoods collide with broader social, economic, and ecological processes (see Rocheleau et al., 1996). A more complete and holistic explanation for the diverse local adaptation strategies also requires additional consideration of how the material productive chores are connected through daily practice to more abstract, culturally significant meanings of identity. Successful adaptation strategies must accommodate material needs and culturally specific identities and gender roles, which, as we have seen, can vary from one settlement to another depending on household gender demographics and employment opportunities. The presence of men in the household or the length of their absence significantly influences the trajectories of work, identities, and local places, particularly in cultural regions where seclusion defines the geographic spaces in which reproduction and production occur.

In Maatarka, the daily work of collecting wood fuel and water compels women to be visible in the public space of the village. This public visibility challenges seclusion ideologies that define the geographic spaces of production and reproduction in previously mobile pastoral households, which are usually isolated from non-kinship-based associations. The settled village context disrupts the traditional social system and produces new insecurities around women's visibility, status, and images. This is particularly true in households where the men are absent most of the time. Women in Maatarka have opted to invest capital and labor resources into raising milk cows because this activity perpetuates cultural ideologies of pastoral production and accommodates the seclusion of women's activities and social networks from public to private spaces.

Pastoral women have always cherished their control of milk, cheese, butter, and buttermilk. Women use these resources to develop social and distribution networks outside the confines of the home. These contacts increase access to a larger range of social, political, and economic resources (Kerven, 1987; Waters-Bayer, 1988; Herren, 1990). These informal livestock by-product associations serve the same function for women as the formal men's livestock cooperatives do for men. In both cases the institutions create a forum for exchanging important information and resources across a large area.

Beni Guil women say that they use their milk exchange systems to create links between village households, between the village and tent households in surrounding areas, and between village households and households in towns like Tendrara. Women in Maatarka rely heavily on these links to towns because they provide access to commercial resources like grain fodder, which women need for their own goats and cows.

Interviews with groups of women from different socioeconomic classes in Maatarka, however, revealed several potential problems with their desire to raise more milk cows in the village. The women identified insufficient investment capital and the maintenance costs as the two biggest problems. Indeed, in 1997, only four households in Maatarka owned cows, and all but one of these was wealthy enough to sustain feed inputs for the livestock. They also had reliable connections with male family members who carried out commercial transactions. One poor woman, Fatna Jenfi, also had a cow that she had inherited 6 years earlier from her father. She could barely keep up with the cost of feeding her cow, but she valued the milk for household consumption. She lamented the fact that the cow didn't produce enough milk to generate a little income from selling surplus milk and milk products.

Unlike Mengoub Gare, the household spaces in Maatarka are devoid of any greenery. And future trajectories suggest that these domestic spaces will remain unchanged, except for the possible addition of a cow or two tethered in the barren courtyards of extended family compounds.

THE POSSIBILITY OF CREATING A MILK COOPERATIVE IN MAATARKA

Group interviews with Fatna and several other poor women in Maatarka indicate that they would buy cows if they could afford them. But they worry about the necessary maintenance costs and the economic risks associated with such high initial investments. The discussions revealed that women wanted to create a cooperative to address these problems. The co-op would develop a rotating capital fund, establish links to markets for fodder supplements, interact with veterinarians, share a stud bull, market milk and milk products, and sell or buy animals at the *souk* (market).

Cultural norms still discourage women from direct commercial transactions in most areas of the livestock sector. But the high rate of male absenteeism in Maatarka has opened a cultural space wherein women can discuss gender-based realignment of household production and the possibility of creating a communal cooperative beyond the individual household. Rocheleau et al. (1996) describe these shifting gendered spatial categories as a continuum from the private homestead to the public spaces of croplands, fields, neighborhoods, or cities. In this case, women's activities of managing cows in the household compound are extended to the public sphere of the dairy cooperative. This type of feminist political ecology analysis highlights the importance of gendered spaces of production and their relevance for household adaptation strategies in pastoral societies that have settled permanently.

DAIRY COOPERATIVES, MORE COWS, AND ENVIRONMENTAL TRAJECTORIES

The discourse about creating a women's dairy cooperative in Maatarka suggests that women there are trying to find new solutions to their sedentary livelihoods and represents an important cue into the construction of new identities and spaces of production. However, whether these ideas and discourses can turn into productive material realities demands the answers to a series of key concerns.

The cultural framework among pastoral societies in the MENA encourages economic power to gravitate toward the men, not the women. Consequently, collective resource management institutions among women have been informal to avoid directly challenging male authority and power. Among the Beni Guil women, a *saadeka* represents an informal economic cooperative. It is simply a gathering of women who pool food or cash to assist someone (usually another woman) in need. The *saadeka* is organic and generated by a self-selected group of participants who unite at a given moment, for a given cause. These associations have always been ephemeral, never formal, and never unifying large groups of women in a permanent affiliation. As such, they never overtly compete with the men's interests expressed through formal organizations at the tribal scale.

Of central concern for the viability of a women's milk cooperative in Maatarka is whether or not women there can transform these traditionally informal cooperative structures into a permanent and formal institution in the village. Would men in the village support the organization? Can such an institution promote equity and empowerment for all members, regardless of class or tribal affiliation? What is the history of the relationship between the village women and outsider institutions like the PDPEO? Can these organizations collaborate more effectively with women to ensure that benefits flow back to the women?

Research from other African and Middle Eastern countries indicates that women's empowerment gained from dairy-marketing projects varies considerably from case to case, depending on the economic status and sex of the household head, location and distance to markets, and gender makeup of marketing associations (Hogg, 1992; Horowitz & Jowkar, 1992).

The idea of a female production system that operates communally inverts the traditional pastoral production model where men control cooperative institutions at the tribal scale, while women remain isolated in individual household units. Evidence from Maatarka suggests that men have and will continue to encourage economic divisions between nonhousehold women. Women's exclusion from participation in the management of the village garden is one example. The strong persistence of a pastoral identity raises the question of whether or not women can break through cultural norms of male dominance at the tribal scale and economic independence of the household unit.

Cooperative systems among pastoral nomads have usually been activated only during times of stress. This chapter has demonstrated that permanent settlement represents "a time of stress" for pastoral nomads. This process produces new livelihood strategies, which destabilize gender roles and identities and lead to diverse transformations of domestic and public spaces in the settlements.

CONCLUSION

In Mengoub Gare livelihood stresses have produced new collective identities and a transformation of village landscapes. The presence of men in the village and their shared work activities with nearby farmers allows for a transformation of daily activities and an evolution of a cultural identity from pastoral nomad to settled agriculturalist. These transformations of identity are accepted and expressed in the domestic space through women's work in household gardens. At the community scale and within the realm of the public sphere, villagers have simply adapted the communal (male) management of water resources for individual (female) household gardens. These adaptations enable the creation of new agricultural land uses in the domestic space without challenging cultural norms that discourage women from cultivating land. And, at the level of public discourse, both men and women claim that only men cultivate land. It is through this shared public discourse that alternative identities and culturally controversial gender-based activities can develop within the private space.

In Maatarka, on the other hand, male absenteeism diminishes the power that women have to challenge cultural norms of production, either within the household or at the scale of the community. Women in this village therefore increase their economic independence by investing cash remittances in livestock, preferably milk cows. This activity reflects the continuation of a strong pastoral identity and does not confront accepted gender roles and responsibilities. Without the men present in the home, few opportunities exist for men and women to negotiate and reassess productive household activities. Nor can women alone confront the realm of public discourse. Yet without a "unified" domestic front, transformation of gendered activities and productive spaces will occur only slowly, if at all.

Rural spaces and places throughout the MENA are produced and maintained through daily practice and activities, which are intimately linked with cultural identities and social relations. How quickly these evolve in response to broader social, political, and economic changes associated with commercialization and globalization depends largely on the dynamics of gender-based negotiations in the domestic space and the defense of those actions in public discourse. The examples raised in this chapter suggest that careful analyses of shifting gender-based activities and identities at the household scale provide important insights into the responsiveness of local production strategies, which produce and reproduce rural livelihoods and places in the MENA.

NOTES

1. The "Project de Développement des Parcours et de l'Élevage dans l'Oriental" (PDPEO) is a state and internationally funded range conservation project, with a budget of $10 million. The project began in 1990 and ended in 2000, and was funded by the African Development Bank, International Fund for Agricultural Development, and the Moroccan government. Its scope included 3.2 million hectares of Morocco's eastern high plateau region. The goals were to diversify fodder resources, restore rangeland cover vegetation, curb sand dune accumulation, create pastoral cooperatives for feed distribution, minimize permanent settlement, and develop income-generating activities for women.

2. *Sheiks* and *mukkadems* are public officials who are elected by local people in the community. Each community represents a tribal lineage (there are 16 among the Beni Guil) and they may elect one *sheik* and up to two *mukkadems* depending on the population of the tribe. These elected officials represent the grassroots level of the Moroccan political administration. These officials create the link between the local people and their government officials, such as the *Caid*, who represents the interests of all the different lineages, and the province governors, who are appointed by King Mohammed VI.

REFERENCES

Abu-Lughod, L. (1986). *Veiled sentiments: Honor and poetry in a bedouin society.* Berkeley and Los Angeles: University of California Press.

Abu-Lughod, L. (1993). *Writing women's worlds.* Berkeley and Los Angeles: University of California Press.

Abu-Lughod, L. (2001). Orientalism and Middle East feminist studies. *Feminist Studies, 27*(1), 101–113.

Ahmed, L. (1992). *Women and gender in Islam: Historical roots of a modern debate.* New Haven, CT: Yale University Press.

Alaoui El Mdaghri, C. (1995). Women, environment, and population: A Moroccan case study. *IDS Bulletin, 26*(1), 61–65.

Ardener, S. (Ed.). (1981). *Women and space: Ground rules and social maps*. London: Helm.

Artz, N. E., Norton, B. E., & O'Rourke, J. T. (1986, April). *Management of common property grazing lands: Tamahdite, Morocco*. Paper read at Proceedings of the Conference on Common Property Management, Washington, DC.

Ask, K., & Tjomsland, M. (Eds.). (1998). *Women and Islamization: Contemporary dimensions of discourse on gender relations*. Oxford, UK, and New York: Berg.

Barbour, R. S., & Kitzinger, J. (Eds.). (1999). *Developing focus group research: Politics, theory, and practice*. Thousand Oaks, CA: Sage.

Beck, L. (1998). Use of land by nomadic pastoralists in Iran: 1970–1998. In J. Albert, M. Bernhardsson, & R. Kenna, (Eds.), *Transformation of Middle Eastern natural environments: Legacies and lessons* (pp. 58–80). New Haven, CT: Yale University Press.

Bedrani, S. (1991). Legislation for livestock on the public lands in Algeria. *Nature and Resources, 27*(4), 24–30.

Bencherifa, A. (1996). Is sedentarization of pastoral nomads causing desertification?: The case of the Beni Guil of eastern Morocco. In A. Bencherifa & W. Swearingen (Eds.), *The North African environment at risk* (pp. 117–130). Boulder, CO: Westview Press.

Bencherifa, A., & Johnson, D. L. (1991). Changing resource management strategies and their environmental impact on the Middle Atlas Mountains of Morocco. *Mountain Research and Development, 11*(4), 183–194.

BenJelloun, S. (1996). *Promotion des activités feminies: Resultats de l'enquete realisées dans la région du projet de développement des parcours et de l'évage dans l'oriental*. Rabat: Institut Agronomique et Vétérinaire Hassan II.

Blunt, A., & Rose, G. (Eds.). (1994). *Writing women and space: Colonial and postcolonial geographies*. New York: Guilford Press.

Bourdieu, P. (1973). The Berber house. In M. Douglas (Ed.), *Rules and meanings* (pp. 98–110). Harmondsworth, UK: Penguin Books.

Bourdieu, P. (1977). *Outline of a theory of practice*. Cambridge, UK: Cambridge University Press.

Bourqia, R. (1989). *Rapport sur la composante féminine dans la région du projet de développement pastoral et de l'élevage dans l'oriental*. Rabat: L'Institut Agronomique et Vétérinaire Hassan II.

Chambers, R. (1983). *Rural development: Putting the last first*. Harlow, UK: Longman Press.

Chambers, R. (1997). *Whose reality counts?: Putting the last first*. London: Intermetidate Technology.

Chatty, D. (2000). Women working in Oman: Individual choice and cultural constraints. *International Journal of Middle East Studies, 32*, 241–254.

Chodorow, N. (1974). Family structure and feminine personality. In M. Rosaldo & L. Lamphere (Eds.), *Women, culture, and society* (pp. 43–66). Stanford, CA: Stanford University Press.

Davis, D. K. (1996). Gender, indigenous knowledge, and pastoral resource use in Morocco. *Geographical Review, 86*(2), 284–288.

Davis, D. K. (2000). Environmentalism as social control?: An exploration of the transformation of pastoral nomadic societies in French colonial North Africa. *Arab World Geographer/Le Géographe du Monde Arabe, 3*(3), 182–198.

Direction Provincale de l'Agriculture de Figuig. (1997). *Projet de développement des parcours et de l'élevage dans l'oriental: Rapport annuel.* Bouarfa, Morocco: Ministère de l'Agriculture et de Mise en Valeur Agricole, Direction Provinciale de l'Agriculture de Figuig.

Direction Provincale de l'Agriculture de Figuig. (2001). *Projet de développement des parcours et de l'élevage dans l'oriental: Rapport annuel.* Bouarfa, Morocco: Ministère de l'Agriculture et de Mise en Valeur Agricole, Direction Provinciale de l'Agriculture de Figuig.

Dresch, J. (1959). *Le Maroc: Bilan d'une colonisation.* Paris: Éditions Sociales.

El Guindi, F. (1999). *Veil: Modesty, privacy, and resistance.* Oxford, UK: Berg.

Escobar, A. (1996). Constructing nature: Elements for a poststructural political ecology. In M. Watts & R. Peet (Eds.), *Liberation ecologies: Environment, development, and social movements* (pp. 46–68). London and New York: Routledge.

Foucault, M. (1980). *Power/knowledge: Selected interviews and other writings, 1972–1977* (C. Gordon, Ed.). New York: Pantheon Books.

Giddens, A. (1984). *The constitution of society: Outline of a theory of structuration.* Cambridge, UK: Polity Press.

Giddens, A. (1991). *Modernity and self-identity.* Cambridge, UK: Polity Press.

Grandin, B. (1988). *Wealth ranking in smallholder communities.* London: Intermediate Technology Press.

Hammoudi, A., Hammoudi, M., Rachik, H., & Tozy, M. (1992). *Projet de développement des parcours et l'Élevage dans l'oriental: ftude sur le changement, l'innovation et les attitudes.* Rabat: Ministère de l'Agriculture et de la Reforme Agraire, Direction de l'Élevage et l'Institute Agronomique et Vétérinaire Hassan II.

Haraway, D. (1991). *Simians, cyborgs, and women: The reinvention of nature.* London and New York: Routledge.

Harvey, D. (1989). *The condition of postmodernity: An enquiry into the origins of cultural change.* Oxford, UK: Basil Blackwell.

Herpin, E. (1956). Géographie du Maroc oriental. *Bulletin de l'Enseignement Public du Maroc, 43*(234), 5–28.

Herren, U. J. (1990). *The commercial sale of camel milk from pastoral herds in the Mogadishu hinterland, Somalia.* London: Overseas Development Institute.

Hogg, R. (1992). NGO's, pastoralists and the myth of community: Three case studies of pastoral development from East Africa. *Nomadic Peoples, 30,* 122–146.

Horowitz, M. M., & Jowkar, F. (1992). *Pastoral women and change in Africa, the Middle East and Central Asia.* Binghamton, NY: Institute for Development Anthropology, SUNY.

Kerven, C. M. (1987). Some research and development implications for pastoral dairy production in Africa. *International Livestock Centre for Africa Bulletin, 26,* 29–35.

Kwan, M. P. (1999). Gender and individual access to urban opportunities: A study using space–time measures. *Professional Geographer, 51*(2), 210–227.

Kwan, M. P. (2000). Introduction: Feminist geography and GIS. *Gender, Place, and Culture, 9*(3), 271–279.

Lauriac, R. (1940). *L'effort de guerre du Maroc oriental.* Casablanca: Impr. Réunies de la Vigie Marocaine et du Petit Marocain.

MacLeod, A. E. (1997). The new veiling and urban crisis. In M. E. Bonine (Ed.), *Population, poverty and politics in Middle East cities* (pp. 304–325). Gainesville: University Press of Florida.

Maher, V. (1974). *Women and property in Morocco.* Cambridge, UK: Cambridge University Press.

Massey, D. (1991, 24–29 June). A global sense of place. *Marxism Today.*

McDowell, L. (1999). *Gender, identity, and place: Understanding feminist geographies.* Minneapolis: University of Minnesota Press.

McDowell, L., & Sharp, J. P. (Eds.). (1997). *Space, gender, knowledge: Feminist readings.* London: Arnold.

Meir, A. (1997). *As nomadism ends: The Israeli Bedouin of the Negev.* Boulder, CO: Westview Press.

Mernissi, F. (1989). *Doing daily battle: Interviews with Moroccan women.* New Brunswick, NJ: Rutgers University Press.

Michael, B. J. (1991). The impact of international wage labor migration on Hawazma (Baggara) pastoral nomads. *Nomadic Peoples, 28,* 56–70.

Mills, S. (1994). Knowledge, gender, and empire. In G. R. A. Blunt (Ed.), *Writing women and space: Colonial and postcolonial geographies* (pp. 29–50). New York: Guilford Press.

Mir-Hosseini, Z. (1996). Women and politics in post-Khomeini Iran. In H. Afshar (Ed.), *Women and politics in the third world* (pp. 142–170). New York: Routledge.

Moore, H. L. (1996). *Space, text, and gender: An anthropological study of the Marakwet of Kenya.* Cambridge, UK: Cambridge University Press.

Morocco, Direction de la Statistique. (1994). *Population légale du Maroc.* Rabat, Morocco: Royaume du Maroc, Ministère Charge de la Population.

Moss, P. (Ed.). 2002. *Feminist geography in practice.* Oxford, UK: Blackwell.

Müller-Hohenstein, K. (1978). *Die ostmarokkanishen hochplateaus: Ein beitrag zur regionalforschung und zur biogeographie eines Nordafrikanischen trockensteppenraumes.* Erlangen, Germany: Erlanger Geographische Arbeiten 7.

Nelson, C. (1973). Women and power in nomadic societies in the Middle East. In C. Nelson, (Ed.), *The desert and the sown: Nomads in the wider society* (pp. 43–59). Berkeley and Los Angeles: University of California Press.

Nelson, C. (1974). Public and private politics: Women in the Middle Eastern world. *American Ethnologist, 1*(3), 551–563.

Okley, J. (1996). *Own or other culture.* London: Routledge.

Paskoff, R. (1957). Les hauts plaines du Maroc oriental: La région de Berguennt. *Les Cahiers d'Outre Mer, 10*(37), 34–64.

Pred, A. (1990). *Making histories and constructing human geographies.* Boulder, CO: Westview Press.

Rassmussen, S. J. (2002). Tuareg labor migration, gendered spaces and the predicament of women. *City and Society, 14*(2), 281–311.

Raynal, R. (1949). *Movements de la population récents et actuels au Maroc oriental.* Paper read at Congresse Internationale de Géographie, at Lisbon, Portugal.

Rocheleau, D. (1991). Gender, ecology and the science of survival: Stories and lessons from Kenya. *Agriculture and Human Values, 8*(1), 156–165.

Rocheleau, D. (1995). Maps, numbers, text and context: Mixing methods in feminist political ecology. *Professional Geographer, 47*(4), 458–466.

Rocheleau, D. (2002). Environmental social movements and the politics of place. *Development, 45*(1), 28–36.

Rocheleau, D., Thomas-Slayter, B., & Wangari, E. (Eds.). (1996). *Feminist political ecology: Global issues and local experiences.* London and New York: Routledge.

Rosaldo, M. Z., & Lamphere, L. (Eds.). (1974). *Woman, culture, and society*. Stanford, CA: Stanford University Press.

Said, E. (1978). *Orientalism*. New York: Pantheon Books.

Said, E. (1993). *Culture and imperialism*. New York: Knopf.

Schaefer-Davis, S. (1993). Changing gender relations in a Moroccan town. In J. E. Tucker (Ed.), *Arab women: Old boundaries, new frontiers* (pp. 208–223). Bloomington: Indiana University Press.

Slocum, R. (1995). Gender myths. In L. W. R. Slocum, D. Rocheleau, & B. Thomas-Slayter (Eds.), *Power, process, and participation: Tools for change* (pp. 105–107). London: Intermediate Technology.

Smith, K. (1998). Sedentarization and market integration: New opportunities for Rendille and Ariaal women of northern Kenya. *Human Organization, 57*(4), 459–468.

Smith, N. (1993). Homeless/global: scaling places. In J. Bird, B. Curtis, T. Putnam, & L. Tickner (Eds.), *Mapping the futures: Local cultures, global change* (pp. 87–119). London and New York: Routledge.

Soja, E. (1989). *Postmodern geographies: The reassertion of space in critical social theory*. London: Verso.

Steinmann, S. (1998a). Gender, pastoralism, and intensification: Changing environmental resource use in Morocco. In J. Albert, M. Berhhardsson, & R. Kenna (Eds.), *Transformations of Middle Eastern natural environments: Legacies and lessons* (pp. 81–107). New Haven, CT: Yale University Press.

Steinmann, S. (1998b). Gender, animal management, and environmental change in eastern Morocco. *Arab World Geographer, 1*(2), 117–135.

Steinmann, S. (2001). *Gender, pastoralism, and intensification: Changing patterns of resource management in eastern Morocco*. Unpublished doctoral dissertation, Clark University, Worcester, MA.

Terranciano, A. M. (1994). *Contested terrain: The changing politics of land use in Tera, western Niger*. Unpublished master's thesis, University of Wisconsin, Madison.

Thomas-Slayter, B., Esser, A. L., & Shields, D. (1993). *Tools of gender analysis: A guide to field methods for bringing gender into sustainable resource management* [ECOGEN Research Project Series, International Development Program]. Worcester, MA: Clark University.

Tozy, M. (1994, 7–9 March). *Les modes d'appropriation, gestion, et conservation des ressources entre le droit positif et communautaire au Maghreb*. Paper presented at the Conference on Land Degradation and Desertification, at Dakar, Senegal.

Turner, M. (1999). Merging local and regional analyses of land-use change: The case of livestock in the Sahel. *Annals of the Association of American Geographers, 89*(2), 191–219.

Waters-Bayer, A. (1988). *Dairying by settled Fulani agropastoralists in central Nigeria: The role of women and implications for dairy development*. Vol. 4, *Farming systems and resource economics in the tropics*. Kiel, Germany: Wissenschaftsverlag Von Kiel.

Women and Geography Specialty Group. (1997). *Feminist geographies: Explorations in diversity and difference*. Harlow, UK: Longman.

Wolf, D. L. (Ed.). (1996). *Feminist dilemmas in fieldwork*. Boulder, CO: Westview Press.

Part II

Geographies of Mobility

5 Transnational Islam

Indonesian Migrant Domestic Workers in Saudi Arabia

RACHEL SILVEY

In the early 1970s, oil-producing states in the Gulf region saw rapidly rising incomes and an increasing demand for foreign labor. By the early 1980s, growing numbers of Indonesian people had begun to respond to this demand (Spaan, 1999). The distinct majority of these migrants were low-income Muslim women from rural areas of Java, and more than half of these found work as housemaids in Saudi Arabia (Robinson, 2000, p. 254). Many migrants entered Saudi Arabia on a *hajj* (or *umrah*) visa that permitted them to stay in the country for 45 days to make the religious pilgrimage to Mecca and to visit other holy sites within the country. The migrants who were seeking work then stayed beyond the *hajj* visa's legally sanctioned time period to pursue employment in the informal sector (Hugo, 1992). Those who entered the country with a regular work contract visa also commonly made the pilgrimage as part of their sojourn abroad. In these ways, religion is linked to the methods these migrants employ for entering the country, and, as this chapter explores, it is also deeply embedded in a broad range of other aspects of their mobility and overseas employment experiences. Yet within migration studies, research on the meanings of Islam, as it intersects with other aspects of migrants' lives, remains limited (though see Robinson, 2000; Ong, 1995; and Abu-Sahlieh & Aldeeb, 1996, for important exceptions).

More than migration studies in general, the growing literature on domestic servants pays attention to women migrants' own interpretations of their mobility experiences (e.g., Huang & Yeoh, 1996; Yeoh, Huang, & Gonzalez, 1999; Radcliffe, 1990; Heyzer, Lycklama a Nijeholt, & Weerakoon, 1994). In addition, researchers who study international and transnational migration have begun to examine the gender dimensions of mobility processes (see Pessar, 1999; Hondagneu-Sotelo, 1999; and Mahler, 1999, for recent reviews). In this chapter, I build on the literature on domestic workers and gendered transnational migration with the goal of placing it in conversation with the growing body of research within geography on the social and spatial dynamics of religion (Kong, 2001). As Kong (2001, p. 212) argues, "Religion deserves to be acknowledged fully and in like manner alongside race, class, and gender in geographic analysis . . . [in order to] underline the geographic significance of examining religion, not least in the intersection of sacred and secular forces in the making of place." Religion, in the case of Indonesian domestic workers in Saudi Arabia, is central to understanding the production of the gender politics among these transnational migrants, and specifically the ways in which the gender differentiation of their migrant networks ties them to particular places and identities.

Indonesia is the country with the largest Muslim population in the world, with approximately 87% of its over 220 million people claiming Islam as their religion in 1999 (Hefner, 2000). Sunni, Shi'ia, and Sufi denominations exist, and each of these is expressed differently in different regions of the nation. Such a large and diverse community is likely to affect the shape and meaning of global Islam in the years ahead. Indeed, Indonesia's Islamic revival over the past several decades has involved a proliferation of types and spaces of Islamic practice and multiple relationships to the concept of the *umma* (Hefner, 2000).[1]

In recent years Indonesian Muslim groups have strengthened their involvement in transnational networks of migration and communication (Jabali & Jamhari, 2002). Gender relations are at the center of understanding the ways that these social networks take shape (Curran & Saguy, 2001), and I am interested in examining the ways that the gender politics of migrants' religious networks vary geographically. Among Indonesian women migrants to Saudi Arabia, religious beliefs and practices shape every aspect of the mobility experience, from the earliest planning stages to the postmigration workers' rights protest actions. Further, religion is enmeshed in women's mobility processes through diverse social networks, each of which has particular spatialities associated with it. The intersection between gender and religion is thus crucial to our understandings of sociospatial networks and the ways these networks shape women's migrations.

Examining various deployments of Islamic morality, as this study aims to do, is aimed at avoiding some of the pitfalls of previous research on women and Islam. Western scholarship on women and Islam has tended to depict Muslim women, especially those from the Middle East, as either victims of an oppressive culture (equated with Islam) or as "behind-the-scenes-but-truly-powerful" agents (Newland, 2000). Lost in this dichotomization, however, is the much richer reality of women's shifting senses of power and religious subjectivities.[2] Also missing in much of the literature on Islam and gender are in-depth analyses of the range of changing religious identities of Muslim women in Indonesia (but see Brenner, 1996; Blackwood, 1995; and Weix, 1998). I am interested here in providing insight into some of these changes and some of this intrareligious diversity through specific attention to the gendered religious geographies of transnational migrants.

The discussion is based on fieldwork in West Java and South Sulawesi that began in 1995, with follow-up visits in 1998, 2000, and 2002. In recent years, I have focused on the dynamics surrounding the large and growing numbers of Indonesian women migrating to Saudi Arabia to work as domestic servants. Building on a longer term project focused on women factory workers in the same communities (Silvey, 2003), I have spoken with men who have recruited migrants to work in Saudi Arabia, women who have returned from work in Saudi Arabia, families and neighbors of migrant women, civil servants at the Ministry of Labor, and leaders of nongovernmental organizations (NGOs) working on behalf of the rights of migrant women (Silvey, 2004). Respondents drew on Islamic codes in different ways depending on their beliefs, goals, and social locations. Examining these differences in various Indonesian people's interpretations and expressions of Islam sheds light on the ways that people employ religion to reaffirm, challenge, or survive the power relations structuring their position in this transnational migration circuit.

This chapter is organized into five main sections. The first reviews theoretical approaches to gender and transnational migration, and focuses on the literature on migration from Indonesia to Saudi Arabia. This section argues that existing approaches are missing important dimensions of the mobility process and its consequences by giving only scant attention to the role of religion. The second section provides an overview of the recent history of migration flows from Indonesia to Saudi Arabia. It demonstrates the importance of Islam to domestic workers' migration processes. The following two sections examine the ways in which Islam matters within two arenas shaping Indonesian women's migration to Saudi Arabia: the recruitment process and the New Order (1965–1998) state's role in promoting women's domestic roles through increasingly Islamist discourses of gendered morality. The concluding section calls for emphasizing the agency and complex subject positions of "Muslim women" as an intervention into the parsimony and dichotomies of much migration research and the debates on women and Islam.

GENDER, ISLAM, AND MIGRATION IN INDONESIA: COMBINING THEORETICAL PERSPECTIVES

There exists a vast, rich literature on migration, very little of which examines the mutual constitution of religion and mobility (but see, e.g., Abu-Sahlieh & Aldeeb, 1996). Recent scholarship (e.g., Portes & Sensenbrenner, 1993; Leinbach & Watkins, 1998; Hugo, 1997; Chant, 1992; Lawson, 1998; Gidwani & Sivaramakrisnan, 2003) has highlighted the importance of bringing together various theoretical approaches to migration. Here, I follow this scholarship by attempting to integrate theories of the household that account for gender hierarchies (Lawson, 1998) and life-cycle transitions (Leinbach & Watkins, 1998) with understandings of the individual migrant as embedded in dynamic social networks (Portes & Sensenbrenner, 1993), as well as in specific regional modernities (Gidwani & Sivaramakrisnan, 2003). My focus on these dimensions of migration is aimed at providing deeper insight into the ways that gendered migration operates differently across populations and places, and the ways that these differences are linked to the structure–agency dialectics of religion.

Theories of gender and migration focus considerable attention on household-scale processes (Willis & Yeoh, 2000). Feminist migration researchers argue that this focus is essential for understanding sex differentials in migration patterns and rates (Chant, 1992; Radcliffe, 1990; Lawson, 1998). For the case of West Java, interpretations of Islam intersect with the meanings of each of these dimensions of household hierarchies, influencing migrants' gender identities, conceptions of appropriate behavior at particular ages, and the significance for migration of specific stages in the household's life cycle (e.g., Leinbach, Watkins, & Bowen, 1992; Hugo, 1992). Feminist research in Indonesia has emphasized the role of power relations and hierarchies within households in determining who migrates and with what effects on livelihood (see Wolf, 1992; and Hart, 1992, who focuses on Malaysia) and the interrelatedness of household structures and dynamics in producing particular mobility patterns and employment behaviors (see Leinbach & Watkins, 1998; Hugo, 1998; and Lawson, 1998, on Latin America). Economic and workload pressures at both individual- and household-level scales intersect with specific religious commitments, and these are linked to migration (Cremer, 1998; Robinson, 1991, 2000; Chin, 1997; Spaan, 1999).

In order to understand the place-based interpretations of gender and religion, I take as a key entry point the geographic literature on these themes. Within geography, Claire Dwyer (1999, 2000) examines the meanings for young British, Muslim, South Asian women of belonging to a "Muslim community," and illustrates the centrality of gender for understanding the ways that community boundaries are forged. In a similar vein, Secor (2002) provides an analysis of veiling in the local production of Islamic regimes of belonging and knowledge construction among Muslim women who are rural–urban migrants in Istanbul. Lastly, Mohammad (1999) analyzes the central role of women in marking internal, class-based divisions among Pakistani Muslims in southern England. Synthesizing much of this research on gender and Islam, Nagar (2000) and Nagel (2001) have called on geographers to expand our explicitly spatial analyses of gender issues in relation to Islamic communities and practices. Nagel's point is relevant to the rapidly growing body of scholarship on the gendered politics of Indonesian Islam (e.g., Weix, 1998; Brenner, 1996, 1998; Bowen, 1998; Sears, 1996; Marcoes, 2002; Newland, 2000; Errington, 1990; Robinson, 2000) in that this literature has explored a range of critical dimensions of gender and Indonesian Islam, but it has not focused on the spatial or transnational aspects.

In research on Indonesian people's migration to Saudi Arabia in particular, religious identity is often mentioned as an aside rather than analyzed as an explicit central feature of migrants' mobility experiences (see, e.g., Spaan, 1999; Hugo, 1992; Ananta, Kartowibowo, Wiyono, & Chotib, 1998; Cremer, 1988; Robinson, 1991—though see also Robinson, 2000, for an important exception). Yet there are numerous ways in which religion affects Indonesian domestics' migration experiences in Saudi Arabia: recruiters deploy religious codes to persuade aspiring migrants of the desirability of specific destination sites; Indonesian civil authorities and Saudi employers view religion as a factor when they encourage migration between Muslim countries; and workers rely on their spiritual strength to help them manage and occasionally thrive in their overseas jobs. In order to better understand migration, it is helpful to query the interaction of religion with each of these aspects of the migration process.

Attention to religion need not be mutually exclusive of an analysis of household hierarchies or community boundary formation. Rather, the ways that religious identity intersects with household relations and state policies to shape gendered migration experiences can be better understood when attention is given to the interrelationships between these dynamic processes and interacting arenas of cultural production. Bringing these foci together can illuminate the processes through which migrants' identities influence the sacred and secular aspects of mobility for this specific group of women.

INDONESIAN DOMESTIC WORKERS
IN SAUDI ARABIA, 1983–2000

Beginning in 1983, the Indonesian government permitted Middle Eastern countries to recruit Indonesian nationals for overseas work (Robinson, 1991). Indonesia's ambassador to Saudi Arabia at the time expressed enthusiasm for the national plan to promote labor export. He noted that overseas employment could provide jobs for Indonesian nationals, who as a population faced high rates of unemployment. Labor export, he argued, could also create much-needed foreign exchange, as migrants would send remittances home (Robinson, 1991).

Within the first year after Indonesia agreed to release workers to the Middle East, 47,000 fully documented workers left Indonesia for Saudi Arabia, a number that grew rapidly every year thereafter until the Indonesian economic crisis began in late 1997 (Ananta et al., 1998). Between 1989 and 1994, the majority (59%) of documented overseas workers from Indonesia migrated to Saudi Arabia rather than to other countries (Hugo, 1995, p. 280), growing from a total of 55,967 over the 1979–1983 5-year period to 223,579 during the subsequent 5-year period. Then again, between 1989 and 1994, the total increased to 384,822 (Amjad, 1996, p. 345), and during the single year of 1998, according to one source, 389,156 formally documented immigrants to Saudi Arabia came from Indonesia (Depnaker, 1998, cited in Krisnawaty, 1999). These numbers dwarf the numbers of Indonesian people legally emigrating to other countries (Amjad, 1996). Since 1998 there does appear to be an increasing tendency for labor from Indonesia to be directed to other countries within Asia, rather than to the Middle East (Ananta et al., 1998; Hugo, 2002). This tendency appears to be a result of the economic crisis (1997–present) in Indonesia, which made it more difficult for low-income people to afford the cost of travel and recruitment to the Middle East. The remittances that migrant workers sent home have also been substantial, with estimates of total official remittances from all destinations to Indonesia in the first 6 months of 2001 reaching US$4 billion (Hugo, 2002, p. 174).

Of this large number of migrants, women make up the distinct majority: two-thirds of the migrants between 1984 and 1994 were women (Amjad, 1996, p. 346), and in 1998 more than 12 times as many Indonesian women as men immigrated to Saudi Arabia (Hugo, 2002, p. 159). Beyond these formal numbers, many people travel from Indonesia to Saudi Arabia without completing the required documentation. Hugo (2002, p. 159) argues that "undocumented migrants certainly outnumber documented migrants" abroad (see also Spaan, 1999; and Jones, 2000, on undocumented Indonesian migration to Malaysia). Migrants without work visas lack state protection, and their undocumented status raises particularly serious issues for women who work as domestic servants. Domestic service jobs are unregulated in Saudi Arabia, such that even those domestic workers who have work visas or contracts do not have an institutionalized right to legal protection as workers (see also Huang & Yeoh, 1996, on Singapore). In addition, because domestic service takes place within the home, defined by the state as the "private" sphere, exploitation and abuse has the potential to be more easily hidden than abuses in the "public" sphere. Moreover, as I elaborate below, employers use religious differences to rationalize either low pay or ill treatment of their domestic workers, even in situations in which the employers and the employees belong nominally to the same religion.

The severe abuses that Indonesian domestic workers face in households in Saudi Arabia came to public attention soon after migrants began overseas work. By 1984 reports were emerging in the Indonesian press about the working conditions faced by many migrants in Saudi Arabia (Robinson, 2000, p. 255). Reporters found that migrant candidates sometimes received false information about the departure date or the availability of work (*Kompas*, April 7, 1984, as cited in Robinson, 2000, p. 255). They also claimed that workers were being treated poorly and that some were sexually abused in the homes of their Saudi employers. Workers were found to be overworked and underpaid, and in a number of cases were forbidden to leave the residence of their employers (Robinson, 2000, p. 255).

In addition, many domestic workers have died while overseas. Activists claim to have evidence that a number of the unexplained deaths were either murders by employers or suicides resulting from unbearable employment situations (Tagaroa & Sofia, 2002). Public opposition to the "export" of Indonesian workers grew within Indonesia as these cases gained widespread attention in the 1980s (Robinson, 1991).

Into the 1990s, the media continued to give prominent coverage to cases of mistreatment, excessively heavy workloads, and rape of overseas domestic workers, and provided regular reports on the increasing numbers of women who had mysteriously disappeared, been murdered, sentenced to death, or committed suicide in Saudi Arabia (e.g., *Tempo*, September 12, 1999). Much of the media coverage was illustrated with photographs of women wearing the *j'illbab* (headscarf). While wearing the headscarf has become an increasingly common practice in Indonesia in recent years, it is by no means a universal practice (Brenner, 1996). The depiction of the headscarf in the media was noteworthy both because of the regularity with which the image was used and because it resonated with widely circulated religious discourses in both countries. The graphic depictions of the assaults on these women, and specifically on their bodies, were picked up and further circulated by activists in NGOs (e.g., Solidaritas Perempuan, Kalyanamitra), which made the plight of these women a central concern.

Despite widespread popular and government pressure to stop sending women overseas, the export of female domestic laborers continued to dominate the official outflow from Indonesia through late 1997 (Hugo, 1995, p. 282; Ananta et al., 1998). Interestingly, even as the migration flows began to change directions in 1997, Islamist discourse remained at the center of government rationales for exporting workers. Specifically, women were called on as Muslims to be "good mothers" and to protect and provide for their "national family" (Pudjosumedi & Rohiim, 1996), which, according to the government, was facing a crisis that the women could help address.

This brief outline of the history of women's labor migration from Indonesia to Saudi Arabia begins to reveal the ways in which religion has figured in the gender politics of migration. The following sections explain in greater detail how Islam has mattered to the labor recruitment process and to the role of the New Order state in promoting women's migration.

SELLING SAUDI ARABIA AS A DESTINATION SITE

> When else could a person like me make the pilgrimage to Mecca and build a house, if I don't go to Saudi Arabia [to work as a domestic]?
> —KODRIAH, a young woman migrant from Salatiga, West Java (Solidaritas Perempuan, 1994, p. 2)

Most potential migrants have heard stories from neighbors or returned migrants about several possible destinations by the time they are recruited by middlemen and labor brokers (Spaan, 1999). These labor recruitment agents tend to have a destination site prearranged at the time they enter the villages to seek workers to hire, and they advertise the idea that they are selling passage to a place where labor contracts are already arranged. When the brokers aim to persuade potential migrants of the appeal of overseas work, they rely on positive descriptions of the place to which they plan to transport the workers. The sales pitches differ depending on the country to which the migrants are being recruited; in the case of Saudi Arabia, they include reference to the religious compatibility of the migrants with potential employers.

When brokers are recruiting migrants in West Java's villages for passage to Saudi Arabia, they tend to focus their efforts at *pesantren*, or girls' Islamic boarding schools. The *pesantren* are preferred sites for this recruitment stream both because the girls who attend these schools are usually relatively devout Muslims, a quality that is often preferred by employers in Saudi Arabia, and because the students have studied some Arabic, and so can communicate with their Arabic-speaking employers. Nevertheless, there are several issues that make it difficult to convince potential migrants of Saudi Arabia's appeal. First, the cost of transportation to Saudi Arabia is higher than the cost to the other possible destinations, such as Malaysia (the least expensive), Singapore, or Hong Kong. In addition, the popular mythology surrounding migration to Saudi Arabia is that while it is possible for some people to earn relatively high incomes while working there, there is also a greater likelihood of extreme abuse (e.g., rape or other forms of sexual physical assault), possibly ending in tragedy (e.g., lifelong handicap, suicide, murder, or the death sentence). In other words, the rewards are thought to be much higher among migrants who dare to migrate to Saudi Arabia, but the risks are also viewed as potentially much greater than those associated with migrating elsewhere.

In villages in Rancaekek and Bekasi (both in West Java), I interviewed people who had returned from Saudi Arabia, people considering overseas migration, and nonmigrants about their experiences and perspectives on migration. Most people in these two villages had been in contact with at least one very successful overseas domestic who had worked in Saudi Arabia. Yet all respondents had numerous tales about the hardships, abuses, and tragedies that had befallen women domestics in Saudi Arabia. These stories were widely circulated and received with rapt attention. Not surprisingly, the possibility of earning what they considered to be extraordinary wealth was still appealing to people in the villages, most of whom had incomes that fell below the national poverty line. Yet it was only with pronounced apprehension that villagers engaged the fantasies of wealth earned in Saudi Arabia.

Brokers sought to allay some of the fears about Saudi Arabia by comparing the situation there favorably with the problems migrants would face in Malaysia. Specifically, when brokers were recruiting for Saudi Arabia, they pointed out to Muslim women that their religious principles would be challenged if they were to work in Malaysia rather than in Saudi Arabia. They told potential recruits that while Malaysia is also a predominantly Muslim country, many employers of domestic servants there subscribe to other religions, including Christianity and Buddhism. Brokers would cultivate fear and disgust for Malaysia on the part of migrant candidates by regaling them with stories of the "sinful" behavior (from a widely accepted West Javanese Islamic perspective) expected of domestic servants there. For instance, they told potential migrants that they would be forbidden to pray in their employers' home in Malaysia. In Saudi Arabia, on the other hand, according to some brokers, because of the highly devout Muslim population, prayer and fasting during the holy month of Ramadan would not only be tolerated, but in fact would be supported. Domestics in Saudi Arabia, they suggested, could win favor with God (*Allah*) through the intensified practice of religious duties that would be supported there.

According to the brokers, if migrants went to Malaysia, they would also be expected to cook and eat pork, which is considered a sin and is forbidden among West Javanese Muslims as well as Muslims in Saudi Arabia. The problem of being expected to touch, cook, or even eat pork was particularly important to many people in both villages. People were additionally warned that if they migrated to Malaysia rather than to Saudi Arabia, they could be expected to worship in a pagoda rather than in a mosque. Yet another serious problem that recruiters argued could ostensibly be avoided by working in Saudi Arabia was the possibility of being forced to care for dogs. A report by an NGO reviewed the case of one woman in particular who was deeply upset (*sangat menyakitkan hati*) by the expectation that she provide dog care. Contact with dogs is forbidden (*haram*) in general West Javanese interpretations of Islam, as it is in Saudi Arabian and Malaysian interpretations of Islam. Caring for dogs is thus reported to be a serious workers' rights issue by the NGO Solidaritas Perempuan. One woman who had returned from Saudi Arabia said, "I felt disgusted/nauseated, fearful, and sinful whenever the time came to take care of those seven dogs. That was every day. Try and think about it, how do you think I felt?" (Solidaritas Perempuan, 1994, p. 9). People in the two villages expressed anxiety about the possibility that they would be expected to bathe dogs, also a sin in their view, and one that some found even more repugnant than caring for dogs.

The brokers thus used potential migrants' anxiety about the unknown, and their fear of religious difference in particular, to encourage people to migrate to Saudi Arabia. Of course, brokers used similar tactics when seeking to sell passage to other countries as well. When aiming to attract workers to countries other than Saudi Arabia, they would denigrate Saudi Arabian Islam by labeling it "fanatical" (*fanatik*). In other words, recruiters cultivated religion-based preferences regardless of the potential destination site, and employed it in the service of their prevailing goals.

The final, perhaps most influential, method that brokers had of using religion to persuade potential migrants to select Saudi Arabia as their destination site is the fact that Mecca, the Muslim religious center and holiest city, is located there. Migrants can make the holy pilgrimage to Mecca as part of their overseas travel for work. As Eickleman (1990, p. 5) puts it, "Muslim doctrine explicitly enjoins or encourages certain forms of travel. One is the express obligation to undertake the pilgrimage to Mecca (*hajj*)." The *hajj* is the pilgrimage to Mecca during *Dhul Hijjah* (the month for *hajj*). The *umrah*, when performed independently of the *hajj*, is the optional lesser pilgrimage and may be accomplished any time during the year (Denny, 1994). Making the *hajj* pilgrimage is one of the Five Pillars of Islam, and is to be undertaken by all believers if they have the means to do so. It was this desire on the part of many potential migrants to make the *hajj* that underlay the appeal for them of Saudi Arabia as a destination site. As the opening quotation to this section points out, low-income people ("people like me") are generally not able to afford to make the pilgrimage. To return to Indonesia having made the pilgrimage, and thus to have become a *haji*, is a great honor, substantially raising one's social standing and prestige within the home community.

Pilgrims' sense of having fulfilled their religious duty in some cases comes along with an improvement in their financial standing as well. Those few migrants who returned with substantial savings were able to buy or remodel homes in their villages. In each village it was clear which households had been successful, either abroad or in Indonesia's urban economy, because the household members displayed their success in the consumption of new paint, expanded porches and fences, and occasionally the installation of a satellite dish. While it has been reported that successful return migrants purchase land in Central Java, in the villages in Bekasi and Rancaekek this was not the case. In the village in Bekasi there was no arable land to be purchased, while in Rancaekek the land was reportedly growing increasingly degraded as a result of factory pollution. Nevertheless, the highly visible home improvements that successful migrants exhibited in the villages played an important symbolic role in feeding the fantasies of potential future migrants. Villagers conveyed honor on those return migrants who in their eyes had risen in class standing, and they were particularly respectful of those who were both wealthy and had made the pilgrimage to Mecca.

Yet among the return migrants I interviewed, the motive for making the pilgrimage was not simply, or even primarily, based on migrants' desires for improved social standing in the village. Women who made the pilgrimage also expressed the deep spiritual meaning that the *hajj* held for them. As one woman put it, "You are completely pure afterward, like a newborn all over again, without sin, thoroughly cleansed. I would go again and again if I could." In other words, while making the pilgrimage did enhance status, many pilgrims were also interested in expressing the holy aspects of their journey. A central goal for them was to be closer to God. While it is impossible to know exactly what combination of goals and desires drive these pilgrims, it is important to avoid reducing their experience to status concerns. Indeed, in their life histories, migrants and nonmigrants alike repeatedly articulated the importance they attach to Muslim spirituality. That is, rather than focusing only on religious practices, or what they saw as the organized social expectations of Muslims, migrants spoke of their own subjective powerful experiences of spirituality in relation to religion. Their spiritual drives, then, were tied to both their deep sense of fulfillment if they did make the pilgrimage and the ways in which the recruiters could use religion to manipulate them into choosing Saudi Arabia as a destination site.

THE INDONESIAN NEW ORDER
STATE'S DEPLOYMENT OF ISLAM

As private recruitment agents have mobilized Islamist discourses in support of their aims, so too have Indonesian state actors employed Islamic rationales in their efforts to promote women's overseas labor migration. I am specifically concerned in this section with the particular interpretations of women's labor migration put forth by Indonesia's New Order (1965–1998) state.

In the 1980s state officials argued that women migrants would be safe in Saudi Arabia because it was a devoutly Muslim environment (Robinson, 2000, p. 254). Indeed, as the Indonesian ambassador for Saudi Arabia put it, "Islamic tradition and Islamic law is very strong in Saudi Arabia, not like in developed Western nations. Over there, men and women who are not *muhrim* [closely related, so that marriage is prohibited] rarely meet, let alone 'interfere with' [*mengganggu*] each other. If this law is violated the punishment is harsh" (*Kompas*, April 7, 1984, as cited in Robinson, 2000, p. 256). In other words, according to the ambassador, the strength of the religious belief among the Muslims in Saudi Arabia would create a disciplined populace within which Indonesian women could be assured of their safety.

Similar to the ambassador's view of Saudi Arabian Islam was the idea that by sending Indonesian nationals to work in the Middle East, Indonesia could ostensibly uphold Islamic moral codes by keeping labor migration within the *ummat* (community of Islam) (Robinson, 1991). Interestingly, however, while this notion of the community of Islam was deployed in the service of sending women abroad, the Indonesian state denied responsibility for nationals living "illegally" in Saudi Arabia. Abdul Latief, for example, the minister of manpower (Menteri Tenaga Kerja, or Mennaker), argued that "all citizens have the right to go abroad, but the government can't protect all nationalities" (*Kompas*, October 28, 1997). This notion of the limits to the state's responsibility to a community was in sharp contrast to the one on which the ambassador had called when he encouraged women to migrate abroad.

At the same time that the New Order state was encouraging women's migration (however inconsistently), several state institutions and policies were actively reproducing the view that the appropriate place for women is within the home. Such bourgeois ideals were introduced well before Indonesia's postcolonial period (Stoler, 1995), but since 1965 the New Order state had vigorously promoted them in the name of national economic development and political stability. Familism, "mother-ism", and "housewifization" were all central elements of the gender politics of the New Order (Sunindyo, 1996; Suryakusuma, 1996). Such ideals were embodied in organizations such as Dharma Wanita (Women's Duty), which promoted the idea that women's positions were subordinate to those of their husbands.

Yet in order to earn foreign exchange, the state was willing to extend the spaces within which low-income women could perform these idealized practices, thereby providing ideological space within which women, as devout, pious, morally upstanding mothers and wives, could migrate (see Sen, 1998; and also see Robinson, 2000, on religious tensions surrounding women's migration). For female migratory domestic servants, Dharma Wanita's idealized mother/wife ideology was simply transposed to the domestic sphere of the employer. The state's discourse shifted to make the domestics "heroes of national development," and extended their maternal role to serve the needs of their families as well as the economic needs of the entire nation. In meetings of Dharma Wanita that were held in Rancaekek and Bekasi, leaders invoked explicitly religious rationales to further promote the state's class-specific idealization of women's roles as "transnational" mothers and wives. Increasingly, over time, the state relied on religious language and scriptures to support its goals, and Dharma Wanita and other state institutions[3] marshaled Islamist language and beliefs in the service of the state.

State ideologies of masculinity were more implicitly coded than those of femininity, but were—and continue to be—similarly pervasive and at least as influential. Male civil servants, for instance, are conceived by the state as the heads of household, and their rank determines the social status of all members of their family. As household heads, men in this discourse are expected, first and foremost, to provide food and shelter for their families. Census identification placards are placed outside of all households listing the "household head," assumed to be male, followed by the name of his wife. While these placards are used for a number of purposes, as Blackwood (1995, p. 137) points out, they reflect and reinforce a hierarchical division between the household head and his subordinate wife.[4] This official conceptualization of gender relations becomes significant in the Saudi Arabian context in that male migrants remain substantially more mobile and autonomous than do their female counterparts. Within Saudi Arabia, state policies that influence gendered mobility are also explicitly religious, drawing on the moral authority of religious edicts to reinforce particular gendered labor patterns.

The development policies of the New Order state, in sum, established contradictory messages for the construction of gender. Since the 1980s and continuing through the present, the government has promoted women's labor migration to the Middle East (Hugo, 1996) in an effort to encourage much-needed foreign exchange flows via migrant remittances. At the same time, the state has idealized the domestically located mother and wife and her counterpart, the sole, male breadwinner. To reconcile these conflicting aims, the state has relied upon and reproduced an Islamist discourse of women's self-sacrifice to family and nation, in which the migratory income-earning woman becomes a provider of economic development for the "national family." Because most of these women continue to be involved in domestic work overseas, their mobility and labor market participation ultimately aligns with the state's view of domesticated femininity. Indeed, women migrants can continue to perform the dual roles set forth in the widely circulated handbook, *Islam and the Role of Women as Housewives and Pillars of the Nation* (Rohiim, 1996), which draws on the growing moral authority of Islam to produce, support, and reinforce the gender ideologies of the state.

CONCLUSIONS

Women's religious beliefs do not simply allow them to be further exploited, though in some situations religion is manipulated in the service of women's exploitation. Nor does religion primarily provide oppositional strength to women involved in combating their oppression, though it can also be mobilized in this way. Rather, the range of ways in which Islam is deployed in domestic workers' recruitment processes, state policy, and the organization of overseas domestic work experiences reveals the multiple meanings of Islam to different actors.

The use of religious ideology for the purposes of the state or migrant recruiters is not of course unique to Islam. Attention to the ways in which religion is embedded in migrants' individual lives, households, and social networks serves to destabilize and deessentialize gender norms and the meanings of religion. As Eickleman (1997, pp. 4–5) puts it, "Religious communities, like all imagined communities, change over time. Their boundaries are shifted by, and shift, the political, economic, and social contexts in which these participants find themselves." The spatial boundaries of the "community" of Indonesian Muslims is expanded when women from Java migrate to work in Saudi Arabia, and gender norms are produced in conjunction with specific and shifting invocations of religion.

President Suharto (1965–1998) managed through a variety of strategies to keep Islamist political interests subordinate to the overall will of the New Order regime (Hefner, 2000). However, since 1998, increasingly vocal Islamist political constituents have entered Indonesian public political life and have gained more overt political power than at any other time since independence (in 1945). Indeed, Indonesian president Abdurrahman Wahid (Gus Dur, October 1999–July 2001) was himself a Sufi cleric and the leader of the large, national Islamic group Nahdlatul Ulama.

The surge of sectarian violence and violence against women in Indonesia since 1998 has been widely represented as reflective of Christian–Muslim tensions (Robinson & Bessell, 2002). Women's bodies, dress, sexuality, and "autonomy" have been cast at the center of these "religious" struggles, and at the center of contemporary international justifications for war (Moghadam, 2002). Migrant women in particular are wrapped up in the symbolic contestations over national pride, religious value, and cultural status. Increasingly, for some, migrant women are not "in their place"; their mobility may threaten the gendered order and their sociospatial transgressions are regularly punished or controlled.

For many years now feminist geographers have stressed the "need to think of home in terms of dominance and resistance; to consider how and why a particular ideology of home maintains its hegemonic position and how this might be contested through alternative interpretations" (Gregson & Lowe, 1995, p. 226, as cited in Sparke, in press). Indonesian–Saudi women migrants carry with them a religiously rationalized view of home that serves to locate them as housemaids in the "private" spaces of their Saudi employers. But women migrants also employ religion as part of the justification for leaving their own homeland and families to make the pilgrimage to Mecca. On the one hand, women who migrate transnationally are claiming new spaces within which religious prestige and small fortunes are potentially available to them. On the other hand, they can be manipulated and victimized through gendered religious forms of domination that can and sometimes do also travel transnationally. It is through attention to such contradictions and complexity that migration research can contribute to understanding specific gendered and religious meanings of particular departures from home.

ACKNOWLEDGMENTS

An early version of this chapter was presented in March 2001 at the Association of American Geographers' Conference, held in New York City. I would like to thank Richa Nagar for the comments she provided as discussant of the session. My thanks also go to Amy Freeman, Caroline Nagel, and Ghazi-Walid Falah for helpful commentary on a previous draft. The research, reported here was funded by Grant No. 9911510 from the National Science Foundation. That support is greatly appreciated. For valuable research assistance, I'd also like to thank Klara Mezgolits, Monica Ogra, and Nyne van der Berg.

NOTES

1. For a recent overview of the voluminous literature on Islam in Indonesia, see Hefner (2000).
2. For a more nuanced take on gender and Islam, see Ong (1995) on Malyasia.
3. In rural areas, the Pembinaan Kesejahteraan Keluarga (PKK, Family Welfare Guidance) was another New Order state institution geared explicitly toward the

production and maintenance of the state's idealized version of domesticated femininity. The PKK, designed to build "community well-being" (Sunindyo, 1996, p. 124), served to disseminate the state's moral code for women, or the Panca Dharma Wanita (Five responsibilities of women), to rural people. The PKK's stated responsibilities for a woman were listed in order of importance as: "1) support her husband's career and duties; 2) provide offspring; 3) care for and rear the children; 4) be a good housekeeper; and 5) be a guardian of the community" (Sunindyo, 1996, p. 125). The PKK also provides training for low-income women to become proper, or as Suzanne Brenner (1998, p. 245) puts it, "middle-class" mothers and housewives.

4. A specifically militarized version of masculine strength, aggression, and supremacy is also manufactured at all levels of the armed services (Sunindyo, 1996). Military masculinity involves clear parallels with the state's "Bapakism" (father/man-ism) in that both are justified by the argument that such a hierarchy and male supremacy is necessary for the protection of the citizenry and the subordinate members of the household.

REFERENCES

Abu-Sahlieh, S., & Aldeeb, A. (1996). The Islamic conception of migration. *International Migration Review, 30*, 37–57.

Amjad, R. (1996). Philippines and Indonesia: On the way to a migration transition. *Asian and Pacific Migration Journal, 5*, 339–366.

Ananta, A., Kartowibowo, D., Wiyono, N. H., & Chotib (1998). The impact of the economic crisis on international migration: The case of Indonesia. *Asian Pacific Migration Journal, 7*, 313–338.

Blackwood, E. (1995). Senior women, model mothers, and dutiful wives: Managing gender contradictions in a Minangkabau village. In A. Ong & M. Peletz (Eds.), *Bewitching women, pious men: Gender and body politics in Southeast Asia* (pp. 124–158). Berkeley and Los Angeles: University of California Press.

Bowen, J. (1998). Islam and law—Qur'an, justice, gender: Internal debates in Indonesian Islamic jurisprudence. *History of Religions, 38*, 52–79.

Brenner, S. (1996). Reconstructing self and society: Javanese Muslim women and "the veil." *American Ethnologist, 23*, 673–697.

Brenner, S. (1998). *The domestication of desire: Women, wealth, and modernity in Java.* Princeton, NJ: Princeton University Press.

Chant, S. (Ed.). (1992). *Gender and migration in developing countries.* London: Belhaven Press.

Chin, C. B. (1997). Walls of silence and late twentieth century representations of the foreign female domestic worker: The case of Filipina and Indonesian female servants in Malaysia. *International Migration Review, 31*, 353–385.

Cremer, G. (1988). Deployment of Indonesian migrants in the Middle East: Present situation and prospects. *Bulletin of Indonesian Economic Studies, 24*, 73–86.

Curran, S. R., & Saguy, A. C. (2001). Migration and cultural change: A role for gender and social networks? *Journal of International Women's Studies, 2*, 54–77.

Denny, F. (1994). *An introduction to Islam* (2nd ed.). New York: Macmillan.

Dwyer, C. (1999). Contradictions of community: Questions of identity for young British Muslim women. *Environment and Planning A, 31,* 53–68.

Dwyer, C. (2000). Negotiating diasporic identities: Young British South Asian Muslim women. *Women's Studies International Forum, 23,* 475–486.

Eickelman, D. F. (1997). Trans-state Islam and security. In S. H. Rudolph & J. Piscatori (Eds.), *Transnational religion and fading states* (pp. 27–46). Boulder, CO: Westview Press.

Errington, S. (1990). Recasting sex, gender, and power: A theoretical and regional overview. In J. M. Atkinson & S. Errington (Eds.), *Power and difference: Gender in island Southeast Asia* (pp. 1–58). Stanford, CA: Stanford University Press.

Gidwani, V., & Sivaramakrishnan, K. (2003). Circular migration and the spaces of cultural assertion. *Annals of the Association of American Geographers, 93*(1), 186–213.

Hart, G. (1992). Imagined unities: Constructions of the "household" in economic theory. In S. Ortiz & S. Lees (Eds.), *Understanding economic process* (pp. 111–129). Lanham, MD: University Press of America.

Hefner, R. (2000). *Civil Islam: Muslims and democratization in Indonesia.* Princeton, NJ, and Oxford, UK: Princeton University Press.

Heyzer, N., Lycklama a Nijeholt, G., & Weerakoon, N. (Eds.). (1994). *The trade in domestic workers: Causes, mechanisms and consequences of international migration.* London: Asian and Pacific Development Centre.

Hondagneu-Sotelo, P. (1999). Introduction: Gender and contemporary U.S. immigration. *American Behavioral Scientist, 42*(4), 565–576.

Huang, S., & Yeoh, B. (1996). Ties that bind: State policy and migrant female domestic helpers in Singapore. *Geoforum, 27*(4), 479–493.

Hugo, G. (1992). Women on the move: Changing patterns of population movement of women in Indonesia. In S. Chant (Ed.), *Gender and migration in developing countries* (pp. 174–196). London: Belhaven Press.

Hugo, G. (1995). Labour export from Indonesia. *ASEAN Economic Bulletin, 12,* 275–298.

Hugo, G. (1996). Asia on the move: Research challenges for population geography. *International Journal of Population Geography, 2,* 95–118.

Hugo, G. (1997). Changing patterns and processes in population mobility. In G. Jones & T. Hull (Eds.), *Indonesia assessment: Population and human resources* (pp. 68-100). Canberra: Australian National University, Research School of Pacific and Asian Studies.

Hugo, G. (1998). International migration of women in Southeast Asia: Major patterns and policy issues. In C. M. Firdausy (Ed.), *International migration in Southeast Asia: Trends, consequences, issues, and policy measures* (pp. 98–131). Jakarta: Indonesian Institute of Sciences, Southeast Asian Studies Program.

Hugo, G. (2002). Women's international labour migration. In K. Robinson & S. Bessell (Eds.), *Women in Indonesia: Gender, equity, and development* (pp. 158–178). Singapore: Institute of Southeast Asian Studies.

Jabali, F., & Jamhari (Eds.). (2002). *IAIN dan Modernisasi di Indonesia* [State Institute for Islamic Studies and Modernization in Indonesia]. Ciputat, Java: Logos Wacana Ilmu.

Jones, S. (2000). *Making money off migrants: The Indonesian exodus to Malaysia.* Hong Kong and Wollongon, New South Wales, Australia: Asia 2000 Ltd., Hong Kong Centre for Asia Pacific Transformation, and University of Wollongon.

Kong, L. (2001). Mapping "new" geographies of religion: Politics and poetics in modernity. *Progress in Human Geography, 25*(2), 211–233.

Krisnawaty, T. (1999). *Merajut Angin: Kumpulan Cerita Duka Perempuan Pekerja Migran.* Jakarta, Indonesia: Yayasan Hapsari.

Lawson, V. (1998). Hierarchical households and gendered migration: A research agenda. *Progress in Human Geography, 22,* 32–53.

Leinbach, T., & Watkins, J. (1998). Remittances and circulation behavior in the livelihood process: Transmigrant families in South Sumatra, Indonesia. *Economic Geography, 74,* 45–63.

Leinbach, T., Watkins, J., & Bowen, J. (1992). Employment behavior and the family in Indonesian transmigration. *Annals of the Association of American Geographers, 82,* 23–47.

Mahler, S. (1999). Engendering transnational migration. *American Behavioral Scientist, 42,* 690–719.

Marcoes, L. (2002). Women's grassroots movements in Indonesia: A case study of the PKK and Islamic women's organizations. In K. Robinson & S. Bessell (Eds.), *Women in Indonesia: Gender, equity and development* (pp. 187–197). Singapore: Institute of Southeast Asian Studies.

Moghadam, V. (2002). Afghan women and transnational feminism. *Journal of Middle East Women's Studies, 16*(3/4), 1–12.

Mohammad, R. (1999). Marginalisation, Islamism and the production of the "Other's" "Other." *Gender, Place, and Culture, 6*(3), 221–240.

Nagar, R. (2000). Religion, race and the debate over Mut'a in Dar Es Salaam. *Feminist Studies, 26*(3), 661–690.

Nagel, C. (2001). Contemporary scholarship and the demystification—and remystification—of "Muslim women." *Arab World Geographer, 4*(1), 63–72.

Newland, L. (2000). Under the banner of Islam: Mobilising religious identities in West Java. *Australian Journal of Anthropology, 11*(2), 199–222.

Ong, A. (1995). State versus Islam: Malay families, women's bodies, and the body politic in Malaysia. In A. Ong & M. Peletz (Eds.), *Bewitching women, pious men: Gender and body politics in Southeast Asia* (pp. 159–194). Berkeley and Los Angeles: University of California Press.

Pessar, P. (1999). Engendering migration studies: The case of new immigrants in the United States. *American Behavioral Scientist, 42,* 577–600.

Portes, A., & Sensenbrenner, J. (1993) Embeddedness and immigration: Notes on the social determinants of economic action. *American Journal of Sociology, 98,* 1320–1350.

Pudjosumedi, S., & Rohiim, A. T. (1996). *Islam dan Peranan Wanita: Sebagai Ibu Rumah Tangga dan Tiang Negara* [Islam and the role of women as housewives and pillars of the nation]. Solo, Indonesia: C.V. Aneka.

Radcliffe, S. (1990). Ethnicity, patriarchy, and incorporation into the nation: Female migrants as domestic servants in Peru. *Environment and Planning D: Society and Space, 8*, 379–393.

Robinson, K. (1991). Housemaids: The effects of gender and culture in the internal and international migration of Indonesian women. In G. Bottomley, M. de Lepervanche, & J. Martin (Eds.), *Intersexions: Gender/class/culture/ethnicity* (pp. 33–51). Sydney, Australia: Allen & Unwin.

Robinson, K. (2000). Gender, Islam, and nationality: Indonesian domestic servants in the Middle East. In K. Adams & S. Dickey (Eds.), *Home and hegemony: Domestic service and identity politics in South and Southeast Asia* (pp. 249–282). Ann Arbor: University of Michigan Press.

Robinson, K., & Bessell, S. (Eds.). (2002). *Women in Indonesia: Gender, equity and development*. Singapore: Institute of Southeast Asian Studies.

Sears, L. J. (Ed.). (1996). *Fantasizing the feminine in Indonesia*. Durham, NC, and London: Duke University Press.

Secor, A. (2002). The veil and urban space in Istanbul: Women's dress, mobility, and Islamic knowledge. *Gender, Place, and Culture, 9*(1), 5–22.

Sen, K. (1998). Indonesian women at work: Reframing the subject. In K. Sen & M. Stivens (Eds.), *Gender and power in affluent Asia* (pp. 35–62). New York: Routledge.

Silvey, R. (2003). Spaces of protest: Gendered migration, social networks, and labor protest in West Java, Indonesia. *Political Geography, 22*(2), 129–157.

Silvey, R. (2004). Transnational domestication: Indonesian domestic workers in Saudi Arabia. *Political Geography, 23*(3): 245–264.

Solidaritas Perempuan. (1994). *Kasus-Kasus, TKI* [Tenaga Kerja Indonesia, Indonesian. Indonesian Labor Cases]. Jakarta, Indonesia: Solidaritas Perempuan.

Spaan, E. (1999). *Labour circulation and socioeconomic transformation: The case of East Java, Indonesia*. Groningen, The Netherlands: Rijksuniversiteit Groningen.

Sparke, M. (in press). *Hyphen-nation-states: Critical geographies of displacement and disjuncture*. Minneapolis: University of Minnesota Press.

Stoler, A. (1995). *Race and the education of desire: Foucault's history of sexuality and the colonial order of things*. Durham, NC, and London: Duke University Press.

Sunindyo, S. (1996). Murder, gender, and the media: Sexualizing politics and violence. In L. J. Sears (Ed.), *Fantasizing the feminine in Indonesia* (pp. 120–139). Durham, NC, and London: Duke University Press.

Suryakusuma, J. (1996). The state and sexuality in New Order Indonesia. In L. J. Sears (Ed.), *Fantasizing the feminine in Indonesia* (pp. 92–119). Durham, NC, and London: Duke University Press.

Tagaroa, R., & Sofia, E. (2002). *Buruh migran Indonesia: Mencari keadilan* [Indonesian migrant workers: Searching for justice]. Bekasi, Indonesia: Lembaga Advokasi Buruh Migran—Solidaritas Perempuan [Migrant Workers Advocacy Institute—Women's Solidarity].

Weix, G. G. (1998). Islamic prayer groups in Indonesia: Local forums and gendered responses. *Critique of Anthropology, 18*(4), 405–420.

Willis, K., & Yeoh, B. (Eds.). (2000). *Gender and migration*. Cheltenham, UK, and Northampton, MA: Edward Elgar.

Wolf, D. L. (1992). Women, employment and the family in the international division of labour. *Signs, 18*, 214–218.

Yeoh, B., Huang, S., & Gonzalez, J. (1999). Migrant female domestic workers: Debating the economic, social and political impacts in Singapore. *International Migration Review, 33*, 114–136.

6 Moral Geographies and Women's Freedom

Rethinking Freedom Discourse in the Moroccan Context

AMY FREEMAN

Traditional economic theories of migration treat migrants as rational individuals whose decisions to move reflect the aim of maximizing income or some other "utility." In such accounts, migrants are viewed, above all, as free: free from social constraints, free to move, and free to pursue labor market activities. Recent contributions from feminist migration scholars, however, question the assumption of individual freedom, and focus instead on the position of male and female migrants in webs of social relations—including but not limited to patriarchy—that may serve both to enable and to constrain mobility. This literature emphasizes the importance of migrants' narratives and contexts in understanding the complex social factors that enter into migration decisions, outcomes, and experiences (Boyle & Halfacree, 1999; Goss & Lindquist, 1995; Lawson, 2000a, 2000b; Silvey, 2004; Silvey & Lawson, 1999).

Informed by and building on critical migration theory, this chapter addresses mobility and freedom as they relate to Moroccan women living both in Morocco and in France. Investigating women's freedom and mobility points to the social construction of women's morality and the spatialization of moral codes of behavior—that is, the creation of "moral geographies" (see Silvey, 2000a; also see Domosh, 2001). Moral geographies significantly influence mobility and experiences of place at multiple scales—

for example, within villages, between country and city, and transnationally. As Silvey (2004, p. 498) argues, "mobile subjects are policed by discourses defining the boundaries of appropriate gendered, place-based behavior" (see also Hubbard, 1998; Silvey, 2000a, 2000b; Yeoh & Huang, 1998), and much research has demonstrated the ways that women's bodies, in particular, are used in the boundary-making processes of migrant and ethnic communities (Dwyer, 1999; Mohammad, 1999; Nagar, 1998; Ong, 1995; Ong & Peletz, 1995; Yuval-Davis, 1997).

Moral geographies have a relevance to Muslim Moroccan women in particular and to Muslim women more generally. There is a widespread and often erroneous perception that Arab and Muslim women—as an undifferentiated group—are more restricted in their activities and movements than women in the "west" (see Abu-Lughod, 1985/1995; Ahmed, 1994). This chapter does not attempt to answer the question of whether Moroccan women are truly "free" or "unfree," but rather it explores women's ideas about freedom, the moral geographies that shape their mobility, and the potential shifts in subjectivity brought about by their movement in and through spaces. Moroccan women's diverse and often ambivalent narratives of freedom indicate that Western liberal conceptions of freedom, as expressed both in migration theory and in political discourse, merit greater reflection. I do not wish to suggest that Muslims or Moroccans as a group have a fundamentally different notion of freedom than do Christians, Jews, "Westerners," or Europeans. Such a claim, made frequently by both Muslim and Western scholars, essentializes group identities and traits and ignores the historical construction of these identities.[1] Instead, in critiquing universalistic notions of freedom and of the subject, I demonstrate that multiple conceptions of freedom that make reference to different ideologies and contexts are relevant to understanding the moral geographies that shape women's mobility and experience of place.

FREEDOM'S GENDERED SUBJECTS AND MORAL GEOGRAPHIES

The figure of the universally free, disembodied, rational individual found in neoclassical economic theories of migration is a reflection of modernist liberal notions of the subject that emerged out of 18th-century Enlightenment thought (Smith, 1993). While posited as a universal subject that embodies autonomy, equality, and personal freedom, "the individual," in fact, has been defined and enabled by membership in exclusive social groups, such as "free," white, property-owning males (see Rose, 1993). Feminists and critical scholars across disciplines have amply demonstrated and critiqued the degree to which this universalized notion of the autonomous subject and citizen was, and still is, highly exclusionary and hegemonic (Rose,

1993; Yeğenoğlu, 1996), particularly in terms of the normative subject of the public sphere (Bondi, 1998; Domosh, 1997). In its place many feminists have argued for notions of multiple and relational identities and subjectivities (see Bloom, 1999; Domosh, 1997; Nagar, 1997; Young, 1997).

However, despite demonstrating the shortcomings of this hegemonic and essentialist notion of the subject, feminists and critical scholars have devoted much less attention to the ways in which people's everyday ideas of freedom remain tied up with this essentialist view of the individual. While, on the one hand, particular notions of freedom, autonomy, and equality underlie neoliberal practices at the heart of global capitalism and geopolitics, these same values continue to serve as the basis for emancipatory movements for many different groups of people—including women—in a multitude of societies and contexts. Yet there are many different ways people have thought about and relate to the idea of freedom (see Chakrabarty, 1992, 1997; Foner, 1998, 2003; Hirschman, 1998, 2002; Laroui, 2001; Majid, 2000; Young, 2002), and, not surprisingly, there are important gender differences as well. For women more than for men, the notion of personal freedom poses a moral dilemma, as freedom and mobility may challenge the moral order of patriarchal societies—a moral order that rests, in part, on ideas about women's sexuality and the policing of women's bodies (Cresswell, 1999; Dwyer, 1999, 2000; Kofman, Phizacklea, Raghuram, & Sales, 2000; Nagar, 1998; Ong, 1997; Ong & Peletz, 1997; Radcliffe, 1990; Yuval-Davis, 1997). Spaces are coded as morally correct or incorrect and regulated based on the practices known (or believed) to take place there and the reputation of the people occupying those spaces. The existence of these moral geographies influences the range of possibilities for women's mobility and the consequences of transgressing dominant moral codes (Massey, 1994).

The centrality of women's bodies to the construction of moral orders has been well documented in a multitude of geographical and historical contexts. Bondi and Domosh (1998), McMillan (2000), and Wilson (1991) have illustrated how this was explicitly the case in urban areas of Europe and the United States in the 19th and early 20th centuries, where women's mobility in cities was to varying degrees shaped by the normative ideas of the time concerning women's appropriate behavior at particular times and in particular places (for contemporary accounts, see Cresswell, 1999; Hubbard, 1998; Laws, 1997; and Valentine, 1989, 1992). Concerning "non-Western" people and places, Silvey (2000a) has shown in contemporary Indonesia how ideas about women's sexual morality increasingly influence their mobility and migration decisions as the economic crisis there has deepened. In addition, research by Dwyer (1999, 2000) on Pakastani Muslim women in Britain, by Nagar (1998) on women in Tanzania, and by Radcliffe (1990) on Peruvian migrant women demonstrate the ways that women's bodies are policed and used to mark community boundaries.

In the "East" and the "West" alike, fears and anxieties concerning women's freedom and emancipation have been related to a community's desire to control women's sexuality and to ensure their "purity." This intersection between morality and mobility is one of many factors that shape women's access to and experiences of migration and movement at different scales (see Mills, 1999). Hence, as the processes of modernization and global capitalism encourage and impel women to earn wages and spend more time in public (visible) spheres, moral codes of behavior are brought into question.

Yet, in making this critique, some feminist scholars also caution against reinforcing and reproducing essentialist notions of the public as masculine and the private as feminine (Staeheli, 1996). Moral orders and moral geographies, while in some ways rigid and uncompromising, are in other ways fluid, flexible, and open to challenge, and it needs to be recognized that the opening of certain spaces to women has increased opportunities for some, created greater hardships for others, and brought about greater scrutiny of all women (see Abu-Lughod, 1998). Just as notions of public and private spheres have been shown to be overlapping rather than discrete spaces in Western contexts, these spatial divisions have also been shown to overlap and to work differently for Muslim women in a variety of contexts (Bekkar, 1997; Belarbi, 1997; Göle, 1997; Guénif Souilamas, 2000; Joseph, 1997; Secor, 2002).

In the following sections, before reviewing the context of the study and its research design, I briefly discuss the importance of freedom in colonial and postcolonial discourses. Then I draw from interview material to investigate Moroccan women's discourses of freedom, and how these discourses are instrumental in constructing and challenging the moral geographies that shape their mobility and subjectivities. Following feminist and antiessentialist positions (e.g., Hirschmann, 1998, 2002), these accounts highlight, among other things, the interconnectedness of individuals rather than their autonomy, and problematize dominant (neo)liberal conceptions of freedom.

POSTCOLONIAL DISCOURSES ON FREEDOM

Central to European colonial projects of modernity in North Africa and the Middle East was the construction of the Muslim woman as oppressed and in need of liberation, juxtaposed with the European woman defined as "free" and "emancipated." Yet the emancipatory potential and promise of modernity, so celebrated in Europe under the banner of *liberté, égalité et fraternité*, could only reveal its inherent contradictions and exclusions in the context of colonialism. As Homi Bhabha has asked, "What is modernity in those colonial conditions where its imposition is itself the denial of historical freedom, civic autonomy, and the ethical choice of self-fashioning?" (1991, p. 198, cited in Pratt, 2002, pp. 32–33).

The concept of freedom necessarily encompasses conflicting and ambivalent ideas in societies, like Morocco, that have lived through the violence of colonial occupation. Western discourses of the colonial period often expressed the view that colonial subjects, their cultures, and their religions were uncivilized and, as such, not fit or ready for the civil liberties of the metropole (Young, 2002). "Native" women in particular were seen as lacking in freedom—as defined by the European bourgeoisie and colonialists—and the status of Muslim women and their alleged lack of freedom vis-à-vis European women became central to claims about the superiority of Western society (see Collier, 1995).

As Europeans called for the freedom of Muslim women from their oppressive cultures, some Muslim thinkers in Morocco and elsewhere countered that the freedom enjoyed by European women was excessive, immoral, and a sign of the impure and inferior nature of European civilization (see the writings of al-Tahtawi in Louca, 1970, and Tavakoli-Targhi, 1994). The link made between the seclusion and the oppression of women in Arab/Muslim countries and the backward condition of its people, religion, and culture only emboldened certain nationalists to take up the protection of women's status from within Islam and reinforced the need to strictly control women's movement.

While the facile distinctions between "free" and "oppressed" women are no longer widespread in academic work, they continue to hold sway in popular and politicized descriptions of Muslim women, particularly in this post-9/11 era.[2] In the months following the September 11 attacks, for instance, there was a flurry of press articles and television programs dedicated to examining women's lives in Afghanistan and the potentially liberating effects for women of the war the United States was waging against the Taliban regime.[3] Voices from both the "West" and Muslim societies have engaged in a debate about which group of women is "repressed" or "manipulated" and which is "free." Muslim women have not been absent from these debates. Kandiyoti (1994, p. 380) has argued that feminist discourse in Islamic countries often takes one of two forms: either it contrasts the commodified, sexually exploited Western woman with the dignified, protected Muslim woman, or it embraces the "golden age myth of an uncorrupted original Islam against which current discriminatory gender practices may be denounced as actually not Islamic." In all of these cases, women's bodies are used to represent essentialist definitions of culture—representations that have become global in scope.

The question of women's freedom thus remains highly problematic in many postcolonial contexts because of the way that the issue of women's status and emancipation has been deeply politicized and racialized by colonial powers, local nationalist elites, and more recently by neoimperial leaders, religious fundamentalists, the global media, "public intellectuals," and feminists of every stripe. In Morocco, as elsewhere, freedom tends to be defined (particularly by religious conservatives and Islamists) in relation to their experience with Europe (and increasingly the United States), so that while political freedom has usually taken on a positive and necessary connotation, individual freedom, and particularly women's individual freedom, is seen as fundamentally negative and immoral. When freedom is embraced and defended on a personal level, especially in any public/political context, it often must accompany a discourse of anti-Westernism so as not to risk being interpreted (and used against women) as antinationalist or anti-Islamic. In their narratives of mobility and freedom, however, the Moroccan women with whom I spoke revealed much more ambivalent and antiessentialist notions of modern subjectivity and freedom than that allowed for by either (neo)liberal thought or religious conservatives.

CONTEXT OF THE STUDY

Moroccan Political Economy and Migration

Prior to France's colonization of Morocco (officially a French Protectorate from 1912 to 1956), the country was governed by rival tribal groups and essentially overseen by a sultanate whose primary role was to collect taxes, maintain an army, and suppress threats to his power (Waterbury, 1970). France used the position of sultan as a way for the colonial administration to govern with the allegiance of hand-picked local elites. In the aftermath of Morocco's nationalist movements and the fight for independence, the sultan (Mohammed V)—who had gained the support of many nationalists— retained ultimate power and established the monarchy as the ruling system. Today, Morocco is a constitutional monarchy with a parliamentary system (the king is chief of state, and he appoints a prime minister who is head of government). In recent years, there have been attempts by former King Hassan II and now his son, King Mohammed VI, to move Morocco toward a system of greater democratic governance (e.g., through the creation of a bicameral legislature, the appointment of an oppositional leader as prime minister, efforts to implement more open elections, and recognition of Berber languages). Like most poor countries, Morocco maintains a high external debt, has undergone a series of structural adjustment programs, and has embraced neoliberal austerity measures in an attempt to encourage economic activity, foreign investment, and job creation. While the Moroccan economy did show some signs of improvement in the early 1990s, the most recent indicators available showed a reversal of this trend with worsening poverty and unemployment.[4]

Since the 1960s, a constant factor of Moroccan political economy has been the massive migration of both skilled and unskilled labor to Europe, especially to France. In the aftermath of decolonization, France was in need of workers in its factories and facilitated the migration of North Africans for this purpose. Remittances sent back to Morocco from migrants abroad quickly became a primary source of revenue for the national economy. By 1976, migrant remittances surpassed sales from the primary export of phosphates (see Schaeffer, 1999), and in 2002 migrant remittances reached 31.7 billion DH, with remittances from France accounting for almost half of all transfers.[5] Without this source of income from abroad, many Moroccan families, particularly in the rural areas, would find themselves among the ranks of the poor.[6]

As the income gap between Morocco and neighboring Europe continues to grow, so has the migration of Moroccans.[7] According to official data, there were 1.6 million Moroccans living in Europe in 1996, with the greatest number, approximately 653,000, residing in France (Centre d'Etudes et de Recherches Démographiques [CERED], 1996).[8] The percentage of Moroccan women residing in France increased significantly from 26.7% in 1975 to 44.4% in 1990, due primarily to changes in immigration and family reunification policies (CERED, 1996). Many migrant women arrive in France with little or no formal education and no knowledge of French (Tribalat, 1997), and as such they often find themselves even more dependent on and constrained by male family members than they were in Morocco.

In the 1970s, as France attempted to stop immigration from North Africa through restrictive legislation and to encourage migrant repatriation, many Moroccans opted to remain in France and to send for their families. From this point on, the Moroccan population in France increased significantly, and the regular circulation of and contact between people and families in Morocco and France became commonplace. By the mid-1980s, economic crises and global competition made Muslim North African immigrants in France easy targets for anti-immigrant and racist sentiment (Ogden, 1991). In contrast to previous migrants from Spain, Portugal, and Poland, migrants from North Africa are often considered "unassimilable" because of their cultural and religious practices (House, 1995). The controversy that began in the late 1980s over female Muslim students wearing the *hijab* (headscarf) in public schools (resulting in the girls being expelled from school) led the French government in late 2003 to propose banning all students from wearing any conspicuous signs of their religious beliefs. Such a measure, aimed clearly at Muslim girls in particular (since wearing Jewish yarmulkes and Christian crosses had not been debated previously), demonstrates the continued association of "Muslim difference" with women's bodies and the degree to which the presence of a significant Muslim population and identity in France threatens the rigid and exclusive conception of what it means to be French.[9]

Changes in Moroccan Women's Lives and Spaces

Although much of the anthropological and social science research on Morocco does not address issues of women's freedom or mobility directly, this literature discusses various aspects of Moroccan women's use of and access to place and space (Belarbi, 1999; Bourqia, 1996; Davis, 1983, 1987; Davis-Taïeb, 1998; El Harras, 1996; Kapchan, 1996; Maher, 1974; Mernissi, 1987; Naamane-Guessous, 1997; Ossman, 1994, 1998). In addition, the extensive literature on Moroccan women's employment and education implicitly addresses issues of mobility and use of space because such activities usually entail women spending more time outside of the home (see Benzakour Chami, 1999; CERED, 1998; Griffiths, 1996; Ministry of Foreign Affairs and Cooperation, 1996; Moghadam, 1998; Naciri & Barkallil, 1989; and Temsamani Haji, 1997).

On the whole, this literature attests to the enormous changes Moroccan society has undergone in the past 20 years, particularly in relation to women's greater presence in the public sphere in urban areas through paid employment, education, and activism. At the same time, the available indicators make evident the growing disparities in young girls' and women's lives in urban and rural areas. For example, between 1982 and 1998, urban women's illiteracy decreased from 57.6% to 42%; illiteracy for rural women decreased over the same period, but at 82% remained substantially higher than for urban women (Boukous & Agnaou, 2001; Ministry of Foreign Affairs and Cooperation, 1996). And while the gender gap in illiteracy continues to close in urban areas, it has only widened in rural areas (CERED, 1998). Large disparities also exist in primary-school enrollment between rural and urban areas. Although the percentage of boys and girls being schooled in both areas is increasing, improvements have been meager in rural areas, with only 26.6% of girls enrolled in 1994, compared with 80.4% of urban girls (Direction de la Statistique, 1996). In turn, more women are attending high school and university in urban areas, making them more qualified for professional jobs. In terms of employment, women represented 25.5% of the labor force[10] in 1991, up from 11.6% in 1982 (Temsamani Haji, 1997). Although women are concentrated in low-paid jobs in the service and manufacturing industries in urban areas and agricultural work in rural areas, nearly a third of state employees are women (Griffiths, 1996) and an increasing number of women are present in teaching, scientific, and liberal professions (Direction de la Statistique, 1996; Ministry of Foreign Affairs and Cooperation, 1996). Another indication of women's increased participation (and continued struggles) in the labor force is their elevated unemployment rate which, in urban areas in 1995, was 32.2%, compared with 18.7% for men (Direction de la Statistique, 1996).

Furthermore, in the September 2002 legislative elections, following a bill passed by Parliament requiring political parties to include a quota of women nominees, 35 women were elected to the 325-seat House of Representatives, making Morocco the Arab country with the greatest percentage of elected women officials (11%).[11] In October 2003, after over 50 years of struggles by women's rights activists, Mohammed VI announced sweeping changes to Moroccan family law, attesting, hopefully, to the current favorable climate concerning Moroccan women's status.[12]

Improvements in Moroccan women's representation in the political arena and their legal status are important and encouraging steps toward normalizing their greater mobility and visibility. But legal and political victories do not easily or quickly translate into changes in women's everyday lives. Some scholars and activists have noted the continued difficulties and violence women face in Morocco and have questioned the degree to which changes in women's status have affected their access to public, male-dominated spaces (or vice versa) (Association Démocratique des Femmes du Maroc [ADFM], 2001; Bekkar, 1997; Collectif 95 Maghreb Egalité, 1998; Naciri & Barkallil, 1989). At the same time, generalizations are difficult to make since women's use of space, and the moral codes regulating that use, varies in Morocco depending on region, age, social status, and ethnicity (among others), and there is not necessarily unanimity about such norms within any given group (Bennani-Chraïbi, 1995; Davis, 1987; Ossman, 1994). What is considered acceptable behavior, and where such behaviors are sanctioned to take place, is not fixed, but changes in concert with other societal shifts, producing varying outcomes and consequences for women and men.

The Study

The research for this project was carried out over a period of 14 months in 2000 and 2001 in Montpellier, France, and in various locations in Morocco (primarily Rabat, Salé, and Casablanca). The types of Moroccan women I met and spoke to cannot be neatly categorized. In France, the women I interviewed (*n* = 23) were living in France for different reasons: women who were born in France of Moroccan parents, women who migrated with their families as part of reunification policies (as either wives or daughters, migrating at different ages), women who came to France to pursue university studies and stayed, and women who came illegally to find work and/or a husband. In Morocco, I spoke primarily with unschooled women of different ages in literacy classes in Rabat and Salé (*n* = 39), women residing in France and visiting Morocco during their holidays (*n* = 13), and educated women's rights activists in Rabat and Casablanca (*n* = 20).[13] I met Moroccan women by volunteering in literacy centers in both France and Morocco (teaching French), taking the ferry between Morocco and France during the summer, using snowball sampling techniques, and relying on personal contacts. With French-speaking women I conducted the interviews one-on-one; with Moroccan Arabic and Berber-speaking women, an interpreter accompanied me.

The overall research project of which this chapter is a part investigates

questions of postcolonial identity and modernity of Moroccan women living in France and in Morocco through their experiences of political activism, migration/mobility, and literacy classes (see Freeman, 2004a, 2004b).
In an effort to explore women's expressions of their identity and experience
of place, I asked questions related to their upbringing, daily activities and
outings, changes perceived over time and between places, and about their
views of women's rights and freedoms in Morocco. Speaking with Moroccan women in both France and Morocco allowed me to consider the role
that (national) place and transnational migration play in the construction
of women's modern gender identity, including their views and experiences
of freedom. Of the eight interviews I draw from in this chapter, seven of the
women had not received any formal education, and two resided in France
(one was a graduate student, the other was unschooled).

MOROCCAN WOMEN'S NARRATIVES OF FREEDOM

The Moroccan women's narratives I present here offer perspectives on
women's freedom that at times counter and conflict with the dominant notions of freedom implicit in liberal and neoliberal ideology and politics, and
at other times reproduce certain aspects of this freedom. Their experiences
of place and mobility and their views on women's freedom stem from a
complex interconnection of their family situation, the moral geographies
regulating Moroccan social life, and the postcolonial context, which is sat-
urated with references to "life in the West," and which is often defined by
relations of domination with that West. In such a context, it is not surprising that Moroccan women express notions of freedom that are heterogeneous, and at times ambivalent and contradictory. It is also not surprising,
however, that the Moroccan women I met frequently referred to Europe,
North America, and, at times, women's lives there. With very few exceptions, the women I interviewed in Morocco have family members living
abroad (primarily in France, Belgium, Italy, and Spain), and a few from
more well-off families have even visited Europe and the United States. The
women's narratives do not provide a unified alternative to dominant
neoliberal discourses of freedom. They do, however, offer antiessentialist
accounts of freedom and the subject that provide insight into the moral
geographies that shape Moroccan women's mobility, while complicating
the facile equation of the "West" with freedom and "the Arab world" or
"Islam" with a lack of freedom.

In my discussions with Moroccan women in France and in Morocco
about their everyday experiences of place, mobility, and freedom, two general themes emerged: the notion of freedom as relational (i.e., connected to
other individuals) and the notion of freedom with limits. I discuss these two
notions of freedom in separate sections, and in a third section I consider the

intersections of women's narratives of freedom and the moral geographies that influence their mobility and behavior.

Freedom as Relational

While many women were, to varying degrees, critical of societal and familial constraints on both their mobility and identity, most, but not all, of the women expressed themselves in relation to their family or the community, and few seemed willing or able to jeopardize their family's support. Many of the women articulated, in different ways, the constant and often acute tension between family/societal constraints and individual desires (see Mills, 1999, "good daughter" vs. "modern woman," p. 92). As Ruggerini (1997) also found in her work with Moroccan and Tunisian women, tensions between individual aspirations and family expectations and cultural norms do not result in a blanket rejection of one or the other. With more limited access to educational and employment opportunities than men, women find that family relations and networks are essential for them to maintain, and for many women family ties are a strong source of pride and identity (see Ruggerini, 1997). Women across the socioeconomic spectrum adhere to gender-appropriate norms—at times in order to maintain their honor and standing in the family so as not to jeopardize their access to basic resources, and at other times simply in order to avoid the often painful and ostracizing consequences of their transgressions.

This tendency to express identity in relational terms is not, however, necessarily feminist or counterhegemonic to essentialist notions of the subject as free and autonomous. Nonetheless, expressions of relational identity and freedom do reflect alternative accounts of the subject that neither assume nor deny individual autonomy. In arguing that Moroccan women articulate a notion of relational freedom and identity that is different from Western liberal conceptions of subjectivity and freedom (see Hirschmann, 1996), I do not wish to romanticize the existence of "community" in Morocco or to suggest that women do not simultaneously have or wish to have a certain degree of autonomy. The notion of interconnectedness does not exclude the existence of individual identities and differences (Young, 1986/1995). Rather, to say that freedom and identity are relational for many of the Moroccan women I met is to underline the fiction of the unfettered, disembodied, autonomous, and universal subject (see Smith, 1993) of hegemonic discourses of freedom and modernity.

In their respective works, Ossman (1994) and Bennani-Chraïbi (1995) investigate how Moroccan youth negotiate their "self-making" in a world of competing images and models of "ways of being." The young people with whom they spoke often expressed tensions between individual desires and the expectations or restrictions of family, religion, and/or society. Likewise, Guénif Souilamas (2000), in her research with women in France of

North African origin, found that women are often not willing to sacrifice either their bonds to their families or the personal adventure that freedom offers. Instead, they construct their own type of freedoms and identities that she (along with others; e.g., Bennani-Chraïbi, 1995; Mills, 1999) has labeled "mutations." These tensions between personal desires and expectations of families are readily apparent in these interviews, as well.

Halima,[14] a 28-year-old divorced woman from a rural region of Morocco, left her son with her parents in order to find work in France. As Halima's narrative elucidates, her expression of relational freedom underlines the opportunities that such connectivity has afforded her. Her story stresses how one way for women to ensure their safety and the maintenance of their honor with increased mobility is to be accompanied by family members and to extend the definition of family to include people considered as family, but who are not.

> "I came [to Montpellier] with a man from my village, his wife and children. . . . My father wasn't too crazy about me coming, but my father isn't very strict. Mostly I'm afraid of my oldest brother. He said it was shameful that I leave like that, but I don't think so. I just went to my aunt's, that's all! In general, they weren't against it. The girls encouraged me to leave, my aunt talked to my parents about it. I didn't have the courage to talk to them. My father preferred that my brother go in my place because he needed to work . . . thanks to my aunt [I was able to come]. I could never have come by myself. There's also my aunt's husband who thinks of me as his daughter, and he said that to all the people from my village here [in Montpellier]."

Halima and the people from her village use the notion of "family" to include fellow villagers, rendering her mobility outside the village morally acceptable. In essence, her narrative creates a constant presence of family at all points during her move to and within France as a way to counteract the "shamefulness" of her mobility. Halima's experience suggests that, even when women may have the financial means to travel or migrate, the possibilities for both small- and large-scale mobility are often significantly reduced if the proper familial networks are not in place. Thus, mobilizing family networks may offset some of the restrictions on women's mobility, in part by providing an acceptable justification for altering gendered moral geographies. In turn, and in the case of Halima—as we will see later—this may open up other opportunities for women's mobility in and through new spaces, further transforming normative moral geographies.

Rabéa is a severely disabled 41-year-old woman who came to Rabat from a rural area with her daughter after her husband divorced her. She eventually remarried and now lives in a small one-room windowless apartment with her husband and her daughter's 3-year-old child. When I asked her if she thought Moroccan women needed more freedom, along with making reference to education and religious beliefs, she articulated the importance of considering the self and the community in relation to freedom.

> "Women need a type of freedom that they will know how to manage. For example, [freedom is] for educated women, not uneducated women! First of all, a woman has to be afraid of God. She shouldn't do anything that will bring on the anger of God or that of her household. For example, a woman who has freedom must know how to manage it, so that she uses it for her own good and for the good of others, not the woman who does things that are harmful to herself, to society, her husband, and her home. This type of woman should not have her freedom. [It must be] a freedom that will serve her interests, the general interest and that of her children."

Clearly, Rabéa approaches her understanding of women's freedom from within the confines of religion and the patriarchal nuclear family. Her narrative echoes nationalist religious discourse on women's role in society, underlining the importance of women being educated in order to be able to "manage" (through self-discipline) herself and her household. To be sure, the type of relationality that Rabéa expresses can be interpreted as condoning and reproducing patriarchal control over women (see Joseph, 1997). Her narrative recalls the discourse of early 20th-century Moroccan nationalists who focused on women's central role as guardians of the community—Islamic and national—and who rejected certain notions of women's rights that they associated with the West and colonialism. At the same time, Rabéa does not erase herself or the possibility of individual desires and interests in her narrative, but rather objects to a type of freedom that she thinks would be harmful to both women and others. This notion of respect for and consideration of others reflects Rabéa's religious beliefs, and also her adherence to a particular moral order.

However, the type of relationality that she expresses when speaking directly to issues of women's freedom and indirectly of their morality does not preclude her embracing individual identity and desires that may run counter to community norms elsewhere. [15] For example, later on in the interview Rabéa said, "I hope to go to Spain or France someday, to discover another world and other peoples." At another point she contended that "women must be able to choose the man they want to be with, because often the family intervenes [to impose a choice]. . . . she needs to be with the man she wants, that she knows well and gets along with," making it clear that she does not always think women should be subsumed by the interests of the family. Furthermore, the importance and weight of language should not be overlooked in considering the types of responses that my questions on women's freedom elicited.[16] Many women I spoke to implied that they have or would like to have certain types of freedom, but when I used the word in French (*liberté*), or its Arabic equivalent (*hurriya*), it was necessary for me to be more specific about what I meant by the term in order for us to come to a common understanding.[17] Otherwise, I soon realized, we both made certain presumptions about what the word meant without knowing we had different definitions.

As I suggested above, relational freedom can also present obstacles for women. Leila, a 36-year-old single, unschooled woman, articulates how she has "total" freedom, but only insofar as she is accompanied by her father.

> "My father gives us total freedom. We can swim in front of him at the sea . . . he brings us to the beach, to the café. Wherever we go, he's with us. But for us to go out without his permission, he doesn't accept that. . . . [Women in Europe] live better than we do. They rent [their own apartments]. Here, you can't rent an apartment and live alone. Plus, you wouldn't have the means to do it. [In Europe] girls have their freedom when they're 18 years old, they have the means [to take advantage of it]. Our society is bad. If you leave home [before you get married], they interpret it differently. It's as if you're leaving so you can go do bad things, when you just want to be independent."

Leila expresses her frustration with Moroccan society that equates women's desire for independence and autonomy with wanting to do "bad things." She articulates, then, how women's individual freedom and mobility are restricted through their association with immoral behavior and sexual promiscuity; their bodies are thus used to define and regulate the community/ national moral order. Leila refers to women's lives in Europe in order to negatively evaluate Moroccan women's inability to live independently. She contrasts their lives and means with her own as she regrets that her only option for freedom in absence of her father is to get married—this being the only legitimate reason (and economic possibility) for many Moroccan women to leave home. In this respect, relational freedom for many Moroccan women can be rather limited. At the same time, as in Halima's case, the freedom to be mobile can, at times, be made possible only through such relationality as family networks.

Freedom with Limits

In addition to expressing tensions between constraints on identity/mobility and individual desires, a number of women spoke of the notion of "freedom with limits." Ossman (1994, p. 145) mentions how the youth she interviewed spoke about desiring freedom, but not "total" freedom. She interprets this articulation of a limited freedom as an expression of the fear of transgressing boundaries. Alternatively, one could understand this desire for freedom with limits as a way that women claim a certain agency over their lives and actions—in essence, by accepting and reproducing the constraints on their mobility and identity that patriarchal society imposes. Embracing a notion of freedom with limits could also be considered as an oppositional stance (whether conscious or not) toward the dominance and perceived freedom of the "West," where women (often equally essentialized) are believed to have "total" freedom that has resulted in nefarious self-indulgence, the breakdown of the family, and a general loss of morals.

Some of the Moroccan women with whom I spoke reacted negatively to the idea of women's freedom because they, like Leila's narrative highlighted, associate women's freedom with sexual promiscuity. Thus, when I asked the questions "Do you feel you have the freedom to do what you want?" or "Do you think Moroccan women need more freedom?" quite often women assumed that I was asking if they do or want to do things that are considered immoral for "well-educated" and "respectable" women to do. Khadija, a 35-year-old single woman I met in a literacy center in Rabat (she was originally from a rural town) associates having her freedom with acting in a "respectable" manner:

"Up until now, I have my freedom, but a limited freedom, not so you can do whatever you want, but within what's respectable. For example, not in order to go to a seedy place, but a freedom that I have to be responsible about. I don't have the idea to go do something bad because I have my freedom, no. . . . It depends on the person's upbringing, you understand. There are girls who say to their family that they're going to their girlfriend's house, but they go someplace else. Or her girlfriend goes someplace too, and she doesn't have a good reputation. Maybe someone saw her [someplace she shouldn't have been] so they don't give her her freedom anymore. Me, no. They see that I do fine and I don't do anything bad, so they give me my freedom."

Like Rabéa, who spoke about women needing to know how to "manage" their freedom, Khadija talks about being responsible about her freedom. In both cases, it is women's own self-discipline that determines whether they should be able to keep their freedom. For Khadija, freedom is her reward for not transgressing social norms of women's appropriate behavior—in short, for adhering to the dominant moral geographies for women.

Some women like Khadija spoke about "limited freedom" or "freedom with limits" to express the idea that they felt having total freedom would mean they were not virtuous women, but to have limited freedom means they are masters of their freedom, can use it wisely to good ends, and will not let it get out of hand. Rather than seeing themselves as "unfree" or "oppressed," some women feel that to limit their own freedom, to be in control of their freedom and mobility, they can be sure to be perceived as virtuous and "well-educated" women, which reflects back on their honor and that of their family, and, which, if they are single, bears on their marriage prospects.

I met 23-year-old Fatima in a literacy center in Salé. She had worked for a number of years as a "maid"[18] for her uncle and had never gone to school. She recently married and is living with her husband's family until she is able to join him in France.

> "I have my freedom, but I can't go past my limits. I'm free now [that I'm married], I can do what I like. . . . I set my own limits, because you shouldn't abuse your freedom. . . . I don't even go out with my sister. I come to the center, I go straight home, I do my prayers, I study a little, that's it. [My husband's family] knows that I won't go past my limits. . . . I set them for myself, I'm self-taught. I give myself the freedom I need. When I was younger, my father would send me to get something. I could have gone walking around Rabat, for example, but I didn't do it. I always came home at the time he told me to. I could leave school and walk around town if I wanted, but I don't like to do such things."

Khadija and Fatima both talked about "freedom with limits," and their narratives imply the close connection between the way a woman limits her own freedom by controlling her visibility and behavior in particular places—thereby respecting the dominant moral geographies—and, in return, securing her "good reputation" and ensuring that she be allowed to keep this "limited" degree of freedom.[19] Limited freedom can thus be understood as Moroccan women's maintenance of gendered moral codes of behavior and mobility through their own self-discipline. These seemingly contradictory impulses between freedom and self-restraint are in fact part and parcel of the construction of the modern woman in many Middle Eastern contexts (see Abu-Lughod, 1998).

On the other hand, if I asked questions related to (rather than directly about) women's freedom and their freedom of movement—their desires for the future or their children's future, their hopes to travel, to go to school, to get a job, to choose a husband—then women did not assume I was asking about the freedom to do "bad things," and their narratives surrounding potential acts of freedom were often much more positive. By distancing myself from the explicit use of "freedom" language that both implies (and, to a certain degree, imposes) a comparison with "Western" women and suggests the transgression of social mores, some Moroccan women offered more critical accounts of their situation. When I spoke with Iman, a 45-year-old married woman studying in a literacy center in Rabat, about her opportunities to work outside the home and how life has changed for women in Morocco, she said:

"I had the opportunity [to work overseas], twice. . . . I had an opportunity [to leave] but we grew up in a place where it was shameful for girls to do the most normal things, we weren't allowed to speak, to do certain things. So how do you expect me to have the courage to go live by myself and confront another way of life? . . . Today, I try to take my revenge through my children . . . I won't let my daughter get married if she doesn't have a weapon under her arm. What is her weapon? It's her work. Because times have become difficult. Today, if a girl doesn't work, no one will want her [for marriage]. And for yourself, you'll end up bored just staying at home, all day at home, it's not possible. That's life, it's in this way that life has changed. But before, women didn't go out, it was shameful! I had several opportunities to work, but my husband didn't want me to go out. Today, if a job came along, he would accept it! Why? Because he'd like me to. Conditions don't permit us to sit around doing nothing. If a person can help out, she does."

Iman gives an impression of a very strict moral geography during her youth, one that was both externally and internally imposed. Ingrained feelings of shame and fear prevented her from taking an opportunity to go to France that perhaps few women would turn down today. She contrasts that with current times, when economic hardship has made it both possible and necessary for women to leave home and be more mobile, and presumably this means that the shame previously associated with women leaving the home has dissipated to a certain degree. But she also says that having a job and being financially independent have become very important in order for women to find a marriage partner. A certain amount and type of freedom is therefore necessary in order to find a good husband, keeping the notion of women's freedom and mobility in order to earn wages in an acceptable realm of family and community values. But Iman also brings up the issue of women being bored at home, how it is not possible to sit home all day, as she implies women were expected to do when she was younger. When she says that "it is in this way that life has changed," it seems that in part she is referring to the development of women's independent interests outside the domestic sphere and their desire and ability to be a visible, if not an active, participant in public life.

Intersection of Women's Freedom, Discourse, and Moral Geographies

Feminist research has suggested the role that the development of capitalist consumer culture has played in challenging gendered moral geographies, by increasing women's mobility and freedom (although circumscribed and differentiated) through leisure and consumer activities outside the home (see Bondi, 1998; Bondi & Domosh, 1998). Linda McDowell (1999) has referred to this as "consumption as (partial) liberation" (p. 160)—"partial" because when constructed primarily or solely as consumers rather than as producers, women are manipulated by, rather than active agents in, capitalist relations of production. In this section, I draw on feminist research that addresses the intersection of consumption and place to analyze the narratives of some Moroccan women who express their experiences of freedom by referring to the different moral geographies that shape their mobility—geographies which often are accompanied by shifts in their subjectivity and modes of dress as well.

Bondi and Domosh (1998) have noted how the increased surveillance of urban consumer spaces offers safety and reassurance for middle-class women, whereas women's nighttime mobility remains problematic because they fear more for their safety when streets become deserted. While this is also true to a certain degree in the Moroccan context, the moral geographies that result from cultural norms surrounding women's honor can make this same daytime surveillance of consumer spaces a factor that limits rather than expands women's mobility because they risk being seen in the "wrong" place with the "wrong" person (much like Bondi & Domosh, 1998, describe for a 19th-century woman in New York City). In Morocco, the surveillance provided by consumer culture does at times provide greater safety and mobility for women, but at other times it comes at the expense of the anonymity often required for women to express themselves in ways that challenge societal norms (Davis-Taïeb, 1998; Wilson, 1981).

Davis-Taïeb (1998) investigates how changes in the Moroccan and global economies have come together with changes in women's individual desires, showing how a certain type of visibility for Moroccan women has become acceptable in particular urban establishments, such as "salons du thé" and "glaciers" (teahouses and ice cream parlors) and, more recently, McDonald's, as opposed to the morally suspect locations of cafés and bars. "Being seen" in a place considered morally inappropriate for women jeopardizes her reputation (bringing her "purity," [i.e., virginity] into question), affecting both her prospects for marriage and the honor of her family. To be sure, women of all ages in Morocco have forged paths into male-dominated spaces—and often with the help of consumer culture as well as women-oriented nongovernmental organizations (NGOs)—but women are not equally positioned to benefit from these opportunities. Furthermore, increased opportunities for some women have been dependent on the existence of large inequalities between women in Morocco.[20]

Modes of dress—often articulated as the juxtaposition of the *hijab* versus the miniskirt—is central to many Moroccan women's narratives, notably those who have migrated to France. When talking about the *hijab*, Halima (identified and quoted above) articulates the variable nature of the moral geographies that influence her behavior and mobility, and how she has considered the ways in which this flexibility might give her more freedom:

> "If [women] want to take the *hijab* off, they have to put it back on once they go back to the village because people know one another there. Once you leave the village, you can do what you want. . . . I said to myself that once I'm in France I can take off the *hijab* and even wear a miniskirt, but once you go back home, you have to respect the people of the village and their traditions. . . . For us, we say that it's shameful to do this thing or that thing, that you have to fear God. We put limits on ourselves. . . . In Rabat . . . you can find older women who don't wear the *hijab*. But back home in our village, even if you get married young, you automatically have to wear the *hijab* after getting married, whether you pray or not, in both cases you have to wear the *hijab*. If you don't do it, it's considered shameful. When you see women in Casablanca and Rabat on television, you see that they are dressed exactly the same as women here [in Montpellier]. . . . At home, I would go with my neighbors to the boule-vard [main street], we'd laugh, go to the gardens, it was good. Here, I haven't yet gone out in the streets, I just know the road between the house and the store. Back there I have the neighbors and the neighbors' daughters for company . . . I haven't yet tried to see if there's more free-dom [in France], but according to people, there's more . . . Here [women] can work, do what they want, buy what they want, not like in the village. If you need something, you have to ask someone to buy it for you, and they can accept or refuse. You can't go buy things you want by yourself."

For Halima, the shift in her sense of having to answer to her community and their norms of moral geography is not a question of being in Morocco or in France, but of being inside or outside her village, suggesting (as mentioned earlier) the importance of a certain anonymity for women's freedom that urban life can provide. She defines a stricter moral geography connected to her village of origin and a greater sense of freedom away from the village. But at the same time, ironically, her mobility is more limited in France than it was in her village because she does not have her village neighbors to accompany her and she does not speak French. In addition she lives in a close-knit Moroccan community in France where she knows many people who know her family or people in her village and who consider her like family, and this extension of the "gaze" of her village limits her mobility as well. But what is important in Halima's mind is that the gender-appropriate behavior of dressing a certain way is valid primarily in her village, where she feels most known and responsible for respecting the norms of the community. At the end of this excerpt, Halima brings up the idea of freedom as the right of a divorced woman to share in the wealth of her household, the freedom for a woman to work, and also the freedom to consume, to buy what she wants. She expresses here her frustration with having desires and entitlements that could not be fulfilled within the confines of Moroccan village life and as a divorced woman there. And more explicitly than Iman above, she mentions the freedom to be able to choose what she consumes as something she desired but did not have in the village, suggesting that, for her, consumption is a morally appropriate form of freedom that can address her sense of individual desires without significantly affronting community norms.

Another woman with whom I spoke at one of the literacy centers, Laetifa, talked about her preference for city life and brought up the issue of there being nothing to do (for leisure) in the country. Laetifa, a 35-year-old single woman, moved to Rabat with her three sisters from a rural village when she was 23 years old after her mother passed away and her father remarried. She asked, "Freedom to go where?"

> "Life in the country is monotonous. You spend your days in the same house, there's nowhere to go. If you go somewhere, to do what? But in the city, when you're bored and you put on your *djellaba*[21] to go out, no one asks you where you're going. You go out for a bit for a change of scenery. In the country, no, you stay at home. There's nowhere to go. . . . Now it's over. I have my freedom, but it's too late. What am I going to do with this freedom, you understand? You need it when you're 18 or 16 years old, you have to take advantage of it . . . go out with boys, hang out in cafés with them, [that way] you're not ashamed of them. Today, we have our freedom but at a late age. Even if we live in the city now, we got our freedom too late."

Laetifa's thoughts on freedom underline the association she makes between women's freedom and urban life, something at least partially related to her sense that there are more places to go and things to do there. Yet, now that she lives in the city, Laetifa says that she feels she is too old to take advantage of the freedom she has and is past the likely marrying age, implying that having freedom earlier in life is desirable, particularly for going out with boys and learning how to feel comfortable around them (in her words, so "you're not ashamed"). For Laetifa, life in the country did not provide her with the sort of freedom she desired, in part because of her daily responsibilities, but also because, having not been sent to school, she did not have access to the primary place where it is appropriate for girls and boys to intermingle. Further, while she is deeply unhappy about being unmarried and without children, this is not so strong that she is willing to go back to the country to live. Laetifa thus expresses her sense that having freedom in the Moroccan countryside is almost like not having it all, since it did nothing to alter the type of life she had there. One of her brothers who lives in

France has provided Laetifa and her sisters with a house in Rabat to live, however, and through this she expresses at least one type of freedom that many other women do not have: to choose whom she will or will not marry and where she will live, as she imagines a different type of life and future for herself than the one she experienced in the country.

Najia, a 30-year-old graduate student I met in France, initially left Morocco to pursue graduate studies. Unlike Halima—and the majority of unschooled Moroccan women I met in France—she was able to leave Morocco without being accompanied by a family member. This fact, along with her education level, ability to speak French fluently, and relative financial independence, enables her to experience a degree of autonomy and freedom of movement that she juxtaposes to more constrained moral geographies in Morocco. At the time of our interview, Najia had recently married a French man without her father's knowledge and was planning to move to Montreal with him.

> "I feel more independent in France. . . . I'm from a very, very traditional family. I was independent during the day, but still my father didn't come to see what I was doing during the day, because for them I was at the university. . . . But at night, well, friends wanted to go out and everything, but it wasn't possible for me. . . . It's true that at the time I needed that freedom, but when you know the risks that there are in Casa and everything, we didn't even want to take them. Go out at night, where? To go to the discos? It wasn't my thing. . . .
>
> "In Morocco I feel good, and here I feel good too. Here I can allow myself to do anything. When I say anything, I mean, dress the way I want, how I feel. Back home in Morocco, that's just not possible. Not because women there don't dress like they do here, but they go to the beach, to bourgeois neighborhoods, or whatever. But to put on a miniskirt in a working-class neighborhood, it's out of the question, it's difficult. Plus [in Morocco] my father is traditional, and I can't allow myself to wear a miniskirt in front of him because it's an insult. . . . So there are restrictions, you can't be comfortable everywhere, you always have to pay attention to what you wear."

Najia's moral geographies are temporal as well as spatial—going out at night in Morocco was not possible for her not only because her family did not allow it, but also because of the real danger involved, as well as a lack of desirable places to go. For Najia, her freedom is defined in relation to her sense of independence, notably, a certain distancing from her family. In France, she says she dresses how she pleases, partly because she does not worry about her father seeing her, partly because she implies that it feels generally safer. In Morocco, in contrast, what she and other women wear varies depending to a greater degree on the specific places they go. Interestingly, she expresses more freedom in the way one can dress in the bourgeois neighborhoods of Casablanca and the beaches, where certain "Western" or "modern" modes of dress and behavior are more common (and where more foreigners go), and so are perceived as less shocking and provocative. In making the distinction between bourgeois and working-class neighborhoods, Najia alludes to the notion of class-based definitions and modes of freedom for women that feminist scholars have discussed in other contexts. If, as Bondi (1998, p. 179) asserts, "class privilege may be a pre-condition for the 'feminization' of urban space," without the widespread economic development required for the establishment of a large middle class with surplus income, leisure time, and the corresponding activities and spaces, it is uncertain to what degree women in Morocco can normalize their presence in public spaces—even as consumers—and especially at night.

What seems clear, however, is that for Najia a certain bourgeois lifestyle and identity is associated with a particular type of mobility and freedom for women. In part, her socioeconomic and educational status, urban origin, and fluency in French enable her to easily identify with and reproduce European constructions of modern women's freedom and mobility. For this reason, there is a clear distinction in her narrative between the moral geographies regulating her mobility in France and those in Morocco. Halima, on the other hand, who "hasn't yet tried to see if there's more freedom" in France, grew up in a rural village, did not go to school, and speaks very little French or Arabic, expresses a distinction between village and city life within Morocco, but she perceives city life in Morocco and city life in France to be basically the same. Like Laetifa, it is the urbanness of Halima's life, as well as Najia's, that provides the potential at least for new forms and expressions of freedom, but certainly no guarantees. While there are significant differences between Najia, Halima, and Laetifa's experiences of freedom and mobility—due in large part to their different educational and financial situations—they are all equally aware of the different moral geographies regulating their lives and the need to modify their behavior accordingly.

FREEDOM'S FUTURES

Many Moroccan women I spoke with expressed, implicitly or explicitly, a desire to have more freedom of choice in their daily lives. But because the use of freedom discourse has always been political (see Foner, 1998), it is important to think about freedom in more critical and contextual ways. It is counterproductive to resort to simplistic oppositions between "free" and "oppressed" women, or to engage in discourse that argues for the "emancipation" or "liberation" of essentialized groups of women. As long as particular forms of cultural identity and associated freedoms are perceived as emanating from places (e.g., Western Europe and the United States) that have long treated Muslim countries and peoples with disdain, hatred, and violence, many Muslim women and men (including decision makers) will continue to embrace aspects of their cultural heritage that firmly run counter to those forms of identity and definitions of freedom.

In this chapter, by taking into consideration the changing nature of moral geographies and the role that different notions of freedom play in this process, I have explored how Moroccan women's mobility is at times facilitated and at other times constrained depending on political economic processes as well as on a woman's particular family and socioeconomic context. The notions of freedom that Moroccan women have articulated here—freedom as relational and freedom with limits—and their expression of the interconnection between freedom and moral geographies demonstrate both the multiple and contextual nature of freedom discourse, and also offer nonessentialist accounts of the subject and of place. Such accounts of freedom and moral geographies are a beginning place for understanding the complex and changing factors influencing Moroccan women's mobility and experiences of place, and for providing alternative narratives to divisive discourses on "free Western" and "oppressed Muslim" women.

ACKNOWLEDGMENTS

This chapter is based on a paper given at the annual conference of the Association of American Geographers in New Orleans in March 2003. Many thanks to Rachel Silvey for organizing the session, and to both her and Vicky Lawson for comments on a previous draft. Special thanks to Caroline Nagel for her helpful comments and extensive editing of this chapter. I am especially grateful to all of the Moroccan women who shared their stories with me. All views presented and any errors in the chapter remain my own. I gratefully acknowledge dissertation research grants from the National Science Foundation (No. BCS-0082253), Foreign Language Area Studies, and the American Institute for Maghrib Studies, and dissertation write-up support from the American Association of University Women (Educational Foundation American Fellowship).

NOTES

1. Claims that culturally specific notions of freedom do exist are often founded on culturally specific understandings of the individual or personhood. For example, both Majid (2000) and Sadiqi (2003) argue for a notion of the collective self (for Muslims and Moroccans, respectively) based on according primary importance to religious/community identity. This leads, in Majid's case, to the assertion that there exists a specific Muslim notion of freedom.
2. For example, in his editorial "Saudis in Bikinis" (*New York Times*, October 25,

2002), Nicholas Kristof embraces the project of "liberating" Muslim women. He concludes the article, based on interviews conducted with Saudi women, by saying: "I kept asking women how they felt about being repressed, and they kept answering indignantly that they aren't repressed. So what should we make of this? Is it paternalistic of us in the West to try to liberate women who insist that they're happy as they are? No, I think we're on firm ground. If most Saudi women want to wear a tent, if they don't want to drive, then that's fine. But why not give them a choice?" For similar patronizing rhetoric, see also Maureen Dowd's "Frederick's of Riyadh," *New York Times*, November 10, 2002. Hirschmann (1998) offers an insightful feminist reading of veiling that attempts to address the issue of women's free agency.

3. For example, on February 28, 2002, Diane Sawyer aired *Journey Out of Darkness* to recount her trip to Afghanistan to interview women she had met during her previous visit there in 1996; Oprah aired a show on "Women of Afghanistan" on June 27, 2002; on September 29, 2002, the *New York Times Magazine* featured a piece on Afghan girls going back to school after the U.S. invasion, "Shabana Is Late for School." Similar claims about the liberating effects for Iraqi women of the United States-led war have been made; for a critique, see, for example, the editorial on *Middle East Report, 230* (Spring 2004), "Sexuality, Suppression, and the State" (available online at *www.merip.org/mer/mer230/mer230_ editorial.html*).

4. For the early 1990s, see "Le Maroc commence à obtenir des resultats économiques encourageants," *Le Monde*, May 24, 1994, and "Its Economy Rising, Morocco Lures Investors," *New York Times*, November 11, 1993; for both 1991 and 1999 indicators, see World Bank (2001).

5. Data on remittances are from the official website of the Moroccan Office des Changes at *www.oc.gov.ma*. In June 2002, US$1 = 10.8 MDH (Moroccan dirhams).

6. "Les transferts contribuent à l'atténuation de la pauvreté," *La Gazette du Maroc*, No. 222, July 4, 2001, p. 36.

7. Since the creation of the European "Schengen Space" in 1990, visas to Europe have been even more difficult for Moroccans to obtain. Even so, according to one survey, in 2001, almost one out of every four high-school graduates in Morocco applied for a student visa to study in Europe, while 82% of high-school students said they would like to leave Morocco (Vermeren, 2002). Despite the increased difficulties that Moroccans face in France (and Europe in general), the number of illegal immigrants detained in Spain and Morocco or who have drowned attempting to cross the Strait of Gibraltar separating Morocco and Spain continues to mount. Every year an estimated 100,000 Moroccans attempt to illegally migrate (Vermeren, 2002) and between 1997 and November 2001, 3,286 Moroccans drowned attempting to do so (see "Immigration clandestine: 4000 "Harragas" morts en 5 ans," *La Vie Economique*, August 31, 2001, and "La ruée vers l'autre," *La Verité*, July 6–12, 2001).

8. Numbers vary greatly depending on data source; estimates are as high as 5–7 million Moroccans living in all foreign countries (Vermeren, 2002); France's 1999 census records the Moroccan population at 529,059, in Institut National de la Statistique et des Etudes Economiques et Ministère de l'Economie, des Finances et de l'Industrie (2003).

9. For the 1989 event, see Gaspard and Khosrokhavar (1992); for the 2003 debate, see "Ban Religious Attire in School, French Panel Says," *New York Times*, December 12, 2003, and Paul Silverstein's "Headscarves and the French Tricolor," *Middle East Report*, January 30, 2004 (available online at *www.merip. org/mero/mero013004.html*).

10. See Griffiths (1996) on the difficulties of estimating women's employment rates in Morocco.

11. For coverage of the election results, see *www.arabicnews.com*.

12. See Freeman (2004b) for a discussion. See also "Le nouveau code de la famille annoncé par S.M Mohamed VI devant le parlement," *Libération*, October 13, 2003; "Le roi, les femmes et les frères," *L'Intelligent.com* (online publication of Jeune Afrique), October 21, 2003; and "Morocco Adopts Landmark Family Law Supporting Women's Equality," available online at *www.learningpartnership. org/events/newsalerts/morocco0204.phtml#adfmdoc*.

13. While there is a small Jewish population in Morocco and there are many Jews of Moroccan descent in France, I only interviewed Muslim Moroccan women for this study. I refrain from repeatedly designating these women as "Moroccan Muslim women" since I believe that there is a tendency to point out religious belonging where Muslims are concerned, but the same is not true for other religions (see Nagel, 2001).

14. Pseudonyms are used for all women interviewed.

15. See Chapter 3 in Gokariksel (2003) for an interesting discussion of communitarianism versus individualism in the contemporary narratives of Turkish women.

16. Escobar (1995) and Laroui (2001) have noted the importance of paying attention to the way European-defined modernity imposes itself via language.

17. In addition, my status as a white, French-speaking "Western" woman certainly influenced the types of responses elicited, although it is difficult to know how exactly. I discuss at length the relevance of intersubjectivity in my research in Freeman (2004a).

18. Seventeen of the 39 women I interviewed in literacy centers in Morocco were working or had previously worked as live-in maids. The terms used in Moroccan Arabic (*kheddama*) and French (*bonne* or *petite bonne*) are both pejorative; thus, I prefer to use the English term "maid" rather than the more politically correct "domestic worker," which I believe erases some of the stigma and disrespect the women working in this position carry around with them.

19. There is obviously a difference between the articulation of beliefs and norms and actual behavior, and women's narratives need to be interpreted primarily as expressions of norms (see Davis, 1987; Ossman, 1994).

20. A prime example of such interdependence is the prevalence in urban areas of live-in maids who are recruited from rural areas. Girls are hired, sometimes at a very young age (7–10 years old), and often work long hours for low wages—usually all of which is sent back to their families. In a context where gender roles at home have remained unchanged for most Moroccan families, the need for domestic help has increased as more urban women are employed outside the home.

21. A *djellaba* is a one-piece garment that many Moroccan women wear, with or without a headscarf. Although there are many different styles and fabrics, it is often used as an easy, comfortable item to put on over whatever one happens to be wearing at home.

REFERENCES

Abu-Lughod, L. (1985/1995). A community of secrets: The separate worlds of Bedouin women. In P. A. Weiss & M. Friedman (Eds.), *Feminism and Community* (pp. 21–44). Philadelphia: Temple University Press.

Abu-Lughod, L. (1998). Introduction: Feminist longings and postcolonial conditions. In L. Abu-Lughod (Ed.), *Remaking women: Feminism and modernity in the Middle East* (pp. 3–31). Princeton, NJ: Princeton University Press.

Ahmed, L. (1994). *Women and gender in Islam.* New Haven, CT, and London: Yale University Press.

Association Démocratique des Femmes du Maroc. (2001). *Convention CEDAW: Rapport parallèle.* Rabat, Morocco: Author.

Bekkar, R. (1997). Statut social des femmes, accès à l'espace et à la parole publique. In H. Davis-Taïeb, R. Bekkar, & J.-C. David (Eds.), *Espaces publics, paroles publiques au Maghreb et au Machrek* (pp. 83–90). Lyon, France: Maison de l'Orient méditerranéen.

Belarbi, A. (1997). Réflexions préliminaries sur une approache féministe: De la dichotomie *espace public/espace privé.* In R. Bourqia (Ed.), *Etudes féminines: Notes méthodologiques* (pp. 73–82). Colloques et Séminaires, no. 73. Rabat, Morocco: Faculté des Lettres et des Sciences Humaines.

Belarbi, A. (1999). La quête et la conquête d'un espace de vie: Contraintes et opportunités pour les femmes migrantes. In A. Belarbi (Ed.), *Initiatives féminines* (pp. 63–75). Collection Approches. Casablanca, Morocco: Editions Le Fennec.

Bennani-Chraïbi, M. (1995). *Soumis et rebelles: Les jeunes au Maroc.* Casablanca, Morocco: Editions Le Fennec.

Benzakour Chami, A. (1999). Femmes et dynamiques innovantes. In A. Belarbi (Ed.), *Initiatives féminines* (pp. 13–29). Casablanca, Morocco: Editions Le Fennec.

Bloom, L. (1999). *Under the sign of hope: Feminist methodology and narrative interpretation.* Albany: State University of New York Press.

Bondi, L. (1998). Gender, class and urban space: Public and private space in contemporary urban landscapes. *Urban Geography, 19*(2), 160–185.

Bondi, L., & Domosh, M. (1998). On the contours of public space: A tale of three women. *Antipode, 30*(3), 270–289.

Boukous, A., & Agnaou, F. (2001). *Alphabétisation et développement durable au Maroc.* Essais et études no. 28. Rabat, Morocco: Faculté des Lettres et des Sciences Humaines.

Bourqia, R. (1996). Habitat, femmes et honneur: Le cas de quelques quartiers populaires d'Oujda. In R. Bourqia, M. Charrad, & N. Gallagher (Eds.), *Femmes, culture et société au Maghreb* (Vol. 1, pp. 15–35). Casablanca, Morocco: Afrique Orient.

Boyle, P., & Halfacree, K. (Eds.). (1999). *Migration and gender in the developed world.* London and New York: Routledge.

Centre d'Etudes et de Recherches Démographiques. (1996). *Migration Internationle.* Actes du séminaire. Rabat, Morocco: Author.

Centre d'Etudes et de Recherches Démographiques. (1998). *Genre et développement: Aspects socio-démographiques et culturels de la différenciation sexuelle.* Rabat, Morocco: Author.

Chakrabarty, D. (1992). Postcoloniality and the artifice of history: Who speaks for "Indian" pasts? *Representations, 37*(4), 1–26.

Chakrabarty, D. (1997). The difference—Deferral of a colonial modernity. In F. Cooper & A. Stoler (Eds.), *Tensions of empire: Colonial cultures in a bourgeois world* (pp. 373–405). Berkeley and Los Angeles: University of California Press.

Collectif 95 Maghreb Egalité. (1998). *Violations flagrantes des droits et violences à l'égard des femmes au Maghreb* (Rapport annuel, 1996–1997). Rabat, Morocco: Friedrich Ebert Stiftung.

Collier, J. (1995). Intertwined histories: Islamic law and Western imperialism. *Stanford Humanities Review, 5*(1), 152–164.

Cresswell, T. (1999). Embodiment, power and the politics of mobility: The case of female tramps and hobos. *Transactions, Institute of British Geographers, 24*(2), 175–192.

Davis, S. (1983). *Patience and power: Women's lives in a Moroccan village.* Cambridge, MA: Schenkman.

Davis, S. (1987). Changing gender relations in a Moroccan town. In L. Beck & N. Keddie (Eds.), *Women in the Muslim world* (pp. 208–223). Cambridge, MA: Harvard University Press.

Davis-Taïeb, H. (1998). "Là où vont les femmes": Notes sur les femmes, les cafés, et les fast-foods au Maroc. In S. Ossman (Ed.), *Miroirs maghrébins: Itinéraires de soi et paysages de rencontre* (pp. 217–225). Paris: CNRS Editions.

Direction de la Statistique. (1996). *Annuaire statistique du Maroc, 1996.* Rabat, Morocco: Royaume du Maroc, Ministère Chargé de la Population.

Domosh, M. (1997). With "stout boots and a stout heart": Historical methodology and feminist geography. In J. P. Jones III, H. J. Nast, & S. M. Roberts (Eds.), *Thresholds in feminist geography* (pp. 225–237). Lanham, NY, Boulder, CO, and Oxford, UK: Rowman & Littlefield.

Domosh, M. (2001). The "Women of New York": A fashionable moral geography. *Environment and Planning D: Society and Space, 19,* 573–592.

Dwyer, C. (1999). Contradictions of community: Questions of identity for young British Muslim women. *Environment and Planning A, 31*(1), 53–68.

Dwyer, C. (2000). Negotiating diasporic identities: Young British South Asian Muslim women. *Women's Studies International Forum, 23*(4), 475–486.

El Harras, M. (1996). Féminité et masculinité dans la société rurale marocaine: Le cas d'Anjra. In R. Bourqia, M. Charrad & N. Gallagher (Eds.), *Femmes, culture et société au Maghreb* (Vol. 1, pp. 37–56). Casablanca, Morocco: Afrique Orient.

Escobar, A. (1995). *Encountering development: The making and unmaking of the third world.* Princeton, NJ: Princeton University Press.

Foner, E. (1998). *The story of American freedom.* New York and London: W. W. Norton.

Foner, E. (2003, April 13). Not all freedom is made in America. *New York Times,* section 4, p. 2.

Freeman, A. (2004a). *Contingent modernity: Moroccan women's narratives in "post" colonial perspective.* Unpublished doctoral dissertation, Department of Geography, University of Washington.

Freeman, A. (2004b). Re-locating Moroccan women's identities in a transnational world: The "woman question" in question. *Gender, Place, and Culture, 11*(1), 17–41.

Gaspard, F., & Khosrokhavar, F. (1992). *Le Foulard et la République*. Paris: La Découverte.

Gokariksel, B. P. (2003). *Situated modernities: Geographies of identity, urban space and globalization*. Unpublished doctoral dissertation, Department of Geography, University of Washington.

Göle, N. (1997). The gendered nature of the public sphere. *Public Culture, 10*(1), 61–81.

Goss, J., & Lindquist, B. (1995). Conceptualizing international labor migration: A structuration perspective. *International Migration Review, 29*(2), 317–351.

Griffiths, C. (1996). Social development and women in Africa: The case of Morocco. *Journal of Gender Studies, 5*(1), 63–79.

Guénif Souilamas, N. (2000). *Des "beurettes" aux descendants d'immigrants nord-africains*. Paris: Grasset.

Hadraoui, T. (1988). Ces petites qui travaillent pour vous. *Kalima, 30*, 16–19.

Hirschmann, N. J. (1996). Revisioning freedom: Relationship, context, and the politics of empowerment. In N. J. Hirschmann & C. Di Stefano (Eds.), *Revisioning the political: Feminist reconstructions of traditional concepts in Western political theory* (pp. 51–74). Boulder, CO, and Oxford, UK: Westview Press.

Hirschmann, N. J. (1998). Western feminism, Eastern veiling and the question of free agency. *Constellations, 5*(30), 345–368.

Hirschmann, N. J. (2002). Toward a feminist theory of freedom. In C. L. Mui & J. S. Murphy (Eds.), *Gender struggles: Practical approaches to contemporary feminism* (pp. 47–68). Lanham, MD, Boulder, CO, New York, and Oxford, UK: Rowman & Littlefield.

House, J. (1995). The "space" for Muslim identities in modern and contemporary France. In S. Taji-Farouki (Ed.), *Muslim communities in France* (Occasional Paper No. 51, pp. 7–25). Durham, UK: University of Durham.

Hubbard, P. (1998). Sexuality, immorality and the city: Red-light districts and the marginalisation of street prostitutes. *Gender, Place and Culture, 5*(1), 55–72.

Institut National de la Statistique et des Etudes Economiques et Ministère de l'Economie, des Finances et de l'Industrie. (2003). *Annuaire statistique de la France*, (Vol. 106), Paris: Author.

Joseph, S. (1997). The public/private. The imagined boundary in the imagined nation/state/community, The Lebanese case. *Feminist Review, 57*, 73–92.

Kandiyoti, D. (1994). Identity and its discontents: Women and the nation. In P. Williams & L. Chrisman (Eds.), *Colonial discourse and post-colonial theory: A reader* (pp. 376–391). New York: Columbia University Press.

Kapchan, D. (1996). *Gender on the market*. Philadelphia: University of Pennsylvania Press.

Kofman, E., Phizacklea, A., Raghuram, P., & Sales, R. (2000). *Gender and international migration in Europe: Employment, welfare and politics*. London and New York: Routledge.

Laroui, A. (2001). *Islam et modernité*. Casablanca, Morocco: Centre Culturel Arabe.

Laws, G. (1997). Women's life courses, spatial mobility, and state policies. In J. P. Jones III, H. J. Nast, & S. M. Roberts (Eds.), *Thresholds in feminist geography* (pp. 47–64). Lanham, MD, New York, Boulder, CO, Oxford, UK: Rowman & Littlefield.

Lawson, V. A. (2000a). Questions of migration and belonging: Understandings of migration under neoliberalism in Ecuador. *International Journal of Population Geography*, 5, 261–276.

Lawson, V. A. (2000b). Arguments within geographies of movement: The theoretical potential of migrants' stories. *Progress in Human Geography*, 24(2), 173–189.

Louca, A. (1970). *Voyageurs et écrivains égyptiens en France au XIXè siècle*. Paris: Didier.

Maher, V. (1974). *Women and property in Morocco*. London: Cambridge University Press.

Majid, A. (2000). *Unveiling traditions: Postcolonial Islam in a polycentric world*. Durham, NC, and London: Duke University Press.

Massey, D. (1994). *Space, place and gender*. Minneapolis: University of Minnesota Press.

McDowell, L. (1999). *Gender, Identity and Place: Understanding feminist geographies*. Minneapolis: University of Minnesota Press.

McMillan, J. F. (2000). *France and women, 1789–1914: Gender, society and politics*. London and New York: Routledge.

Mernissi, F. (1987). *Beyond the veil: Male–female dynamics in modern Muslim society*. Bloomington and Indianapolis: Indiana University Press.

Mills, M. B. (1999). *Thai women in the global labor force: Consuming desires, contested selves*. New Brunswick, NJ, and London: Rutgers University Press.

Ministry of Foreign Affairs and Cooperation. (1996). *Socioeconomic Indicators on Moroccan women's integration in development*. Rabat, Morocco: Directorate of Multilateral Cooperation.

Moghadam, V. (1998). *Women, work, and economic reform in the Middle East and North Africa*. Boulder, CO, and London: Lynne Rienner.

Mohammad, R. (1999). Marginalisation, Islamism and the production of the "other's" "other." *Gender, Place and Culture*, 6(3), 221–240.

Naamane-Guessous, S. (1997). *Au-delà de toute pudeur*. Casablanca, Morocco: Editions Eddif.

Naciri, R., & Barkallil, N. (1989). Les femmes au Maroc ou les contradictions d'une évolution récente. *Corps Ecrit*, 31, 153–162.

Nagar, R. (1997). Exploring methodological borderlands through oral narratives. In J. P. Jones III, H. J. Nast, & S. M. Roberts (Eds.), *Thresholds in feminist geography* (pp. 203–224). Lanham, MD, New York, Boulder, CO, and Oxford, UK: Rowman & Littlefield.

Nagar, R. (1998). Communal discourses, marriage and the politics of gendered social boundaries among South Asian immigrants in Tanzania. *Gender, Place and Culture*, 5(2), 117–139.

Nagel, C. (2001). Contemporary scholarship and the demystification—and re-mystification—of "Muslim women," *Arab World Geographer*, 4(1), 63–72.

Ogden, P. (1991). Immigration to France since 1945: Myth and reality. *Ethnic and Racial Studies*, 14(3), 294–318.

Ong, A. (1995). State versus Islam: Malay families, women's bodies, and the body politic in Malaysia. In A. Ong & M. Peletz (Eds.), *Bewitching women, pious men: Gender and body politics in Southeast Asia* (pp. 159–194). Berkeley, Los Angeles, and London: University of California Press.

Ong, A., & Peletz, M. (1995). Introduction. In A. Ong & M. Peletz (Eds.), *Bewitching women, pious men: Gender and body politics in Southeast Asia* (pp. 1–18). Berkeley, Los Angeles, and London: University of California Press.

Ossman, S. (1994). *Picturing Casablanca: Portraits of power in a modern city.* Berkeley, Los Angeles, and London: University of California Press.

Ossman, S. (1998). Savoir se montrer: Modèles, modes et salons de coiffure à Casablanca. In S. Ossman (Ed.), *Miroirs maghrébins: Itinéraires de soi et paysages de rencontre* (pp. 227–239). Paris: CNRS Editions.

Pratt, M. L. (2002). Modernity and periphery: Toward a global and relational analysis. In E. Mudimbe-Boyi (Ed.), *Beyond dichotomies: Histories, identities, cultures, and the challenge of globalization* (pp. 21–47). Albany: State University of New York Press.

Radcliffe, S. (1990). Ethnicity, patriarchy and incorporation into the nation: Female migrants as domestic servants in Peru. *Environment and Planning D: Society and Space, 8,* 379–393.

Rose, G. (1993). *Feminism and geography.* Cambridge, UK: Polity Press.

Ruggerini, M. G. (1997). Expérience et vécu au féminin entre tradition et modernité. In *Droits de citoyenneté des femmes au Maghreb* (pp. 225–247). Casablanca, Morocco: Le Fennec.

Sadiqi, F. (2003). *Women, gender and language in Morocco.* Leiden, The Netherlands, and Boston: Brill.

Schaeffer, F. (1999) *Champ. réseau et circulation migratoires: Articulation de ces trois notions à travers l'étude de la migration marocaine. L'exemple de la communauté marocaine de Strasbourg.* Poitiers, France: Université de Poitiers, Département de géographie.

Secor, A. (2002). The veil and urban space in Istanbul: Women's dress, mobility and Islamic knowledge. *Gender, Place and Culture, 9*(1), 5–22.

Silvey, R. (2000a). Stigmatized spaces: Gender and mobility under crisis in South Sulawesi, Indonesia. *Gender, Place and Culture, 7*(2), 143–161.

Silvey, R. (2000b). Diasporic subjects: Gender and mobility in South Sulawesi. *Women's Studies International Forum, 23*(4), 501–515.

Silvey, R. (2004). Power, difference, and mobility: Feminist advances in migration studies. *Progress in Human Geography, 28*(4), 490–506.

Silvey, R., & Lawson, V. (1999). Placing the migrant. *Annals of the Association of American Geographers, 89*(1), 121–132.

Smith, S. (1993). *Subjectivity, identity, and the body: Women's autobiographical practices in the twentieth century.* Bloomington and Indianapolis: Indiana University Press.

Staeheli, L. (1996). Publicity, privacy, and women's political action. *Environment and Planning D: Society and Space, 14,* 601–619.

Tavakoli-Targhi, M. (1994). Women of the West imagined: The *farangi* other and the emergence of the woman question in Iran. In V. Moghadam (Ed.), *Identity, Politics and Women* (pp. 98–120). Boulder, CO, and Oxford, UK: Westview Press.

Temsamani Haji, T. (1997). Analyse socio-économique de la condition de la femme au Maroc. In *Droits de citoyenneté des femmes au Maghreb* (pp. 77–92). Casablanca, Morocco: Editions Le Fennec.

Tribalat, M. (1997). Chronique de l'immigration. *Population, 1,* 163–220.

Valentine, G. (1989). The geography of women's fear. *Area, 21,* 385–390.

Valentine, G. (1992). Images of danger: Women's sources of information about the spatial distribution of male violence. *Area, 24,* 22–29.

Vermeren, P. (2002, June). En guise d'avenir, l'exil: Les marocains rêvent d'Europe. *Le Monde Diplomatique,* pp. 1, 16–17.

Waterbury, J. (1970). *The commander of the faithful: The Moroccan political elite—A study in segmented politics.* New York: Columbia University Press.

Wilson, E. (1991). *The sphinx in the city.* London: Virago.

World Bank. (2001). *Morocco, country assistance strategy, 2001–2004.* Available online at *wbln0018.worldbank.org/mna/mena.nsf/attachments/CAS+2001.1/ $File/22115-1.pdf*

Yeğenoğlu, M. (1996). *Colonial fantasies: Towards a feminist reading of orientalism.* Cambridge, UK: Cambridge University Press.

Yeoh, B., & Huang, S. (1998). Negotiating public space: Strategies and styles of migrant female domestic workers in Singapore. *Urban Studies, 35*(3), 583–602.

Young, C. (2002). Itineraries of ideas of freedom in Africa: Precolonial to postcolonial. In R. Taylor (Ed.), *The idea of freedom in Asia and Africa* (pp. 9–39). Stanford, CA: Stanford University Press.

Young, I. M. (1986/1995). The ideal of community and the politics of difference. In P. A. Weiss & M. Friedman (Eds.), *Feminism and community* (pp. 233–258). Philadelphia: Temple University Press.

Young, I. M. (1997). *Intersecting voices: Dilemmas of gender, political philosophy, and policy.* Princeton, NJ: Princeton University Press.

Yuval-Davis, N. (1997). *Gender and nation.* London, Thousand Oaks, CA, and New Delhi, India: Sage.

7 Negotiating Spaces of the Home, the Education System, and the Labor Market

The Case of Young, Working-Class, British Pakistani Muslim Women

ROBINA MOHAMMAD

Different forms of nationalism draw on and reinforce very different ideas of womanhood (Yuval-Davis, 1997). A common feature of right-wing nationalist discourses is the centrality of women to the collective identity. The burden of bearing this collective identity is demanding. Women are called on to perform the ideal of womanhood that marks the collectivity, which in turn circumscribes their experiences and access to social and economic advancement.

As Graham (1995) notes, collective responses to political and socioeconomic instability and/or marginalization tend toward a reactionary retreat into "tradition" that has implications for the position of women and the performance of womanhood. Discourses that promote a "return to tradition," often to recover a mythical golden age, may be underpinned by regressive, radically conservative interpretations of religious ideologies, as, for example, in the *Franquista* project (1939–1975) in early 20th-century Spain. General Franco's coup in 1936, a reactionary response to the social instability generated by the progressive reforms of the secular, democratic, Republican regime, was supported by the Catholic Church. General Franco's governance drew on and formulated a nationalist form of Catholicism that emphasized the hierarchically organized Catholic family as a foundation of the nation. The centrality of the Catholic family and women's role within it as mothers and wives was a significant (but not the only) factor in circumscribing women's experiences and opportunities in Spanish society during the *Franquista* period. In a contemporary example, radical, right-wing Hindu nationalism (termed *Hindutva*) is on the rise in the "new India" that is emerging with economic and social changes unleashed by economic liberalization. *Hindutva* ideology prioritizes the Hindu family as the basis of the Indian nation, promoting a vision of womanhood that foregrounds their role within the family.

Regressive nationalisms that draw on Islamist ideologies can be understood as a response to Western imperialisms and the failure of Western modernity to deliver progress. Islam acts as a sign around which alternative modernities can be forged. These modernities are marked by culturally specific and radically conservative interpretations of Islam that, as with the discourses of National Catholicism and Hindu nationalism, place stress on the family (Taraki, 1995) and the role of women as mothers of the collectivity (see Afshar, 1988, for the case of revolutionary Iran, and O'Kane, 1997, for the case of the Taliban's Afghanistan; for post-Zia Pakistan, see Mumtaz & Shaheed, 1987, and Chenoy, 2002).

In this chapter I situate working-class, British, Pakistani Muslim women within the context of a global decline of secularism and reassertion of right-wing religious—in this case Islamist[1]—ideologies to offer at least a partial explanation of their continued social and economic marginality in Britain. Drawing on data from an empirical study conducted in Reading, UK, I highlight how Pakistani communities in Britain retain and continuously renew links with a simultaneously real and imaginary homeland through economic interests as well as social and kinship networks strengthened by marriage. Thus the ideals of womanhood promoted by right-wing forces in post-Zia Pakistan travel through these networks to influence, albeit unevenly, working-class Pakistani communities in Britain. These ideals, as I have noted, emphasize women's place within, and relationship to, the Islamic family, which is perceived within British working-class Pakistani communities to be under threat from Western values, a threat whose confirmation is found in the high divorce rates in the West (e.g., Sarwar, 1980).

A twin approach is utilized to ensure that women conform to this ideal. First, there is an emphasis on the socialization of children and the transmission of values to future generations (which, in itself, stresses the significance of the mothering role) that promote self-regulation. Second, a regulatory framework involving parents and the local Pakistani community is put in place to ensure that women comply. Parental regulations supported by community surveillance seek to control and limit women's access to particular spaces and times that may be perceived as a threat to the Islamic family. The constraints imposed on women are by no means imposed

in a uniform way and, in fact, are negotiable to varying extents. The degree
of constraint also appears to be dependent on the socioeconomic status of
the family and, within this, the level of parental education: the higher the
level of parental education, the greater the possibilities for negotiating parental constraints. It is also important to bear in mind that constraints are
not imposed on inactive, passive objects, but on subjects who are always in
the process of becoming. These women, whose subjectivities are produced
across a matrix of discourses—Western liberal, secular, consumerist, as well
as Islamist—may not respond to parental and/or community regulation in
accordance with expectations. They may comply with, reject, negotiate, or
reinterpret the ideals required of them. The discussion that follows highlights working-class British Pakistani women's struggles to perform ideals
of Pakistani Muslim womanhood, to participate in post-16 education, and
to have access to opportunities not just for paid work but to aspire to a
range of careers beyond the professions. In the next section I discuss the
history of Pakistanis in Britain and their ongoing relationship to the homeland that supports the concern for and maintenance of a Pakistani Muslim
identity in Britain.

IN THE GRIP OF THE HOMELAND:
PAKISTANI MUSLIMS IN BRITAIN

The women interviewed for this study are from families who originate in
the region of Mirpur in Pakistan. Migration to Britain from the South
Asian subcontinent was facilitated initially by the existence of colonial
ties, which allowed Indians and Pakistanis to cross political boundaries
with relative ease. Mirpuris in particular constituted a large percentage of
recruits for the British Army and Navy, opening up the possibility of settlement in Britain. Thus, early migrants from this region in the period
immediately prior to and after World War II were primarily seamen settlers. The majority of other early migrants were from the professional
classes. These settlers, in turn, opened up the possibilities of migration
for other Pakistanis as they became the first link in a process of chain migration. Subsequent migrants, however, were largely from working-class
rural origins.

Push-and-Pull Factors

Anwar (1979) notes three main "push" factors influencing outward migration: the partition of the subcontinent in 1947; the construction of the
Mangla Dam in Mirpur in the early 1960s, which displaced a large percentage of the population and which amplified the chain migration opened up
by early settlers; and the low productivity of agricultural lands in Mirpur,

which encouraged young men in the region to seek livelihoods elsewhere (Anwar, 1979).

At the same time, the availability of work and British policies for the recruitment of cheap labor provided significant "pull" factors. In the pre-1960 period, the Pakistani government, like the Indian government, had placed stringent controls on intercontinental travel, which kept outward migration to a minimum. But in 1960 the Indian Supreme Court ruled that it was unconstitutional for the Indian government to deny passports to Indian nationals, leading to the relaxation of these restrictions and promoting parallel developments in Pakistan. At the same time, immigration restrictions imposed by the British government in the 1962 Commonwealth Immigrants Act led, ironically, to an acceleration of immigration from South Asia as those already in Britain sought to make their living arrangements more permanent and to "beat the ban" by bringing in family members (Hiro, 1991).

The majority of Pakistani arrivals in the early 1960s had been males who saw their residence in Britain purely as a means of making money. Their stay in Britain was seen as a temporary sojourn away from home. But the imposition of restrictions beginning with the 1962 Commonwealth Immigrants Act changed this attitude and forced a reconsideration of the nature of their presence in Britain. The arrival of wives and children to join husbands and fathers in Britain led to the beginnings of "communities" among Pakistanis (Hiro, 1991), most notably in Manchester (northwest), Bradford (Yorkshire and Humberside), Birmingham (West Midlands), and London (see Table 7.1).

Marginality and the Grip of the Homeland

Pakistani settlement in Britain has not, as one might expect, resulted in a detachment from or loss of connections with the homeland; nor has it diminished the sense of being Pakistani and Pakistani Muslims. Rather, the links between the homeland are continuously renewed, facilitated by transportation and technological developments, and reinforced through marriage. Ballard (1991) noted over a decade ago that as the second generation of Pakistanis was coming of age, the trickle of young women and men arriving in Britain as brides or bridegrooms of young British Pakistanis was rising again. Aziz al Azmeh (1993) has also remarked on the practice of British Pakistanis seeking conservative ("traditional") young women from rural regions as brides for their British-born sons. At the same time, as many of my respondents highlighted from their personal experience (see Mohammad, in press) and the experiences of their friends and relatives, some British Pakistani women continue to be encouraged or even to be coerced to marry men from Pakistan.[2]

As Ang (1993, p. 40) argues, this concern with homeland religiocul-

TABLE 7.1. Regional distribution of Pakistanis in the
United Kingdom

Region	Percentage
Northeast	1.88
Northwest	15.16
Yorkshire and Humberside	19.58
East Midlands	3.72
West Midlands	20.68
East	5.19
London	19.10
Southeast	7.83
Southwest	0.90
Wales	1.11
Scotland	4.25
Northern Ireland	0.09

Total population of British Pakistanis: 747,285

Note: U.K. Census 2001, Office of National Statistics (2004b).

ture and the "identification with an imagined 'where you are from' is . . .
often a sign of, and surrender to, a condition of actual marginalization in
the place 'where you're at.' "[3] This "semi-industrialised, newly urbanised,
working class community that is only one generation away from rural peas-
antry" (Modood, 1992, p. 261) is so economically and socially marginalized in British society (as I explain in greater detail below) that it may be
referred to as an "underclass." It is in this context that the family becomes
significant. As Taraki (1995, p. 645) has highlighted, "Radical Islam . . .
created an area of [Muslim] cultural resistance around women and the family which came to represent the inviolable repository of Muslim identity."
Thus the family offers working-class British Pakistanis both a refuge from
marginalization and a means of resistance, through the marking and maintenance of a Pakistani Muslim identity that centers on women.

Marginalization, Collective Identity, and Womanhood

Kandiyoti (1993, p. 376) argues that women often find themselves the
"privileged signifiers of difference." As mothers they bear the responsibility
for the reproduction of the collectivity not only in physical terms, but also
in ideological terms through the transmission of culture to future generations. As the guardians of collective identity, women are guarded and their
bodies ordered in space and time (Afshar, 1994). Their bodily presence and
visibility in spaces defined as masculine become subject to varying but strict

regulations. Thus, in the Pakistani context,[4] the process of Islamization proceeded, in part, through the regulation of women's bodies, as did the Islamization of Iran following the revolution in 1979 and the Talibanization of Afghanistan during the 1990s. Women's bodies are made central to the construction, maintenance, and performance of a collective identity. Such rigidly constructed and imposed gender divisions mark the domestic place of the home and family as distinct from the public sphere that lies beyond these. Women's roles as mothers of the collective naturalize their place within the home and family and make marriage discursively and in practice a key marker that shapes the trajectory of their lives. Their (future) marriage mediates their place within the natal family as well as the family of future in-laws.

Women's (hetero)sexual purity[5] is represented as key to marriage and the formation of Muslim families. At the same time, women's bodies are perceived to exude sexuality that is seen to entice and distract men, thereby threatening their (hetero)sexual purity (Afshar, 1988; Mernissi, 1975). Women are scripted as "naturally" sexually provocative, hence their association with *fitna* (chaos) in Islamic society (Badran, 1995; Mernissi, 1975). Women must be kept separate from unrelated men by restricting them to domestic spaces within the confines of the family. If they do enter public, masculine space, then they must ensure that their sexuality is firmly contained through coverage of head and body. Hair is regarded as being as sexually enticing as the body. It forms part of what the Qur'an refers to as women's "ornaments" that they must hide from the gaze of unrelated men. Thus, prior to venturing out, they must cover their hair and hide the contours of their body by creating a private space around the body, thus desexualizing it.

Veiling, or *purdah*, can take a variety of forms (including the *chador* and the *burqa*), but often involves a total coverage of the body, including the face.[6] When veiling[7] is an imposition rather than a free choice,[8] it can be experienced as a cumbersome and disabling confinement (Mumtaz & Shaheed, 1987).

The fixation on women's (hetero)sexual purity and its impact on women's spatial mobility may become especially significant in the diasporic context, as evidenced by the case of working-class Pakistani Muslims. Yuval-Davies (1997) notes that in situations in which individual men and collectivities feel threatened by "others," the regulation of women is intensified. Saifullah Khan's (1982) study of Bangladeshi women in Bradford, England, for example, found that the practice of *purdah* was more extreme and rigid there than in Bangladesh. As noted earlier, working-class British Pakistanis respond to racialized and class-based marginalization, as well as to the traumas of dislocation and resettlement in a new and often hostile world, by seeking a refuge in collective identity. As bearers of this identity, women become subject to tighter regulations that are similar to those imposed on women in the homeland but also differ as they are adapted to the particular requirements of the diasporic context (see Mohammad, 1999).

METHODOLOGY

The data for this chapter are drawn from a 1995 study undertaken in Reading, England, investigating the barriers to Pakistani women's participation in the labor market (see Bowlby, Lloyd-Evans, & Mohammad, 1997). The project was funded by the Reading Borough Council in conjunction with the Pakistani Community Centre.

Socioeconomic Profile of British Pakistanis

A glance at the socioeconomic profile of Pakistanis across the United Kingdom confirms their marginal status among ethnic minority groups. Data for levels of educational attainment at the age of 16 suggest that out of all ethnic groups, Pakistanis achieve the fewest GCSE[9] grades A through C, with the exception of black Caribbean and "other black" groups. In all ethnic groups girls did better than boys (see Figure 7.1). With the exception of

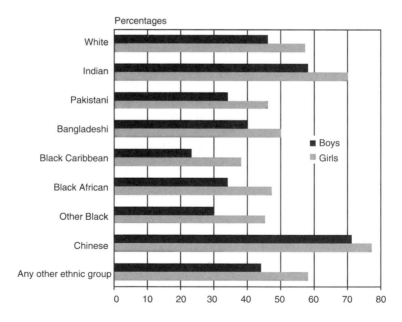

FIGURE 7.1. Educational attainment at 16 by ethnic group and sex, 2002. Source: National Pupil Database, Department for Education and Skills (2002).

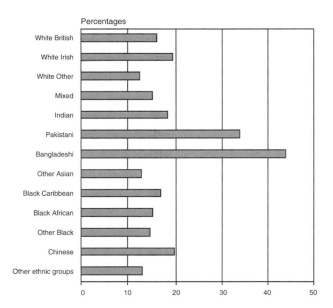

FIGURE 7.2. People of working age with no qualifications, by ethnic group, shown as a proportion of the total working-age population (males ages 16–64, females ages 16–59), 2001–2002. Source: Annual Local Area Labour Force Survey 2001–2002, Office for National Statistics (2004a).

Bangladeshis, Pakistanis are most likely to leave school with no formal qualifications (see Figure 7.2).

Figure 7.3 shows that, with the exception of Bangladeshis, Pakistanis in Britain have the highest unemployment rate of all ethnic groups, with female unemployment being slightly higher than that for males. Economic inactivity rates are, again with the exception of Bangladeshis, the highest for Pakistanis. Those for Pakistani women, standing at 72%, are far higher than for Pakistani men at 28% (see Figure 7.4), though it is important to remember that this only records economic activity in the formal labor market, while many Pakistani women engage in the informal economy to generate income (see Brah, 1996). It is notable, however, that Pakistani women have a rate of entry into the professions which, at 11%, is higher than that for British white women, although it is lagging in comparison with "other white," Indian, and Chinese women (at 21, 16, and 15%, respectively). Pakistani women's entry into professional occupations is considerably higher than that for Pakistani men, which, at 9%, is among the lowest of all the ethnic groups. This reveals Pakistani women's preference for professional occupations, which is encouraged and supported by their parents, as I discuss below.

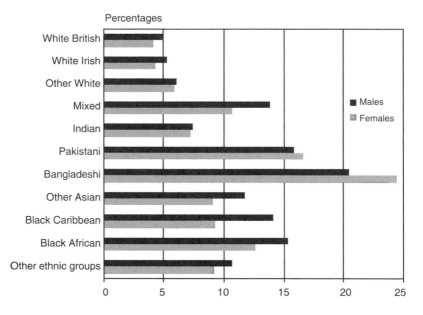

FIGURE 7.3. Unemployment rates by ethnic group, 2001–2002. Source: Office of National Statistics Office (2004d).

The Study

The empirical study was carried out using semistructured, in-depth interviews with 25 women between 15 and 30 years of age. Respondents were recruited through local schools and contacts within the Pakistani community using the snowball method. The areas covered by the questionnaire were as follows: school experiences (including subjects taken at GCSE and A-level,[10] level and form of participation in extracurricular activities, relationship to teachers, and access to career advice); labor market participation (including work experience, training, access to transportation, and employment held at the time of the interview); labor market expectations (including future career plans, preferences for full-time or part-time employment, wage expectations, and ideas about "good" and "bad" jobs); and finally, home and family (including the family's length of time in Britain and parents' occupations and education levels). The questionnaire presumed that the respondents had free choice in making key decisions about their lives, but as one 15-year-old girl remarked in response to the question "Would you like to be in paid work?," "Asking this of people with no control over their lives is stupid."

Twenty of the respondents were between 15 and 19 years of age. Two respondents were 20, and three were 25 and above. Of the 20 respondents ages 15–19, all but two (both 16-year-olds) were students. The majority of

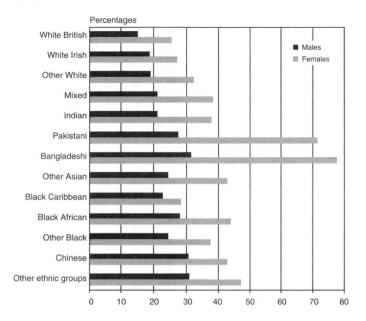

FIGURE 7.4. Economic inactivity rates for people of working age, by ethnic group and sex, 2001–2002. Source: Office of National Statistics (2004c).

the respondents over age 15 had achieved at least six GCSEs on completion of a 2-year course of study. Of those in post-16 education, five were studying for vocational qualifications (or NVQs[11]), and six were either studying for or had achieved three A-levels. Only three respondents, Zara, Reena, and Tara, had attended or were attending college. For these women, the path from school to university was neither smooth nor direct, and the issue of space–time constraints dominated all the interviews.

Only three respondents at the time of interview were in paid work: Selina (age 20), Sharon (age 20), and Nina (age 25). Selina had held a variety of jobs and was working on the shop floor of a major supermarket. Sharon was working on the shop floor of a department store. Nina, who took a Youth Training Scheme (YTS) placement after leaving school, worked as an administrator and had changed to part-time work after having a baby.

The main concern of the majority of young women interviewed was negotiating parental permission to access post-16 education (including university) and/or entry to the labor market. Few felt that they were in a position to think more concretely about the direction they were taking and where they wanted to be in terms of future careers. It is important to note that the questions of space–time constraints that I discuss below do not relate simply to social marginality, but to interlocking multiple exclusions, and that there is a considerable variation in the imposition and negotiation of constraints even among this small, relatively homogenous group. It is also notable that women who were higher academic achievers were those whose parents had higher levels of education. Parents with a higher level of education were also less restrictive of daughters. It appeared that those parents with the lowest levels of education did not prioritize the education of their daughters, and that they, moreover, seemed to view education as an obstacle to their daughters' true vocation in life: the formation of a Muslim family through marriage and the roles of wife and mother.

OBSTACLES TO EDUCATION

"Pakistani girls and women have a lot to offer. Unfortunately, we are denied our right to go further and to pursue our goals, dreams, and ambitions. Our families are still living in the dark ages, and instead of encouraging . . . us to blossom, attempt to stifle any growth they feel threatens their control over us and place unjustified obstacles in our paths to keep us isolated and trapped." (—SEEMA, age 25)

Women's educational trajectories are directed by the concerns relating to collective identity in four related ways. First, the centrality of the family to processes of collective identity construction and maintenance means that in the diaspora, as in the homeland, Pakistani Muslims, particularly those who are working class and of rural origin, place a stress on marriage when considering the future for Pakistani Muslim women. Second, the importance of marriage raises concerns for women's (hetero)sexual purity, which leads to restrictions on women's spatial mobility that indirectly undermine women's access to education. Third, for some parents education is viewed as loosening familial control over women by encouraging independent thought and by enabling social mobility and assimilation into wider, white society, which is seen to undermine the very foundations of collective identity. Fourth, even when parents are not concerned with the influence of education per se, they may prohibit their daughters from continuing in education when it comes into conflict with parental marriage plans.

Often, women are prepared for their roles as wives and mothers from birth. Farah, age 16, whose engagement for marriage was decided by her parents upon birth, comments, "Women are sold at an early age." Another respondent, 17-year-old Layla, declares: "Marriage is something that I feel is emphasized too much in our religion. Everybody has to get married. I am not against people getting married as long as they want to." Farah and another respondent, Zubia, left the education system at age 16, that is, at the earliest opportunity. They are both engaged to be married and have not been permitted by their parents either to continue in education or to enter the labor market. They are to "sit at home" until marriage. After marriage, as Farah, who is betrothed to her paternal cousin, explains, "They expect you to cook and clean, no chance to work outside the home." Undertaking housework is part of the training of daughters. As a respondent in Afshar's study (1994, p. 135) pointed out, "We have to teach our children two separate sorts of things; one is about cooking and cleaning and things like that." My respondent Sabia confirms this reality when she argues that "teachers, especially males, should be more understanding toward the difficulties we have to face at home. We have to do housework, which affects the time we have left to do other work."

Thus an emphasis on marriage means that women's formal education cannot be allowed to undermine the important skills they need to develop for their roles as wives and mothers. Neither the participation in post-16 formal education nor participation in the formal labor market can be taken for granted as a choice to be exercised by women. The idea of marriage stresses that daughters are *paraya dhan*—that is, they are a form of wealth that belongs not to their parents, but rather to their future in-laws. This means, as Sheena's father reminds her, that the decision for her to pursue a career after marriage is in the hands of her future husband and in-laws.

The importance of women's (hetero)sexual purity, both real and imagined (being seen as [hetero]sexually pure is as important as actually maintaining purity) means that women's access to spaces perceived to be threatening to (hetero)sexual purity is regulated and limited, thus affecting women's participation in the education system and the labor market. In the diasporic context, as in the homeland, public space is coded as masculine. But in Britain, public space is also liberal in that there are no state regulations prohibiting and policing relations between men and women in keeping with the requirements of the Pakistani Muslim community. Moreover, the presence of Western values beyond the front door means that there is an absence of a wider community framework of surveillance as there might be in the homeland. In addition, the spaces of education such as schools, colleges, and universities, as well as those of the labor market, are often closed, opaque spaces that block the policing gaze of parents and the Pakistani community.

SPACES OF SCHOOL:
OBSCURING THE PARENTAL GAZE

Pakistani parents perceive their daughters' (hetero)sexual purity to be put at risk by the existence of opportunities for them to develop relationships with unrelated men in spaces outside the home, particularly when encouraged and supported by the immorality of liberal Western culture (Modood, 1992). This culture not only exists outside the front door but also manages to pervade the home through television and other media (Ahmed & Hastings, 1994). Parents seek to control these risks by drawing on Islamist discourse produced within the homeland that sets out ideals of Muslim womanhood, and by socializing girls to conform to these ideals through self-regulation. In addition, parents seek to control daughters' access to what they consider dangerous spaces that may threaten their (hetero)sexual purity. Many respondents, for example, agree with another respondent's claim that "hanging around town is [seen as] wrong because men are around. Girls aren't allowed in town for very long."

The space of the school, although clearly Western and liberal, may be a single-sex one, and hence feminine (this option is popular within the Pakistani community; indeed, a number of my respondents attended single-sex schools) (see also Afshar, 1994). These are some of the concerns that have encouraged a demand for Muslim schools (see Joly, 1986; Kelly & Shaikh, 1989). The space of the school tends to be perceived by parents as highly regulated and disciplined in a way that certain spaces of post-16 and certainly post-18 education (i.e., college and university) and labor markets are not. The significance of this distinction is stressed by a number of respondents. Rhea defined for me the difference between "school" and "college" or "university":

> "What they [parents] believe is at school you have the supervision of teachers. At our school that is definitely what it is. If they find some of the Asian girls doing things they shouldn't be doing, then, because the teachers are so aware of Islamic culture and the Hindu culture and all the other multicultures, they do inform the parents, and the parents are aware of that...."

Zara also drew attention to the fact that

> "lessons [at college] are not controlled that strict. Teachers are more liberal. If you want to do the work it is up to you to get it done. They won't hassle you or anything. Schools are not like that: a couple of absences and they [the teachers] would notice and get in touch with the parents."

As the first substantial space outside a home environment to which Pakistani children are exposed and in which they spend a significant amount of time, school is the place in which the respondents first experienced the issue of spatial constraints. Not only their presence within the school but also their movements between home and school are often tightly regulated. This is particularly evident in the area of extracurricular activities. As Sharon remarked, "Most [extracurricular] activities were after school. Therefore restrictions from home caused problems." Selina also pointed out that she was unable to participate in extracurricular activities "because they were after school and parents didn't want me out after school." It is notable that only the three respondents who attend a girls-only grammar school have participated in the full range of extracurricular activities irrespective of the timing of the activities. Another two respondents were able to participate because the extracurricular activities that interested them took place at lunchtime, and so did not raise the issue of being present in school after hours when school regulations might be relaxed.

Some parents, especially those who themselves have a limited education, are not just concerned about the threat to (hetero)sexual purity produced by women's access to particular spaces but are concerned with the psychological influence of education they might receive. Historically, in South Asia "education was seen as a means for loosening the control exercised by men over women. . . . It is precisely for this reason that it played a central role in the struggle for women's rights in India" (Mumtaz & Shaheed, 1987, p. 38). Selina, for instance, enrolled in a sociology major against her parents' wishes. She told me that her parents were concerned about its influence on her. They would not allow her to spend much time in her own room—time they felt would facilitate contemplation and questioning. Under pressure from them, she abandoned her major. In her study of the Yorkshire-based Pakistani community, Afshar (1994) discusses two sisters who were chaperoned daily to and from school by their father and who were closely supervised at all times. These sisters responded by "breaking out." They left home, cut their hair, and later married white men. Similarly, Selina and her twin sister responded to strict regulation by their family (see Mohammad, 1999) by leaving home. Both went on to undertake university degrees. Selina's twin, Anila, took a degree in English and published a book of poetry. Selina herself undertook a foundation course that provided access to university to study sociology. While Anila has consistently refused contact with her family, Selina has gradually reestablished relations with her family, who are now prepared to accept her on her own terms. On my last contact with Selina she had suspended her studies during her final year because her father had a terminal illness. Temporarily, she was at home supporting her mother following her father's death.

By contrast, 25-year-old Seema's parents were less concerned about the influence of education on her thinking than they were with ensuring that her marriage, arranged with a relative in Pakistan, would not be put in jeopardy by his difficulties in gaining a British visa. British fiancées of overseas Pakistanis must be in paid work to show that they are able to support their fiancés in order to strengthen their application for a British visa. After her engagement, Seema was forced to leave school at the earliest opportunity (after GCSEs). She entered the labor market and worked for 2 years. During this period her fiancé failed to get a visa. She then made a decision to study for her A-levels part-time. With her fiancé's visa still held up, she decided to attend university to study law. When she informed her family of her decision, her father refused to speak to her for 6 months. On completion of her degree, she married her fiancé, who had finally arrived in Britain by then. After marriage she found that her husband didn't approve of her undertaking paid work. She notes that she would like to undertake paid work because "I'm bored! I need to use my brain to do something worthwhile. I feel like I'm wasting precious time and could be doing so much." She has applied for several jobs in a variety of fields, including charities, but has "been unsuccessful because they usually don't want someone who's genuinely interested but has no experience." Seema's path to higher education and her negotiation of entry into paid work has involved many twists and turns. It is difficult to retain a clear sense of direction. In part, this relates to uncertainties over marriage and opportunities to pursue paid work. In part, it relates to the difficulties of following a straight trajectory in the context of the different demands made on British Pakistani women. At another level, some Pakistani women, as many respondents noted, may not have any particular trajectory in mind because they view continuing in education as a means to defer marriage for a few years.

The presence of Pakistanis in higher education is among the lowest of all the ethnic groups with the exception of Chinese and Bangladeshis. Pakistani women participate in higher education at a rate lower (by about a third) than that of Pakistani men (Higher Education Statistics Agency, 1995). The most recent data available confirm that Pakistani and Bangladeshi women are the least likely to hold degrees (Office of National Statistics, 2004). Of my respondents, only the seven working toward their A-levels seemed able to develop a clear direction for their studies. These young women hope to pursue studies in law, medicine, pharmacology, and languages at university. While women from less-educated backgrounds are subject to tighter spatial constraints on their home ground, these women are able to consider courses at the universities away from home. One of these seven women remarked, "Generally I feel luckier than some other Asian girls who have been prevented from studying exactly what they want because of parents."

However, the opportunities available to the young women planning to study away from home must not be taken to suggest that their parents do not share concerns about their daughters' (hetero)sexual purity and their reputations within the community. For the more educated parents, there is a tension between a desire to educate daughters and concerns of honor and standing within the community (Afshar, 1988). Moreover, it is often the community that questions, criticizes, and goads parents about their decisions to allow daughters to study at university, particularly where these are away from home. As Polly explains,

"As the time approached for me to leave, friends of my father began to turn him against the idea. One friend warned him 'they get up to all sorts of things, I know because my son is at university and he tells me what girls get up to.' "

Mona, whose father is a research scientist, has been permitted to pursue a career in medicine away from home. A major factor in this relaxing of regulations is that she has spent the last 5 years in Pakistan. She tells me that her family moved to Pakistan when she was 12 so that "we, the children, would have the same values as our parents." This parental strategy to ensure against their children's assimilation to the West has encouraged a more liberal approach toward their daughters.

THE GENDERING OF JOBS AND THE WORKPLACE

One means of negotiating parental constraints in the pursuit of higher education, particularly with educated parents, is the study of subjects that are highly valorized within the Pakistani and more broadly the South Asian communities. As one respondent noted, "Medicine [is a] prestige career. People like to say 'My daughter is a doctor.' " It is in this context that the majority of the respondents placed professions such as doctor, dentist, lawyer, and pharmacist in the category of "good" jobs.

Apart from jobs that are usually perceived as "bad," such as cleaner and refuse collector, respondents also mentioned nursing as a relatively low-status occupation. One respondent said that nursing is "not approved of because it is considered a dirty job changing bed pans." Nursing is an extension of women's caring role in the home, but, unlike in the home, nurses are not caring for their own family members but for unrelated men and women. Waitressing is also "disapproved of because of the male factor," that is, interactions with men.

Respondents were asked to name typical men's jobs and typical women's jobs. Three that crop up repeatedly are taxi driver for men and sewing (factory work) or shop assistant for women. Taxi driving is popular among Pakistani men (most respondents have a relative or know someone who drives taxis) because they make good money on the job, but it is a low-status occupation. In Pakistan historically, for those women who are uneducated or less educated, as one respondent states, "if you are going to work, you either teach or sew. To them these are perfectly respectable jobs, [particularly] sewing, because you are at home."

As this quote indicates, the spaces and times in which jobs take place are gendered, in that the place and time in which paid work is performed is significant in dictating the form of work Pakistani women are able to consider. Taxi driving, an example of a "man's job," is a relatively fluid occupation in terms of both space and time. It involves mobility and travel and is also less fixed to particular hours: shifts can be stretched and juggled.

"Women's jobs," identified as shop or factory work, are far more spatially and temporally fixed. Women are contained within the shop or on the factory floor where they typically work set hours. Both spaces are shared with other employees and, in the case of the shop floor, also with members of the public. Both of these spaces are relatively open to a range of gazes that may serve to constrain or to enforce particular behaviors. The disciplinary gaze of the employer, for instance, regulates workers not only for their efficiency but also, particularly in the case of the shop floor, appropriate behavior in dealings with members of the public. The shop floor is also open to the gazes of parents who can come in to inspect their daughters at work. In contrast, the taxi, in addition to being a mobile space, is also a relatively closed, individualized space that does not require or allow the same level or type of discipline that exists on the shop floor or in the factory. The discipline that is imposed on the taxi driver relates more to the operation of his vehicle on the road than to the individual himself.

The time and place of work was stressed by respondents as significant in persuading parents of their entry into the labor market. It is notable that only three respondents—all pursuing professions—and Selina, who has left home, were open to the idea of working "anywhere." Sana, who has a place at university to study medicine, is keen to go "wherever my job takes me"; Zena would like to work in London because the city offers the "best opportunities." The majority of respondents, whether single or married with children, stressed that if they were to look for paid work they would only consider Reading. The farthest they would contemplate were the surrounding areas. Some, like 17-year-old Marina, who is studying for her A-levels, reminded me that "my parents don't allow me to be outside anywhere alone," and that jobs involving distance away from the home are not suitable.

Many of the younger respondents had negotiated parental permission to work very locally during school holidays (for a discussion of how young women negotiate parental constraints, see Mohammad, 1999). The majority were required to be home by early evening, which also restricted them to the proximity of their locality. They did not see this situation changing if and when they were in permanent employment. These constraints prohibit entry into jobs that involve evening or night shifts or that require attendance at training courses away from home. Sharon recalled how she has had to turn down a number of work opportunities that required her to do evening hours on a regular basis. She has also had to turn down opportunities for promotion within her present job which would move her from general sales to becoming a representative for a cosmetic house—such a promotion would involve spending a week away from home on a training course.

Tara noted that when travel away from home is required as part of paid work or for educational purposes, places that are familiar—those perceived by her parents as culturally similar to the everyday home environment—are much more likely to see an easing of parental restrictions than those places that seem foreign. A school or work trip to Edinburgh, for example, would be more likely to find parental approval than one to Paris despite the geographical proximity of Paris. Tara told me that it is very difficult for Pakistani women like her to embark on careers that might involve regular travel away from home. She suggested that the most she can expect to negotiate is a few, occasional, nights away from home during the week. Weekends, she argued, are a different matter. She drew attention to the ways in which particular times such as the weekend, like particular spaces, are seen to be more conducive to immoral activity "because of all the stuff you can get up to. The weekend is free time for you to do what you want." It is a time–space that offers greater opportunity to socialize with the opposite sex and hence to encourage office romances and liaisons.

Parental concerns are heightened with respect to the opacity of particular spaces such as the office. Unlike in South Asia, working-class, British, Pakistani women are required to be simultaneously visible and invisible. Although a number of women defined waitressing as a bad job because it encourages encounters and interactions with men, in practice it is accepted that women will encounter men in the public arena. But when these encounters and interactions take place in spaces that are relatively open to the public/parental/community gaze, then this gaze works to discipline, limit, and control them. So while women must avoid drawing the attention of the masculine gaze in public spaces, they must also ensure that they remain visible to their families to facilitate parental policing. This means that some parents may show a greater preference for their daughters to work on the shop floor (in their own locality) than in the office. Although on the shop floor women may be more subjected to the male gaze and have the possibility of a greater number of encounters with men, these encounters are regulated by the disciplinary gaze of the store and the public as a whole, including parents, who can make an inspection of their daughters' performance anytime.

Thus the requirements of maintaining a distinctly bounded collective identity ensures that the access of women to post-16 and higher education cannot be taken for granted. Some women are able to negotiate the pursuit of education and subsequent entry into the labor market by studying for a few high-status careers. This finding helps to explain the statistical evidence highlighted earlier showing the high percentage of Pakistani women in the category of professionals relative to white women. For Pakistani women, the preference for and stress on entering the professions is likely to be greater than for British white women. However, the education system as a mechanism for sorting and sifting out high achievers for the professions means that access is not possible for the mass of Pakistani women who aspire to them. For the mass of young women, negotiation of parental permission for entry into the labor force is contingent upon many factors, including the timing of marriage and the nationality of the future fiancé. If and when they are able to enter the labor market, they may have to confront a whole set of racist stereotypes that block their progress. At the same time, they may remain subject to tight regulations that limit and prohibit participation in many forms of paid work, particularly of a more professional nature, that might involve travel. Such constraints serve to undermine women's progress in paid work and access to promotion. Thus the majority of Pakistani women remain in low-level jobs that hold limited possibilities for financial independence, and therefore do not challenge women's position within the Pakistani community.

CONCLUSION

I started the chapter by looking at the rise of conservative, radical, religious nationalisms in the context of the decline of secularism and the loss of faith in Western rational modernity. Religious nationalisms place a stress on the family and on women's roles as the bearers of collective identity and as the mothers of future generations. Women are the public face of the collectivity and custodians of its cultural and religious values. This makes women both the "guardians" and the "guarded" and legitimizes the imposition of physical and spatial constraints. I traced the impact on women of the rise of Islamism in Pakistan and how Islamism has informed the ideals and practices of Muslim womanhood in the Pakistani diaspora.

The requirements for the performance of Muslim womanhood in Great Britain, however, is not the same as it is in the homeland, but is adapted to take into account different spatial practices and norms in the country of settlement. The national space of the homeland is regulated to maintain the segregation of unrelated men and women. State and societal surveillance ensures against any visible signs of activities of a sexual nature. By contrast, the liberal Western state and society allows the free mingling of unrelated men and women and does not exercise moral disapproval of pre-/extramarital (hetero)sexual activity, which is a key concern for the Pakistani community, as women's purity is linked to marriage, the family, and collective identity. I then discussed the ways in which the relationship of the family and marriage to nationhood and collective identity prioritizes the roles of wife and mother for women. The idealization and performance of Muslim womanhood mediates women's access to and participation in the education system and labor market, and in some instances enables and even compels their entry into the labor market. Zubia, for example, laments that her fiancé was not from Pakistan. If he had been, she would have had to take on paid employment to secure a British visa for him. As it stood, her parents did not believe that she needed to continue with her education, so prior to marriage she remained at home.

I have highlighted how, within the broad requirement of the performance of Muslim womanhood, the level of education of parents seems to be a key factor influencing the nature and extent of the spatial and temporal constraints on women with respect to the education system and labor market. Parents who were relatively more educated encouraged the academic education of their daughters. Daughters who were more academically able were better positioned to negotiate parental and community concerns to pursue the high-status and highly regarded professions such as medicine and law. They seemed to be subjected to fewer restrictions with respect to how long and where they studied and with respect to their entry into the labor market.

Respondents' vision of good jobs broadly reiterated the consensus of the Pakistani community. "Good" jobs are those that are visible and that allow young women to be monitored. It is interesting to note that one explanation given for judging a job to be "bad"—that it involves encounters with men—was not applied to the professions, which almost always require such encounters. According to this criterion, childcare and infant-school teaching would have been at the top of the "good job" list, but such "female jobs" did not feature on the good job lists of any respondents.

The number of young women able to achieve entry into the professions even with the support of parents and the education system is limited. For the majority of British working-class Pakistani women, access to higher levels of education and entry into the labor market cannot be taken for granted. They have to negotiate parental and community religiocultural restrictions, and even if they are successful in this task, they have to negotiate racialized sexisms in the education system and the labor market. Moreover, when women are able to negotiate an entry into the labor market, parental constraints ensure that they are restricted to work that is undertaken at a set place near the parental or marital home and that has fixed hours. This precludes higher status, better paid work that might require training away from the regular work site, travel, or longer, more fluid hours. It reinforces the glass ceiling that undermines women's rise in the labor market.

NOTES

1. Islamist discourses are those that promote the production of specifically Muslim subjectivities. It is important to note, however, that these discourses are not singular but multiple and contradictory (Sayyid, 1997).
2. It is important to bear in mind that forced marriage is not a practice legitimized by Islam, even in its most conservative forms.

3. In this regard, it is important to note that links with the homeland and homeland religioculture intersect with more localized processes to produce particular identities. For British Pakistanis, identification as Muslim was greatly enhanced by the "Rushdie Affair" (see Modood, 1992).

4. Although Pakistan was founded on the basis of religious identity, it was broadly committed to secularism until Zia-ul-Haq's coup (1977–1989). Since its founding in 1947, in return for women's support for the nationalist movement, successive governments had promoted women's rights. This changed with the dictatorship of General Zia. His form of Islamism saw a significant erosion of women's rights (Mumtaz & Shaheed, 1987).

5. Women's (hetero)sexual purity is intimately linked to the concept of *izzat*, or honor of her father and her family. Afshar (1988) points out that women's (hetero)sexual purity is made a condition of making (a good) marriage and that marriage is a means for parents to transfer the responsibility of guarding their daughters' bodies to more able young men.

6. According to Hansen (1967, p. 71), the practice of veiling was not introduced by Islam: "Seclusion and veiling are phenomena . . . foreign to Arabs and unknown at the time of Mohammad," but were present for millennia in the Mesopotamian/Mediterranean region (see also El Guindi, 1999).

7. A veil/headscarf has become (both for Muslims themselves and for the West) a primary signifier of Islam. Yet Shaarawi (1986), writing on Egypt in the 1920s, argued that veiling was a social convention connected with class (see also El Guindi, 1999). The veil is read as an instrument of women's oppression, yet the veil also acts as a symbol of liberation and/or resistance. Women may veil in order to achieve greater freedom from social constraints through maintaining an image of purity, and the veil may symbolize a conscious rejection of Western values or an assertion of nationalism or revivalism (Afshar, 1994, p. 135).

8. The notion of free choice, of course, is problematic because discourses work not by controlling people from above but by promoting self-regulation. Discourses seek to produce particular subjectivities, meaning that subjects will "freely" choose to perform in particular ways (see Rose & Miller, 1992). This is not to say that there can be no resistance.

9. "GCSE" refers to the General Certificate of Secondary Education, which involves a 2-year course of study undertaken from the age of 14. It provides young people with a basic grounding in a range of around 10 subjects. Students may leave school at the age of 16 with the GCSE qualifications or stay on to undertake a 2-year course of advanced-level ("A-level") studies in up to four subjects, which enables access to university education.

10. The structure of A-level study has undergone some changes in recent years but my respondents followed the format described in Note 9.

11. This stands for National Vocational Qualification. These are post-16 vocational qualifications that prepare students for employment. They are undertaken at colleges of further education, which are distinct from universities in that they rarely if ever offer degree courses. By contrast, colleges of higher education, like universities, offer degree courses.

REFERENCES

Al-Azmeh, A. (1993). *Islam modernities*. London: Vaeso.

Afshar, H. (1988). *Islam and feminisms: An Iranian case study*. Basingstoke, UK: Palgrave.

Afshar, H. (1994). Muslim women in West Yorkshire growing up with real and imaginary values amidst conflicting views of self and society. In H. Afshar & M. Maynard (Eds.), *The dynamics of "race" and gender: Some feminist interventions* (pp. 127–147). London: Taylor & Francis.

Ahmed, A., & Hastings, D. (1994). *Islam, globalisation and postmodernity*. London: Routledge.

Ang, I. (1993). Migrations of Chineseness: Ethnicity in the postmodem world. In D. Bennett (Ed.), *Cultural studies: Pluralism and theory* (pp. 32–44). Melbourne, Australia: University of Melbourne.

Anwar, M. (1979). *The myth of return Pakistanis in Britain*. London: Heinemann.

Badran, M. (1995). *Feminists, Islam, and nation: Gender and the making of modern Egypt*. Princeton, NJ: Princeton University Press.

Ballard, R. (1991). The Pakistanis: Stability and introspection. In C. Peach (Ed.), *The ethnic minority populations of Great Britain* (Vol. 2, pp. 121–149). London: HMSO.

Bowlby, S., Lloyd-Evans, S., & Mohammad, R. (1997). Becoming a paid worker: images and identity. In T. Skelton & G. Valentine (Eds.), *Cool places: Geographies of youth cultures* (pp. 229–248). London: Routledge.

Brah, A. (1996). *Cartographies of diaspora: Contesting identities*. London: Routledge.

Chenoy, A. M. (2002). *Militarism and women in South Asia*. New Delhi, India: Kali for Women.

Department of Education and Skills. (2002). National pupil database. Retrieved from National Statistics online: *www.statistics.gov.uk*

El Guindi, F. (1999). *Modesty, privacy and resistance*. Oxford, UK: Berg.

Graham, H. (1995). Women and social change. In H. Graham & J. Labanyi (Eds.), *Spanish cultural studies: An introduction* (pp. 99–116). Oxford, UK: Oxford University Press.

Hansen, H. H. (1967). *Investigations in a Sh'ia village in Bahrain*. Copenhagen: National Museum of Denmark.

Higher Education Statistics Agency. (1995). *Ethnicity in higher education*. Cheltenham, UK: Author.

Hiro, D. (1991). *Black British white British: A history of race relations in Britain* (2nd ed.). London: Paladin.

Joly, D. (1986). *The opinions of Mirpuri parents in Saltley, Birmingham, about their children's education* (Research Paper 2). Warwick, UK: University of Warwick, Centre for Research in Ethnic Relations.

Kandiyoti, D. (1993). Identity and its discontents: Women and the nation. In P. Williams & L. Chrisman (Eds.), *Colonial discourse and post-colonial theory: A reader* (pp. 376–391). New York: Harvester Wheatsheaf.

Kelly, A., & Shaikh, S. (1989). To mix or not to mix: Pakistani girls in British schools. *Educational Research, 31*, 10–19.

Mernissi, F. (1975). *Beyond the veil: Male–female dynamics in a modern Muslim society*. London: Schenkman.

Modood, T. (1992). British Asian Muslims and the Rushdie Affair. In J. Donald & A. Rattansi (Eds.), *Race, culture and difference* (pp. 260–277). London: Sage, in conjunction with Open University.

Mohammad, R. (1999). Marginalisation, Islamism and the production of the "other's" "other." *Gender, Place, and Culture, 6*, 221–240.

Mohammad, R. (2004). British Pakistani Muslim women: Marking the body, marking the nation. In L. Nelson & J. Seager (Eds.), *A companion to feminist geography*. Malden, MA: Blackwell.

Mumtaz, K., & Shaheed, F. (1987). *Women of Pakistan: Two steps forward, one step back?* London: Zed Books.

Office of National Statistics. (2004a). *Annual local area labour force survey, 2001/ 2002*. Retrieved from National Statistics Online: *www.statistics.gov.uk*

Office of National Statistics. (2004b). *Census 2001*. Retrieved from National Statistics Online: *www.statistics.gov.uk*

Office of National Statistics. (2004c). *Economic inactivity rates for people of working age, by ethnic group and sex, 2001/2002*. Retrieved from National Statistics Online: *www.statistics.gov.uk*

Office of National Statistics. (2004d). *Unemployment rates by ethnic group, 2001/ 2002*. Retrieved from National Statistics Online: *www.statistics.gov.uk*

O'Kane, M. (1997, 29 November). A holy betrayal. *Guardian Weekend*, pp. 38–44.

Rose, N. & Miller, P. (1992). Political power beyond the state: Problematics of government. *British Journal of Sociology, 43*, 173–203.

Saifullah Khan, V. (1982). The role of the culture of dominance in structuring the experience of ethnic minorities. In C. Husband (Ed.), *"Race" in Britain: Continuity and change* (pp. 197–216). London: Hutchinson.

Sarwar, G. (1980). *Islam: Beliefs and teachings*. London: Muslim Educational Trust.

Sayyid, B. S. (1997). *A fundamental fear: Eurocentrism and the emergence of Islamism*. London: Zed Books.

Shaarawi, H. (1986). *Harem years: The memoirs of an Egyptian feminist* (Trans. & Ed. by Margot Badran). London: Virago Press.

Taraki, L. (1995). Islam is the solution: Jordanian Islamists and the dilemma of the "modern woman." *British Journal of Sociology, 46*, 643–661.

Yuval-Davis, N. (1997). *Gender and nation*. London: Sage.

Part III

Discourse, Representation, and the Contestation of Space

8 Islamism, Democracy, and the Political Production of the Headscarf Issue in Turkey

Anna Secor

What has come to be known as the "headscarf issue" (*başörtüsü meselesi*) has taken up a prominent position in the symbolic lexicon of the struggle between political Islamism and state secularism. In the mid-1980s, protests erupted in major Turkish cities, as students mobilized against the state's enforcement of antiveiling dress codes in spaces such as the universities, courts, and state offices. With the Islamist party achieving electoral successes in the mid-1990s, the headscarf issue has continued to operate as a flashpoint for Turkish politics. In Turkey, as in France and Egypt, protestors and Islamists have argued that state regulations restricting veiling discriminate against pious Muslim women who feel pressured to choose between their faith and their education or profession.[1] Further aggravating the conflict, the Turkish government passed a law in 1997 that increased compulsory primary-school education from 6 to 8 years in the public, secular schools. Previously, girls could be withdrawn from the secular schools after the sixth grade and enrolled in the religious (*imam-hatip*) middle schools, where veiling was permitted and gender segregation practiced. Under the new legislation, adolescent girls were forced either to attend school unveiled or not at all.[2] The impact of the 8-year education law on the *imam-hatip* schools and women's veiling practices was not incidental, but rather occurred as part of the "February 28th Process" through which the secular establishment, led by the military, forced the elected Islamist party prime minister, Necmettin Erbakan, from office and sought to (re)establish secular control over the public sphere (Yavuz, 2000).

Along with other elements of dress and adornment, veiling is an embodied spatial practice through which women are inserted into relations of power in society.[3] These relations of power inscribe "regimes of veiling," or spatial hegemonies (however partial and impermanent) within which particular veiling laws, rules, or norms hold sway (Secor, 2002). For example, while veiling may represent an informally and unevenly enforced norm in particular neighborhoods, in other spaces (such as university classrooms) *not* veiling is the dominant and formally regulated mode of attire for women. Through these sociospatial regimes, veiling practices become intelligible—that is, they come to be seen and understood in particular ways that are often tied up with ideas of womanhood, honor, and shame. As women traverse urban spaces, their mobile and embodied practices of veiling or not veiling contribute to the production, and sometimes subversion, of these spatial regimes. At the same time, formal and informal veiling regimes are bound up with the techniques of government, such as policing, that regulate particular spaces. Veiling thus becomes a site for both the disciplinary administration of bodies and the regulation of populations—what Foucault calls "biopower," referring to the forms of power that interweave sexual and bodily conduct with questions of national policy (Foucault, 1978).

This chapter is concerned with how the sociospatial practice of veiling has come to function as a site of politics in Turkey. It begins from several, interrelated questions, each of which is explored through the discursive analysis of focus-group texts. First, *How are veiling practices constituted through a diversity of practices and associated meanings in Turkish society?* I begin with a discussion of the way veiling has been constituted through the practices of nation-state formation in Turkey. Using focus-group texts, this section also draws forward the complexity of veiling practices as they are differently enacted and interpreted across urban communities in Istanbul. The second overarching question that this chapter addresses is: *How is the practice and regulation of veiling (or "the headscarf issue") constituted as a political issue?* I argue that veiling practices, and the related debate surrounding religious education, work as points of capture within the powerful, competing discourses of democracy and Islamism in Turkey. Finally, I pose the question, *How do regimes of veiling or not veiling situate individuals and populations in relation to governmental practice and technologies of citizenship?* By "technologies" of citizenship, I refer to what Nikolas Rose (1999) calls "an assembly of forms of knowledge with a variety of mechanical devices and an assortment of little techniques oriented to produce practical outcomes" (p. 52). Regimes of veiling, whether formal or informal, are instrumental in promoting the citizenship rights and identities of certain subjects as opposed to others; such processes can be traced in the ways in which focus-group participants experience and represent their own relationships to the police, the military, and the courts, as well as to such mythical entities as "the state" (*devlet*), "the people" (*halk*), or "the nation" (*millet*). Furthermore, the spatiality of veiling practices and regulations means that these techniques are deeply implicated in contests over "public" and "private," the limits of state intervention, and the power of Islam.

Together, these questions contribute to an understanding of the spatial production of veiling regimes that links practices of government to questions of identity. Drawing on Foucault's idea of "governmentality," this approach anticipates the problem of "*who* we are when we are governed in such a manner" (Dean, 1999, p. 17, emphasis in original; see also Foucault, 1994). That is, I am interested both in how the regulation of veiling positions individuals and populations as *objects* of government, and in how veiling becomes a channel through which individuals constitute their own self-identities as political *subjects*, and thus as citizens. Giorgio Agamben (1998) argues that these two lines of analysis, which Foucault terms "political techniques" and "technologies of the self", converge to constitute the citizen, "the new biopolitical body of humanity" (p. 9). In this chapter, I seek to demonstrate how this convergence takes place through the production of veiling as a political issue in Turkey.

This chapter is based on fieldwork carried out in Istanbul at various times between 1998 and 2003. Over this time period, I conducted 22 focus groups with differently positioned Istanbul residents: rural–urban migrants, Kurds, Alevis, Islamists, and so on. In each case, focus groups consisted of 7 to 10 participants who did not previously know each other and who were selected as part of a target group (e.g., younger migrant women who had been in the city for less than 10 years, or lower-class men who had been active in political parties, or Alevi youths). These participants were identified either through informal networks or through a database compiled from survey research. While many of my general observations are based on impressions gathered from all of these discussions, this chapter will draw mostly from two focus groups, one with women and one with men, conducted in the summer of 2003.[4] Part of a larger project on civil society in Istanbul, these groups were comprised of people first contacted through a representative survey of Istanbul residents.[5] Focus groups provide particularly rich texts for the discursive analysis of meaning as contingently and collaboratively constructed through social interaction (Wilkinson, 1998).

Discussants in these two groups were invited to participate based on their involvement in some kind of religiously oriented associational activity, whether as Islamist party members, participants in nongovernmental Islam-oriented organizations or charities, attendees at informal religious meetings, or as protestors and activists in the headscarf campaigns. Because of their involvement in these activities and their support for Islamist political parties,[6] I refer to these participants as "Islamist" men and women. However, this should not be taken to imply that all of these participants subscribe to a clearly articulated, consistent political agenda. As the criteria for selection indicate, "Islamism" in this case may refer to religious, social, and political engagement. Furthermore, it is more and more understood that political Islamism in Turkey is an umbrella movement, striated by different perspectives, interests, and social positions (Buğra, 2002; Houston, 1999; White, 2002). For these reasons, the term should be understood in such a way that does not presume particular positions or ideologies, but rather serves as shorthand for participation in a set of diverse practices.

VEILING PRACTICES AND
CONTESTED MEANINGS IN TURKEY

Practices of veiling have been bound up with questions of national identity, ideology, and state practice throughout the 20th century. As in other Middle Eastern contexts, the scripting of veiling practices in Turkey has taken place in dialogue with European imperial discourses that cast the veil as a synecdoche for the "barbarity" of Muslim societies (Göle, 1996; Ahmed, 1992). In a spirit of Westernizing reform that can be traced back to the *Tanzimat* (reorganization) of the late Ottoman era (1839–1876), Mustafa Kemal "Atatürk," the former Ottoman general who led the Turkish revolution, founded the Turkish republic in 1923 based on secularist, modernist principles. Adopting European legal codes, banning the Islamic caliphate, and creating a department, the Directorate of Religious Affairs (Diyanet İşleri Bakanlığı), for the management of religion and religious education, the laic republic[7] attempted to reorient the Turkish population toward secularist, modernist, and nationalist ideals. As part of this project of reculturation, Atatürk denounced the practice of veiling and encouraged women to don European dress. Men were also directed to adjust their self-presentation; not only was the new face of the republic a shaven one, but the late Otoman fez was banned and replaced by the brimmed hat in public affairs.

The republican elite initiated a transformation of everyday life that ranged from language reform to the construction of new urban spaces and the promotion of "Westernized" lifestyles. Not only were girls to become educated alongside boys in public school, but many also attended vocational women's schools and became active in the workforce of the new state. As Navaro-Yashin (2002) has argued, new consumer habits, focusing on dress, were to define the "modern woman" as distinct from "the backwards Islamist woman" in the discourses of the secular mainstream (p. 86). Through the reorganization of elements of dress, bearing, and manners, the Kemalists[8] attempted to create embodied cultural forms that would facilitate the inscription of a new Turkish national identity (Bourdieu, 1997). In the process, a new spatial imaginary was asserted over and against previous forms of sociospatial organization.

In her work on veiling and civilization, Nilufer Göle (1996) describes how the Turkish *mahrem* (the sphere of domesticity, secrecy, the family, and the forbidden) had been the object of modernizing reform since the *Tanzimat* period. She argues that "the most resistant antagonism between the Islamic and the modern Western civilizations" can be grounded "in the organization of interior and exterior spheres, as well as in the separation of male and female" (p. 14). "Women's place," that is, their visibility in public or their presence in the *mahrem*, has come to define the degree to which society has been either Westernized or Islamicized. It was in this context that the Kemalist state sought to shift the boundaries of the *mahrem* and the *namahrem* (exterior) and to redefine women's roles in society through education and entrance into waged labor. At the same time, the project of Kemalism was neither absolute nor internally coherent, and its effects on gender, spatial practices, and culture have registered unevenly across Turkish society.

The simple headscarf, a square of fabric used to cover a woman's head and hair to varying degrees, never did disappear from practices of dress in Turkey. According to a nationwide survey conducted by Ali Çarkoğlu and Binnaz Toprak (2000), only about 27% of Turkish women go out on the street with their heads uncovered today, though this national statistic masks a great deal of rural–urban and regional variation. Despite the consistent presence of head covering, the growing popularity of veiling among the middle classes in the 1980s and 1990s has been interpreted as indicating "the re-Islamization of personal relations, public spaces and daily practices" (Göle, 1997, p. 51). In part, this (re)interpretation of the headscarf has stemmed from the new forms of veiling that have become popular among lower-middle-class and middle-class university students in urban areas. While their mothers may have worn a simple headscarf (*başörtüsü*), or may have left their heads uncovered, these young women have adopted new styles of "turban" (*türban*) that reflect both changing class dynamics and the politicization of Islam in Turkey. Combined with other elements of dress such as raincoats, the new headscarves are larger, more colorful, and more likely to be tightly pinned under the chin and draped fully over the shoulders than the older forms. This form of veiling, called *tesettür*, registers particular class- and consumption-based identities at the same time as it is often interpreted through the lens of Islamist political mobilization in Turkey (Kılıçbay & Binark, 2002; Saktanbar, 1994). According to the survey conducted by Çarkoğlu and Toprak (2000), 15.7% of Turkish women adopt this "turban" style of veiling, while 53.4% wear the headscarf. A third mode of veiling that has also gained in popularity in recent decades is the black *çarşaf*, or full body veil. Unlike the other "headscarf"-based veiling forms, the *çarşaf* may sometimes include facial covering as well, leaving only the eyes or the eyes and nose exposed. The *çarşaf* remains a garment worn by a small minority of women (3%, according to Çarkoğlu & Toprak, 2000) and is frequently associated with *tarikatlar*, the Islamic brotherhoods that are officially outlawed but nonetheless thriving in urban areas.

Veiling practices vary in form and meaning. In focus-group discussions, women both distinguished their own veiling (or not-veiling) practices from others and debated the meaning of personal and community practices. Part of the mobility of veiling as a symbol derives from its shifting position within different interpretations of Islamic doctrine and the requirements of religious practice and belief (see Secor, 2002). Further, the articulation of veiling practices within Islam varies across the local contexts of villages, communities, and neighborhoods. In focus-group discussions, the meanings of veiling practices were contested, unfixed, and charged with controversy. Is veiling about sin (an issue between the individual and God) or about the preservation of women's honor (a social issue)? Is veiling something that should be understood as forced on women (by communities, families, or male relatives), or something that women choose as an expression of inner faith? When is veiling a traditional practice, when is it a sign of religiosity, and when does it function as a political symbol? Played out through women's conversations and debates, these questions speak to the ways in which veiling practice is modulated across different sociospatial contexts.

While much of this chapter will concentrate on the headscarf in political discourse and practice (particularly drawing on the focus groups with "Islamist" participants), the following dialogue, which took place among older Kurdish women, is intended to highlight the range of veiling practices and regimes of social control within which women negotiate their everyday lives in Istanbul. Nazan, [9] who wears a casual headscarf, is a 40-year-old mother of seven children who migrated from Siirt 14 years ago. Semiha, who wore a headscarf to the focus group but removed it once seated with the women, is 50 years old and the mother of six children. She is from Diyarbakir and came from the Bismil district to Istanbul 5 years ago. Güldem did not wear any kind of headscarf. She is 41 years old, has three children, and migrated from Malatya 14 years ago. Finally, Feriha, who wears a headscarf, migrated from Bitlis 15 years ago and is the mother of eight children. Although this dialogue is telescoped at two points for brevity, its flow and rhythm are preserved to illustrate how questions of representation and meaning are interwoven through a debate over the politics of veiling, both within local communities and the wider national context.

MODERATOR: I'd like to pass to another topic. Among us there are two ladies who wear the headscarf. Why do you wear it?

NAZAN: The headscarf is in our traditions, in our hometown [*memleket*] we should not show our hair, even a strand of hair, it must be covered. But to cover we don't wear the turban [*türban*], we wear a scarf. Everybody according to their own desires. If I want I can uncover, but this is what is natural for me.

SEMİHA: I don't agree with you.

NAZAN: I wanted it like this, I liked it like this. I liked myself dressed like this. It is something from within me.

. . .

GÜLDEM: When it is bound up with tradition, that is one thing, but some use it politically.

NAZAN: That is not us.

GÜLDEM: I wasn't talking about you.

MAKBULE: In our villages it comes from our mothers and our fathers. Our traditions are like this, yes.

GÜLDEM: I'm saying, if it is covering for tradition, my mother covered her head lightly and so did my grandmother. But when this is carried out for political reasons, that is when I find it wrong. There are many who use it politically.

SEMİHA: Our friend [Makbule] said, "I am free, I can wear it or not." I definitely didn't agree. Without a doubt, for us in the east [of Turkey], our elders don't accept you if your head is uncovered, "You, you're going to hell, or you'll be a whore". . . . I am not free, my daughter is not free. . . . I mean, nobody goes to heaven or to hell with their clothes.

NAZAN: I wear a headscarf. An uncovered woman, a covered woman, how do I know that I will go to heaven? Maybe she will go to heaven.

. . .

FERİHA: Actually, I used to have my head uncovered. When I was single I wore it but not this often. But after I was married I covered my head like this. I definitely covered it myself. Look, I am married for 30 years, and not once has my husband told me to wear this. We don't have that problem.

SEMİHA: But most of the pressure comes from the community, from society.

FERİHA: We also have daughters, and all of them have their heads uncovered. There is no pressure among us.

SEMİHA: We cannot go outside with our heads uncovered.

FERİHA: No, there is no pressure among us.

When Nazan is asked why she veils, she immediately points out both that she does not wear the kind of headscarf associated with the Islamist political movement (the turban) and that she has chosen to veil of her own volition. Later in the focus-group discussion, she reiterates that her community does not veil "fanatically" (*aşırı kapanmıyorduk*), and further asserts that there is no tie between religiosity and covering, that it is just "normal." Likewise, in the above dialogue, she assures Semiha that she does not expect covered women to be more likely to go to heaven than uncovered women. This is a case in which the headscarf is worn neither as a political marker nor as a sign of Koranic literacy or piety. Both Güldem and Nazan draw a stark line between this "traditional" veiling and the kinds of practices they associate with political Islam. This delineation reproduces elements of public discourse (both secularist and Islamist) surrounding the headscarf issue in Turkey. For example, it echoes the distinction made in a 1990 advertisement, placed in an Islamist women's magazine, for *tesettür* garments, that proclaimed "Veiling is not a tradition, but a law of Allah" (Kılıçbay & Binark, 2002, p. 503). Veiling for reasons of tradition is thus distinguished from the new "conscious" veiling practices of the Islamist movement.

Finally, a second fault line appears in the above dialogue when Semiha airs her disagreement with Nazan over the issue of veiling choice. In the conversation with Feriha that follows, it becomes apparent that the two women's communities practice very different veiling regimes. This diversity of practices across localized migrant networks undermines attempts to generalize about veiling as a discipline and a choice. Thus the headscarf maintains an ambiguous and shifting relationship to constellations of gender relations, community norms, religion, and politics in Istanbul. The following section seeks to position the veil within political discourses that transect local, national, and international scales.

THE "HEADSCARF ISSUE" AS SITE OF ISLAMIST/DEMOCRATIC POLITICS

Veiling, in all its various forms, did not become a site of political intensity in Turkey (or elsewhere) because it is inherently controversial or peculiarly political as a form of dress (Eickelman & Piscatori, 1996). On the contrary, the symbolic potency of veiling derives in large part from its historical inscription within orientalizing discourses (Yeğenoğlu, 1998) and the ways in which it was subsequently swept up within the modernizing currents of nationalist imagination (Göle, 1996). In addition, I argue that the contemporary political significance of the headscarf arises from the nodal function it has come to play within Islamist, secularist, and democratic discourses. The "headscarf issue" has been, in effect "issue-tized"[10] through discourses of Islamism and laicism, and within a transnational "individual rights" discourse that claims democracy as its organizing term. As such, veiling is also taken to represent a particular ideal of gender relations, although in fact there is no simple or stable relationship between veiling practices and regimes of gender. In short, the headscarf has become a point of capture, a site of intensity, for the ongoing negotiation of powerful and competing ideologies circulating in Turkish society.

The function of the "headscarf issue" within the currents of Islamist and democratic politics in Turkey can be identified in the invocation of regulatory veiling codes in the conversations of Islamist participants and others. When discussing the necessity for Islamicization in Turkey, movement participants very often point first to the injustice of the formal and informal regulation of women's veiling in public institutions such as schools, universities, courts, and the spaces of the state, especially the Turkish Grand National Assembly (parliament). In my focus groups with Islamist participants, the question "Is Turkey a democracy?" led directly to the question of the headscarf and its regulation by the state. Restrictions on veiled women's mobility within public spaces function both as evidence against the state and its claims to democratic legitimacy and as proof of the need for Islamicization of the public sphere.

The following dialogue between women in the group of Islamist participants provides a window into the rights-based discourse within which the headscarf issue is called forth. It begins with Meryem, a 49-year-old illiterate woman who wears a full black *çarşaf* pinned under her chin, describing her experience at a march against the headscarf regulations. Havva, who is 41 and a primary-school graduate, wears a scarf that is wrapped loosely, but thoroughly, and pinned under her chin. Ceren, who wears a headscarf as well, is 45 years old and has a middle-school education. Like the others, she is a housewife and a mother.

MERYEM: What we enjoyed was like this, I mean, we were the people [*bütün halk biz*]. It was like this, I mean: Let them remove the headscarf! Covered people want to dress like this and they won't be excluded! No one will go to school! We watched the evening news. They went and took the diploma wearing a wig. Why must it be like this, how did this situation come to be?

HAVVA: There are human rights. It is said that everyone is equal, and equality is taken from your hand.

CEREN: Pardon, can I say something? Twenty-four years old, with an *imam-hatip* degree from Istinya Imam Hatip school, she cannot find work and now sits at home for 3 years . . .

MODERATOR: Your daughter?

CEREN: My daughter.

There are three moments in the above discussion that are particularly significant for an understanding of how the headscarf issue has come to function within political discourse in Turkey. First, Meryem is talking about acts of resistance, about becoming "the people" (*halk*) through public action, at the same time as she is wondering why these actions have become necessary. She invokes both a refusal to be excluded and a willful self-exclusion that presumably would reveal the fragility of the system: "No one will go to school." The incident that she refers to, in which girls attended public school wearing wigs to maintain their modesty, further serves to illustrate the potential for everyday subversion of the formal antiveiling regime. The second significant moment is Havva's appeal to human rights, a term that must be understood as international in provenance and linked to domestic discourses of democracy, Turkey's bid for European Union membership, and the transnationalization of the headscarf issue. In her construction, Havva also highlights the hypocrisy of the Turkish republic's claims to the equal treatment of its citizens. Third, Ceren brings the discussion back to the impact that the headscarf dispute has had on her own life by describing her daughter's situation. Although her daughter was able to attend a religious high school, she has not found work; the unspoken implication is that her unemployment results from the foreclosure of avenues for veiled women and *imam-hatip* school graduates. The headscarf is thus inserted within multiple interrelated frames of reference. As a site of resistance, the "headscarf issue" is paradoxically both the site of the state's failure and a sign of grassroots empowerment. Further, it is a nodal point in national and international discourses of democracy and the state. And finally, the headscarf comes to stand in for the injustice, inequality, and futility that saturate the difficult daily lives of ordinary people who struggle to find work and make ends meet in Turkey's fraught economy.

In the process of its "issue-tization" the headscarf in Turkey has become bound up with an internationalized language of rights, democracy, and equality. When Eren, a theology student in the group of Islamist men, says, "I accept the headscarf as a basic human right," his statement echoes the pronouncement of the head of the Great Mosque of Paris who, in 1989, argued: "If a girl asks to have her hair covered, I believe it is her most basic right" (Soysal, 1997, p. 516). In her study of Muslim communities in Berlin, Birmingham, and Marseilles, Yasemin Soysal (1997) concludes: "The Islamic organizations I study do not justify their demands by reaching back to religious teachings or traditions, but by recourse to the language of rights, and thus, of citizenship" (p. 519). Indeed, participants in the group of Islamist women called upon European and U.S. practices regarding veiling rights and religious education to support their arguments against the Turkish state's laic practices. Although the context for my study is quite different from Soysal's, my point is simply that the connection between women's veiling practices and human rights claims is being formulated in relation to wider articulations of Islamic politics. At the same time, one cannot say that the democratic, rights-based discourse *takes the place* of religious rationalizations for veiling in Turkey, as Soysal implies it does in her study. Rather, it is the failure of the state to put into practice its professed democratic ideals that gives the Islamist movement purchase for its central argument in favor of the Islamicization of the public sphere. Describing the mass media campaign of the Refah Partisi (RP) in the 1991 elections, the first in which the Islamist party positioned itself as a potentially broad-based movement, Ayse Öncü (1995) describes a television spot in which only one of the seven women shown had her head covered:

> The only "turbaned" female was a young girl, directly addressing the viewer to say that she was expelled from the university during her senior year because she used a headscarf (the word "turban" was not used because it signifies radical Islam), followed by a voice-over pledging that no one will be discriminated against because of her beliefs and practices when the RP is in power. (p. 61)

There is thus a double movement: headscarf proponents call upon a powerful, internationally sanctioned discourse of rights, and the Islamist movement takes on the mantle of democratization through its support for veiled women in the public sphere. While staunch secularists continue to claim, in effect, that the headscarf violates the pure realm of the secular state as envisioned by Atatürk, the most common objection voiced among ordinary people is against the politicization of the headscarf and the "use" of veiled women for political ends (as Güldem explains in the first dialogue). The result is the political production of the "headscarf issue," articulated within a relatively consistent set of terms.

AMBIVALENT CONSTRUCTIONS: VEILING RIGHTS AND THE REGULATION OF DRESS AND DAILY LIFE

Among the effects of this production is an ambivalent articulation of "human rights" within Islamist discourses. In the focus group with Islamist women, this emerged most strikingly from their discussion of other spatial practices of dress. In the following dialogue, discourses of morality and public composure veer toward the reversal, rather than the abolishment, of the regulatory regime of public dress legislation and enforcement. We have already encountered Havva and Ceren in the previous dialogue; this discussion also includes Emel, a 29-year-old high-school graduate who is a housewife with one child; Belgin, a 27-year-old housewife and primary-school graduate with no children; and Arzu, a 37-year-old, middle-school graduate, and mother of two children. All of the women wear headscarves, except for Arzu who attended the meeting wearing an elegantly tailored, dark-blue *çarşaf*, one perhaps reserved for special occasions.

EMEL: Covered families see the clothing outside, those whose bellies are uncovered. This can't be. All the men see it and look. I mean, a belly shouldn't be uncovered outside.

. . .

BELGIN: It is necessary not to have an effect [by wearing sexy clothes at school].

HAVVA: There should be a clear rule [for dress in schools]. Of course, they can go with their heads uncovered.

MODERATOR: Who is going to put this in place?

ARZU: The state will implement it, our state.

MODERATOR: But I thought we didn't like the state's dress codes!

CEREN: I mean, it is important to correct the state's rules. Those who go around so uncovered must be removed, I'm very sorry!

ARZU: Maybe we also don't like what the state measures as justice.

CEREN: The state's men make the law. I mean if there is a state, the laws are made within this state. The rights of citizens, the law, can everything be asked from the state?

MODERATOR: I am asking you.

When pushed to address the seeming contradiction between their previously expressed rights-based opposition to state intervention in veiling practices and their support for legislation against immodest dress, Ceren and Arzu argue that it is not a question of attenuating state control over women's dress, but rather of recalibrating the "justice" of the state to better harmonize with their own, Islam-informed perspectives. The state is thus invoked as the source of law and of right, and asked to implement and enforce sanctions against particular modes of dress. At the same time, we can read in Ceren's final question an ambivalence, an uncertainty, as to what exactly the role of the state might be in regard to rights and the law. The discussants are not suggesting that uncovered heads fall in the category of that which should be regulated by the state; like veiled women in other focus groups, participants in this group insist that veiling should not be an enforced practice. However, uncovered bellies and miniskirts are frequently cited (in this group and others) to illustrate the cultural politics of the formal enforcement of the antiveiling regime. Indeed, the 1980 "Dress and Appearance Regulation" (issued by military leaders who had then seized power through a coup d'etat) not only barred headscarves from university campuses but also contained directives against long hair and facial hair for men and miniskirts for women (Olson, 1985). Yet, while measures have been taken against veiled women, the policing of hemlines on university campuses has been a low priority. The question thus becomes one of governance, as state interventions reinforce lines of distinction in Turkish society by positioning female subjects in different ways depending on their dress and adornment in the public arena.

The ambivalence of veiling rights discourses can also be read in the representation of male bearding in focus-group discussions. Aspects of self-presentation, such as facial hair, prayer beads, and the typical collarless shirt, function to mark men as Islamist in Turkish society—though certainly not unambiguously, since beards, for instance, have also carried a leftist meaning. Although beards were cited alongside veiling as marking certain people and communities as "others" in opposition to the practices of secularism, women expressed mixed views regarding the significance of bearding both in Islam and as a "right." When discussing formal and informal regulations against facial hair in professions and schools, Belgin and Ceren had the following exchange:

BELGİN: A person with a beard can cut it. The beard isn't that important. I mean so what if a man has a beard? I think men are better looking without beards anyhow.

CEREN: In the view of our religion, a woman with the *çarşaf* and her husband with a beard are put into practice in the Sunna. The Prophet had a beard, and a robe [*cüppe*], of course.

For Belgin, the beard is simply not that significant, perhaps in part because, unlike the veil, it does not operate to signify, however ambivalently, particular formations of gender ideology, honor, and purity. However, Ceren's reply situates the beard within the same set of Islamic practices as the *çarşaf* (though she herself does not wear this garment). In any case, sanctions against beards fail to spark the same moral and political discourses that are mobilized around questions of veiling, further illustrating the specificity of the headscarf issue as a nodal point in political discourse in Turkey.

The idea of veiling as a human right represents a particular conjuncture of democratic and Islamist politics, a point at which these powerful legitimizing discourses interact to catalyze the "headscarf issue" as a shared construction and political focus. By understanding the political production of the headscarf issue in this way, we are also able to unravel some of the seeming contradictions of Islamist political discourse. For while rights are invoked in support of veiling practices, headscarf supporters otherwise express a desire for the Islamicization of governance rather than its "democratization" per se.[11] An example from the group of Islamist men illustrates this dynamic and further evokes the headscarf as an issue situated within everyday practices of government. Adem is an unmarried, 30-year-old high-school graduate and the owner of a shop that sells watches and cell phones.

"The headscarf is forbidden at the university, fine; why isn't the miniskirt forbidden? I mean, when we talk about human rights, one is below and another is above. When we talk about human rights, one person's rights will not be another's. I mean they say that one tyrannizes the other, but it also goes the other way. What one of them does is right, but according to whom? What you did is wrong according to me, what is right to me is wrong to you. Politics is found in the center of this, but we can't find the center. We have no politics."

Adem's statement encapsulates a sense of "rights" in Turkey as being not only unevenly protected by the state, but profoundly incommensurable. In this discourse, the (iconic) miniskirted woman is shown to have more rights than the (iconic) veiled woman under the current state-enforced secular hegemony: "One is below and another is above," as Adem says. However, there is no resolution of this problem possible through a universalist human rights regime within which, presumably, everyone's rights are protected. Instead, the secular–Islamist contest is seen as a zero-sum game being played out in the Turkish political field, a jockeying for position within a hierarchy of rights. For Adem, this represents a failure of politics, not because secular–Islamist positions should be equally valued or protected—which he sees as impossible due to their differing ethical systems—but because there is no consensus taking shape, no middle ground between these polarities. Without this shared ethical ground, no "politics" is possible. A particular understanding of "rights" (as hierarchical) and "politics" (as premised upon shared ethics) is thus filtered through the practices and discourses that have come into play around questions of veiling in Turkey.

Participants in the group of Islamist men grappled with questions of veiling and other norms of dress in relation to government, law, and rights. In the dialogue that follows, these issues are discussed among three of the men. Eren is a 27-year-old theology PhD student; because of his education, he was frequently looked to as an authority in the group. In terms of age and education, Hakan is at the other end of the spectrum in the group; a 49-year-old fisherman, watermelon peddler, and father of three children, he has only a primary-school education. While Eren is clean-shaven and wore a neatly pressed white shirt to the meeting, Hakan, with his skull cap and long beard, presented a markedly "Islamic" appearance. Barış, who drives a taxi, is 42 years old, has a high-school education, and is the father of three children.

EREN: . . . I accept the headscarf as one of the basic human rights. At the very least this is a symbol of religion. I see it as a necessity, and as such a human right. . . . This is a commandment of religion, they [women who wear the headscarf] view it as necessary and they have completely internalized this, and when this comes off, a person feels naked, but from above there is this insistence that you come out from under it.

HAKAN: Excuse me, can I ask something, to get help with it? Now, I didn't go to school, I struggled with primary school and dropped out. Now, as I understand it, to go to university with a headscarf is forbidden. Is there any law like that for an earring? A boy wears an earring, can he also not enter, doesn't this also break the law? I mean they talk about documents of human rights, is there a difference between them?

EREN: Well, the one who wants to wear a headscarf, and the one who wants to wear an earring—

HAKAN: Is there a difference? Seeing that the law is broken, whether you enter with an earring or with a headscarf, is there a difference? I'm thinking like this but then . . . it's because I'm ignorant.

MANY AT ONCE: *Estağfurullah* ["Please don't say such a thing about yourself"].

EREN: I think there is something theoretically different about the situations . . . I view the headscarf as a basic human right.

MODERATOR: Okay, I will ask something. Is the headscarf a political issue in Turkey?

BARIŞ: Now when I am starting to eat I say *bismillah* [thanks be to God], but another eats without saying this. This is also a symbol. One begins saying *bismillah*, one doesn't, if that [the headscarf] is a symbol, this is a symbol. If to say *bismillah* is harmful to the foundation of this country, it [the headscarf] is also wrong, the two are tied.

After Eren reiterates the oft-cited basis of veiling as a human right, Hakan intervenes with his sheepishly posed question. Although it is somewhat ambiguous, in my understanding Hakan's question goes to the issue of why certain aspects of dress codes (such as prohibitions against earrings for men) are not policed, while the secularist antiveiling regimes are formally enforced. Hakan presents this as an arbitrary application of the law. In my interpretation, he does this to highlight the cultural politics behind the headscarf regulations (just as the women did by pointing out the lack of antiminiskirt enforcement), rather than as a true confession of ignorance. In response, Eren distinguishes the veil as a particularly significant, religiously commanded, article of dress that can therefore be counted as a "human right." He thus makes a distinction between the legislation of veiling regimes and other kinds of dress codes based on their status in relation both to human rights and to Islam. Finally, Barış's analogy between the headscarf and the Muslim practice of saying *bismillah* situates the headscarf within the symbolic lexicon of Islam. By suggesting that these practices and the threat that they pose to the state are equivalent, Barış elides the differences between them (e.g., that one is public and visible while the other is private and aural) in order to magnify their similarity within the repertoire of Islamic symbolism. The state is thus seen as operating within an anti-Islamic register that seeks to criminalize habitual "private" religious practices.

The production of the headscarf as an issue that stitches together democratic and Islamist discourses gives rise to some ambivalent constructions in Turkish political discourse. While the headscarf is framed in terms of human rights, everyday understandings of rights and government are formulated within the context of the daily negotiation of politics and identity in Turkey. In a milieu where the state is understood as acting to assert the rights and interests of one group (the secular elite) over another (the Islamic folk), rights come to be understood as a product of cultural hegemony. The strategy of Islamist politics, then, is both to condemn the hypocrisy and violations of the secular establishment and to advocate for an Islamicizing corrective.

BIOPOWER AND THE DISCIPLINING
OF ISLAMIST SUBJECTS

In this section, I turn to the question of how veiling and other Islamist practices situate subjects in relation to governmental practice and the technologies of citizenship. I argue that the administration of veiling practices performs one aspect of *biopower*, which refers to the exertion of power over life through both the disciplining of bodies and the regulation of populations (Foucault, 1978; on veiling, see also Ong, 1990). As a technique of biopower, the spatial regulation of women's dress is enacted by a range of institutions (e.g., families, police, courts, and the army), and works at multiple levels, from the delineation of secular spaces to the prescription of bodily conduct. Situated within this web of regulation, veiling practices become a critical site for struggles over the delineation of public and private realms, the limits of state intervention, and the enactment of citizenship rights. It is within these struggles that liberal ideas of rights and privacy are called forth to assert the limits of state power over bodies, lives, and spaces.

Veiling regulation as a technique of biopower takes place within the context of broader practices of laicism in Turkey. While these practices have a long history, arguably the most recent secularist intervention was what has come to be known as "the February 28th Process," an 18-point antifundamentalist program initiated in 1997 by the National Security Council, a military–civilian state advisory body established by the 1982 constitution. Focus group participants referred to this process as marking a shift in the position of Islamism in Turkey. For example, in response to one of the first questions asked, "How have you come into contact with state institutions in your daily life?", Eren discussed the headscarf issue and his sister's inability to continue studying due to the 8-year education law. He went on to add the following:

> "The Constitutional Court closed the Refah Partisi [in 1998]. They had a concept of laicism, if I remember correctly, that defines laicism as extending into the family. It used a concept of laicism in the family, like religion. After seeing this you say, now this here, if it will enter to here, to my *mahrem* [private, domestic] arena, then nothing remains. It will be able to penetrate all areas. There is such an image. In that case there is a destruction of trust. Like it or not, ownership is reduced [*sahiplenme azalıyor ister istemez*]. The situation when the military comes up against the nation, like in the 28 February situation, has this kind of psychological effect. I mean, in general I have not come into confrontation with the state, except as a family and psychologically. . . ."

In this statement, Eren is referring to the January 1998 Constitutional Court ruling that shut down (not for the first or the last time) the Islamist party (RP), which had come to power having gained a plurality of votes in the previous elections. Hakan Yavuz (2000) summarizes this ruling as follows:

> In its decision, the Turkish court argued that *laicism* is not only a separation between religion and politics but also a necessary division between religion and society. This justified regulation of social life, education, family, economy, law, daily code of conduct and dress-code in accordance with the needs of everyday life and the Kemalist principles. (p. 38)

This court decision figures in Eren's narrative as a moment of realization, the point at which he comes to understand that the state's laicism is a legitimizing discourse for biopolitical techniques of government that operate on, through, and potentially against populations, or what he calls "the nation" (*millet*). He locates his encounter with the state within the realm of psychology, in that he was disturbed personally by the implications of the court's ruling, and within his family, where his sister was affected by the state's regulation of veiling practices. While his statement that "ownership is reduced" translates oddly into English, I have preserved the construction rather than trying to smooth it out because it expresses a particular conception of governmental practice and that which escapes its grasp. The *mahrem*, that is, the domestic, feminine sphere, is thus pictured as that which is owned—in other words, private—and also that upon which the laws of Islam alone are expected to act. In Eren's statement, it is thus not simply that the Turkish state has sought to cleanse Islam from the public sphere, but rather that it has sought to organize populations through intervention in the conduct of everyday life. Furthermore, what is at stake is not only the specific issues of women's dress, mobility, and education, but the very boundary between the private and the public in Turkish society and the limits of state intervention.

These biopolitical practices situate "Islamist subjects" in relation to the police, the courts, and "the state" as it is mythologized in the Turkish context (see Navaro-Yashin, 2002). Such practices beg the question posed by Mitchell Dean (1999) and quoted at the outset of this chapter: Who are we when we are governed in such a way? The question calls for an analysis of how practices of government and authority are linked to modalities of identity and citizenship. Some of these social effects can be traced through the everyday practices narrated by focus-group participants. In particular, encounters with the police and the military figure as sites of government and "subjectification," that is, as spaces where individuals find themselves taking up particular positions in relation to other entities (such as "the na-tion," "the people," or "the state") and establishing themselves as political subjects. In the group of Islamist women, participants discussed how their veiling practices prevent them from attending military ceremonies for their sons. Moreover, both men and women talked of police discriminating against their communities and families because of the presence of veiled women and bearded men; Barış referred to "insinuations" being made at the police station because the men in his community are bearded, and Arzu, whose son did not pass the police academy exam, surmised that the reason might have been that "they do research, our men are bearded." In this way, practices associated with the police and the military delineate spaces both for the regulation of Islamist identities and for the identification of Islamist subjects.

Islamist women's discussions of the impact of the 28th February pro-cess on the *imam-hatip* schools reiterated their impression that juridical and policing practices place their communities under a cloud of suspicion. Havva was especially agitated as she demanded to know: "How many peo-ple have *imam-hatip* graduates killed? Why are these forbidden? How much damage have they done to this country?" Later, she again brought up the way that *imam-hatip* schools, their graduates, and their proponents were cast as somehow dangerous or criminal.

In fact, in some of their everyday religious practices, focus-group par-ticipants found themselves coming under the discipline and surveillance of the police:

EMEL: In our house we had religious meetings, these were taken from our hands.

MODERATOR: How? Who took them?

EMEL: They came from the police station and forbade us to have one more meeting.

CEREN: They [neighbors] must have complained.

EMEL: And for one year we didn't go, why? I want to learn religion, and other things.

CEREN: They are done in secret.

EMEL: They are done in secret. At one house today, we become afraid . . .

CEREN: From the point of view of religion, we are not free.

EMEL: It's just a conversation after all! [*Sohbet ya!*]

CEREN: Women get Koran lessons in secret. You can't gather with 10 women, immediately the police come down, as though there is a complaint.

MODERATOR: In your nearby environment, in your neighborhoods, is it like this?

CEREN: Yes. One by one we go out to the house where the discussion [*sohbet*] will be . . .

Emel and Ceren's discussion of clandestine meetings for Koranic study and conversation among women draws attention to how complaints by neighbors and police surveillance work to position Islamist women as criminal in relation to the disciplinary biopolitical technologies of government.[12] It is not that Koranic study is illegal in Turkey; on the contrary, after 5 years of primary school, students have the option of signing up for extracurricular Koran courses that are organized through the Directorate of Religious Affairs—in other words, under state supervision. In this context, Ceren and Emel's dialogue captures feelings of unease and reveals the tactics, such as changing the place and going to the house stealthily, one by one, which are used to keep these meetings under the radar.

In these discussions, participants both recount how the practices of government have situated Islamist subjects and voice objections to what they see as processes of marginalization and criminalization. In these ways, the discussions among focus-group participants express an awareness of how the Islamist–laic contest continues to play out through policy, enforcement practices, and political discourses. The "issue-tization" and ambivalent construction of veiling practices in Turkey take place within this context of governmentality and biopolitical production.

CONCLUSION

What remains unspoken in this chapter is what is perceived to be at stake for the secularist state in the regulation of veiling practices. It is not simply a desire for power that has led to regulations over women's dress in certain spaces in Turkey, but rather a particular constellation of fears and desires through which the veil has come to be seen as a symbol of resistance to Ataturk's modernizing reforms, especially concerning women's roles in society, and of the potential for Islamist revolution. As Esra Özyürek (2003) shows in her discussion of the 1999 controversy sparked by Merve Kavakcı, the Refah Party parliamentarian who attempted to take her oath of office while wearing a headscarf, the incursion of veiling into regulated spaces is often seen as the potential harbinger of an Iranian- or even Taliban-style reconfiguration of space, gender, and power in Turkey. Newspapers, protestors, and other analysts accused Kavakcı, who had both Turkish and U.S. citizenship, of being at once an American provocateur and an Iranian agent. Along with then prime minister Bulent Ecevit's famous statement, "Please let this woman know her place," these events once again positioned the headscarf as a symbol of the dangerous porosity of boundaries.

Finally, what is at stake in the contest over the headscarf in Turkey is the question of how the techniques of government, operating on and through populations, structure and define the gendered spaces of political, social, and religious life. In the attempt to delimit state intervention and to assert the political subjectivity of citizens, liberal democratic discourse (momentarily, contingently) articulates with pro-veiling arguments in Turkey. I argue that the assembly of knowledge and practices surrounding women's head covering works to situate individuals within particular relations of power that are articulated at once through Islamist and liberal-democratic discourses. When the "headscarf issue" thus operates as a point of capture for Islamist and liberal-democratic arguments, this both affects how rights are understood in the Turkish context and positions Islamists in a particular way vis-à-vis society, the state, and international human rights discourses. The discipline and regulation of veiling thus operates as a technique of biopower that is encountered within the everyday spaces of the police, the military, the army, schools, and legal rulings. Certainly, there is much at stake in the headscarf contest, both for Islamists and for secularists. Furthermore, these discourses and practices are themselves mobile; not only is the correspondence between veiling and particular sociospatial regimes of gender itself multiple and shifting, but so too are conceptions of rights, democracy, and the state. Let this study appear not to arbitrate the Islamist–secularist conflict, but to provide a partial window into its political production.

ACKNOWLEDGMENTS

I gratefully acknowledge the support of Grant No. BCS-0137060 from the National Science Foundation for this research. I would also like to thank the team at the Social Research Center (Sosyal Araştırmalar Merkezi) in Levent, Istanbul, for all their help with this project. This chapter has benefited from the comments of participants at the Pennsylvania State University Geography Department Coffee Hour, where I presented a previous version of this argument. I would also like to thank Banu Gökariksel and the editors, Ghazi-Walid Falah and Caroline Nagel, for their helpful comments on an earlier draft. I alone am responsible for the contents of this chapter.

NOTES

1. See Elizabeth Özalga (1998) for a discussion of the legal history of veiling in the Turkish republic. See also Emelie Olson's (1985) work on the headscarf dispute in the early 1980s.

2. The *imam-hatip* schools, or preacher schools, were first opened in 1950 by the state Directorate of Religious Affairs, which regulates all mosques in Turkey. Their purpose was to train imams, who would then be employed by the mosques as civil servants. In 1973, their charge was expanded as they began to admit girls as well. By the late 1990s, the *imam-hatip* middle schools and high schools graduated far more people than were employed by the mosques and had simply become a religious alternative to secular education. After the 1997 law went into effect, the middle schools were gradually shut down, though *imam-hatip* high schools are still in operation.

3. In Turkish, what I am calling "veiling" is most often referred to in terms of "covering," and in the specific terms of the headscarf or turban. I use the term "veiling," as it has been used elsewhere in the literature on gender and Islam, to refer to practices of covering women's heads, hair, and sometimes bodies and faces for the purposes of modesty and honor and as an Islamic practice.

4. The group with Islamist women was facilitated by a trained female moderator and myself. The group with Islamist men was facilitated by a male moderator while I observed, with the consent of the participants, on a closed-circuit television in another room. I chose to absent myself from the room for this discussion because I thought that my presence, as a woman in a male space, might exert some effect on the conversation. I found the experience of watching the group on television alienating and afterward decided it was probably unnecessary or not worth the peculiarity and the feeling of surveillance. This was the first focus group I had done with men, and for later focus groups with men I participated in person. The discussions were loosely structured but guided by questions about associational life and everyday encounters with state institutions.

5. The survey was of 4,005 Istanbul residents and was conducted in the summer of 2002 as part of a project sponsored by the National Science Foundation called "Reshaping Civil Society: Islam, Democracy and Diversity in Istanbul" (BCS-0137060). Fourteen of the focus groups were also conducted as part of this project. I received assistance with the survey and focus groups from the Social Research Center (Sosyal Araştırmalar Merkezi) in Levent, Istanbul.

6. Because of occasional shut-downs by the Constitutional Court and an internal split, it is worth clarifying the lineage of Islamist parties in Turkey. First orga-

nized (under different names) in the 1970s, the Refah Partisi (RP), led by Necmettin Erbakan, came to municipal power in Istanbul and Ankara (and other municipalities) in 1994, and to national power with a plurality of the vote (around 20%) in 1995. It was shut down in 1997, whereupon the Fazilet Partisi (FP) took its place. The FP did not garner a plurality in the 1999 national elections, but did make it into parliament once more. However, it too was shut down and subsequently replaced by two parties, the Saadet Partisi, which continues under Erbakan's leadership, and the more popular Adalet ve Kalkınma Partisi, more commonly called Ak Parti, led by Recep Tayyip Erdoğan. The Ak Parti, which has eschewed the "Islamist" label and prefers to be considered "Muslim democrat," garnered an unprecedented 34% of the national vote in November 2002.

7. Laicism (*laiklik*) is the Turkish term for secularism and reflects the particular form that secularism has taken in Turkey, with the institutionalization of state control of religion.

8. "Kemalists" refers to the political elite who practiced the reformist and Westernizing principles of Mustafa Kemal Atatürk.

9. All names are pseudonyms.

10. See Ayşe Öncü's (1995, p. 53) discussion of how "Islam, as packaged for consumption by heterogeneous audiences becomes an issue, something that has to be addressed and confronted—provoking pro and con positions" within the Turkish mass media in the 1990s. I borrow the term "issue-tization" from her provocative argument.

11. As Jenny White (2002, pp. 166–170) points out in her study, and as my focus-group discussions also illustrate, one response of Turkish Islamists to the question of whether Islam and democracy are compatible is to argue that "Sharia is democracy," since contained within Islam are all the general goods associated with democracy. Thus the Islamicization of society would obviate the need for "democracy," at least by that name.

12. I am reminded that when this focus group was assembling and the group of veiled women disembarked from the van in the street in Levent and entered the research quarters, we joked about how the neighbors would become suspicious of our activities.

REFERENCES

Agamben, G. (1998). *Homo sacer: Sovereign power and bare life.* Stanford, CA: Stanford University Press.

Ahmed, L. (1992). *Women and gender in Islam.* New Haven, CT: Yale University Press.

Bourdieu, P. (1977). *Outline of a theory of practice.* Cambridge, UK: Cambridge University Press.

Buğra, A. (2002). Labor, capital and religion: Harmony and conflict among the constituency of political Islam in Turkey. *Middle Eastern Studies, 38,* 187–204.

Çarkoğlu, A., & Toprak, B. (2000). *Türkiye'de din, toplum ve siyaset* [Religion, society, and politics in Turkey]. Istanbul: Türkiye Ekonomik ve Sosyal Etüdler.

Dean, M. (1999). *Governmentality: Power and rule in modern society.* London: Sage.

Eickelman, D. F., & Piscatori, J. (1996). *Muslim politics.* Princeton, NJ: Princeton University Press.

Foucault, M. (1978). *The history of sexuality, Vol. 1: An introduction.* New York: Vintage Books.

Foucault, M. (1994). Governmentality. In J. D. Faubion (Ed.), *Power* (pp. 201–222). New York: New Press.

Göle, N. (1996). *The forbidden modern.* Ann Arbor: University of Michigan Press.

Göle, N. (1997). Secularism and Islamism in Turkey: The making of elites and counterelites. *Middle East Journal, 51,* 46–58.

Houston, C. (1999). Civilizing Islam, Islamist civilizing?: Turkey's Islamist movement and the problem of ethnic difference. *Thesis Eleven, 58,* 83–98.

Kılıçbay, B., & Binark, M. (2002). Consumer culture, Islam and the politics of life-style: Fashion for veiling in contemporary Turkey. *European Journal of Communication, 17,* 495–511.

Navaro-Yashin, Y. (2002). *Faces of the state: Secularism and public life in Turkey.* Princeton, NJ: Princeton University Press.

Olson, E. A. (1985). Muslim identity and secularisms in contemporary Turkey: "The headscarf dispute." *Anthropological Quarterly, 58,* 161–170.

Öncü, A. (1995). Packaging Islam: Cultural politics on the landscape of Turkish commercial television. *Public Culture, 8,* 51–71.

Ong, A. (1990). State versus Islam: Malay families, women's bodies, and the body politic in Malaysia. *American Ethnologist, 17,* 258–276.

Özdalga, E. (1998). *The veiling issue, official secularism and popular Islam in modern Turkey.* Richmond, UK: Curzon.

Özyürek, E. (2003, December 12–14). *The headscarf knot in the Turkish Parliament.* Conference paper presented at the American University in Cairo for the workshop "Gendered Bodies, Transnational Politics: Modernities Reconsidered," organized by the Institute for Gender and Women's Studies at the American University in Cairo and the Center for the Study of Gender and Sexuality at New York University.

Rose, N. (1999). *Powers of freedom: Reframing political thought.* Cambridge, UK: Cambridge University Press.

Saktanber, A. (1994). Becoming the "other" as a Muslim in Turkey: Turkish women vs. Islamist women. *New Perspectives on Turkey, 11,* 99–134.

Secor, A. (2002). The veil and urban space in Istanbul: Women's dress, mobility and Islamic knowledge. *Gender, Place, and Culture, 9,* 5–22.

Soysal, Y. N. (1997). Changing parameters of citizenship and claims-making: Organized Islam in European public spheres. *Theory and Society, 26,* 509–527.

White, J. (2002). *Islamist mobilization in Turkey.* Seattle: University of Washington Press.

Wilkinson, S. (1998). Focus groups in feminist research: Power, interaction, and the coconstruction of meaning. *Women Studies International Forum, 24,* 111–125.

Yavuz, M. H. (2000). Cleansing Islam from the public sphere. *Journal of International Affairs, 54,* 21–42.

Yeğenoğlu, M. (1998). *Colonial fantasies: Towards a feminist reading of orientalism.* Cambridge, UK: Cambridge University Press.

9 Social Transformation and Islamic Reinterpretation in Northern Somalia

The Women's Mosque in Gabiley

ABDI ISMAIL SAMATAR

Transformations in the lives of Muslim women are overlooked or misunderstood when seen solely in terms of Islam or religious revival. The focus of Islam as determinant of women's place has largely ignored the role of the world system and capitalist expansion in shaping gender relations, emphasizing instead unchanging religious texts and traditions. Studies of women's integration into the world system, on the other hand, often analyze the material changes in women's lives without connecting them to processes of religious and cultural transformation.

—BERNAL (1994, p. 59)

Precolonial Islamic practice in Somalia was among the most liberal in the Muslim world regarding gender relations and women's involvement in economic and social life. The country's colonization and the economy's commercialization induced contradictory social processes. These processes simultaneously intensified men's control over women and their resources and created new opportunities for women's advancement. The dynamics generated by these twin processes conditioned emerging patterns pertaining to women's role and social location in Islamic northern Somalia. An issue central to these patterns was women's access to Islamic and secular education.

Most Islamic societies have denied women the opportunity to gain significant training in Islam, although the holy Qur'an and the prophet's Hadith urge all Muslims to seek knowledge:

> God will exalt those who believe among you, and those who have knowledge, to high ranks. (Qur'an xx, 114)

> The search for knowledge is a duty for every Muslim, male or female—Hadith. (May, 1980, 386-6)

The denial of Islamic education to women and girls for several centuries led to an absence of Muslim women educated in Islamic affairs and of female religious leaders. This established a tradition in which only men interpreted the holy text and the prophet's sayings. In the process, women lost many freedoms they had gained in Islam's early years. For instance, the opportunity to interpret Islamic canons and to lead prayers, both of which were possible for learned women during the prophet's life, almost vanished.

Muslim women in many Islamic societies have struggled to regain lost ground and to empower half of the Islamic *umma* (the community of all Muslims) in accordance with Allah's sense of justice (Afshar, 1996). Central to these engagements has been access to Islamic education, in particular, and to the opportunity to gain leadership in Islamic affairs. The establishment (1970–1972) of a women's mosque in the town of Gabileh, located in northwest Somalia, was a historic benchmark in the annals of the Somali and Islamic worlds.[1] My claim is that the women who built possibly the first women's mosque in the world had two goals. Their first and foremost objective was to create an autonomous space that would allow women to join men in prayers and other religious rituals without transgressing on Islam's tenets.[2] Their second purpose was to establish a center where women could learn and deepen their understanding of the Qur'an and other Islamic texts. Such a center suggested an implicit criticism of Islamic practice, which did not provide women with the opportunity to study Islam. This censure also challenged men's interpretation of Allah's fairness and justice. For example, the Qur'an and the Hadith do not mandate that women pray in the back of the mosque. As a result, the essence and spirit of Islam do not prohibit women from praying in a separate but adjacent mosque. According to this interpretation, women would stand in lines parallel to the men's lines, rather than behind them. This practice could suggest that men and women are equal in Allah's eyes, as both submit to Allah's will in their prayers. The introduction of such a practice is also in accord with the *hajj* (Islamic pilgrimage) convention where women and men perform their obligations without regard to sex segregation and gender hierarchy in terms of geographic location (Nanji, 1996).

Finally, the women's mosque in the seemingly conservative small town of Gabiley signals the availability of a progressive Islamic alternative to a Euro-Americacentric view of women's liberation. This alternative liberation disconnects Islam from the patriarchal practices of different cultures in the Muslim world. Islam-based women's liberation will help eliminate women's isolation and redefine the public–private divide without abandoning the decency and mutual respect stipulated by the Qur'an and Hadith.

The rest of this chapter is divided into four parts. The first section schematically outlines the structure of northern Somali society's precolonial pastoral economy, its division of labor, and the political and religious role of men and women. The second section highlights the ways in which colonialism and intensified commercialization affected women's role in the economy, the consequent redefinition of Islamic practice regarding middle-class women's dress code and mobility, and the secular education of girls. The patterns set during the latter years of colonial rule gained strength after independence in 1960. This long historical outline is necessary to contextualize the establishment of the women's mosque in Gabiley. The third section narrates the story of the women's mosque. The chapter's conclusion assesses the significance of the mosque's establishment and its limited contribution to progressive Islamic reform in Gabiley and the rest of Somalia.

PRECOLONIAL POLITICAL ECONOMY, WOMEN, AND ISLAMIC PRACTICE

Precolonial northern Somali society consisted of two distinct but connected parts: the commercially oriented small towns dotted along the Gulf of Aden and the pastoral interior. Among the major coastal towns were Zeylac, Bulaxaar, Berbera, Maydh, Calaula, Hobyo, Muqdisho, Marka, and Barawa. The story of these port towns is told elsewhere (Alpers, 1983; Kapteijns & Spaulding, 1989; Kassim, 1995; Reese, 1999). The focus of this chapter is the predominantly pastoral northern Somali society.

The division of labor in this pastoral society dovetailed with patriarchal, but relatively open, cultural norms (Kapteijns, 1999; Samatar, 1989)[3] and a relaxed interpretation of Islam. Men and women were fully involved in the production of necessities for the family, although in different spheres. Women were responsible for building portable homes in pastoral areas and mud huts in settled communities. Their responsibilities also included maintaining the house and managing small ruminants such as sheep and goats. When rainwater was within easy reach of the community, women took sheep and goats to the watering holes. The small stock had to stay close to settlements as it required frequent (alternate days) watering, unlike camels, which could go without water for up to 15 days. Girls looked after these animals as long as they stayed within a half-day walk of the village. Furthermore, married women and their unmarried daughters traveled some distance to collect firewood and reeds for making house mats and carpets. Married women had more mobility, while their teenaged daughters faced greater restrictions, particularly as they approached marriage age (15–20). Finally, although women were restricted to the domestic sphere, they were still allowed to participate in a wide array of productive and social activities that took them away from home.

In contrast, men, particularly young ones, tended to large livestock, such as camels, and maintained water wells. They would regularly be away in distant grazing areas for months. During the wet season, men and their camel herds traveled some distance to save the rangeland close to the settlement for the dry season. Men also left home when they went out to explore new grazing areas. Men plowed the fields, using a hoe or oxen-mounted wooden plow, weeded the farm, and harvested the produce, usually sorghum, maize, and beans, in the few farming communities in the western areas of northern Somalia. They protected the fields from scavenging beasts and birds and maintained the underground granaries.

Livestock was the main form of capital in this mainly pastoral society. Access to rangeland and water were the conditions necessary for this capital's reproduction. A household or an individual family owned neither the rangeland nor the water resources. Men from several families dug and maintained water wells. These families shared use of the wells. The whole community or several communities had usufruct rights to rangeland within reasonable proximity of the settlement. Rangelands, except those that were closed off (*xidhmo*) to save them for needier times, were open to all members. The elder's council was responsible for deciding to close off a grazing area. In addition, the area surrounding a community was not used for grazing during the rainy season. Most livestock did not need to stay close to the village when water and grass were plentiful.

Unlike this relatively complementary division of labor in the economy, men were hegemonic in the domains of formal politics and religion. The council of elders responsible for managing community affairs was exclusively male. Although all adult men did not necessarily participate in the council's deliberations, the process was open and fairly democratic. Despite the absence of bureaucratically sanctioned mechanisms for selecting elders and council leaders, individuals rose to prominence and gained respect for their ability to clearly articulate issues and to render fair and balanced judgments in disputes. The council had the authority to ensure that community members abided by the dictates of Islam, Somali *Xeer* (customary law), and the edicts of tradition. The council's authority extended to deciding on women's role in the economy, their claim to property, and their treatment by kinfolk. Although women were physically absent from these councils, they significantly influenced the elders' deliberations and decisions. Women who were culturally knowledgeable used their superior understanding of tradition to influence community affairs through their husbands, fathers, and brothers.[4]

Men held sway in religious affairs and related scholarship and ceremonial matters. Women were not formally barred from studying Islam, but they were not encouraged to do so.[5] Their knowledge of Islam was limited to what they learned as children from their mothers and as adults from their husbands. In Somali mythology, there were no women whose religious reputation, even in fiction, came close to the fame of the Somali ruler Araweelo. This mythical female became the lord of the land. Araweelo had the reputation of being a tough ruler who is said to have castrated all men except those from whom she wanted to have children. There are no other known women who presided over such councils or who became rulers of their communities. Muunisa is the only mythical religious female leader. The devil is said to have seduced her on her way to prayers. Consequently, she lost both faith and face. The only female religious leader whose life is documented historically is Sheikh Dada Masiti, who became a leading Islamic figure in her hometown of Barva in the latter part of the 19th century (Kassim, 1995). The religious division of labor reinforced what patriarchal culture already sanctioned.[6] Women were relegated to work in the domestic sphere and excluded from gaining religious titles, such as wadaad, sheikh, or imam.

These political and religious demarcations partially governed sociospatial practice and gender ideology. Women's mobility was not severely restricted. Kapteijns and Spaulding (1989) note that a few women may even have been key links in the trade between pastoralists and coastal towns. Although women were barred from certain public spaces, such as the elders' council, and from conducting religious ceremonies, such as the *Mowleed* (the prophet's birthday celebrations), they participated in many other outdoor economic and social activities. For example, unlike in some Islamic societies, northern Somali women openly and publicly participated in ceremonial dances with men.

In addition, men were excluded from intruding into the women's arena. In fact, men who partook in a women's gathering were labeled *dumar shaneyeh* (he who is the women's fifth column). Fearing such a biting label, most men did not interfere with women's spaces. Women protested when men intruded into their domain, and the elders' council acted swiftly to correct such contravention. In summary, women were not confined to the home, except during the last month of pregnancy and the 40 days after the birth of a child. Beyond these limits, women went almost anywhere necessary to accomplish their tasks.

Finally, women's and men's traditional dress was relatively unrestrictive. Women's dress consisted of a long wraparound cotton sheet (*qayd*) that left a woman's neck, face, hands, and part of the shoulders uncovered. This dress was similar to the *guntiimo* used in more recent years in southern Somalia. In contrast, two cotton sheets constituted men's traditional pastoral dress.

COLONIAL TRANSFORMATION, WOMEN, AND SECULAR AND ISLAMIC EDUCATION

Colonialism and the commercialization of social life and subsequent transformations in the northern Somali pastoral economy inevitably entailed changes in the practice of Islam and other cultural norms (see Figure 9.1) (Samatar, 1997).[7] This section briefly describes how the dynamics of colonization and commercialization affected the division of labor, and the reinterpretation of Islamic practice to sanction housewivization of middle-class women and to impose a new dress code on women. Furthermore, it sketches the manner in which colonial secular education was introduced into northern Somalia and how it reinforced discrimination against girls.

The colonial state reinforced Somali patriarchy in the way it reinterpreted Islamic law (*Shari'ah*) with the help of native *ulema* (the body of mullahs). The state promulgated new laws that enhanced male dominance and control. At the same time it also opened career opportunities for women by establishing girls' schools during the final days of colonial rule. Similarly, commercialization induced parallel processes that led to the housewivization of women in middle-class families and the entry of poor urban women into market opportunities.

As in other African regions, colonialism in Somalia brought new processes of articulation in the regional and global economy. The changes colonialism induced included commercialization of key resources and rapid urbanization. The division of labor described above remained intact in the

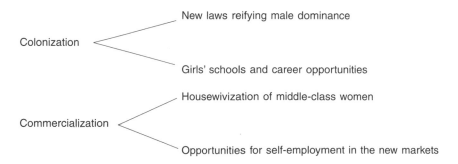

New laws reifying male dominance

Colonization

Girls' schools and career opportunities

Housewivization of middle-class women

Commercialization

Opportunities for self-employment in the new markets

FIGURE 9.1. Impact of colonization and commercialization on gender division of labor in northern Somalia.

rural areas until the middle of the 1930s (Samatar, 1989). However, the control and use of small livestock was noticeably changed, as they were quickly and progressively commoditized. Women's grip over small ruminants began to loosen. This stock became the colony's chief trade commodity, and men were the principal organizers of this trade. They marketed and sold the animals. Although cash from the sales technically belonged to the household, the men retained full control over its distribution. The wife received some money to be used for family sustenance, while the man retained some for his use. This change indirectly, but radically, undermined women's access to and control over this key resource. It also increased a patriarch's control over the labor of women and female children.

The establishment of colonial urban centers and the expansion of old coastal towns, both linked to the new commodity economy, accompanied the commercialization of the rural economy. The growth of urban centers gained momentum as trade increased briskly between 1925 and 1940 (Samatar, 1989). The principal towns were Hargeisa (the colonial capital), Berbera, Burco, Boraama, Cerigabo, Gabiley, and Laas Canood. The expansion of the colonial urban economy led to the emergence of an urban-based class social structure. The dominant players in this new social economy included traders, the staff of the colonial administration, and teachers. This transformation led to the development of a new family type and new household relations.[8] Men in the emergent class whose income or salaries were high enough sought housewives rather than wives who remained active in the economic sphere. Members of this group who had livestock in the countryside often had second wives to attend to their property. This new relationship confined the wives to the home and separated them from domestic work altogether if their husbands' incomes were sufficient to pay for domestic help. Middle-class households borrowed girls from their rural relatives and paid them a token wage in return. The higher the wealth and income of a household, the more domesticated were its female members. These household arrangements were the ideal image of the urban, middle-class Somali family. Families whose wealth or income was not sufficient to hire domestic help had to resort to old ways. Women in these families became village or urban market women, such as butchers. Others, particularly in smaller towns and villages, practiced rural occupations, such as rearing livestock.

Islam was also redefined as social differentiation unraveled. The first sign of this was using Islam to defend housewivization.[9] Such use of Islam was evident in work and dress. Middle-class wives were excluded from productive economic activity outside the home. Moreover, this group's movements were curtailed, although they could visit friends and relatives.

Dress vividly captures the changing conceptions of appropriate conduct and presentation. In pastoral communities, the traditional wrap-around, white, cotton sheet with no sleeves and a scarf (*masar* or *gambo*) covering the hair of married women were the norm. In the new urban society, the one-piece dress (*toob*) with sleeves (or sleeveless if the woman worked outside the home) and an extra shawl became requisite. The *toob*, adopted from coastal towns, was accompanied by a heavy, long, flowing skirt (*googarad*) that covered all of the lower body except the heels. The shawl was not required inside the home unless men were visiting. In some instances, the new dress code included the *shadir* and the *hijab*. This urban dress code became the norm for females, starting at age 14. Wives of the commercial and administrative classes could afford this attire, but even lower-class women attempted to follow suit, given the higher status conferred by the dress code.[10] Currently, in a phase of intensified conservatism,[11] the shawl is tied under the chin, protecting the neck and much of the face from vision.

The *toob–googarad–masar–gambo–shawl* dress code made some headway in the countryside until recently. However, given its restrictiveness, it never became the norm in pastoral–farming communities. The old dress code prevailed in the countryside for the most part. Rural women wore urban dress if they could adapt it to their work demands. In later years a more flexible and lighterweight sleeveless dress, called the *diric*, replaced the *toob*, particularly with the younger generations. Finally, the determinant for urban versus rural dress codes was and still is the degree of a woman's involvement in productive labor.

Colonialism set in motion a number of processes that gave men greater opportunities to secure their interests. Women's autonomy worsened, and they became more dependent on men, who interacted with the increasingly commercialized and bureaucratized society. Pastoral women had to rely on men to sell their animals so they could have cash to purchase the needs of the household, and urban middle-class women became relatively isolated housewives. While the middle-class, housewife-based urban family became idealized, poor women in towns could not afford this lifestyle and had to engage in petty trade and other means to support their families (Cabdillahi, 1998).

By the mid-1950s a clear rural–urban divide in economic organization, hierarchical structure, and gender ideology existed in northern Somalia. Although the new economy and the reinterpretation of Islam disadvantaged women, most women who were poor and mostly rural escaped the ideal family code's restrictions. However, the unavailability of Qur'anic and secular education to women blocked their participation in the higher echelons of the new economy and society whether they were rural or urban, middle class or poor. Western and Islamic education proved to be critical in forming gender roles. Qur'anic schools were accessible to small numbers of children in traditional pastoral communities. These were boys' schools, and the duration of training was rarely more than 2–3 years. The boys were then expected to contribute to the household. Only a few exceptional boys were trained beyond this to become religious authorities, or *waddads*. The young men who pursued Islamic teaching then had to travel beyond their villages and live in Islamic centers, such as Harar, under an accomplished sheikh's tutelage. Young girls did not receive similar Islamic training (Xassan, 1999).

Colonial education entered this terrain. Unlike in many parts of colonial Africa, Christian missionaries did not venture deep into Somali territory. There was one mission school for orphans in the port town of Berbera in the 19th and early 20th centuries. The Muslims' early-morning call to prayers irritated those staffing the small colonial administrative station in Berbera. The officers felt that the call disturbed their sleep and ordered its discontinuation. This raised the ire of a young dynamic sheikh who had recently returned from a long tour of Islamic training in Mecca and Medina. Sayid Moxamed Cabdullah Xassan defied the order and had several confrontations with colonial authorities. In the end he left for the interior to organize a liberation war to rid the country of colonial infidels and missionaries. He almost succeeded in doing so in 1910, when the British evacuated the last stronghold of Berbera. The liberation war lasted until 1921, when British war planes bombed Sayid Moxamed's forts. This was the first time British war planes were used in subjugating local resistance in the colonies. Sayid Moxamed fled deep into the Somali–Ethiopian region. From that time Islam became the main source of resistance to British rule, and the authorities never dared to restrict prayers again.

The British attempt to establish secular education confronted the community's suspicion regarding the real agenda behind such a program. The colonial authorities and several Somalis who supported secular education constantly argued with religious leaders (Somaliland Protectorate, Education Department, 1956; Celmi & Muxumed, 1999). Two incidents highlight these confrontations. First, colonial education authorities wanted to use Latin script to write the Somali language in order to teach it in schools. This experiment was modeled after the Kiswahili experiment in British East Africa. Community elders and religious leaders vehemently opposed this effort, and it was shelved until 1971, 11 years after the British and Italian Somalilands united to form the Somali Republic. Those who opposed Latin script claimed that it was a colonial strategy to introduce Christianity and to reduce the proud Somali to the status of the East African Bantus (Samatar, 1989).[12] The only Somalis who were educated beyond basic literacy in Arabic and arithmetic were sons of notables sent to Aden and Sudan (British Somaliland Protectorate, 1934).

The second instance exemplifying the resistance to colonialism occurred in Gabiley. A British colonial education officer and his Somali assistant[13] came to town in 1951 to convince village elders to establish an elementary school. Primary schools had already been established in Hargeysa, Boorama, and Berbera in the 1940s. In spite of this, Gabiley residents pelted the officers with stones and ran them out of the village (Cabdillahi, 1986). The elders claimed that establishing an elementary school was another Christian ploy. Only one village resident stood up to the crowd in support of the school.[14] Despite massive resistance, the school was built in 1953.

The larger community and those who resisted secular education demanded that boys be educated in Islam and be able to read the Qur'an as prerequisites for enrolling in secular schools. The colonial authorities ceded to this agenda. With this concession, the number of secular and Qur'anic schools increased. Boys learned the Arabic alphabet and memorized the Qur'an. Although these schools were for boys only, a few girls attended them. The main Qur'anic school in Gabiley, established in the late 1940s, grew substantially once secular education was promulgated. Macalin Xassan Fahiye ran this Qur'anic school. Many villagers who attended this school fondly call it Ma'alin Hassan University. The few girls who attended Macalin Xassan's school did so in the early 1960s. The girls of that generation do not have similar nostalgic memories of the institution (Cusman, 1998).

Boys began attending Qur'anic and secular schools in Gabiley. The prerequisite for secular school admission was a child's ability to recite all the chapters in the first Giz of the Qur'an.[15] Many boys who met this requirement never entered secular school due to the scarcity of these institutions.

In contrast, girls could not attend secular schools because they did not have the requisite Qur'anic knowledge and because of the patriarchal prohibitions imposed on women. This systematic exclusion of girls from Qur'anic and secular education reinforced the middle-class notion of the ideal family and of women's role in it. Girls did not need an education as they were expected to marry young. The colonial government did not allocate any resources for girls' education until the last years of colonial rule.

The first and only girls' elementary school was established in Burco, a town that was at the forefront of antisecular education resistance, in 1953. The school started with two European mistresses and 30 Somali girls. Twelve of the girls were borders (Somaliland Protectorate, Education Department, 1953). This school was turned into a girls' intermediate school in 1957. Another girls' intermediate boarding school was established in Hargeisa in 1962. Science and math were not taught in girls' schools, as students were prepared to become housewives for the emergent male elite (Xudhuun, 2000). Only a few escaped this fate. The two most illustrious exceptions became a nurse and a school principal in the late 1960s. Others became government clerks, some leaving the service when they married. This environment did not nurture confident young women. In fact, a large number of girls who went to school dropped out as their parents tacitly encouraged them to marry before they became "too old."[16] In contrast, the boys received lifelong professional skills training through the Clerical Training Center in Hargeisa, the Teachers' Training Center in Camoud, several intermediate boarding schools, and two senior boarding secondary schools in Sheikh and Camoud. These boys became independent Somalia's administrators, teachers, medical professionals, and political leaders.

The Somali government's view regarding girls' education was ahead of public sentiment. Steeped in patriarchy and mesmerized by the seeming glory of daughters and sisters living as housewives of well-to-do men, Somali men were not inclined to push a public agenda centered on girls' education. Despite this unsupportive social climate, the new government opened up schooling opportunities for girls. By the late 1960s, many girls' elementary schools existed across the country. Additionally, a large number of girls were also attending what were previously boys' intermediate schools.

Expanding secular education for girls induced growth in girls' Qur'anic schools. In Gabiley, Macalin Xassan University became a coeducational institution in the early 1960s. Later other coeducational Qur'anic schools were established.[17] For the first time in Somali history, girls had open access to religious education. Once girls learned the requisite first Giz, they went to government schools. Islamic history and the Qur'an were among the subjects taught in the secular schools. Moreover, some students in secular schools spent their summer vacations in Qur'anic schools to deepen their knowledge of Islam.

Gabiley's first girls' elementary school was established in 1964 as part of the independent government's national education initiative. The school consisted of one rented room in the center of the town's main street. Eleven girls were enrolled in standard one. The 11 girls faced adjustment problems during the early days, as some men and boys opposed this development. Some boys in the town harassed these first-graders; the school uniform that included a short skirt exacerbated this harassment. Despite these problems, many of the opinion makers in the village, such as Haji Asker Cabdillahi, fully supported girls' education and the new school in Gabiley. Three years later the school moved to a new building adjacent to the boys' elementary school. By this time, more than 100 girls were enrolled in this coeducational day school. The school had male teachers except for the recently hired religious instructor.

A Somali family from Allah-Ibadey, a town on the Somali–Ethiopian border, settled in Gabiley in the early 1960s. Sheikh Ismail, the father of the family, was hired as a religious education teacher in the boys' elementary school. His wife, Sheikh Marian Sheikh Ismail,[18] was also a student of Islam, trained by her father and her husband. Sheikh Marian's skills found a ready market in the community.

A small but vibrant women's center called Sitaad existed in the village from the late 1950s (Kapteijns & Ali, 1996).[19] A number of middle-aged and older women established the Sitaad center.[20] A few of the older widows supported themselves and their families. These women's meager resources built the small mud-adobe building that housed the center. All women were practicing Muslims who observed the five prayers of the day and fasting during Ramadan month.

While men could gather and pray at the main mosque to celebrate religious occasions and gather at the teashop for socializing, women had no similar public gathering spot. The Sitaad center, located on the periphery of the main village, was the only public space where women could gather. It was a devotional space where women sang religious songs and attended to some of their collective concerns. Since none of the center's founding members were trained in Islam, Sheikh Marian was an Allah-sent blessing for the group. The sheikh was immediately inducted and began leading prayers and preaching in the center. She also began to teach the women basic Islamic history and the Qur'an.

With the increased demand for girls' religious education, Sheikh Marian began running her own Qur'anic school a few months after she arrived in Gabiley. She became an instant celebrity as the only female Qur'anic teacher in town and in the region. The Qur'anic school gave her exposure in the community and with public officials. The girls' government elementary school then recruited her as the school's religious teacher. The author was a junior colleague of Sheikh Marian during his national service years in 1972–1973.

The development of secular education opportunities for girls and the concomitant demand for Qur'anic education generated a self-reinforcing dynamic where women gained access to two spheres heretofore forbidden to them. Knowledge of the Qur'an as a prerequisite for secular school admission created, in this instance, a new tradition in which Islam and secularism mutually reinforced each other's growth, defying the often-noted immutuality of tradition and modernity.

THE WOMEN'S MOSQUE

Gabiley was established as an agricultural village in the early 1930s. Gabiley had six teashops and 26 retail stores in 1945. The expanded transit trade between Ethiopia and Somalia during the Italian occupation of the region in the period 1939–1941 significantly stimulated the village's economic activity (Samatar, 1989). Despite trade expansion, Gabiley remained a sleepy religious village until the late 1950s.

Gabiley's first permanent mosque was built in the late 1940s and renovated in 1958. A second and smaller mosque was established in 1963. Men used the two mosques for prayers and other Islamic functions. These mosques were not called "male" mosques, although they were essentially for males. Women rarely prayed or worshipped in the mosques. Occasionally women prayed in the back of the mosques, particularly during the two annual Islamic celebrations, the *Eid*s.

Nearly 10 years after the establishment of the Sitaad center (1968–1969), the Sitaad community members considered expanding the center into a mosque and women's community center. They sought financial help from town merchants and the district commissioner.[21] Their request was turned down; indeed, the women received no assistance from any man or authority they approached. The men told the women that the Sitaad center did not need to be upgraded into a mosque. Furthermore, the women were told that they could pray in the verandahs of the existing mosques. The women were angry and felt betrayed because some leaders ridiculed their plan. However, these setbacks simply fortified their resolve to establish their own mosque.[22]

After noting the town leaders' behavior, the women reorganized themselves and resolved to build the mosque on the empty plot straddling the main mosque and Macalin Xassan's Qur'anic school.[23] The group applied for a land grant for the plot from the local government. They received the permit for the 2-acre plot free of charge. Such a grant was not unusual, since all unoccupied land belonged to the state. What is not known is why the town leaders and the district commissioner who ridiculed the women's request for help did not block the land grant. Possibly the application for the plot went to a low-level clerk who was not informed about what the leaders thought of the women's request. Moreover, it is also possible that everybody knew about the land grant application, but the officials could not legally stop it. The land and the building were not subject to any taxes.

The construction of the first women's mosque in Somalia, and possibly the first mosque built by women for women in the world, began in 1970.[24] Organizers included Sheikh Marian Sheikh Ismail, Xalimo Cabdillahi, Amina Sheikh Muse, Casha Maweel, Fatimo Kahin, Cibado Celmi, Casha Sultan, Tusmo Abrar, Laqanyo Cabdillahi, Mako Ismail, Casha Haji, and Khadija Hashi Booni. The group had limited resources, no more than a few hundred shillings (about US$200) they had scavenged from their paltry savings. The mosque's construction was a painstakingly slow process, given the women's lack of financial resources and the townsmen's unwillingness to contribute. The men's attitudes contrasted sharply with the generosity of poor rural women in the surrounding villages and settlements. Each rural woman contributed a penny or two from her daily milk sales in town. Some who did not donate cash gifts enthusiastically contributed their labor to the effort. Other women from as far away as Djibouti sent their contributions. Despite these donations, the Sitaad group and other women in Gabileh had to provide most of the resources to sustain the project.

A committee managed the building process. They hired local masons, carpenters, and some laborers. In addition, many women worked as mortar and cement mixers. They built the mosque with locally quarried, flat, clay stone instead of the more expensive and attractive block-like sandstone or concrete block. The main mosque was built with sandstone blocks. The women used mud, a standard construction method for houses built since 1970, to cement the stones together. They then plastered the walls with a mix of fine-grained sand and cement. The roof of the mosque is made from corrugated iron. Buildings constructed this way are prone to termite infestation. Termites usually destroy all wooden building parts. Although the construction cost of the women's mosque was relatively low compared to that of the adjacent main mosque, its maintenance cost is high.

The women completed the mosque in 1972. Islamic and secular local authorities never recognized or celebrated this national accomplishment. Although District Gabileh won a national medal for its civic and development undertakings in 1973, the women's mosque was not even mentioned. The absence of official recognition was even more obvious given the government's concerted and highly publicized efforts to encourage community-wide projects.[25] Today, the mosque's founders insist that they did not establish the mosque to receive recognition from the authorities. They say, "Hooshayedu meeaheyiin in la nasheego," which means "Our project was not about getting credit." These women noted that the mosque is not a women's place, but a "Bayt Allah" (House of Allah). They hasten to add that all the women who selflessly contributed their efforts, not just the Sitaad group, felt proud of serving Allah's will.

The women's mosque is about half the size of the main mosque and can accommodate 300 women at full capacity. This many women may come to the mosque to pray on major Islamic occasions. The women's mosque shares a wall with the men's mosque and its height is several feet shorter than the adjacent male mosque. In some minds the difference in the heights of the two mosques signifies the lower status of the women's mosque.

From the start Sheikh Marian could lead prayers in the new mosque; however, the group wanted to share the leadership of the main mosque's imam.[26] The trouble was that they could hear the call to prayers, but not hear the imam's voice once prayers started, because of the wall separating the two mosques. They asked the men if a door could be built into the dividing wall. The men denied the women's request and told them to pray in the main mosque's verandah. This suggestion offended the women. They decided that Sheikh Marian would lead their prayers until the men agreed to install the door. Sheikh Marian made sure that her physical location when she led prayers was slightly behind the male imam's. This gesture reassured male leaders that the women were not intent on running a separate, parallel, and equal operation in "their" mosque.[27]

The women persevered in their request for the door. Sheikh Marian's husband, Sheikh Ismail, finally and openly came to their assistance and persuaded the men to build the door. He advised them that by letting the women follow their call they would be reaffirming men's leadership of prayers. The implicit idea in Sheikh Ismail's plea was that if the men did not concede to the women's request, the women might have no choice but to call and lead their prayers independently. He also reminded them that Islam prefers a united community of prayers. Finally the men agreed and fitted the door into the wall in 1973. A curtain was hung over the opening of the door to prevent the women and men from seeing each other. This link has worked flawlessly ever since.

Not only is the mosque a holy place where women can come to pray, but it is also a place where they can learn the Qur'an, the Hadith, and the Tafsiir.[28] Old Sitaad functions are conducted in the small Sitaad center. Ten women were studying advanced Tafsiir in 1998–1999. The religious training and expertise of four of these women, Shukri Osman, Zahra Abdi, Amina Aden, and Safia Aw Aden, is almost equal to that of the late sheikh Marian. The mosque also took on the function of providing temporary refuge for homeless or destitute women.[29] This function gained greater importance as a result of the destruction and chaos produced by the 1988–1994 Somali civil war.

The civil war destroyed civilized life. The state collapsed and the country disintegrated into warlord fiefdoms (Samatar, 1992). Although the war only moderately affected Gabiley, many public and private buildings and homes were destroyed. Some destruction resulted from indiscriminate use of military firepower. Marauding thieves who looted everything that could be removed, including corrugated iron roofing and window frames, caused the majority of the damage. The two mosques sustained damage from the firepower, but fortunately the looters spared these structures. The roofs of the two mosques were badly damaged. The main mosque was closed in 1993 for repair. The townsmen mobilized support for its rehabilitation. A wealthy businessman, a relative newcomer, financed the entire operation. The repairs were completed in the same year.

The men who rehabilitated the main mosque did not consider the needs of the adjacent women's mosque. Initially, the main mosque's wealthy benefactor thought about paying for repairing the women's mosque, but he later changed his mind. The structure of the women's mosque deteriorated significantly as water leaked through the holes in the roof and into the mud cement holding the flat stones together. The women pleaded with the men to give them the main mosque's undamaged corrugated sheets of old roofing and the ceiling beams. The men denied the women's request and sold these items. When asked why they denied the women's request, the men said that there was no need for a separate women's mosque. In fact, some younger and more militant men threatened to dismantle the women's mosque.[30] The women said they were prepared to defend Allah's House from misguided zealots and refused to succumb to these threats and pressures. The women selectively replaced the damaged sheets of metal and restored areas needing immediate attention. Despite their effort, the mosque's structure continues to deteriorate, and the women lack the resources to pay for necessary repairs.

The women who founded the mosque are now too old to manage its daily affairs. Sheikh Marian remained the mosque-based community's leader until her death in 1987. Sahra Abdi, a younger, self-educated, local government employee who was trained by Sheikh Marian, then assumed the responsibility of managing the mosque. Currently, Safia Aw Aden, a small merchant, oversees the mosque's daily affairs. A committee consisting of Safia Aw Aden, Amina Aden, Zahra Abdi, and Shukri Osman is responsible for general management of the mosque.

Five mosques currently exist in Gabiley. A more modern one was built at the southern end of town in the late 1980s with a grant from a Middle Eastern religious foundation. This male mosque is the center for young radical Islamists. They have attracted a contingent of young women to their fold. These women are trained in Islamic affairs along purist lines that sanction women's traditional roles. These women pray in the back of this mosque. Women followers of this purist but traditional interpretation of Islam and those of the women's mosque disagree on many issues. The two groups of women regularly debate about the appropriate role of women in Islam.

Deqa Jama, an old matriarch, singlehandedly financed the fifth mosque. Deqa used remittance money sent by her sons and daughters who work in the Middle East, Europe, and the United States and some of the wealth she inherited from her late husband. The mosque is affectionately called "Deqa's mosque." This is a conventional male mosque where women can pray in the back. Deqa's mosque is located in the northern perimeter of town in an area that was farmland. It is about the same size as the women's mosque, but it is well kept and maintained.

CONCLUSION

Somali society went through fundamental changes since its contacts with the outside world intensified through colonization and the establishment of the postcolonial state. Major areas of change include women's role in the economy and the family and their access to Islamic and secular education. Women lost *and* gained from these changes. Women's foremost loss, particularly prior to the 1980s, was their reduced role in the cash economy. The old pastoral world in which the division of labor between women and men was complementary and premised on use-value production gave way to a two-tier economy in which men controlled access to the market. The men also determined what pastoral household resources were to be marketed and how most cash earnings were to be used. Second, denying women access to opportunities, such as secular education, reinforced their marginality in this sphere. Third, colonial education reinforced the idea that Islamic education was under men's purview. Fourth, social transformations under colonialism generated a new form of servitude for middle-class women. Housewivization increasingly became the norm. Finally, middle-class women lost much of their independence as Islamic practice was reinterpreted to sanction greater restrictions on their mobility.

Women made several gains as a result of this process. First, most women were not constrained by the new middle-class morality and entered the emerging markets, particularly the informal ones. Women, increasingly since 1980, are becoming significant actors in commercial and formal sectors of the economy. Second, with the close of the colonial era, girls gained access to secular education and consequently to Qur'anic training. The proportion of girls in school grew substantially until the disintegration of the Somali state in 1991. The entry of large numbers of girls in to secular schools meant an even larger number attended Qur'anic schools. Although gains in women's education have improved many women's livelihood chances, many discriminatory barriers remain in place. These discriminatory practices became more onerous with the disintegration of national state institutions in 1991.

The notion that Islamic revival is reactionary in nature appears to be a misrepresentation. The establishment of the world's first women's mosque in the traditionally religious town of Gabiley, Somalia, proves the open-ended nature of Islamic reinvention. The women pioneers who planned and built the mosque were neither informed by Western feminist ideology nor by anti-Islamic sentiments. Instead, they felt that Islamic practice in this society unduly restricted women's opportunities to learn and interpret Islamic texts and traditions. Establishing a holy place of their own where they could learn and ultimately interpret Islam without a male filter was a radical social and religious project. This was an important departure from the practice of having a women's prayer room or even a chamber adjacent to the men's mosque. What made this project radical is that it questioned the peripheralization of women in prayers and Islamic learning and leadership. The establishment of the women's mosque challenged prevailing Islamic practice. It sought to highlight the "female" question within Islamic tradition. It also raised another question: If Islam is meant for a community of people (not men only), and since Allah did not ordain that only males learn and interpret the meaning of the Qur'an, then how can Islamic practice exclude women from these enterprises?

Despite its radical intent, the women's mosque has had a limited positive impact on Islamic practice in Gabiley and the country. First, the mosque's existence is accepted as a normal part of Islamic reality in Gabiley. Only a few misguided individuals still feel that it should not exist.

Second, the mosque is a legitimate and autonomous public space where large numbers of women can meet, discuss religious affairs, study Islam and the Tafsiir of the Qur'an, and say their prayers. Third, more women, young and old, have become more informed about Islam. Although more women are better educated in Islamic matters, only a handful have gained advanced knowledge of Islam, and none has earned the title of sheikh. This is largely due to the fact that Sheikh Marian was not able, due to the demands of her family and her job in the secular school, to devote sufficient time to training women and girls. Moreover, the 1988–1993 civil war disrupted all forms of educational activities, including Islamic training. Male religious leaders, who do not see the need to train young women to become religious leaders, have compounded the issue. Another obstacle to women becoming sheikhs is the expectation that once married a woman will devote her energies to her husband and children. The end result of all of this is that insufficient numbers of women are trained to challenge the male interpretation of Islam and its practice. To realize this progressive Islamic project's potential will require significantly expanded Islamic and secular educational opportunities for a large number of women. Fourth, regular debates take place in Gabiley between women from the women's mosque and younger women who follow a more conventional interpretation of the woman's role in Islam. These debates between learned women with differing renditions of Islam could not have happened without the establishment of the women's mosque. Fifth, the mosque and its associated women's community is an alternative resource for younger women who want to learn about Islam without fully falling victim to some of the reactionary interpretations of the Qur'an and Islamic tradition peddled by some religious men and most laymen. Currently, a group of 10 women study the Tafsiir in the mosque under the tutelage of a male sheikh. Some sheikhs are not hostile to women's training in Islamic affairs, but nearly all of them will have difficulty accepting the leadership of a female sheikh. Finally, the limited impact of the women's historic mosque on Islamic practice in Gabiley and the country is in part due to the stagnation and ultimately the collapse of the modernity project, including secular education, professionally managed public institutions, and economic development (Pasha & Samatar, 1996).[31] This points to the important, but not linear, relationship between the interpretation of religious doctrine and the quality of life in general (Bernal, 1994).

ACKNOWLEDGMENTS

This chapter is adapted from an article published in *The Arab World Geographer*, Vol. 3, No. 1 (2000), pp. 22–39. Reproduced by permission of AWG—The Arab World Geographer, Toronto, Canada.

NOTES

1. In earlier times royal and other wealthy women built mosques in South Asia and the Middle East, but these were not intended for women's use. See the list of eight mosques built by various women from Morocco, Turkey, and India in Qureshi (1989, p. 97).

2. For the restrictiveness of spaces in "male" mosques allocated for women, see Holod and Khan (1997). According to this authoritative text, most modern mosques have a relatively small area in the mosque for women prayers. There are rarely any mosques that allocate equal space for both sexes. One of the rare exceptions is Bail-ul-Islam in Toronto, Canada:

> The men's prayer hall, measuring 80 X 60 ft . . . can accommodate up to 720 worshippers. . . . A separate well-defined entrance leads to a women's prayer hall of equal size on the level below. This is a rare instances in which the women's prayer hall is the same size as the men's. (Holod & Khan, 1997, p. 223)

3. Although all northern Somalis were Muslims, the manner in which Islam was practiced in this society was very different from those of Arabian countries. Here, there was no seclusion of women, and no *hijab*. All women wore the one-piece wrap (*qayd*) and headscarf. Married women wore black scarves while unmarried women used multicolor scarves. The arms, face, and neck were not covered. For one interpretation of women's history, see Kapteijns (1999).

4. Group interview, Gabiley, July 18, 1997.

5. For comparative work in other Muslim societies, see Sabbazah (1994). Al-hibri (1982), Kandiyoti (1991), and Afkhami (1995).

6. For a discussion of how male interpretation of the Qur'an and Hadith reinforced patriarchy in other Islamic societies, see Khan (1988), Qureshi (1989, pp. 95–97), Barazangi, Zaman, and Afzal (1996), and Ong (1990). Barazangi et al. illustrate the male interpretation of the centrality of Friday prayers and its injustice to women:

> Thus, a dual injustice has been committed against women: they are prevented from attending a mosque, and their Wajib to attend Friday prayers has been revoked. Hence, Friday prayer is now considered a Wajib for mature, sane, free males only. Women are classified with . . . boys, and the insane (p. 83).

7. A broader application of this framework in explicating transformation in Somali society is found in Samatar (1997).

8. For a similar discussion of the changes, such as the domestication of women and the emergence of a new morality induced by the integration of rural life into the world system, see Bernal (1994).

9. On the issue of class and the status of women, see Baffoun (1982).

10. For a discussion of the relationship between dress codes and class in some Islamic societies, see Ramazani (1983). Also see MacLeod (1992).

11. Whatever image the *hijab* conjures in the Western world, many women and men in the towns in northwest Somalia noted that this new dress code enables women to freely move around even in places where they could not go in the

past. The advantage of the new dress is that no one can determine the identity of women under cover.

12. Farah Omaar, a well-known Somalia activist, articulated these concerns.

13. This assistant was Mr. Mohamoud Ahmed Ali, who was later recognized as the father of modern Somali education.

14. The man's name was Ismail Samatar Mohamed. He volunteered to send his underage child to school as a test. In a year's time others joined the pro-school agenda. Haji Asker Cabdillahi, Interview, Gabiley, July 10, 1986.

15. The Qur'an is divided into 30 Giz. Each Giz consists of a number of chapters.

16. I observed this process at work when I was a national service schoolteacher in Gabiley in the early 1970s.

17. For a discussion of the relationships between Islamic learning and its relationship to Western education in Africa, see Reichmuth (1993).

18. Note that her father's name was the same as that of her husband. In Somali culture, women retain their family surname after marriage.

19. This discussion of the Sitaad center is based on a conversion I had with some of the founding mothers of the women's mosque. For a discussion of the Sitaat in general, see Kapteijns and Ali (1996).

20. Interview, Laqanyo Cabdillahi and Halimo Cabdillahi, Gabiley, July 18, 1997. For a general account of the struggle of Muslim women, see Mernissi (1996).

21. The government designated Gabileh as the capital of a new administrative district in 1963 after an intense lobbying effort by local residents. The district instantly became a viable unit and one of only a few districts that contributed more to central government revenues than it received from the treasury.

22. The women's strategy was not to alienate anyone and to make their demands on the basis of their need for a holy place of worship in which women had some privacy. This strategy paid off, as noted in the discussion below. I should also mention that such a strategy has its limitation as it constrained the long-term development of the women's Islamic agenda. For a treatment of the importance of social context in strategy development, see Kandiyoti (1988).

23. The women who took part in these discussions do not remember whose idea it was to build the mosque. They feel that this was an idea they all shared as a group.

24. In Africa, from east to west and from north to south, the women's prayer room is usually a small room attached to the main mosque. Although the Qur'an emphasizes the importance of collective prayers and communal gatherings, in practice women are excluded from these due to patriarchal interpretations of Islamic edict. For an earlier discussion of this, see Bevan-Jones and Bevan-Jones (1941, pp. 258–259).

25. The military regime that came to power in October 1969 formally ushered in a new era for Somali women. The regime enacted progressive laws that embodied women's equality with men and the right of married women to divorce their husbands if they were so inclined. Some religious leaders contested these laws in Mogadishu, but there was little organized resistance to it in the Gabileh District. These laws, in principle, meant that the district government leaders should have supported women's activities, such as building the mosque. However, in

practice, it made no difference to the women's effort. The effort to build the mosque was the only organized women's movement not inspired, controlled, or manipulated by the regime. Most women in this movement, nonetheless, contributed substantially to most government organized civic efforts to establish and improve public facilities. Many informers note that women were the backbone of these projects.

26. Although women play critical roles in many facets of Muslim life, we know very little about imam women. For a discussion of related issues, see Walther (1981). One of the earliest women imams lived at the time of the prophet.

> The early historians mention only one woman, Umm Waraqa Bin Abdallah, who acted as the prayer leader of a mixed community [male and female], that of her clan, so numerous that it had its own muezzin. Prophet Mohamed himself is said to have instructed her to serve as prayer leader. She was also one of few women who handed down the [Q]oran before it was put in final written form. (Walther, 1981, p. 111)

27. Shaaban (1995), using the work of Lebanese Islamic analyst Nazira Zin al-Din, exposes that much of what constrains Muslim women's freedom is fundamentally due to male interpretation of the holy texts. The issue that most concerned builders of the women's mosque was finding space where women could fulfill their religious duties and deepen their knowledge of Islam.

28. *Tafsiir* means interpretation of the Qur'an by a learned Muslim.

29. The number of such women (and men) have increased significantly since the mid-1980s although the Somali extended family system still cares for lots of individuals who are unable to care for themselves. The civil war in the late 1980s and 1990s, and associated disruptions of all livelihoods, added large numbers of people to these rolls.

30. Interview, Sahra Abdi, Gabiley, July 20, 1997.

31. For an examination of the relationship between religious interpretation and modernity, see Pasha and Samatar (1996).

REFERENCES

Abdi, S. (1997, July 20). *Interview*, Gabiley, Somalia.

Afkhami, M. (Ed.) (1995). *Faith and freedom: Women's human rights in the Muslim world*. Syracuse, NY: Syracuse University Press.

Afshar, H. (1996). Islam and feminism: An analysis of political strategies. In M. Yamani (Ed.), *Feminism and Islam: Legal and literary perspectives* (pp. 197–216). New York: New York University Press.

Al-hibri, A. (Ed.) (1982). Women and Islam [Special Issue]. *Women's Studies International Forum, 5* 207–220.

Alpers, E. (1983). Muqdishu in the nineteenth century: A regional perspective. *Journal of African History, 24,* 441–459.

Baffoun, A. (1982). Women and social change in the Muslim Arab world. *Women's Studies International Forum, 5,* 227–242.

Barazangi, Ni, Zaman, R., & Afzal, O. (Eds.) (1996). *Islamic identity and the struggle for justices.* Gainesville: University Press of Florida.

Bernal, V. (1994). Gender, culture, and capitalism: Women and the remaking of Islamic "tradition" in a Sudanese village. *Comparative Studies in Society and History, 36,* 36–67.

Bevan-Jones, V. R., & Bevan-Jones, L. (1941). *Women in Islam: A manual with special reference to conditions in India.* Lucknow, India: Lucknow Publishing House.

British Somaliland Protectorate. (1934). *Annual report.* London: HMGS Printers.

Cabdillahi, L. & Cabdillahi, H. (1997, July 18). *Interview,* Gabiley, Somalia.

Cabdillahi, H. A. (1986). *Interview,* Gabiley, Somalia.

Cabdillahi, L. 1998. *Interview,* Gabiley, Somalia.

Celmi, H. D. & Muxumed, H. J. (1999). *Interview,* Borama, Somalia.

Cusman, S. (1998). *Interview,* Gabiley, Somalia.

Holod, R. & Khan, H.-U. (1997). *The mosque and the modern world: Architects, patrons and designers since the 1950s.* London: IC Publications.

Kandiyoti, D. (1988). Bargaining with patriarchy. *Gender and Society, 2,* 271–290.

Kandiyoti, D. (1991). *Women, Islam and the state.* Philadelphia: Temple University Press.

Kapteijns, L. (1999). *Women's voices in a men's world: Women and pastoral tradition in northern Somali culture c. 1880–1998.* Portsmouth, NH: Heinemann.

Kapteijns, L., & Ali, M. (1996). Sittaat: Somali women's songs for the "mothers of the believers." Kenneth Harrow (Ed.), In the marabout and the muse, (pp. 124–141). Portsmouth, NH: Heinemann.

Kapteijns, L., & Spaulding, J. (1989). Class formation and gender in precolonial Somali society: A research agenda. *Northeast African Studies, 11,* 19–38.

Kassim, M. (1995). Aspects of the Benadir cultural history: The case of the Bravan Ulama. In A. J. Ahmed (Ed.), *The invention of Somalia* (pp. 29–42). Lawrenceville, NJ: Red Sea Press.

Khan, Q. (1988). *Status of women in Islam.* Lahore, Pakistan: Islamic Book Foundation.

MacLeod, A. E. (1992). Hegemonic relations and gender resistance: The new veiling as accommodating protest in Cairo. *Signs: Journal of Women in Culture and Society, 17,* 533–557.

May, D. (1980). Women in Islam: Yesterday and today. In C. Pullapilly (Ed.), *Islam in the contemporary world* (pp. 370–401). South Bend, IN: Cross Roads Books.

Mernissi, F. (1991). *Can we women head a Muslim state?* Lahore, Pakistan: Simorgh Publications.

Nanji, A. A. (Ed.). (1996). *The Islamic almanac: A reference work on the history, faith, culture and people of Islam.* New York: Gale Research.

Ong, A. (1990). State versus Islam: Malay families, women's bodies, and the body politic in Malaysia. *American Ethnologist, 17,* 258–276.

Pasha, K. M., & Samatar, A. (1996). The resurgence of Islam. In J. Mittleman (Ed.), *Globalization: Critical reflections* (pp. 187–201). Boulder, CO: Lynne Rienner.

Qureshi, M. S. (1989). *The role of the mosque in Islam.* Lahore, Pakistan: Publishers United.

Ramazani, N. (1983). The veil—Piety or protest? *Journal of South Asian and Middle Eastern Studies, 7,* 20–36.

Reichmuth, S. (1993). Islamic learning and its interaction with "Western" education in Ilorin, Nigeria. In L. Brenner (Ed.), *Muslim identity and social change in sub-Saharan Africa* (pp. 179–197). London: Hurst & Company.

Reese, S. (1999). Urban woes and pious remedies: Sufism in nineteenth-century beaadir (Somalia). *Africa Today, 46,* 169–192.

Sabbazah, S., (Ed.). (1994). *Arab women: Between defiance and restraint.* New York: Olive Branch Press.

Samatar, A. (1989). *The state and rural transformation in northern Somalia, 1884–1986.* Madison: University of Wisconsin Press.

Samatar, A. (1997). Leadership and ethnicity in the making of African state models. *Third World Quarterly, 18,* 687–707.

Samatar, A. (1992). Destruction of state and society in Somalia: Beyond the tribal convention in Somalia. *Journal of Modern African Studies, 30,* 625–641.

Shaaban, B. (1995). The muted voices of women interpreters. In M. Afkham (Ed.), *Faith and freedom: Women's human rights in the Muslim world* (pp. 61–77). Syracuse, NY: Syracuse University Press.

Somaliland Protectorate, Education Department. (1953). *Annual report.* Hargeysa.

Somaliland Protectorate, Education Department. (1956). *Annual report.* Hargeisa.

Walther, W. (1981). *Women and Islam.* New York: Markus Wiener.

Xassan, M. (1999). *Interview,* Gabiley, Somalia.

Xudhuun, Q. (2000). *Interview,* Minneapolis, MN.

10 Contesting Space

Gendered Discourse and Labor among Lebanese Women

MALEK ABISAAB

Every year when we finished sorting and baling raw tobacco we would send it from the Ghaziyya to other branches of the Regie, mainly Beirut. We would then clean the warehouse and the stacks. The Regie's supervisor (male) overlooked and checked our activities. We would split up into groups, some carrying brooms, others standing on the tables to wash windows. During one of these cleaning episodes, the supervisor turned to a male employee saying aloud: "Don't they all look like cows?" Afterwards, whenever we cleaned the building after the end of the tobacco season, we would angrily remind each other of the supervisor's demeaning statement.[1]

Approximately 144 Lebanese tobacco workingwomen and 33 men employed as temporary tobacco workers went on strike in the south at the Ghaziyya branch of the Regie (the French Lebanese Tobacco Monopoly) on June 23, 1970.[2] Their major demands were job permanency and better working conditions. Since the establishment of that branch in 1964, the Regie had been violating Lebanese labor law by employing these workers only as seasonal laborers. In addition to their being deprived of the basic job benefits, female workers in particular faced denigration and humiliation through the verbal expressions and physical manners of their male superiors. They hoped that the strike would achieve not only their demands but also bring a recovery of respect, and dignity. The women's refusal to be "cowed" became a rallying point for their protest. They objected to being

249

associated with the barn and the rural household. The women were being told by the male employees that their labor was essential, yet devalued, and that their presence at the Regie was "temporary," because the factory remained the "male" world of paid work. By striking, the women contested ownership over the factory space and its interpretation. At the same time, they drew meaning from the personal and social spaces of the farm and the home.

From the beginning of the strike, both the Regie and the government continued to deny Ghaziyya workers job permanency. Moreover, during the strike rumors spread that the Regie was planning to close the factory, which exacerbated the tense situation and prompted the workers to occupy the factory. The police force suppressed them, but a few weeks later the workers resorted to another type of protest. For hours, they disrupted the traffic on a major highway in south Lebanon. These and other similar confrontations with the Regie and the police resulted in a number of casualties; many women were seriously injured and others were arrested. Throughout the strike the female Ghaziyya workers strove against both family resistance and social condemnation that at times threatened to overwhelm them. As they sharpened their methods of collective bargaining and radicalized their form of confrontation with the Regie, they pushed their way through social spaces largely claimed by men. For them, "permanency" meant their "permanent" right to the space of the factory. Once achieved, this permanency also would prove to men, to the Regie, and to society at large that they were not "cows" who belonged on the farm or in the home, but workers who "belonged on the factory floor, and the latter to them. As I show below, the strike gradually turned into an event that involved the exploration and expansion of distinctly new spatial claims for Lebanese women tobacco workers.

It is problematic to select and artificially separate "public" from "private" with the rich and complex history of women's labor culture, social experiences, and personal lives. Private and public sources of women's labor, social experiences, and self-image shift and evolve under distinct historical conditions, which make it difficult to generalize about them across class, culture, or geography.[3] In the last few decades, a number of scholars, particularly anthropologists and geographers, have studied gender and identity production in public space, thus providing new insights into the complex relation of gender and public space and challenging the private–public dichotomy. Caroline Nagel (2001) noted that Muslim women's literature reflects how space is regulated in ways that challenge gender roles.[4] Peter Gran argues that the state and the various ideologies of the family have a stake in maintaining the separate domains of spaces.[5] Most of the existing and evolving scholarship on public space in Arab Middle Eastern and North African societies focuses on cultural and patriarchal mappings of the home as women's space, and explores the sacred geography, including mosque, shrine, and pilgrimage in Islamic societies.[6] Still, there is no comprehensive study to date that examines the social arrangement of public space and the interconnected and shifting constructs of "public" and "private" in the lives of protesting and militant workingwomen in diverse Arab/Islamic societies.

The evidence used in this chapter suggests that women resisted this public–private dichotomizing, demanding that both farm, home, or factory are spaces where they belong. In other words, women tobacco workers refused the public–private split that some scholars assume is generally operating in the Arab/Muslim world. This chapter explores labor strikes as public sites of feminine radicalism that shape and are shaped by a range of private–public arrangements of social and economic activities for women outside the industrial workplace. I take as a case study the women tobacco workers of Ghaziyya, a rural town in south Lebanon, who went on strike in 1970 against the Regie in pursuit of job permanency. For months the Ghaziyya workingwomen campaigned to raise awareness about their labor grievances among government officials, union members, national, religious figures, and even university students in the capital city, Beirut. When they failed to change their labor conditions through peaceful mediation with community leaders or by resorting to legal means, they escalated the strike and turned to organized radical confrontations with the Regie and the Lebanese government. As young, determined women who moved to occupy and claim public spaces dominated by men, they stirred up in both the onlookers and the media reactions and images ranging from feminine empowerment and heroism, to moral laxity.[7] State officials, like several male family members of the strikers', associated these acts of striking and militancy with "masculinity." By doing so they were rejecting political public roles for women, and depicting them as "abnormal," that is, as an aberration to femaleness. Diverse newspaper accounts both supporting and opposing the strike, supplemented by the oral accounts of Ghaziyya workingwomen themselves, reflect a gendered struggle over the manipulation and political appropriation of public space. For the duration of the strike, Ghaziyya women challenged the state's gendered hierarchies of power that positioned female citizens, especially workingwomen, in subordination to men and treated their factory work as marginal and appropriate to their gender role and the patriarchal expectations of their society. Indeed, the state had the ability to promote certain public roles for women in the line with its economic interests while suppressing others.[8] While the state sought female labor, it also had to negotiate physical and social limits for women, who no longer directed their productivity within the household alone.[9] Despite the tensions between familial and state control over female labor, they both converged on the importance of weakening women's ability to challenge men's political and economic prerogatives.

Several facets of the Ghaziyya workingwomen's backgrounds and experiences reveal the complex ways in which private and public roles were intertwined.[10] For one, the Regie, rather consciously, harnessed the skills rural women developed in the household and through cottage industries and invested them in wage labor. Women, for instance, figured prominently and at times almost exclusively in the department of sorting (al-farz), where their "delicate hands," accustomed to special forms of rural labor, sorted and packed tobacco leaves.[11] Second, even though Ghaziyya lies in the Lebanese countryside, women's trips from home to work were too short to truly separate the two worlds. Third, most of the workingwomen who led the strike were Shi'i Muslims who actively participated in a range of public religious events that contributed to their skills in labor activism and striking.[12] Women found new meanings in factory labor but these did not replace meanings derived from the domestic sphere or from village social and religious engagements.[13] Rather, women's roles were rearranged and negotiated in relationship to each other. Curiously, none of the Ghaziyya women who went on strike in 1970 were affiliated with leftist political parties, particularly the Communist Party, which supported their strike. Neither the Communist Party nor the labor union emerged as an attractive public forum for the majority of workingwomen or a platform for developing their new public roles. Nevertheless, the Ghaziyya women drew upon a fluid network of informal relations, personal ties, and friendships with Communist male colleagues at the factory. Outside the formal circles of the party and the union, women succeeded in communicating, planning, organizing, and radicalizing protest against the Regie. Overall, Ghaziyya militant women sought their own styles of leadership and accessed the types of public spheres they found most congenial to their experiences and self-identity.

RURAL DISPLACEMENT
AND SECT AT THE WORKPLACE

From the mid-1950s to 1969 a decline in the agricultural revenues of the Lebanese countryside, a lack of government-initiated reforms, land shortages, overpopulation, and dramatic urban prosperity led to rural–urban migrations from the areas of 'Akkar in the north, the Biqa' in the east, and the south to Beirut.[14] From 1969 onward, political instability and civil violence contributed to a new wave of migration from the south and the Biqa' to Beirut.[15] The biased development policies of the Lebanese state also proved to be a potent factor in transforming the regional and sectarian character of the Regie tobacco workers, both women and men. The Shi'ite population, concentrated in the "peripheral" rural regions of the country, such as the south where the Ghaziyya branch lies, seemed to have borne the brunt of underdevelopment and government mismanagement, thus driving hundreds of thousands of them to the city.

The major rural regions of Lebanon, namely, the Biqa', the north (particularly 'Akkar), and the south, exhibited common features of underdevelopment, population growth, unemployment, and high rates of illiteracy from the mid-1950s until the early 1970s. These conditions were accompanied by a conscious governmental policy of marginalizing the countryside and strangling opportunities for social development and economic growth there, which, in turn, accounted for the expansion of the rural lower class. Subsequently, there were large waves of migration to the urban centers, particularly Beirut, beginning in the late 1960s and intensifying after 1970.[16] The south, unlike other regions, also became the stage for an additional social process, namely, political instability and radicalization after the eruption of the Lebanese Civil War in 1975.

Various Lebanese regions also reflected particular sectarian configurations. The Biqa' had large Christian communities—both Maronite, Catholic, and Greek Orthodox—but even a larger Shi'i one. The south was predominantly Shi'i but had a significant Sunni community and a smaller Maronite one. The north had a mixed Muslim–Christian population of various denominations. A major wave of migration from these rural regions to the coastal cities, particularly Beirut, began in the mid 1950s in reaction to interdependent processes of population growth, land shortage and official policy.[17] In rural Lebanon, the natural rate of increase of Muslim populations seemed more rapid than that of Christians.[18] It is possible that, by the mid-1950s, Shi'i Muslims had already become the largest sectarian group in Lebanon.[19] This put greater pressure on the Shi'i regions in the south and the Biqa' than on their Christian counterparts.

Erosion and the decreasing return on agricultural land pushed many peasants to sell their lands and to take work as agricultural laborers or to move to the city. In 1961, approximately 92% of peasants owned 5 or fewer hectares while less than half of 0.5% owned from 50 to 100 hectares.[20] The breakup of land ownership due to inheritance and sale created many tiny lots that were insufficient to support a rural household (typically a family of five).[21] By 1965 rural–urban migration accounted for 65% of Lebanese urban growth, which was the second highest level of urban growth in the Middle East, surpassed only by that of the Yemen Arab Republic.[22]

Infrastructure, health, and educational facilities in rural districts were generally underdeveloped. The south, much like the north (especially the 'Akkar region), and the Biqa' had for decades formed a human reservoir for most industrial work, particularly at the Regie.[23] Meanwhile, from 1969 onward, a Palestinian and Lebanese armed resistance to Israel emerged in the south. The south gradually became a staging area for Israel's systematic military attacks, causing the dislocation of thousands of southerners and triggering waves of migration to Beirut. The rise in the number of Shi'i laborers, both male and female, at the industrial sites of Beirut from 1969 onward reflected these dislocations. A number of industries, including carpentry, mechanics, printing presses, construction, and shoemaking, claimed they needed to maintain their profits by laying off workers. They asked for government permission to dispense with half of their workforce or to reduce workers' salaries by half.[24] At the same time, Shi'i youth in the south were embracing the Palestinian cause. Many Maronite political leaders in the south, however, felt that the Palestine Liberation Organization (PLO) and the leftist Lebanese National Movement offered Israel a reason to transform the south into a war zone.

The full ramifications of the demographic transformation in different Lebanese regions cannot be understood without taking into account of state ideology and policy. The economic policies of Bishara al-Khuri (1946–1952) and Camille Chamoun (1952–1958) had far-reaching effects on the social composition of the industrial workers in major cities, including those at the Regie. One consequence of these policies was the deterioration of Muslim rural regions, which pushed its inhabitants to join the industries of the cities. Muslim workingmen and workingwomen at the Regie as a whole were most numerous between 1954 and 1969 (see Table 10.1).

Al-Khuri's and Chamoun's governments promoted Lebanon as a lib-

TABLE 10.1. The Sectarian Background of the Regie Female Workers, 1954–1969

| | 1954 | | 1969 | |
	N	%	N	%
Christian Maronite	350	44	424	32
Muslim Sunni	18	2	79	6
Muslim Shi'i	168	21	554	42
Christian Catholic	50	6	64	5
Christian Orthodox	105	13	129	10
Muslim Druze	3	0	6	1
Armenian	86	11	53	4
Syriac	5	1	7	1
Christian Protestant	—	—	—	—
Latin	3	0	4	0
Chaldean	—	—	—	—
Muslim 'Alawite	—	—	1	0
Jews	—	—	—	—
Total	788	100	1,321	100
Missing	153	16	105	7

Note. Rounded to the nearest whole number.

Source: Union of the Regie Workers and Employees, Union Membership Dues (1954), and Personnel Department of the Regie, Liste Nominative du Personnel (January 11, 1969).

eral, pro-Western, service-based polity in which the Maronite elite and a few Muslim allies enjoyed political and economic dominance. They focused their efforts on developing Beirut and Mount Lebanon, where Maronite Christians were concentrated. Little attention, if any, was devoted to the south, the Biqa', or 'Akkar because they seemed irrelevant to tourism, commercial planning, or banking and financial development. Only the industrial regions closest to the capital city received government support and protection in the hope that this would strengthen the transportation and banking sectors.[25]

Due to reinvestments in the service sector rather than in the productive sectors, industrial undertakings did not become a major part of the economy.[26] President Fuad Shihab (1958–1964) and his successor, Charles Helou (1964–1970), hoped to restore economic growth in peripheral regions outside Beirut and respond to the needs of their Muslim populations.[27] During Shihab's presidency, the Regie planned to open new branches in these peripheral districts, including Nabatiyya and Ghaziyya in the south. But in the long run, none of these branches matched Hadath in Beirut in the scope and size of tobacco production.

These socioeconomic and demographic changes have had a significant impact on the structure of the migrant families and the role of women within them, yet this does not mean that the new and old worlds of women had strictly been separated. It is true that coming to the city had opened new social avenues for women, but their association with rural life had not been severed. The interplay between public and private spaces is evident in the case of Zaynab Zu'aytir, a female Regie worker. "I was born to a peasant family," Zaynab told me,

> "that lived from farming. We used to work on a land that was owned by relatives. I was 10 years old when we left for Beirut. Then, at 21, I joined the Regie. Every summer my family and I would go back to Ba'labak to cultivate the land and prepare the food provisions for the winter. We, the people of Ba'labak, don't like to see our men doing household work. I managed to save some money from my work at the Regie and was able to buy a land up in our village. One day, a man offered to buy it from me, but I refused. I told him that I wanted to preserve my ties to my village. When I die I would like to be buried here."[28]

WOMEN'S TASKS AND WORK ENVIRONMENTS

Between 1954 and 1969, more than 40% of Regie workers were women (see Table 10.2). The company's administrators were almost exclusively men drawn from wealthy and educated Lebanese families, mostly Sunnite Muslims and Maronite Christians.[29] Women were hired as workers. Since

TABLE 10.2. The Gender Distribution of the Regie Working Force,
1954–1969

	1954		1969	
	n	%	*n*	%
Female	941	46	1,426	43
Male	1,121	54	1,855	57
Total	2,062	100	3,281	100
Missing	2	0.1	—	—

Note. Rounded to the nearest whole number.
Sources: Union of the Regie Workers and Employees, *Union Membership Dues* (1954), and
Personnel Department of the Regie, *Liste Nominative du Personnel* (August 11, 1969).

its founding in 1964, the Ghaziyya branch of the Regie hired, for the most part, laborers for a 6-month period, then laid them off for the rest of the year. A major station in south Lebanon for sorting out the Regie's raw tobacco harvest, Ghaziyya processed 800,000 kilograms of the 1,800,000 kilograms that passed through the Regie's central plant in Hadath, a suburb of Beirut. Two hundred laborers worked at that branch, the majority of whom were women. These were mostly young, single, Shi'ite Muslims who worked for a little less than $3 per day.[30] Only 33 workers, mostly men, were permanent.

The raw tobacco at Ghaziyya was classified into three grades: "clean," which was ready for exportation; "medium," which was mixed with foreign tobacco to produce the most popular Lebanese cigarettes (Bafra, Okay, and Cedars); and "Inferior," which was used for low-quality local cigarettes. Two male supervisors, one tobacco expert, and a manager formed the administrative body of the Ghaziyya plant that overlooked the production process.

The process of production itself was divided into several components. Eighty-four women stripped off the leaves, another 50 sorted out the decayed leaves, and a group of 15 women processed the sorted leaves and arranged them into bales. A group of 35 men then lifted the bales and stored them in a warehouse. At work, four women would sit around one table and sort out the leaves to produce 20 bales of the medium and 13 bales of the clean grades daily. Then another group of six women would sift the decayed and low-quality leaves and arrange them into 10 bales daily. When asked why sorting (*al-farz*) was an "unskilled" labor task relegated to women, Regie male managers and workers alike noted that it needed "delicate hands" and "a lot of patience." In other words, the skills that men ignored but that women developed in the private domestic circles were put to use in the public workplace of waged labor. Management thus emphasized the continuity between domestic and factory labor for women.[31]

Ghaziyya temporary tobacco workingwomen, along with their female and male allies, fought ardently for the implementation of a labor law that was promulgated in 1946. They hoped, unfortunately to no avail, that legal channels would improve their labor conditions.[32] The government dismissed the women's demands, claiming that the limited quantity of raw tobacco annually stored at Ghaziyya would not provide them with work beyond 6 months.[33] The workers challenged this ruling by pointing out that more than 50% of the Regie's annual production came from south Lebanon, the region of Ghaziyya.[34] They also argued that many of their colleagues in other branches that sorted and stored much less tobacco than Ghaziyya did had acquired permanent employment.[35] Moreover, they emphasized that Lebanese labor law itself stipulated that seasonal laborers had the right to become permanent after 3 months of uninterrupted work.[36] The Regie and the government alike turned deaf ears to such demands and continued to find them unworthy of serious consideration, let alone implementation.[37]

State legislation pertaining to women's waged work, whether during the period of French colonial rule (1920–1946) or in independent Lebanon, reflected patriarchal tensions, gender biases, and a spirit of paternalism. The French colonial government issued its first legal document on labor relations in 1935; 2 years later it promulgated a new law regulating the employment of women and children in industrial plants.[38] On the one hand, the state removed some areas of control over women away from the family, but, on the other hand, it introduced new forms of restraint. For instance, it prohibited women from driving "machines with big engines" or engaging in alcohol production.[39] In 1948, the state issued new laws prohibiting women from working in the evening or at night, except in a family business or in food-handling jobs where products could decay quickly.[40] "I was probably the first female adolescent," Hannih Dib, a principal female activist in the strike, says,

"to take up a man's work at a gas station. It was shameful for a girl to take up men's trades, especially in an open setting like a gas station, where I was continuously exposed to men. For this reason, my family opposed the job but I defended it and insisted I could protect myself and protect the family's honor because it was my honor. But I suffered greatly from confrontations with my brothers in connection with my job. In the end, my brothers accepted my decision. When I think about it, I have no doubt that the goal of the owners of that gas station behind hiring a woman was to attract the male drivers who like to see a girl work at a gas station."[41]

Hannih rejected preindustrial notions of male protection, and instead saw her waged work as a route to self-empowerment. But the picture is complex and, at times, contradictory. She was appropriating, quite consciously, a male-associated space and questioning sexual boundaries, yet she was also putting herself in a position of being sexually exploited. She was trading this exploitation for a new spatial arrangement as both the contractor and the object of spatial empowerment.

Laws prohibited women from working in factories that manufactured explosives, molten iron, chemicals, and dyed textiles. Officials pointed to the legitimate hazards such jobs might pose to women's reproductive health. But the government offered no clear rationale for prohibiting other types of work.

Women professionals in the fields of music, theater, and the arts, however, were exempt from such laws. This gender–class bias was mixed with patriarchal protection. The state emphasized in 1946 the centrality of the mother–child relationship and its contribution to familial and national cohesion, thus decreeing that women receive a 40-day maternity leave with full pay and preventing employers from allowing them to return to work for 30 days after giving birth. The laws also preserved men's dominance in waged work and emphasized women's domestic roles. In 1951 state laws gave women—but not men—the right to end a labor contract instantly upon marriage, but not in cases of illness or childbirth. Women received less recognition at the workplace and fewer vacations and promotions.[42] In retrospect, the state's project of turning colonial subjects into national citizens, manifested in the body of labor laws, was challenged by gendered lower class models of nationalism deemed "unorthodox" by the bourgeoisie and the state. In the process of citizen-subject formation, the state promoted gendered constructions of the public and the private that had direct implications for women and gender relations.

A close analysis of the attitudes of the government and the Regie officials shows that they both ignored and violated labor laws more easily when it came to southern Shi'i women like those of Ghaziyya than when it came to Beiruti workingmen of diverse sectarian backgrounds, namely, Christian and Sunni Muslim. Ghaziyya women responded to this gendered and regional discrimination with defiance. They tried to obtain the support of a public network of national and communal associations through collective organization. The strike gradually turned into a place for the exploration and expansion of distinct public roles for Lebanese women tobacco workers. Several Ghaziyya parents threatened their own daughters with death were they to strike.[43] These threats disclosed the weakness rather than the stability or potency of patriarchal and familial control. In Lebanese rural and urban households alike, men were slowly but surely losing to women some control to women over the gender politics of public spaces. The women's act of striking was at once a statement about private sources of identity and about public experiences at the industrial workplace.

GHAZIYYA WOMEN IN A SIT-IN
(*I'TISAM*) AT THE SUPREME SHI'I COUNCIL

Lebanese tobacco women have a long history of labor activism and struggle against the French colonial authorities, and the Lebanese state.[44] This tradition of resistance was also a feature of the relationship between women workers and the Regie since its inception in 1935. Thus, the Ghaziyya strike should be viewed as a continuation of that tradition.

The temporary workers of Ghaziyya, mostly women, started their strike on June 23, 1970.[45] Prior to the strike in May 1970, the Ghaziyya workingwomen decided first to seek the support of Imam Musa al-Sadr, a prominent national religious leader and the head of the Supreme Shi'i Council.[46] At this time, they staged an *i'tisam* at the council to express indignation and to attempt to win public support using at this point nonmilitant confrontation. Al-Sadr gained popularity among southern Shi'i families with his support of social justice and economic stability for Shi'i Muslims against their marginalization by the Lebanese government and powerful sectarian organizations. The women's decision to have al-Sadr petition the government on their behalf was significant. On the one hand, it showed that, at this early stage of the strike, the women decided to work through paternalism and male religious authority in order to win sympathy from their communities and government officials. They emphasized their subservience in the patriarchal hierarchy in order to force the male elite into fulfilling their paternalist obligations to protect women from harm. "Two or three busses," 'Itaf Tutanji remembers,

> "full of workingwomen went to see the Imam. That was our first visit. We entered the garden outside the building, but the Imam did not want to meet with us. He told his assistants, 'I don't want to see them.' We did not dress up formally and had no scarves to cover our heads. We remained in the front yard until dusk, for he prevented us from entering the building. Eventually, the council employees asked us to leave. During our second visit we dressed up in an acceptable way [she meant formally], but still we did not cover our heads. The council employees, however, gave us scarves because the Imam would not allow us to enter the building without head covers. Then he came out from his office and met with us. We explained our grievances and demands to him and he promised to help."[47]

The choice of al-Sadr was meant to embarrass a government that Lebanese Shi'is, including al-Sadr, criticized as discriminating against them in terms of employment, development, promotions, and wages. Furthermore, women leaders of the strike noted that their turning to al-Sadr was a tactical move to gain the support of some of the female workers who were confused or hesitant about the strike and whose families viewed "protesting in the streets" as a threat to the "morality and honor of their daughters."[48]

Al-i'tisam at the council failed to achieve the most urgent and immediate goal of job permanency for Ghaziyya women. The women, however, gained social and political visibility early on through this strategy. After several meetings and lengthy dealings with high-ranking government officials, al-Sadr also came back empty-handed.[49] Shortly after, he became ambivalent about his support for the Ghaziyya women and indirectly tried to end *al-i'tisam* at the council. His assistants asked the women strikers to take their protest to the headquarters of the General Federation of Workers (GFW), signaling that al-Sadr no longer wanted to be involved with the protesters. The Ghaziyya women had appealed to al-Sadr as a fellow Shi'i and as a paternal figure. Al-Sadr in turn tried to extricate himself from the relationship with the protesters by voicing his concerns about the women's moral "safety" and "decency" if they continued to congregate at the council.[50] The state police guarded the council, so there were no immediate dangers. A few female tobacco workers noted in interviews with me that al-Sadr may have been using a strategy of wanting to keep the council precincts "pure," that is, properly accessible to male personnel and visitors. The council stood for the Islamic Shi'i community in Lebanon at large, and, as such, it was an extension of its public welfare and collective religious concerns and social affairs. Al-Sadr was in part implying that the presence of women would "contaminate" such an edifice, that is, make it physically and spiritually *najis* (impure) due to the association of women with menstrual blood.[51] By referring to women's sexuality and safety, al-Sadr implied as well a concern with men' s spiritual "safety" by emphasizing the council as the site of male—not female—public activity. He was also asserting that the council, as an extension of a holy place of worship, like a mosque, which should not be "overtaken" physically or politically by women.

This was a turning point in the women's struggle against the Regie. They then decided to turn to the Union of the Regie Workers and Employees (URWE), the only official union at the Regie.[52] It is important to note, however, that the women did not have great confidence in the URWE, as it was a company union that discriminated against temporary workers and women. The URWE gave exclusive rights of membership to permanent workers and aimed to organize labor for the benefit of capital and the male working elite.[53] Moreover, since the URWE's inception, its leadership had been drawn from high-ranking male directors and supervisors of the Regie.[54] Only one post on the executive council was reserved for a woman, even though women comprised more than 40% of the total labor force.[55] The URWE used this "women's" post to communicate the union's decisions and instructions to women workers.[56]

The URWE showed little interest in espousing the cause of Ghaziyya women who moved in their strike (*idrab*) from the phase of *al-i'tisam* to street demonstrations (*muzaharat*). Behind closed doors, the URWE's executive board reiterated the government's argument against the workers, namely that the Ghaziyya plant lacked the quantities of raw tobacco necessary for permanently hiring more than the existing 33 full-time (mostly male) workers.[57] Because the URWE denied daily workers membership in its ranks, Ghaziyya workingwomen had no legal space, so to speak, from which to force the URWE and the Regie to enter into a discussion about their status and fate. Nonetheless, the women struggled to end this legal vacuum by obtaining some formal acknowledgment of their position. Curiously, Hannih Hakim, the only female tobacco worker on the URWE's executive council, played a marginal role in the URWE's deliberations and did not even question its opposition to the strike. Only Hasan Hamid, a Communist worker, upheld (if only for a while) the demands of Ghaziyya strikers. He questioned the Regie's anticipated action, supported by the government, to close down the Ghaziyya branch and keep the two factories in Bikfayya (in Mount Lebanon) and Tripoli (in the north) open.[58] Hamid explained that all these factories were built at the same time and occupied a similar position in the production process of the Regie. Why, then, did only Ghaziyya utilize temporary workers and why was only it to be closed down? Bikfaya and Tripoli, unlike Ghaziyya, Hamid explained, had a mixed-gender Christian–Muslim workforce. Ghaziyya, on the other hand, had an overwhelmingly female Shi'i workforce.[59] In essence, Hamid was accusing the government and the Regie of sectarian discrimination, that is, of preferring to give permanency to men with urban, mostly Christian and Sunni Muslim, backgrounds, rather than to women with rural Shi'i backgrounds. He did not, however, point to the gendered discrimination at the heart of this conflict. Female leaders of the strike also did not express their radicalism in terms of a self-conscious or crystallized feminism. They stressed class and sectarian discrimination on the part of the government and the Regie more than gender discrimination per se.[60]

It is important to pause here and examine the nature of the women's approach to party affiliation, particularly the Communist Party and the Organization of Communist Action (OCA), which upheld their goals and demands. Among the more militant Regie women, only two were active in the unions and were indirectly influenced by socialist views or methods of labor organization.[61] Many women expressed feelings of confusion and uncertainty about joining labor unions, stating that they were "uneducated" and "illiterate" and would not be able to "live up" to union standards and goals. Most of them knew only indirectly—and usually through a man—about the long-term objectives of the union and the Communist Party. Others seemed overburdened with domestic chores in addition to their Regie job that left them little time for other activities.[62] A few also pointed to the aversion of their fathers or husbands to women's involvement in any activity of a political nature that seemed "unladylike." For their part, unionists and Communists seemed uninterested in recruiting women into their ranks or making their meetings and circles more friendly and sensitive to women's domestic and family commitments. Several Communist leaders found it divisive to address gender issues and rarely distinguished between male and female working-class cultures.[63] The Communist Party addressed their audience in the plural masculine as "our male comrades" and "the workingmen of the countryside"—only rarely were women singled out as a group of their own in that audience.[64]

The influence of leftist ideology, particularly that of the Communist Party, found its way into female workers circles after the 1963 strike at Hadath and reached its peak of influence by 1965.[65] Communist influence among Regie workers and involvement in the strike of 1965 in Hadath re-peatedly was emphasized in the police reports and official declarations.[66] "One cannot deny the active and important role of leftist parties in sup-porting the workers," Dib would note and then went to say:

> "Early on at the Regie, I met several workers who belonged to the OCA. I believe that these organizations were created to help the workers become aware of their rights. One day a lady from a leftist background from out-side the Regie came and said that we should get organized."[67]

During the 1965 strike of the Regie workers, among similar claims pro-government newspapers ran headlines such as "Men and Women are Sacri-ficed for Leftist Extremists," "The Communists Exploit the Strike of the Regie Workingmen and Women," and "Communist Agitators Placed Women at the Forefront of the [Strike] Lines."[68] Women's militancy, however, was shaped outside the public space of the party and its formal structure in the complex contexts of professional, social, and personal experiences unique to the tobacco workingwomen in south Lebanon—contexts well described by Hannih. Overall, it seems that neither a conscious, well-articulated femi-nism nor formal socialist or unionist ideals constituted significant sources of public militancy. "I admire the ideas of the parties [mainly socialist and communist]," Dib told me in her statement to me in 1997,

> "that support the workers' rights and strive for their sake. Jesus Christ was also a worker before there were any communists. I did not belong to any Communist organization but I supported them and voted for their candidates during the various parliamentary elections. We did not have any experience in politics or trade unionism, which these people [the left-ists] knew well."[69]

On one hand, Dib stresses that women expressed great commitment to the strike, yet, on the other hand, she complained about the obstacles they faced, for they were "more ignorant about their rights and labor organization than the men" and were negatively influenced by "their families, societies, and religions." According to Dib, the women were sheltered and self-absorbed.[70]

Leftist parties supported the activities of workers in general. Nonetheless, women tobacco workers seem to have developed their own experiences and political awareness from a mix of informal, social, and personal endeavors associated with private space and a continuous tradition of resistance that the Regie workforce had built up over the years. This again shows the interweaving of private and public spaces.

WOMEN IN PUBLICLY CHARGED SPACES: FACTORY, HIGHWAY, UNIVERSITY, AND STREET

On June 25, 1970, the URWE, possibly under the pressure from the strikers and their supporters and sympathizers, was forced to take a slightly more active role in the conflict.[71] The workers on strike elected two of their colleagues, namely, Hannih Dib and Muhammad Husayn Kharrubi, a male temporary worker, to represent them, and urged the URWE to adopt their demands. Their requests split the URWE into two factions for and against adopting the demands of the Ghaziyya strike.[72] Hamid, who insisted on embracing the Ghaziyya strikers' request for permanency, expected the strike to take on more militant forms if the URWE denied its support. He noted that the Ghaziyya workers had struck previously when Jean Tuwayni, the former president of the URWE, whom they expected to support them, told them instead that the Regie would fire them if they insisted on asking for job permanency. Most of the URWE executive board, however, rejected any attempts to adopt or acknowledge the aims of the Ghaziyya strikers. Curiously, the URWE simply agreed to offer "humanitarian" support for the workers exemplified by a small amount of money to help them pay for some logistical expenses. In my opinion, this was an example of the indecisive policies of the URWE and its inclination toward the administration of the Regie.[73] Meanwhile, the government took precautionary steps against the strikers at Ghaziyya by tightening surveillance and security measures. The governor of south Lebanon expected the Ghaziyya working-women to intensify their struggle and escalate the strike. Around the end of July, the governor declared that he had taken extraordinary "security measures" to protect the properties of the Regie against the strikers and to maintain "order" in the region.[74] Indirectly, he hoped to intimidate the women and push them to give up their struggle. Al-Sadr entered the scene again, this time promising to address the grievances of the workers with the government and encouraging them to end their strike.[75] Despite the fact that the strikers finally voted to end the strike, the Regie moved on to discharge both female and male strikers from their jobs on August 28, 1970.

Immediately, the workers went back on strike with renewed commitment and fervor.[76]

Weeks went by and discussions reached a stalemate. The Ghaziyya strikers started to hear rumors that the Regie planned to close the plant permanently.[77] A few days later, in a show of defiance to the government, the workingwomen and men entered the factory by force and organized a sit-in on its premises. Several women, with their male colleagues, pressed their bodies against the main gate of the factory to break it open. The policemen guarding the gate pushed back, but the workers outnumbered them. The strikers poured through the gate and many managed to climb over the wall of the building to occupy the first floor.[78] The Ghaziyya women described these moments with great enthusiasm, recalling their fearless confrontation with the Regie and the government alike and describing an undeniable sense of validation and empowerment that had issued from their action.[79] "We engaged in a kind of fist fighting," said Da'd Ghandur, recalling these moments.

> "The policemen beat me up and I hit back. I saw the officer in charge of the police force flogging a woman colleague. I was outraged and swift. I caught his hand, took the whip, and whipped him back. I gave several lashes until his assistants pointed their weapons at me and ordered me to stop. I was scared then and they arrested me."[80]

The workers' success was short-lived. The policemen crushed their strike by force, attacking them with machine guns and clubs to force them out of the factory. When the police clamped down on them, three leading women in the strike were seriously injured. Different sources depicted differently women's public acts of defiance and militancy. Through their newspapers and reports, unionists and socialists emphasized the heroism of the strikers and the rationality of their cause, at times giving special emphasis to the female character and leadership of the strike.[81] The government and a number of social institutions seemed more conscious of the gender character of the strike, but dismissed its importance or legitimacy on that very basis. Still others condemned the policemen's "cowardly" attack on a "defenseless" group of women.[82]

The Regie proceeded to fire all the strikers. The latter decided a month later, on October 12, 1970, to galvanize the people of south Lebanon to their cause and agitate against the government. They carried their protest to a public site of logistical and geographical significance, namely, a major highway connecting Sidon and Tyre, two central cities in south Lebanon. They blocked the highway with barriers and by burning car tires. The police rushed to quell what was depicted as a *shaghab* (riot), thus treating this outburst of frustration as an isolated act of civil disobedience, rather than as a sustained form of struggle against the government to achieve clear goals. The strikers decided to end the roadblock when the minister of the interior promised to take up their demands with the president and prime minister.[83]

The GFW did not formally grant its support to the strike, claiming instead that the Ghaziyya workers were not registered members of the URWE. The women complained about the GFW's complacency, which weakened their bargaining position and helped the Regie deny them their rights.[84] Consonant with the complacency of the GFW, the prime minister Sa'ib Salam ruled out the possibility of permanency for the Ghaziyya workers. Shrewdly, he proposed to change their status from "temporary" to "seasonal" workers. This shift would have no fundamental bearing on their labor status, salaries, or rank. The workers knew well Salam's history of coercion and aggression against the labor movement in general, and against the activism of tobacco women in particular. Most importantly, they recalled his use of armed force to crush an earlier strike held in 1946 that had infamously led to the death of a female worker named Warda Butrus Ibrahim. With this history in mind, workers rejected Salam's offer, turned away from the URWE, and appealed to all labor unions, community associations, and political parties to support them.[85] This move was noteworthy, for it signaled a new phase in the collective labor organization of the Ghaziyya workingwomen. Soon after, the women began a sit-in at the center of the GFW. "Southern women joined us in the sit-in," Hannih Dib asserts,

> "regardless of the fact that they had big families to take care of. The average size of their families was between five and six, yet whenever they had any free time they joined us in the sit-ins and never wavered in their support. There were around 40 or 50 women who were constantly present. Their shoes became their pillows and the newspapers were their blankets. They would sleep for 2 hours and then others would come and take their place."[86]

The sit-in at the GFW induced the latter to mediate between the strikers and the government. In response, the minister of finance proposed to rehire the workers at the Regie for a little longer than 6 months and to double the quantity of raw tobacco allotted to Ghaziyya.[87] The workers rejected the offer, recognizing that the Regie's intention was to permit them to work overtime for only 8 months (rather than an entire year) and thus to deny them permanency once again.[88] Dib noted that when she complained to the minister of finance about such grievances, he responded, "You should be grateful to God because you are working for 6 months. Other women do not have a job at all."[89] In this and other statements, government officials and Regie male administrators treated women's waged labor as unworthy of serious regulation and as a privilege rather than a right.

The strikers' efforts brought them limited short-term gains. The prime minister and his cabinet, along with the Regie, were forced to abandon any attempts to shut down the Ghaziyya plant, or to hire new workers in place of those fired. The strikers now hoped to achieve their most urgent aim of permanency. The workingwomen mobilized critical links to nationally visible public institutions such as the central plant of the Regie, in Hadath, and the Lebanese University in Beirut. They visited the Hadath plant and called upon their co-workers and the students of the university to support them. Women strikers were empowered by appropriation of masculine spaces that were revered as public realms. At times, the very sanctity of these spaces worked to their advantage. "We knew," explains Hannih Dib,

> "that the major police battalion known as 'The Group of 16' would not violate the sanctity of an educational institution by using violence against us. We wanted to take advantage of every second of that freedom afforded to us at the university campus to organize an important rally in favor of our cause. We anticipated this would also get the attention of the media and consequently pressure the government to renegotiate with us."[90]

A wide range of private–public social and religious experiences and economic activities seemed to have shaped the women's public role in the strike. Among those discussed by the strikers was the economic deterioration of their region, south Lebanon, perceived as the outcome of discriminatory governmental policies against Shi'ite Muslims. Also implicated were a resulting mixed home–farm work pattern and a new overlapping of personal and social ties forged among home, village, and factory. Each of these new circumstances involved distinct changes in private and public roles and self-images for the women of Ghaziyya.

The Regie staff tried unsuccessfully to prevent the Ghaziyya women and men from meeting with their colleagues at Hadath.[91] At this point, the strikers were not merely concerned with achieving permanency but also with returning to their jobs and ensuring that the Ghaziyya plant would not shut down. On January 17, the URWE president told the strikers they could start work in February of the same year, but under the old work conditions. The Ghaziyya strikers refused this offer and threatened to embark on a new *i'tisam* at the office of the URWE. They stood up on the front stairwell of the Hadath plant shouting boldly, "There can be no Regie without the south," or as one woman expressed it to me, "There is no Regie without the labor of our hands at Ghaziyya." The women then entered into the factory building and mixed with their colleagues, singing of their hopes and struggles and shouting labor slogans against exploitation and poverty. When the workday ended, the women and men of Ghaziyya and Hadath marched to the campus of the Lebanese University a few miles away. There, students received them warmly and set up a forum in which the workers discussed issues related to their plight for hours.[92]

The government and the Regie remained intransigent. In January 1971 the government proposed to allow the Ghaziyya workers to resume their jobs immediately and even implied a willingness to discuss compensation for the strike days. But the government was completely silent on the permanency demand.[93] Most labor unions and federations advised Ghaziyya workers to accept these conditions in order to regain their jobs and prevent the Regie from closing the plant.[94] After examining the situation with their colleagues, the Ghaziyya workers decided on January 7, 1971, to accept this proposal and end the strike. This decision can be seen either as a strategic move to gain short-term goals or as an act of resignation.

However compromised by this resolution to the conflict, the workers kept the cause alive through continuous reiteration of the events of the strike. In the years following the strike, many female laborers left the Regie for better paying jobs. Others married and left work altogether. Those who remained at the Regie continued the struggle. Their persistence paid off in 1980, when a group of them met with the then-minister of finance, Ali Khalil, who was from the south and had close ties to the AMAL movement. He was persuaded by workers to sign a decree granting all temporary Regie workers (850) permanent status. The decree reflected both a long difficult workers' struggle as well as new demographic and political realities accompanying the first phase of the Lebanese Civil War (1975–1982). These realities ushered in a reconfiguration of the political power in Lebanon in which the Muslim Shi'ites gained more influence in the power structure of the state. However, as much as a changing political context created new opportunities for workers to press their demands, it must also be acknowledged that such opportunities could only be grasped by workers who came to see themselves as actors and by women workers, in particular, who had become accustomed to thinking of the workplace as part of a sphere to which they rightfully belonged. A recent history of organized struggle left the women and men of Ghaziyya well positioned to reap the advantage of the weaknesses and contradictions at times in the relationship between the state and the Regie. The cracks in this relationship revealed themselves. A change had come, but it had come from within as well as from without to alter the way that women and work intersected in Lebanon in the 1970s.

In conclusion, the militant tobacco workingwomen drew upon multiple private and public social and economic experiences, forging at will dynamic connections among the spaces of home, village, and factory and even protesting in spaces lying outside them. Clearly, it is difficult, if not impossible, to locate identity and self-image in one productive or social sphere exclusively or to talk about set boundaries between public and private. The case of women tobacco workers proves the inadequacy of much of the scholarship on Arab women that first continues to see and locate women almost exclusively within "traditional," "domestic" circles, and second considers the domestic as merely private. One recent example of this scholarship is provided in the work of geographers Leila Ayari and Marc

Brosseau (1995), who argued that Tunisian novelists, writing in French, show male and female characters bridging "tradition" and "forbidden spaces."[95] Ayari and Brosseau stated that there is "little overlap between the two" in the Arab/Muslim context.[96] As this study has shown, it is problematic to view the public and private spheres as static and sharply dichotomized. Protesting women pursued relentlessly communal, sectarian, and domestic support for goals associated with their industrial work. Meanwhile, female radicalism evolved not out of formal professional or political vehicles like the trade union and the party. The women expanded their public world, and experimented with novel public spaces, which became the sites of their particular style of militancy and social identity.

NOTES

1. 'ItafTutanji, interview.
2. *Al-Hayat* (*The Life*; newspaper) (June 24, 1970, p. 5).
3. Afsaruddin (1999, pp. 10–11).
4. Nagel (2001, pp. 69–70). See also Bourdieu (1977). Bourdieu shows how connotations of male/female are shaped by changing contexts, and by what is public and what is private. Geographers Arnesen and Laegran (2003), suggested that male and female youths in Norway "coproduce" places as gendered in distinct ways. At the same place, young men and women do gender "similarly as well as differently." This fluid and multifaceted disposition of gendered public space was useful in looking at Lebanese women and men's differing modes ofusing and projecting their identity at the factory and during protest. See also Annstrong and Squires (2002); Mazumdar and Mazumdar (2002); Slyomovics (1996); and Ask and Tjomsland (1988). Ask and Tjomsland state that even though public–private and male–female spatial categories seem dichotomized in a rigid way in Islamist movements, there are many contraventions to this spatial arrangement. See also El Guindi (1999); Freidl (1991); and Hegland (1991, pp. 215–230).
5. Peter Gran (1996, p. 65).
6. I cite here representative works of this scholarship, namely, Schimmel (1991) and Fischer (1991). See also Salvatore and Eickelman (2003). The authors noted that several contemporary scholars across disciplines exploring the public sphere and public Islam have suggested that the former is constantly changing and that its boundaries continue to be contested by a range of social actors. Scholars of public Islam, however, view social practices and collective ritual as decisive and, at times, primary forces in shaping the politics and economics of Islamic societies. They focus predominantly on religious experiences, identity production, and management of sacred life.
7. *Al-Thaqafa al-Wataniyya* (*The National Culture*; periodical) (September 25, 1970, pp. 21–23); *Al-Huriyya* (*The Freedom*; magazine) (September 21, 1970, p. 7); and *Al-Nahar* (*The Day*; newspaper) (July 3, 1970, p. 4).
8. Afsaruddin (1999, pp. 10–11).
9. See Domosh and Seager (2001, p. 39). Domosh and Seager noted that there

are gaping contradictions between the ideology [of how women and men are "supposed" to relate to work and to each other] and the reality. . . . The confinement of women in households dominated by men, removed from wage-earning possibilities, has social, cultural, financial and emotional limits for both men and women.

10. Domosh and Seager (2001, p. 33).
11. Jacques Daghir, interview.
12. The relationship between the militancy of Shi'i women workers and the practice of certain religious rituals will be studied in a future research project that I will undertake jointly with Rula Abisaab.
13. Domosh and Seager (2001, p. 31).
14. See Abisaab (2001, pp. 154–191).
15. Abisaab (2001).
16. In 1950, those engaged in agriculture—estimated at 40–50% of the population—earned no more than 19% of the total provisional national income, while the industrial population (estimated at the time at 8% of the total population) earned 13% of total income. See Asfour (1955, p. 2).
17. Asfour (1955, p. 1). By 1960 the infant mortality rate in Lebanon was 70 (per 1,000 live births) compared to 130 in Syria. Thus, despite the poor health conditions in rural Lebanon, the national health standards were steadily improving, which in turn signaled a greater population growth. See Richards and Waterbury (1990, p. 97).
18. Richards and Waterbury (1990, p. 106).
19. There were no official censuses for the Lebanese population from 1932 until 1970, and few scholars have attempted to come up with approximate estimates of the size of sectarian groups. See Hudson (1985) and Richards and Waterbury (1990, p. 97).
20. Richards and Waterbury (1997, Table 6.4, p. 150).
21. *Al-Qadaiyyah al-Zira'iyyah Lubnan fi Daw' al-Mariksiyya* (1970, p. 72).
22. Richards and Waterbury (1990, Table 10.1, pp. 26–65).
23. Richards and Waterbury (1990, Table 10.1, pp. 264–265). The Biqa' was more than 41% of the total size of Lebanon. The Biqa' Plain alone was 170,000 hectares (1 hectare = 2,471 acres), or approximately 52% of the total agricultural area in Lebanon. Most of the fertile lands were owned by a handful of families such as Rizk, Bustrus, Eddi, and Skaf. The agricultural products of al-Biqa' composed 30% of the total agricultural production in Lebanon. In the 1960s the Biqa's total population was 368,000, 65% of whom lived in villages and, therefore, relied completely on agriculture. Thirty-five percent lived in towns. See Al-Qadiyyah al-Zira'iyyah fi Lubnan fi Daw' al-Mariksiyya (1970, pp. 104–105, 166–167, 223).
24. Al-Buwari (1986, pp. 297–298).
25. Persen (1958, pp. 227–278).
26. See also Richards and Waterbury (1990, p. 74). Their Table 3.11 assesses sectoral distribution of the labor force in the Middle East (in percentages) from 1950 to 1980. In 1960 the highest percentage of workers could be found in the services sector (39%). Agricultural and industrial workers formed 38% and 23% of the total workforce, respectively. The table shows a 17% decline in the agricultural workforce between 1950 and 1960, a 3% increase in the industrial sector, and a 14% increase in the number of those working in the services sector.

27. Al-Jisr (1988, pp. 84–85).
28. Zaynab Zu'aytir, interview.
29. By "workers," I mean the blue-collar workers, and by "employees," the white-collar staff.
30. The daily wage for those workers 6.60 Lebanese pounds, that is, a little less than $3.00. See *Al-Thaqafa al-Wataniyya* (*The National Culture*; periodical) (September 25, 1970, p. 20).
31. *Al-Hurriyya* (*The Freedom*; magazine) (September 7, 1970, p. 9).
32. Abisaab (1999, pp. 55–66).
33. *Al-Hurriyya* (*The Freedom*; magazine) (September 7, 1970, p. 9).
34. *Al-Hayat* (*The Life*; newspaper) (November 16, 1970, p. 5).
35. *Al-Nahar* (*The Day*; newspaper) (July 23, 1970, p. 4).
36. *Al-Hayat* (*The Life*; newspaper) (November 21, 1970, p. 5).
37. For more on workingwomen's use of labor laws, see Abisaab (2001, pp. 142–150).
38. Qanun Yakhtas, MAE, Syrie–Liban, April 17, 1935, vol. 2921.
39. Shu'ayb (1980, pp. 15–19).
40. Shu'ayb (1980, pp. 15–19).
41. Hannih Dib, interview.
42. Shu'ayb (1980). See also Ghurayyib (1988, p. 330).
43. Hannih Dib, interview.
44. Abisaab (2004).
45. *Al-Hayat* (*The Life*; newspaper) (June 24, 1970, p. 5).
46. Imam Musa al-Sadr started a political movement in 1970, the year of the strike, to address the deteriorating conditions of Shi'ite Muslims in Lebanon. This led to the foundation of a number of sociopolitical organizations, the most important of which were the Lebanese Resistance Army (AMAL) and the Committee for the Support of South Lebanon. See Hannih Dib, interview. On al-Sadr's political movement and life, see Ajami (1986).
47. Ajami (1986).
48. Hannih Dib, interview and 'Itaf Tutanji, interview.
49. Unfortunately, we know nothing about the conversations he had with these officials or the arguments used by either side or the language describing their distinct positions on the matter.
50. *Al-Hurriyya* (*The Freedom*; magazine) (September 21, 1970, p. 7).
51. The women workers in question preferred to remain anonymous.
52. Founded on July 19, 1947 a year after a bloody confrontation between the Regie workers and the Lebanese government. For more details on the strike, see Abisaab (2001, Ch. 3).
53. Rizkallah-Boulad (1972). The executive council of the URWE consisted of two bodies, the consultative and the executive. The former consisted of five posts occupied by the workers' representatives whose roles were confined to deliberation. The executive body was composed of five posts assigned to the Regie's employees. Evidently, the policies and resolutions of the URWE remained in the hands of the active members who cast their votes on whether and when to strike.
54. Rizkallah-Boulad (1972).
55. Abdul Aziz Harfush, interview and also Tabarani (1974).
56. Iqbal Dughan, interview.
57. Others on the executive board argued that the URWE would lose its bargaining

power with the Regie if it were to entertain or adopt the demands of the Ghaziyya temporary workers. Probably the URWE feared that the government might decline to give it a promised loan, among other demands, if it backed the strike. See Union of the Regie Workers and Employees (1970, p. 78).

58. Union of the Regie Workers and Employees (1970, 51–52).
59. Union of the Regie Workers and Employees (1970, 51–52).
60. Oral accounts by several tobacco workingwomen collected between February and July 1997.
61. Mainly, Wasila Dubuq and Hannih Dib.
62. Hannih Dib, interview.
63. Leftist scholars who discussed Communist activism in Lebanon made no mention of women's issues or gendered dimensions of class. See Couland (1979) and Mustafa (1979).
64. *Al-Shuyu'iyyun al-Lubnaniyyun wa Muhimmat al-Marhalah al-Muqbilah* (no date, pp. 72–73). The party also discussed the growth of conscious social awareness in Lebanon at the hands of "male students and teachers, and the sons of the toiling industrial workingmen."
65. This was indicated by the growing number of subscriptions to the Communist daily newspaper *Al-Nida'* (*The Call*) among women and men workers at the Regie. See also *Al-Nahar* (*The Day*; newspaper) (July 16, 1963, p. 6; August 10, 1963, p. 6; October 31, 1963, pp. 5–6); *Al-Hayat* (*The Life*; newspaper) (March 7, 1965, p. 7). Ahmad 'Abdallah interview. 'Abdallah, a principal Communist Regie worker confirmed that 75 tobacco workers (a little more than 2% of the total labor force) subscribed to *Al-Nida'* during that year. Rizkallah-Boulad (1972, p. 6) also asserted the substantial growth in the number of Communist and Phalanges affiliates at the Regie.
66. See *Al-Hayat* (*The Life*; newspaper) (March 9, 1965, p. 5; March 14, 1965, p. 3).
67. Hannih Dib, interview.
68. *Al-Nahar* (*The Day*; newspaper) (March 7, 1965, p. 6; March 13, 1965, p. 3; March 26, 1965, p. 6).
69. Hannih Dib, interview.
70. Hannih Dib, interview.
71. Union of the Regie Workers and Employees (1970, p. 71).
72. George Abu Sulayman and Butrus Ghusayn, a high-ranking male employee, opposed the integration arguing that it would weaken the bargaining position of the URWE. Ghusayn also insisted that there were insufficient quantities of raw tobacco at Ghaziyya that would justify extending permanency to the working-women. See Union of the Regie Workers and Employees (1970, p. 78).
73. Union of the Regie Workers and Employees (1970, p. 78). Eight members out of ten endorsed the decision to adopt the demands of the strikers. This adoption was conditioned to remain secretive until such time when the entire board of the URWE decides to disclose it. In other words, the URWE literally dismissed the demands of Ghaziyya. Moreover, probably due to internal company and Communist party politics, which needs further research, Abu Sulayman voted against the inclusion of Ghaziyya demands and Rizq did not vote at all.
74. *Al-Nahar* (*The Day*; newspaper) (July 29, 1970, p. 4). The second Arab–Israeli war in 1967 had a major effect on South Lebanon that hosted thousands of up-rooted Palestinian refugees and became a hot bed for the Palestine Liberation Organization (PLO) and liberal nationalist and leftist activists who were sym-

pathetic to labor and peasant grievances. One could infer, as such, that the governor's "security measures" reflected the fear that the strikers might empower themselves by drawing on the support of such political activists in the south.

75. *Al-Thaqafa al-Wataniyya* (*The National Culture*; periodical) (December 5, 1970, p. 9)

76. *Al-Thaqafa al-Wataniyya* (*The National Culture*; periodical) (December 5, 1970, p. 9)

77. *Al-Thaqafa al-Wataniyya* (*The National Culture*; periodical) (December 5, 1970, p. 21).

78. *Al-Hayat* (*The Life*; newspaper) (September 12, 1970, p. 5)

79. Hannih Dib, interview; 'Itaf Tutanji, interview; Da'd Ghandur, interview; Husayn Khalifa, interview.

80. Da'd Ghandur, interview.

81. *Al-Hurriyya* (*The Freedom*; magazine) (September 21, 1970, p. 7) and *Al-Thaqafa al-Wataniyya* (*The National Culture*; periodical) (September 25, 1970, p. 19).

82. Hannih Dib, interview; 'Itaf Tutanji, interview; Husayn Khalifa, interview; *Al-Huriyya* (*The Freedom*; magazine) (September 29, 1970, pp. 7–15).

83. *Al-Nahar* (*The Day*; newspaper) (October 13, 1970, p. 5).

84. Hannih Dib, interview.

85. Hannih Dib, interview, *Al-Nahar* (*The Day*; newspaper) (November 19, 1970, p. 5), and *Al-Nahar* (*The Day*; newspaper) (November 19, 1970, p. 5).

86. Hannih Dib, interview.

87. *Al-Hurriyya* (*The Freedom*; magazine) (September 21, 1970, p. 7).

88. *Al-Hurriyya* (*The Freedom*; magazine) (December 14, 1970, p. 15).

89. *Al-Hurriyya* (*The Freedom*; magazine) (December 7, 1970, p. 10) and *Al-Thaqafa al-Wataniyya* (*The National Culture*; periodical) (December 5, 1970, p. 9).

90. Hannih Dib, interview.

91. *Al-Hurriyya* (*The Freedom*; magazine) (December 7, 1970, p. 10) and Hannih Dib, interview.

92. *Al-Nahar* (*The Day*; newspaper) (January 18, 1971, p. 1).

93. *Al-Nahar* (*The Day*; newspaper) (January 10, 1971, p. 7).

94. *Al-Hurriyya* (*The Freedom*; magazine) (December 28, 1970, p. 11).

95. Ayari and Brosseau (1998, pp. 105–106).

96. See also Fischer (1991). Similar views are reflected in Brahimi (1991).

REFERENCES

Primary Sources

Ministère des Affaires Entrangères (MAE). (1935, April 17). Qanun Yakhtas bi Istikhldam al-Awlad wa al-Nis' fi al-A'mal al-Sina'iyya [A law pertaining to the employment of children and women in industrial labor]. Vol. 2921. Personnel Department of the Regie, Liste nominative du personnel (January 1, 1969).

Union of the Regie Workers and Employees (URWE). (1954). Union membership dues.

Union of the Regie Workers and Employees (URWE). (1970). *Minutes of the Meetings.*

Oral Histories

Ahmad 'Abdallah, Interview, Wadi al-Zinih, Lebanon, January 29, 1997.
Jacques Daghir, Interview, B'abda, Lebanon, January 28, 1997.
Hannih Dib, Interview, Ghaziyya, South Lebanon, March 6, 1996.
Wasila Dubuq, Interview, Beirut, Lebanon, January 1, 1997.
Iqbal Dughan, Interview, Hadath, Lebanon, January 1, 1997.
Da'd Ghandour, Interview, Ghaziyya, South Lebanon, March 8, 1997.
Abdul Aziz Harfoush, Interview, Burj al-Barajinah, Lebanon, June 20, 1995.
Husayn Khalifa, Interview, Ghaziyya, South Lebanon, March 8, 1997.
'Itaf Tutanji, Interview, Ghaziyya, South Lebanon, February 2, 1996.
Zaynab Zu'aytir, Interview, Hadath, Lebanon, February 13, 1997.

Secondary Sources

Abisaab, M. (2001). *A history of women tobacco workers: Labor, community, and social transformation in Lebanon, 1895–1997*. Unpublished doctoral dissertation, State University of New York at Binghamton.

Abisaab, M. (2004). At the legal frontiers: Unruly working women between colonial authority and the national state, 1940–1946. *Journal of Women's History, 3*, 55–82.

Afsaruddin, A. (Ed.). (1999). *Hermeneutics and honor: Negotiating female "public" space in Islamic/ate societies*. Cambridge, MA: Harvard University Press.

Ajami, F. (1986). *The vanished Imam: Musa al-Sadr and the Shia of Lebanon*. Ithaca, NY: Cornell University Press.

Al-Buwari, E. (1986). *Tarikh al-Haraka al-'Ummaliyya wa al-Naqabiyya fi Lubnan: 1908–1946* [The History of the labor and syndicate movement in Lebanon, 1908–1946]. Beirut: Dar al-Farabi.

Al-Jisr, B. (1988). *Fouad Chihab: Dhalika al-Majhul* [Fouad Chihab: That anonymous]. Beirut: Sharikat al-Matbu'at lil-Tawzi' wa'l-Nashr.

Al-Qadaiyya al-Zira'iyya fi Lubnan fi Daw' al-Mariksiyya [The agrarian question in Lebanon from a Marxist perspective]. (1970). Beirut: Manshurat al-Hizb al-Shuyu'i al-Lubnani.

Al-Shuyu'iyyun al Lubnaniyyun wa Muhimmat al-Marhalah al-Mughbilah [The Lebanese communists and the missions of the coming period]. (No date). Beirut: Manshruat al-hizb al-Shuyu'i al-Lubnani.

Armstrong, C., & Squires, J. (2002). Beyond the public/private dichotomy: Relational space and sexual inequalities. *Contemporary Political Theory, 3*, 261–283.

Arnesen, K., & Laegran, A. S. (2003). Playing gender in public and community spaces. *Norwegian Journal of Geography, 3*, 164–173.

Asfour, E. (1955). Industrial development in Lebanon. *Middle East Economic Papers, 2*, 1–37.

Ask, K., & Tjomsland, M. (Eds.). (1988). *Women and Islamization: Contemporary dimensions of discourse of gender relations*. Oxford, UK, and New York: Berg.

Ayari, L. & Brosseau, M. (1998). In their rightful place: Gender and place in three novels by Tunisian women writers. *The Arab World Geographer, 2*, 103–116.

Bourdieu, P. (1977). *Outline of a theory of practice*. Cambridge, UK: Cambridge University Press.

Brahimi, D. (1991). *Appareillages: dix etudes comparatistes sur la literature des hommes et des femmes dans le monde arabe et aux Antilles*. Paris: Deuxtemps tierce.

Couland, J. (1979). *Nahwa Tarikh 'Lmi li'l-Haraka al-'Ummaliyya fi al-'Alam al-'Arabi* [Toward a Scientific History of the Labor Movement in the Arab World]. *Al-Tariq* [The Path], *1*, 127–152.

Domosh, M., & Seager, J. (2001). *Putting women in place.* New York: Guilford Press.

El Guindi, F. (1999). *Veil: Modesty, privacy, and resistance.* Oxford, UK: Berg.

Fischer, M. (1991). Sacred circles: Iranian Zoroastrian and Shi'i Muslim feasting and Pilgrimage circuits. In J. Scott & P. Simpson-Housley (Eds.), *Sacred places and profane spaces: The geographies of Judaism, Christianity, and Islam* (pp. 131–144). New York: Greenwood Press.

Freidl, E. (1991). The dynamics of women's spheres of action in rural Iran. In N. Keddie & B. Baron, (Eds.), *Women in Middle Eastern history: Shifting boundaries of sex and gender* (pp. 195–214). New Haven, CT: Yale University Press.

Ghurayyib, R. (1988). *Adwa' 'Ala al-Harakah al-Nisa'iyyah: Maqualat wa Dirasat* [Highlight the modern women's movement: Studies and essays]. Beirut: Institute of Women's Studies in the Arab World.

Gran, P. (1996). Organization of culture and the construction of the family in the modern Middle East. In A. Al-Azhary-Sonbol (Ed.), *Women, the family, and divorce laws in Islamic history* (pp. 64–78). Syracuse, NY: Syracuse University Press.

Hegland, M. E. (1991). Political roles of Alia Bad Women: The public/private dichotomies transcended. In N. Keddie & B. Baron (Eds.), *Women in Middle Eastern history: Shifting boundaries of sex and gender* (pp. 215–230). New Haven, CT: Yale University Press.

Hudson, M. (1985). *The precarious republic: Political modernization in Lebanon.* Boulder, CO: Westview Press.

Mazumadar, S., & Mazumadar, S. (2002). Rethinking public and private spaces: Religion and women in Muslim society. *Journal of Planning Literature, 4,* 561–643.

Mustafa, I. (1979). Tatawwurat Bunyawiyya Hamma [An important structural development]. *Al-Tariq, 1,* 95–108.

Nagel, C. (2001). Review essays. *The Arab World Geographer, 1,* 69–70.

Person, W. (1958). Lebanese economic development since 1950. *Middle East Journal, 12,* 277–294.

Richards, A. & Waterbury J. (1990). *A political economy of the Middle East: State, class, and economic development.* Boulder, CO: Westview Press.

Rizkallah-Boulad, M. (1972). La Regie des tabacs et son syndicat. *Travaux et Jours, 44,* 47–73.

Salvatore, A., & Eickelman, D. (2003). The public sphere and public Islam. *International Institute for the Study of Islam in the Modern World, 13,* 52.

Shimmel, A. (1991). Sacred geography in Islam. In J. Scott & P. Simpson-Housley (Eds.), *Sacred places and profane spaces: The geographies of Judaism, Christianity, and Islam* (pp. 163–175). New York: Greenwood Press.

Shu'ayb, A. (1980). Al-Mar'a al-'Amila fi'l-Qanun al-Lubnani [Workingwomen in Lebanese law]. In *Al-Mar'a wa'l-'Amal fi Lubnan* [Women and labor in Lebanon] (pp. 13–52). Beirut: Institute of Women's Studies in the Arab World.

Slyomovics, S. (1996). "Hassiba Ben Bouali, if you could see our Algeria": Women and public space in Algeria. In S. Sabbagh (Ed.), *Arab women: Between defiance and restraint* (pp. 211–220). New York: Olive Branch Press.

Tabarani, G. (September 27, 1974). Al-Naqabat Lam Ta'ud Lil Rijal. Al-Mar'a Aydan Asbahat Naqabiyya [Trade unions are not only for men. Women also became unionists]. *Al-Hawadith* [The Events], pp. 73–74.

11 Writing Place and Gender in Novels by Tunisian Women

MARC BROSSEAU
LEILA AYARI

> . . . the heart of the house beats in my grandmother's corset
> just as the street pounds in my old man's hand.
> —BÉJI (1993, p. 119)

"Literature is a 'place' of freedom that condenses and disperses the violence of contemporary history" (Harel, 2002, p. 7). On the
one hand, literature *condenses*: indeed, it absorbs, re-creates, sorts, constructs, reproduces, and distorts various aspects of our experience of the social world. These variable degrees of *mimesis* relate to how literature's
grasp on external reality, however slippery, transforms it into an object of
representation. Yet the idea of condensation points to something other than
mimetic representation. It refers to something more generative than straight-
forward reflection, to literature's hermeneutical or interpretive dimensions.
Novels, for example, do not simply represent social, cultural, historical, or
geographical realities: in the process of "reducing their volume" and "increasing their density," novels formulate original interpretations. On the
other hand, literature also *disperses*, a notion that points to its social and
cultural relevance and significance. Literature communicates meanings often not expressed in other discursive forms, it shares interpretations of the
world, reveals the beauties and the atrocities of the human condition, critiques the social and political order, and disseminates alternative under-

standings of what constitutes the "established reality," all of which are open to reinterpretation in different cultural contexts. Hence, it takes part in a wider sociopolitical process. This chapter is an attempt at considering both these dimensions of literature—artistic condensation and social dissemination—in the context of a cultural and geographical interpretation of contemporary novels by Tunisian women writers.

Given the prevalence of the spatial segregation of the genders in the Muslim world (Mernissi, 1985), it is surprising to see how little geographical research has focused on the experience of place by men and women as represented in literature. This type of investigation would not only reveal various aspects of gender relations, but could also lead to a broader examination of literature as a cultural production that embodies, reproduces, or resists cultural and social values. In this interpretation of five novels written by Tunisian women, the description of women's experience of place in Tunisia illustrates how literary representations can be viewed both as a description of various social realities and as a discourse of emancipation that challenges certain aspects of the hegemonic social order. Although their depiction of Tunisian gender relations is far from being radical, these authors reveal how spatial and social segregation is experienced from a woman's point of view. They illustrate how spatiality is not only a useful interpretive device to highlight aspects of women's conditions, but also a central object of their struggle for greater equality. Tradition and "modernity" are not opposed in a simple dualistic manner. Instead, the novels we examine often express an ambivalence between respect for traditional Muslim values and a legitimate desire to overcome some of the limitations imposed upon women by this moral and social order. The clear separation of private and public spaces along gender and age lines is an important aspect of the representation of space and place in these novels. It provides an interesting analytical angle from which to examine aspects of women's experience of space and place in contemporary Tunisia.

Before embarking on this examination of the representation of gender and place in contemporary novels by Tunisian women, we provide a brief overview of the various ways in which geographers have engaged works of literature to help define the contours of the approach we have privileged in this chapter. We then introduce the five novels under examination, accompanied by a brief discussion about Tunisian literature and the particular context from which women authors writing in French have evolved. These works of fiction emanate from a *paradoxical geography*—culturally and linguistically—that is described in some detail. The remainder of the chapter focuses on specific geographical and social themes in the novels that speak to the relevance of a geographically informed analysis of literary works. We discuss how the boundaries between private and public spaces and their crucial gender relevance have been represented in the five novels. In addition, we examine how profound differences that exist between the urban and the rural spheres, as far as gender roles and spatial politics are concerned, have been portrayed. Far from being static or absolute, the boundaries between private (feminine) and public (masculine) spaces are being contested or put into question. In this context, we highlight the role of *intermediaries,* who, in these novels, create precious links between women in the private sphere and what occurs in public places. More openly critical of these spatial boundaries, we also show how the recurring theme of spatial transgression acts as a ritual of resistance that illustrates how space is a key element of women's quest for equality.

LITERARY GEOGRAPHIES OF SPACE AND PLACE

Since the 1970s, geographers and other researchers in the social sciences and humanities have increasingly turned to literature as a source of inspiration. Thirty years later, literary geography, as some like to label it, has become a recognized subfield of the discipline (Claval, 1995; Crang, 1998; Shurmer-Smith, 2002). There are many ways in which to consider literary works from a geographical perspective and reasons for resorting to sources such as the novel vary. The novel can be seen as a documentary source depicting regions and places; as a transcription of the experience of place (in different geographical and cultural settings); as a critique of mainstream social reality (a form of counterdiscourse along political, social, ethnic, or gender lines); or as another representational mode that explores, in a different manner, how language can express or communicate various aspects of geographical reality (Brosseau, 1994, 1996). The first two, regionalist and humanistic interpretations, respectively, have insisted on literature's mimetic abilities: factual mimetism when the novel is considered as a documentary source on place (see Gilbert, 1972; Chevalier, 1993), subjective mimetism when it is seen as an artistic account of the experience of place (Tuan, 1978; Frémont, 1976; Porteous, 1985). Hence, these interpretations have focused mainly on the "condensation" abilities of literature. The third approach, associated with a historicomaterialist epistemology, has been more sociological in scope and therefore more concerned with literature's ideological function or, more generally, its social relevance as a reflection of unfair social conditions (Cook, 1981; Silk & Silk, 1985). The fourth approach has engaged in a more open-ended dialogue with literature about its formal possibilities in expressing meanings about people and place that usually cannot find satisfactory or transitive forms of expression in geography's traditional discursive practices (Robinson, 1977; Lafaille, 1989; Brosseau, 1997). In the context of the rejuvenation of cultural geography— and the emergence of the "new" cultural geography—more recent interpretations of literature have developed diverse analytical strategies that seek to overcome yesterday's epistemological incompatibilities (Cosgrove, 1994).

They have shown the importance of space and spatiality in the understanding of cultural representation and cultural politics (Brosseau, 2003). They are more likely to consider representations, and literary representations more specifically, as "a set of practices by which meanings are constituted and communicated. Such representational practices produce and circulate meanings among members of social groups and these meaning can be defined as culture. . . . Representations not only reflect reality, but they help to constitute reality" (Duncan, 2000, p. 703).

In this chapter, the analysis of women's experiences of place in the novels under consideration leads us to consider them as a form of cultural critique. The representation of subjective experiences of place is a common focus for many humanistic geographers attempting to understand sense of place (Pocock, 1981; Porteous, 1990). Although often considered from an individualistic standpoint, the experience of place in literature can also be examined from a social and critical perspective. The spatial distribution of the characters, who differ in age, gender, class, ethnicity, culture, their movement, their activities, and their relationships, create specific social topographies in novels (Daniels & Rycroft, 1993; Preston & Simpson-Housley, 1994; Brosseau, 1995). Research on the representation of cities in literature has revealed how different groups may experience place (Monk & Norwood, 1990; Teather, 1991; Deslauriers, 1994). When considering gender, private and public spaces are a common theme in such analyses, as illustrated in papers by Gilbert (1994) on Isabel Allende and by Gilbert and Simpson-Housley (1997) on Margaret Atwood. Issues of class, gender, race, and ethnicity, considered by themselves or in a combined fashion, are integrated in the analysis of the representation of social reality in space (McKittrick, 2000; Carter, 2001).

WOMEN WRITERS AND TUNISIAN LITERATURE

Most Tunisian literature is written in Arabic (Fontaine, 1977, 1990; Khadhar, 1987; Bekri, 1999). However, the novels examined for our research were written in French. They are a subset of what is often referred to as the "littérature maghrébine d'expression française" (Dejeux, 1992, 1994). The novels chosen are *Cendre à l'aube* (Ash at Dawn; 1975), by Jalila Hafsia; *Les jardins du nord* (Gardens of the North; 1982), by Souad Guellouz; *L'oeil du jour* (The Eye of the Day; 1985), by Hélé Béji; *Chronique frontalière* (Border Chronicle; 1991), by Emna Bel Haj Yahia; and *L'immeuble de la rue du Caire* (The Apartment Building on la rue du Caire; 2002), by Noura Bensaad.[1] Tunisian women did not write any novels in French until 1975, at which time three were published.

Tunisia became independent in 1956. The "new" Tunisian state set many fundamental transformations in motion in Tunisian society: modernization of the economy, growing urbanization and a widening of the gap between the city and the country, and significant increases in life expectancy and literacy rates, for instance (Camau, 1989). The same year, it implemented the *Code du statut personnel* (Personal status code). According to some observers, this code sets Tunisia apart in the Arab/Muslim world for promoting women's rights and greater gender equality (Charrad, 1998). Along with other social policies, it is responsible for many positive effects: ensuring basic rights for women, abolishing polygamy, outlawing repudiation, promoting education for women, and so on. Since independence, education rates, contraception use, and women's participation in the paid labor force, for example, have been accompanied by a significant drop in birthrates not often observed in the Arab/Muslim world. However, women's social mobility, especially in rural areas, is still slow and incomplete. The quest for full equality in waged work and in public space more generally is, to this day, the object of social tensions. In particular, the growing equality and autonomy of women is nonetheless viewed as a threat to men (Camau, 1989, pp. 102–103).

The novels under consideration provide interpretations of social life in the context of the modernization of social relations in Tunisia from the 1950s to the present. The general process of modernization and the progressive transformation of the traditional extended family into a nuclear one serve as the backdrop for these novels, which often represent social reality at an intimate family scale.

Cendre à l'aube, by Jalila Hafsia, is set between the 1950s and the 1970s and tells the story of a young, upper-middle-class Tunisian girl. In this novel, there is a clear contrast between city and country and between the domestic and public spheres. Transgressing from the woman's (private) sphere to the man's (public) sphere is portrayed as a crucial step toward emancipation.

Souad Guellouz's *Les jardins du nord* has a much lighter and rural flavor. This historical interpretation of Tunisian culture and family life takes the form of a collage that intertwines family memories with the author's personal reflections. Apart from emphasizing the severe restrictions faced by women, the tone of the novel is characterized by a hint of nostalgia for a past era and way of life. It is a novel "about memories and therefore about returning to one's roots" (Déjeux, 1994, p. 125).

L'oeil du jour, by Hélé Béji, presents the author's personal observations on Tunis after she returns on a holiday from her new adopted home, Paris. She finds that the efforts to modernize the city have spoiled its charm. Her grandmother's house is the only place where she feels truly at home. It has been argued that Béji is Tunisia's first French-language woman novelist worth calling a novelist (Déjeux, 1994, p. 53).

Chronique frontalière, by Emna Bel Haj Yahia, is a chronicle of the struggle of two Tunisian women in their quest for equality in a male-dominated society. More openly feminist in its stance, it portrays women on both sides of the Mediterranean, Paris and Tunis, who are disillusioned by tradition and the so-called progress of modernity.

Noura Bensaad's *L'immeuble de la rue du Caire* is the most recent of our novels. Comprising a series of portraits of daily life centered around a single apartment building in Tunis, it captures the diversity of contemporary Tunisian culture. From the street to the roof terrace, from the various apartments to the courtyard, the short novel explores a wide range of characters and relationships.

These five novels are different in many ways. Yet they clearly share a common view about a woman's place in society. They were all written by well-educated Tunisian women from a middle-class background, a fact that clearly shapes their representations of social relations. They challenge mainstream Tunisian culture because their authors wrote and published them in an environment where writing is not considered as an "acceptable" endeavor for women. Until very recently, the novel was a "male" genre and so these novels constitute relative acts of resistance, "an arena for struggles over spatial, social and cultural meanings," as was proposed for other literary works (Gilbert & Simpson-Housley, 1997, p. 245).

East and West: A Paradoxical Geography

While the fact that these women chose to write in French may seem unimportant, it is, in fact, of great cultural relevance. Indeed, many critics have discussed the cultural politics and the existential ambivalence associated with the use of French by authors of the Maghreb (Bekri, 1999). For Tunisians (and all peoples of the Maghreb) who lived through the French occupation, and especially those who attended school during that time, French has long been the language of the colonizer. One needed to master French to work in administrative positions and many thought it would help pave the way to modernization (Déjeux, 1992, p. 52). However, people continued to associate French with the Western world. A Tunisian dialect of Arabic was spoken, but classical written Arabic—the variety shared by the entire Arab world—was not taught in schools. It was up to parents, if they had the desire and the means to do so, to have an instructor come to the house and teach their children the language of the Qur'an. The main characters in the novels by Guellouz and Hafsia often allude to a certain void, a deep regret, and even a sense of shame stemming from the fact that they did not learn classical Arabic. Because language is a social barrier, not knowing "their language" distances them from their history, their ancestors, and even their religion. Guellouz tells of the main character's (young Sophia Chebil) lack of interest in private Arabic lessons. Since Arabic was not a requirement in school, Sofia saw no point in putting effort into learning complex Arabic grammar. At the time, she thought only of the importance of

French, "this French which will help us fight against the French" (Guellouz, 1982, p. 128). Only when she reaches adulthood does Sofia regret her laziness and feel the shame of not knowing "her language." With this passage, it is clear that Guellouz tries to justify and defend her use of French, while still claiming her Arab and Muslim identity. In the household featured in *Cendre à l'aube*, it is the grandfather who tries to teach the children Arabic through history and music.

While some authors reject French because it is the colonizer's language, one viewpoint suggests that some women authors reject Arabic, perhaps subconsciously, because it is the language of patriarchal power and of the Qur'an. The idea that a woman should express herself openly is seen not only as a transgression but also as a *fitna*, a threat to the structure of moral values and religious beliefs that underlie traditional society (Segarra, 1997, p. 17). Some North African feminists advocating emancipation within existing traditional structures see the use of the French language as moving away from this ideal because it brings them closer to Western social and ideological structures (Segarra, 1997, p. 20).

The use of French does provide a "place" of freedom that is quite different from that provided by Arabic. The distance it creates allows the author to cross the barriers of prohibition and social taboos (Déjeux, 1994, p. 130). Since French has no religious significance for Muslims, it acts as a "veil," allowing the writer to express herself more freely without having to reveal the most intimate part of her life: her relationship with God. In fact, Fawzia Zouari, who recently published the novel *La retournée*, which addresses identity issues related to belonging to two very different cultures, directly expresses the freedom associated with the use of French: "In this foreign language, French, I now have the impression of running freely on a field unlimited by borders, of conquering a real independence" (Zouari, 1996, p. 131). She goes on to say that preventing her from writing in French would constitute a condemnation to silence. Hélé Béji, herself at the crossroads of both cultures, puts it in very geographical terms: "The land where I contemplate myself is the Orient, the place where I express myself is the West. The oddness of this position does not escape me, for I experience myself primarily as a form of paradoxical geography in which nothing corresponds but everything is communicated" (Béji, 1997, p. 13).

PRIVATE VERSUS PUBLIC SPACE

Traditionally, private space, especially domestic space, is associated with women, whereas the public domain is a more masculine space. This type of spatial segregation is especially prevalent in the Arab/Muslim context where public and private spheres are well defined with little overlap between the two (e.g., Fisher, 1991). Although it is not applied as stringently to younger generations, and even though its intensity varies with one's age, family environment, and socioeconomic class, spatial segregation of the genders is fundamental in shaping the female characters' experience of space and place in the novels under consideration. For women, home is central to every aspect of their lives and is often the only place where they truly belong. They are confined to the home first by their parents, then, once married, by their husbands. The home, over which the woman has almost complete control—at the cost of turning her back on the outside world—and whose every little nook and cranny she knows, becomes her universe (Segarra, 1997, p. 117).

This intimate knowledge of their space gives some women a sense of security inside their homes. This is especially true of elderly women. For them, home is a peaceful haven in a city and a country undergoing rapid changes and which they no longer recognize. Routine housework also brings with it a sense of security that provides the kind of serenity that comes from living comfortably and having absolute control (Brahimi, 1995, p. 29). Every morning, the narrator's mother in *L'oeil du jour* devotes herself to her housework, always following "her favorite itinerary, unaltered by time" (Béji, 1993, p. 12). Referring to the numerous handkerchiefs that the elderly keep in their pockets and elsewhere in their garments, the narrator describes her grandmother's control over the spatial occupation in her home, while also comparing the intimacy of the home to that of her own body, where she keeps the keys to all the parts of her home.

> My grandmother always keeps many of them on her, hidden deep in her corset, where you think she'll never find them again, considering she puts so many sets, wallets, rosaries, keys, and who-knows-what-else in there: all the tools needed to run the household smoothly, tools without which no one can have access neither to the pantry, nor the kitchen, nor the closets, nor the washrooms, nor the stairs on the first floor, nor the "commodino" in the bedroom. The entire house is inside my grandmother's corset, held together by a strong elastic which forms a large fold on top of her waist; the heart of the house beats in my grandmother's corset just as the street pounds in my old man's hand. (Béji, 1993, p. 119)

In this house, every single object has its place and "only during thorough housecleaning are they moved, for a few hours, from their peaceful throne" (Béji, 1993, p. 86).

This widowed grandmother and the elderly women in *Les jardins du nord* control their domestic space and only rarely leave it. They choose to stay in their homes and have maids, children, a neighbor, or some other intermediary run errands for them. Not only have these women created a peaceful haven for themselves and their families, but they clearly state their intention of not seeing this order disturbed by the French occupation and Western influence in general. The mother in *Les jardins du nord* (Ella Yamina) notices the influence of Christian culture on her daughters, who have befriended a young Italian girl, when one of these daughters imitates a funeral scene to mark the end of her affection for her doll:

> "Fatma, Sofia, Maria, come, women do not attend funerals!"
> "But this is a Christian funeral," answered Fatma. [...]
> Ella Yamina let out a sigh but Sophia saw that she was also smiling.
> "There you are," she said, "even our funerals are going to resemble
> Christian funerals!" (Guellouz, 1982, p. 172)

Later, the same idea is expressed again, but in a more serious tone:

> For her [Ella Yamina, Sophia's and Fatma's mother], it was already sad enough that the country was colonized. But she was determined that colonization would at least stop at her doorstep and, if possible, fall flat on its face there. "They" had taken the land and its fruits, "they" would not take the fruit of her womb. . . . (Guellouz, 1982, p. 175)

Again, parallels are drawn between the home, dominated by the woman, and her body or her children's bodies, which are to be protected to the same extent. This certainly would explain, in part, why many female characters remember their childhood homes with so much tenderness, nostalgia, and respect for tradition. The home is an important part of childhood; it is where girls and women spend most of their time.

This nostalgia and attachment to the grandmother's home is an underlying theme in *L'oeil du jour*. When she arrives in Tunis from Paris, where she now lives, the narrator only feels comfortable in her grandmother's home and thus refuses to venture outside. "Moving about inside apartment spaces leading to the main patio is a pleasure of which she never tires" (Brahimi, 1991, p. 77). Hence her confinement to the domestic sphere has not been imposed on her; it is her choice. In *Les jardins du nord*, the tenderness with which the home is described is even more innocent. There is a metonymical process whereby the house expresses both childhood and the narrator's relationship to her mother:

> . . . for Sophia, that house in Metline is still The House, even though she was not born there. In fact, none of the children were born there. Sofia only lived there during vacations, and even then she rarely stayed more than two months at a time. Furthermore, it was neither luxurious nor even comfortable. They had spent many years in that house without running water and electricity. But Sofia loved it. She still loves it today as a witness to her happy childhood, as the last relic of what they were taught to call, "Mama's days." (Guellouz, 1982, p. 66)

Some characters long for the past, a time when they might have been frustrated by the segregation and yet felt safe knowing that they were not alone. Today, with all the upheaval in traditional society and European-style housing, especially the impersonal apartment buildings, segregation is much harder to bear.

This isolation is even more frustrating and restricting for young educated women who wish to live a lifestyle unlike what their mothers and other women from previous generations knew. A woman becomes aware of a perceived inferiority at adolescence, a time in a young woman's life when the family makes decisions about her engagement (Déjeux, 1994, p. 129). The young woman goes from being controlled by her parents to being controlled by her husband. In *Les jardins du nord*, this spousal control is extreme in the relationship between Sophia's grandfather and his first wife: "Fatma saw her parents, who lived five hundred meters away, once a year" (Guellouz, 1982, p. 32). This makes a strong statement about the extent to which a man can control a woman's movements.

In *Cendre à l'aube*, Nabila's "imprisonment" by her first two husbands is less harsh yet more frustrating because Nabila is convinced that she is entitled to a happier life. Consequently, she withdraws into her own shell and tries to lose herself in books, much to the pleasure of her second husband, Hatem's: "Reading prevented Nabila from going out and that reassured Hatem" (Hafsia, 1975, p. 167). Later, she regrets having tolerated her husband's hold on her occupation of space: "In all the years we lived together, he didn't stop controlling her friendships, watching her comings and goings, imposing set itineraries, and frequently checking up on her" (Hafsia, 1975, p. 198). In the more recent novel by Bensaad (2002), however, we see a wider range of gender relations: traditional couples with stricter gender spatial segregation, more modern couples whose use of space is less clearly demarcated, a young woman living alone and feeling relatively free.

Physical isolation in the domestic sphere, linked to a woman's status, often creates some sort of bond between women. Hafsia describes bonds that develop, sometimes unbeknownst to the women themselves, between women in the same building. Space thus becomes a mediator of social relationships, creating a kinship between individuals who would otherwise be isolated:

> Men were rarely seen during the day. They left early in the morning and returned from work at a set time. [. . .] The building looked like it only had women as occupants. [. . .] In that building, the women felt at ease. [. . .] What created a familiarity between them was this intimate and mutual understanding of the stresses in their lives, of their habits, of their problems, of what they had given up. Unbeknownst to them, an affectionate indulgence connected them to one another. Shielded from the eyes of men, they revealed their true selves, without feeling forced to painfully pretend. All of

them accepted their burden with resignation. Knowing that on the floor below another woman, also wearing a faded *blousa* [traditional blouse] and *fouta* [traditional skirt], was going through the same motions and experiencing the same sorrow filled them with serenity. What a comfort! (Hafsia, 1975, p. 35)

The female characters often try to forget their loneliness by visiting a neighbor, sister, cousin, or friend:

Not a day went by without one of the sisters visiting a sister, a brother, or a cousin. they never tired of it. These visits were part of life. No one could stand loneliness. One had to see somebody, anybody. one was never to stay alone! This was the case for all members of society. (Hafsia, 1975, p. 145)

These meetings allow women to distract themselves from the monotony of housework while providing an opportunity for sharing common experiences: "Freed from their chores for an entire afternoon, women, young and old, felt united by a silent contempt for men and their tyrannical organization" (Hafsia, 1975, p. 29). Assisting a family member, friend, or neighbor is frequently used as an excuse to leave the house:

To hell with husbands and children! This week, the excuse to go-to-Yamina's-house-to-help-her-make-couscous proved to be a nice long break. It was always better than the monotony of other days, than the big or small tasks that enslaved their lives, all women's lives. They shared news, laughed like little girls, exchanged recipes for happiness:
"You want your husband to be blinded with love for you? Blind him!"
Sofia listened more carefully.
Then came the details:
"Give him compliments. Tell him: 'You are the most handsome, the most majestic . . . Even if he is a hunchbacked monkey!' " (Guellouz, 1982, p. 96)

In the *L'immeuble de la rue du Caire*, women meet on the roof terrace with their children, hanging clothes and sometimes hot peppers to dry, exchanging news and gossip:

She saw other women who just like her were busy washing or hanging clothes to dry. There were dozens and dozens of red peppers drying on the ground or hanging on strings. Farida thought to herself the roofs were the housewifes' kingdom. Just like her, nearly all women must have felt a sense of freedom on the roof terrace of their building. (Bensaad, 2002, p. 47)

Women's meetings always take place when "the man of the house" is away, but always in a home, never in a café or a restaurant. The boundaries of the private and the public spheres are generally respected. Ella Yamina is shocked when, in accordance with tradition, she visits a new bride and hears someone breathing behind her: "Well, she says to herself, this is incredible. The husband in his room [. . .], I warned them of my visit. I know he is uneducated but I can't believe that he would stay hidden to hear a conversation between women. . . . " (Guellouz, 1982, p. 223). One exception to this general rule is the apartment courtyard of the colonial city, where men and women, still "protected" from the very public gaze of the street, can actually meet and talk more or less freely, as described by Bensaad (2002) in the *L'immeuble de la rue du Caire*.

In more formal gatherings, such as weddings, where both genders find themselves under the same roof, boundaries exist inside the domestic space: "All of the family, or rather the women, surrounded her. The men were in another room with Youssef. The separation of the genders was automatic" (Hafsia, 1975, p. 61).[2] Segarra (1997, p. 118) notes that inside the houses there is also a division of spaces: women's spaces are usually more humid, darker, and have lower ceilings, whereas men's spaces are generally dry, better lit, with higher ceilings.

The presence of men in the private feminine sphere does seem to change the character, the dynamic, and the freedom of movement in that space. In this sense, some women who are unhappy about their situation dread the time of day when their husband returns from work—as if, upon his return, the woman suddenly loses the power over the space which is normally hers (see Bensaad, 2002, p. 24, for an example). It is unacceptable to do or say certain things in the presence of men, even in the private sphere. In *Les jardins du nord*, little Sophia, who was barely 11 years old at the time, learned this truth and brought shame on her mother in the process:

> "She was combing her hair in front of her grandfather and I was overcome with shame. . . . Ah! It is right to say that any small part of a woman's body is indecent."
> [. . .] *Yet Sophia knew that if one of her brothers had combed his three centimeters of hair in front of his grandfather, her mother would not have felt dishonored. At best, she would have very politely told him to comb his hair elsewhere. But in Sophia's case, because of her long hair, a symbol of femininity, she was pushed over into another world, one of mystery (to be maintained), of shame (that was not to be analyzed to avoid making any troubling discoveries), of taboos (sometimes very useful, even necessary, as barriers, in a patriarchal and chauvinistic society).* (Guellouz, 1982, p. 109)

The purpose of spatial segregation of the sexes is therefore to hide the woman's body from the eyes of men. It is a question of honor for the men responsible for protecting the integrity of girls and women (Mernissi, 1985).

To those visiting Tunisia for the first time, the French influence on the lifestyle and the built environment is evident. However, after the initial impression, "one realizes that the French element is more of a veneer, and that underneath things are fundamentally different. One important factor which creates this difference is Islam" (Beaujot, 1985, p. 5). Although Tunisia and France are two opposing worlds, with two very distinct value systems (Segarra, 1997, p. 111), many elements of the French system crossed over to Tunisia during the colonial period. One element that has had major repercussions on the way people occupy space is city planning.

In cities developed with a European lifestyle in mind, there isn't the sacred physical space needed to protect women from male onlookers, and so this space must somehow be created. In *Les jardins du nord*, Sophia's father did just that when the family moved to Tindja:

> In Tindja, a village next to Ferryville, you might get the impression that you were in Europe, or more precisely in France.
>
> All the houses had roofs covered with red tiles and a small garden. They were all fenced in by low hedges, so low in fact that when the Chebils left the Buonanottes and bought their own house, it was a problem for Ella Yamina, who wore a veil. Also, before they moved into the house, Si Abdelkrim had a two-meter-high wall built around the house to hide Ella Yamina from the eyes of passers-by when she went into the garden. (Guellouz, 1982, p. 133)

The critical boundary is drawn here between the house (feminine) and the street (masculine). *Les jardins du nord* is set in the first half of the century, a time when wearing the veil was a way to extend a woman's private sphere into the streets. In the other novels, there is little mention of veils because very few women in Tunisian urban centers wear them. (In fact, it has been banned in Tunisia's schools, universities, and public administrations since 1990. For a general discussion, see Charrad, 1998.)

The street is much more than a mere space for getting around in Muslim cities. Women who find themselves in streets have to endure aggressive looks and comments from men. They are only there out of necessity, to go from one home to another, to get to school, or to run errands and quickly return home. Men will often accompany women who need to go outside the home in order to protect "their honor." In *Cendre à l'aube*, Nabila's best friend's boyfriend is one of these men who feels he has something to protect:

> When they [Nabila and Monia] stepped outside, they never saw Ahmed. But they promptly found him on their path. He waited on the sidewalk, smoking and watching them walk by with long indifferent glances. [. . .]
>
> He accompanied them to the school's door and walked away with the same discretion that he had used to wait for them. (Hafsia, 1975, p. 62)

A young woman's experience of the street is overseen and controlled by men. Beaujot's viewpoint adds an interesting dimension to this idea.

> In the towns it is the men who are in the cafes. At first, one finds it surprising to see only men in these places of leisure. You realize that you have internalized the local norm when you react with shock to see a woman walking in the street as if she belonged there. The fact is that the public domain is a man's domain. A woman who is being harassed on the street or in a crowded bus has no recourse, because, in effect, she does not belong there. This is not to say that there are no women on the streets, but they must have a definite purpose justifying their intrusion into a domain that is not really theirs. (Beaujot, 1985, p. 9)

His remarks explain the feelings and impressions expressed by the women authors of these novels with regard to a woman's place in Tunisia's public spaces. These feelings are clearly expressed in Bel Haj Yahia's *Chronique frontalière*:

> . . . but the exaggerated stare that she senses behind the dark glasses of the young man with the mustache stops her, follows her, and she understands everything about it: curiosity, arrogance, hate, envy, desire. . . . Indifference, however, is a precious and impossible thing to find in the streets that separate her from Tarek. This is the refuge that she yearns for in vain. (Bel Haj Yahia, 1991, p. 53)

One place that is alluded to only in *Cendre à l'aube,* but which deserves to be mentioned, is the brothel. When her son announces that he is in love with a woman factory worker, the mother, who is from a wealthy family, is driven to despair:

> "I don't want to see you with that worker. . . . Have fun if you like. There are places for that . . . plenty of places . . . there are girls who are made for that. . . . But to be enamoured of a factory worker!" (Hafsia, 1975, p. 76)

This passage suggests that the frequenting of such establishments by men, albeit in secret, is a recognized and accepted practice. Although it is a private space where women are confined, the brothel can be described as a masculine space since the women who find themselves there are "made for that," an outlet for men's frustrations or a simple commodity for their enjoyment. These women do not need to be hidden because they have already lost their virginity, the most important part of "nice girls" that needs protecting.

Our reading of the spaces occupied by women has yet to address class and age more specifically. The women subjected to segregation in our novels are all young women from well-to-do families. Girls under the age of puberty as well as elderly women are not subjected to such strict segregation. In the *L'immeuble de la rue du Caire*, for example, women meet and socialize in their homes or on the roof terraces. Men, on the other hand, encounter each other casually on the street. An older woman, returning home after having run errands, would still observe unwritten rules such as avoiding eye contact with men in public spheres:

> At the other end of the street, they saw Fatma walking hastily and laden with parcels. Despite her old age she was walking very upright. She greeted both men without looking at them and disappeared into the shadow of the doorway. (Bensaad, 2002, p. 120)

This somewhat greater spatial freedom also applies to maids and young women from very poor homes. Segarra (1997, p. 79) explains that excessive exposure to the eyes of others cancels its negative effects, it takes away the restrictions placed on the object and causes the observer to lose all interest in it. Although gender comes first in defining who belongs where, age and class provide some exceptions to the general rule. These exceptions become convenient as they create ways of getting around the rules, as we will see later.

CITY VERSUS COUNTRY

Urban and rural spaces have almost opposite connotations for women and men in the novels of Béji, Guellouz, and Hasfia. Bel Haj Yahia and Bensaad barely mention the latter. In the city, spaces occupied by women are generally limited to the home, whereas in rural environments women have much more freedom of movement, even outside the domestic sphere. Women's experiences of spaces and places are therefore more abundant and varied in the countryside than they are in cities. The greater freedom enjoyed by women in rural areas has to do with very practical circumstances. Houses in these regions are not equipped with all the amenities found in urban settings. In many cases, water must be brought from the village spring and firewood must be gathered in the forest. These chores are invariably women's work. Women also participate in farming tasks, which cause them to rub shoulders with men: "meetings were organized during the olive harvest" (Guellouz, 1982, p. 156). Still, too much familiarity between men and women is not acceptable:

> In the city, seclusion was expected in almost all circles, whereas in the villages, where most women had to work outside, seclusion was reserved for those from the wealthiest families. Therefore, in novels written by women, the city is often compressed into a much reduced space, the home. (Segarra, 1997, p. 113)

These necessary outings away from the domestic space lead to meetings and human relationships inaccessible to isolated women in the cities. Contact between women occurs inside and outside the domestic realm. During one of Nabila's stays in the countryside, Hafsia notes that "all the women come to collect water or chop firewood. But it is also a way to meet, talk and hear the latest news of the village" (Hafsia, 1975, p. 103).

In *Cendre à l'aube*, getting away from the city is the reason for this vacation in the countryside. Nabila travels to the mountains during her first divorce and returns to Tunis only several months later, after the spiteful gossip has died down: "She went far away from Tunis, waiting for the divorce to be granted. It was the first time she had suffered public reprobation" (Hafsia, 1975, p. 83). In that environment, Nabila discovered the kind of freedom and serenity that she had never experienced in Tunis: "Wherever she went in the village, she was in her rightful place; whatever she did, no one bothered her. If she wanted to walk, she walked. If she wanted to disguise herself behind a tree, no one would move her" (Hafsia, 1975, p. 91). The natural space is not exclusive to men or to women: "They [Nabila and her sisters] often went for walks. They walked in the hills, in that oak forest through which stretched beautiful paths full of ferns. They quenched their thirst at the spring" (Hafsia, 1975, p. 97).

In coastal rural regions, the beaches replace the forests as the place of choice for outdoor leisure. At the beach, as in all public places, many women are dressed in such a manner as to shield their body from the eyes of men: "They entered the water with a shirt and a long *serouel* [pants] and even though they could enjoy swimming, sunbathing was prohibited" (Guellouz, 1982, p. 83).

MOVEMENT, PROCESSES, AND TRANSGRESSIONS

"In trying to determine the frequency, the rhythm, the order and, most of all, the reasons behind the changes in setting in a novel, we discover just how important they are in creating the novel's unity and movement, and how much space supports all of its other components" (Bourneuf, 1972, p. 100). We have identified two important vectors that help to create bonds between characters belonging to different types of space, private and public. The first vector, *intermediaries,* allows women in the private sphere to have some understanding of life in the public space. The second vector, *transgression,* implies the crossing over from the private space into the public domain in an act of defiance relative to the context.

Intermediaries

Women confined to their homes often resort to intermediaries, either out of necessity or to satisfy their curiosity about the outside world. The first case is generally that of elderly women who do not want to leave the house or who are unable to do so because their frail health does not allow them enough freedom of movement. As we already mentioned, many of these women seem quite content with their confinement to the domestic space; their house is their universe. The grandmother in *L'oeil du jour* is one such woman. She has two regular intermediaries to run her errands: the maid and her neighbor, Slaymane, with whom she shares a close friendship:

> Slaymane only agrees to leave the deck chair in front of his house for the small favors he does for my grandmother, an errand at the market, small repairs, an invitation for coffee, teatime, an announcement, a joke that she has for him. (Béji, 1993, p. 30)

Consequently, the household "receives only a few indirect, carefully filtered pieces of information from the outside" (Brahimi, 1995, p. 30).

Béji describes entire evenings spent watching television. First comes the soap opera, then the weather report, and finally the political news (Béji, 1993, p. 144). In this house, television is presented as a secondary intermediary. Although it does not provide information on the immediate outside environment, it does present information about a male-dominated sphere: politics. It also enables the viewer to have a "virtual" experience of spaces and places by transmitting images and re-creating scenery.

The most common intermediary is without a doubt the accomplice who facilitates a female character's tricks. This go-between works for men as well as for women. His or her mission is usually to forward letters or messages between men and women who, according to societal norms (in the name of religion), are not allowed to communicate. At an early age, Nabila, from *Cendre à l'aube*, eavesdrops on a discussion between her mother and a neighbor and is shocked by the woman's accounts of her secret relationship with a lover: "There she is describing her outings. They were about lovers meeting and letters delivered to her, in secret, thanks to the young maid" (Hafsia, 1975, p. 32). Intermediaries bridge the gap between women's private space and men's public space, thus enabling couples to maintain these types of relationships.

At times, intermediaries are sent by a woman or a teenage girl to gather information about something or someone mentioned in the home. In this case, the scheme facilitated by an intermediary becomes some sort of indirect transgression where imagination and knowledge of the outside world are nourished by the intermediary's descriptions. Our novels include many examples of this. In *Les jardins du nord*, Sophia and her sister want to know about a new neighbor in Metline, a village where tradition and segregation of the sexes are closely observed:

> She never forgot that Metline-was-Metline-and-that-there-were-things-you-did-not-joke-about. Yet they knew everything about their young new

neighbor, who had a beard like Si Haj Ali's, thanks to their brothers, their cousins, and even their young uncles—their lifelong "buddies" whom they questioned skillfully. (Guellouz, 1982, p. 205)

The intermediary is inevitably an individual who easily has access to the public as well as the private spheres. It is easy to see why men, maids, and young children would be the most obvious intermediaries. Several years ago, women who did not wear a veil because they did not fear a man's gaze could also serve as intermediaries: " . . . she sent a Jewish woman who did not wear a veil to Metline, to speak with your grandfather . . ." (Guellouz, 1982, p. 218).

Transgression

The second interesting phenomenon is the transgression from the private sphere to the public sphere and vice versa. The transgression from feminine and masculine spaces is contrary to social expectations because "the woman is like the seat of disorder, of repression, which will dangerously overflow into the male public space and therefore eroticize it . . . and in so doing drastically disrupt the order designed by God in the Creation and leave society in a chaotic state" (Déjeux, 1994, p. 69). Spatial transgression is nonetheless a goal for many female characters and a recurring theme in all five novels. In many respects, it is a ritual of resistance toward the structure imposed by conventional patriarchal authority. It is a way for women to thwart conventions and impose themselves in an environment that is not theirs.

Spatial transgression is not exclusive to women. In a particularly perceptive scene, Bensaad describes a peculiar form of male transgression into the female domestic sphere. Ever since Mohamed and Habiba's daughter, Rafika, married a French man against her father's best advice, Mohamed refuses to see her or even talk about her with his wife. Still eager to hear about Rafika, but unwilling to admit it, he spies on his wife's conversation with her maid in the kitchen about her weekly visit at her daughter's. The women knew about this indiscretion and made a conscious effort to discuss Rafika's family life. This example shows how the domestic spatial segregation of the genders can be used to the mother's advantage, allowing her to share her daughter's news with her husband while observing the patriarchal moral order that requires her to protect his paternalistic pride.

When they heard him approach and sit in the room contiguous to the kitchen, Habiba and Myriam, who were busy preparing the meal, seemed to react to a signal. The maid winked at her boss and asked:

"Lalla Habiba, how is Rafika? You went to see her yesterday afternoon?"

> [...] every Saturday, the day following Habiba's visit to their daughter, he came searching for news by sitting on the other side of the kitchen wall. (Bensaad, 2002, pp. 106, 108)

There are different types of transgressions, and they vary with the intensity and the intentions of the "transgressor." The transgression may be motivated by innocent curiosity and can be achieved visually. At the other end of the spectrum, the transgression can lead to a woman taking over part of a public space.

In the first section of this chapter, we discussed the looks that women endure from men in the public sphere. For women, watching the outside from the inside is also a part of their experience of space and place. The novels include numerous references to women who observe men's public space from a window or a balcony, without being seen. The narrator in *L'oeil du jour* describes the joy of watching without being seen, even though, unlike most Tunisian women, she is an atheist and therefore has no reason to conceal herself: "Near the window, I can watch everything that goes on without being seen" (Béji, 1993, p. 39).

During the colonial era, female characters wanted to observe not only the male universe but also the foreigners who walked the streets. One often had to be quite clever to achieve this:

> At that time, Bizerte was crowded with not only French, of course, but also with Senegalese soldiers and German prisoners. The ways of the French, in particular those of French women, greatly amused Ella Yamina. Since she wore a veil, she could not stand directly on the balcony, which was also fenced in by a wire net. But she found a way to see some of what went on in the street without being seen. She positioned herself two or three meters behind the balcony, seated on the floor with her legs crossed. That way, she could see everything that happened on the sidewalk out front. As for them, they could not see her or at least not see her properly. (Guellouz, 1982, p. 38)

Like her mother, the daughter is fascinated by the street and the people in it. Whereas her mother focused on French women, Sophia preferred to observe the Senegalese soldiers:

> She always had her observation post, the balcony, and the Senegalese fascinated her even more now that she knew they could scare her. From the balcony, she savored the safety she felt just as one savors ice cream in a movie theater while on the screen characters are killing each other and setting fires. (Guellouz, 1982, p. 40)

This childlike, often feminine, curiosity is also alluded to in *Cendre à l'aube* when it is said of young Nabila that "she spent a lot of her time watching

the street. In those days, few women left the house" (Hafsia, 1975, p. 23).
Here, gazing outside is a substitute for physical transgression of spaces.
These two short sentences also hint at the fact that women "today" (when
the novel was written) go out more than they did when Nabila was a child.
Later, Nabila observes a 14-year-old boy. This type of observation is per-
ceived as a danger when there is a risk of being seen from the outside:

> She stood, as usual, at the window, her observation post. The blinds were
> shut; it was hot. The boy was watching the street, sitting idle on the armrest
> of a bench. His skin was brown. So were his thighs, which stuck out of his
> cotton shorts. Nabila was fascinated. Being that she loved danger, she ap-
> proached cautiously and excitedly. She put her face directly on the window.
> She gazed as much as she wanted to. This interest lasted only ten minutes. It
> was violent. It was the first. (Hafsia, 1975, p. 51)

In the days when young women only met their husbands on their wedding
day, they were able to get to know their fiancé by stealing glances at them.
Ella Yamina explains this to her daughters in *Les jardins du nord*:

> "I knew that he looked like his father and that his father would pass in front
> of our house to get to his law office. So one day, when the whole family was
> taking a nap, I went into a barn filled with bags of barley and where I could
> see the street from a small window. I waited for him to return from the of-
> fice. He passed by. I found him as handsome as people said but he also had a
> rare elegance. I told myself that his son must be like him, handsome, ele-
> gant, and I was very happy." (Guellouz, 1982, p. 219)

Women are not the only ones who wish to see their fiancés; men also try to
see a fiancée or any beautiful woman through a window or a doorway. Visual transgression can be described as "soft" since it does not require a
physical movement from one type of space to the other, yet it remains prohibited.

Grandmothers who are content with their place in the home are illiterate. Schooling does seem to act as a springboard for women's spatial transgression. The fact that women have to travel to school makes them more
aware of the city, or at least parts of it. Also, daily contact with others, both
girls and boys, leads to a level of socialization that is impossible to attain
inside the home. Finally, schooling exposes young women to career options
that are usually incompatible with the values taught by the family circle.
Hence, for many of the more educated women, transgression into the spatial sphere traditionally reserved for men becomes a pressing need with age.

When outings in the city are not permitted, a woman will sometimes
decide to go out even when her family or husband forbid her from doing
so. "The statement 'I'm going out' was said defiantly" (Hafsia, 1975,
p. 31). A woman may also choose to invent an excuse in order to leave:

> One morning, she and Monia went together to see a fortuneteller. For this expedition she had to ask Youssef for a few hours of freedom, inventing some pretext. This subterfuge, and more so, this unusual freedom so early in the morning, rejoiced her. [. . .] Nabila became one of the many women who no longer felt confident and were reduced to depending on magic spells to overcome this. (Hafsia, 1975, p. 81)

Nabila finds it difficult to tell the difference between rebellion and freedom until the last pages of the novel. She is the only character, in all five novels, for whom the partial appropriation of the public space is retraced. For Nabila, physical transgression of spaces allows her to explore a new identity. After having been confined to the domestic realm by her parents and later by her husbands, she rebels because she is "convinced that she is entitled to happiness" (Hafsia, 1975, p. 179). She no longer resigns herself to her lot in life as a woman. Nabila needs to be convinced of her decision because she knows that she will face a wall of opposition; the boundary between both worlds is well guarded. The first step she takes is that of finding a job outside her home: "She was nothing like a rebellious woman. She only wanted to work and do something with her life. She felt she had the right to do away with customs and traditions. But instead of being encouraged, she was banned" (Hafsia, 1975, p. 215). Once she starts working and enjoying it, the physical transgression of space leads to a change in her disposition and in her perception of herself: "She went out. For the first time in her life, she was a free woman" (Hafsia, 1975, p. 217). Even her thoughts and her words are not as restrained as before. She discovers a freedom that makes her happy. In the novel's final scenes, Nabila's emancipation is clearly expressed in terms of spatial experience:

> Nabila is sitting under the vault of a small café in the souk. In the shadow of the Zitouna mosque, she seems calm and healed from her wounds, or, rather, in recovery. She wonders what her husband, or husbands (there is no difference anymore) would think to see her like this, in the little café, her legs stretched out, sipping mint tea. None of them would believe their eyes! [. . .] Not one woman in the café. [. . .] But she felt perfectly happy and drank her tea in public. (Hafsia, 1975, p. 265)

Nabila's emancipation, of which the ultimate accomplishment is her appropriation of her share of the space traditionally reserved for men, is the result of a long process of questioning and protest. It is therefore not something that is accessible to all women. Simply moving from the private to the public sphere, or from the home to the street, does not represent true freedom because women still feel unwelcome in men's spaces. Thus, this emancipation remains elusive until mentalities begin to change.

IN SEARCH OF THEIR *RIGHTFUL* PLACE

It would be hard to claim that these five novels, written by authors belonging to the first generation of Tunisian women novelists, provide an interpretation of the *typical* experiences of women of that country. Because of their
education and professional backgrounds, these authors are among the
intellectual elite who write in the language of the colonizer (French), and
often while in self-imposed exile. Yet this cultural distance gives them a
freedom—writing—and enables them to take a stand—exposing injustice
and segregation—both of which would hardly be conceivable in a traditional context. These authors have found in literature a forum for their critical voices to be heard (or read) both in Tunisia and abroad.

The *paradoxical geography* in which these novels were written—
between Tunisia and France, between Arabic and French, between East and
West—has important implications in terms of reception and interpretation:
with greater cultural hybridity in origin, there exist a greater potential for
multiple interpretations. It would be difficult, without engaging in a different type of analysis, to speculate whether or not their authors intended to
send different messages to different audiences. But they were certainly
aware of the differentiated horizon of reception of their writings. Female
and male readers in Tunisia, in other Arab/Muslim countries where French
is commonly used, in France, among people of Arabic descent or not, or
elsewhere in the world are likely to interpret the cultural and political connotations of these literary works quite differently. Their appreciation of the
cultural politics will vary in intensity, in depth, and in substance. What
would constitute an obvious cultural critique for a woman reading these
novels in Tunisia (e.g., spatial transgression) may very well be overlooked
as a detail of limited importance by an outside reader.

The novels offer insights, sometimes intimate, into the female characters' experiences of space and place. We have tried not only to sketch the
outlines of an interpretation of spatialized gender relations in Tunisia, but
also to see the extent to which space informs the daily practices of women
and to which it functions as a major issue in their quest for emancipation.
Places are mostly important inasmuch as they dictate the limits imposed on
the movements of male and female individuals of different age groups. Furthermore, "Space is not described in and of itself but as it relates to the
characters, and especially their inner lives, that is, their state of mind, pas-
sions and search for identity"(Segarra, 1997, p. 111).

Bekri maintains that most novels written in French by Tunisian
women, apart from those of Bel Haj Yahia and maybe Zouari, are not characterized by a clear feminist stance. Arguably, Bekri writes that emancipation for these women authors is already a given, hence the themes they develop are more or less universal (Bekri, 1999, pp. 38–39). Indeed, it may be
presumptuous to read these novels as militant feminist works. Yet, in our

view, their tone and subject matter clearly challenge traditional cultural and patriarchal values. On the other hand, these novels express the need to find a "middle ground" that accommodates respect for tradition as well as a woman's need for empowerment and equality. In this sense, the words of these women illustrate how literature is a "place of freedom" that "condenses and disperses" the violence but also the challenges of contemporary life.

ACKNOWLEDGMENTS

This chapter is an expanded version of a previously published paper in *The Arab World Geographer*, Vol. 1, No. 2 (1998), pp. 103–116. We would like to thank the editor for permission to publish this new version.

We would like to express our warmest thanks to David Tavares of the Department of Geography, University of Ottawa, for his background research and proofreading of the final draft.

NOTES

1. These novels were written in French and have not been translated into English. The translations provided are those of the authors of this chapter.
2. We could infer from this assertion that the implied reader is not Tunisian but more likely European. This statement would be considered superfluous by a Tunisian reader.

REFERENCES

Beaujot, R. (1985). Cultural constructions of demographic inquiry: Experiences of an expatriate researcher in Tunisia. *Culture*, 5(1), 3–14.

Béji, H. (1997). *L'imposture culturelle*. Paris: Stock.

Bekri, T. (1999). *De la littérature tunisienne et maghrébine et autres textes*. Paris: L'Harmattan.

Bourneuf, R., & Ouellet, R. (1972). *L'univers du roman*. Paris: Presses universitaires de France.

Brahimi, D. (1991). *Appareillages: Dix études comparatistes sur la littérature des hommes et des femmes dans le monde arabe et aux Antilles*. Paris: Deuxtemps tierce.

Brahimi, D. (1995). *Magrébines, portraits littéraires*. Paris: L'Harmattan-Awal.

Brosseau, M. (1994). Geography's literature. *Progress in Human Geography*, 18(3), 333–353.

Brosseau, M. (1995). The city in textual form: Manhattan Transfer's New York. *Ecumene*, 2(1), 89–114.

Brosseau, M. (1996). *Des romans-géographes, essai*. Paris: L'Harmattan.

Brosseau, M. (1997). Géographie, pratiques discursives et ambiance postmoderne. *Cahiers de géographie du Québec, 41*(114), 289–299.

Brosseau, M. (2003). L'espace littéraire entre géographie et critique. In R. Bouvet & B. El Omari (Eds.), *L'espace en toutes lettres* (pp. 13–36). Montreal: Nota Bene.

Camau, M. (1989). *La Tunisie.* Paris: Presses universitaires de France.

Carter, G. (2001). "Domestic geography" and the politics of Scottish landscape in Nan Sheppard's *The living mountain. Gender, Place, and Culture, 8*(1), 25–36.

Charrad, M. M. (1998). Cultural diversity within Islam: Veils and laws in Tunisia. In H. L. Bodman & N. Tohidi (Eds.), *Women in Muslim societies: Diversity within unity* (pp. 63–79). Boulder, CO: Lynne Rienner.

Chevalier, M. (1993). Géographie et littérature. In M. Chevalier (Ed.), *La littérature dans tous ses espaces* (pp. 3–84). Paris: Éditions du CNRS.

Claval, P. (1995). *La géographie culturelle.* Paris: Nathan.

Cook, I. G. (1981). Consciousness and the novel: Fact or fiction in the works of D. H. Lawrence. In D. C. D. Pocock (Ed.), *Humanistic geography and literature* (pp. 66–84). London: Croom Helm.

Cosgrove, D. E. (1994). Worlds of meaning: Cultural geography and the imagination. In K. Foote, P. Hugill, K. Mathewson, & J. Smith (Eds.), *Re-reading cultural geography* (pp. 387–395). Austin: University of Texas Press.

Crang, M. (1998). *Cultural geography.* London: Routledge.

Daniels, S., & Rycroft, S. (1993). Mapping the modern city: Alan Sillitoe's Nottingham novels. *Transactions of the Institute of British Geographers, n.s. 18*, 460–480.

Déjeux, J. (1992). *La littérature maghrébine d'expression française.* Paris: Presses universitaires de France.

Déjeux, J. (1994). *La littérature féminine de langue française du Maghreb.* Paris: Karthala.

Deslauriers, P. (1994). Very different Montreals: Pathways through the city and ethnicity in novels by authors of different origins. In P. Preston & P. Simpson-Housley (Eds.), *Writing the city: Eden, Babylon and the New Jerusalem* (pp. 109–123). London: Routledge.

Duncan, J. S. (2000). Representation. In R. J. Johnston, D. Gregory, G. Pratt, & M. Watts (Eds.), *The dictionary of human geography* (4th ed., pp. 703–705). London: Blackwell.

Fisher, M. (1991). Sacred circles: Iranian (Zoroastrian and Shi'ite Muslim) feasting and pilgrimage circuits. In J. Scott & P. Simpson-Housley (Eds.), *Sacred places and profane spaces: The geographies of Judaism, Christianity and Islam* (pp. 131–144). Westport, CT: Greenwood Press.

Fontaine, J. (1977). *20 ans de littérature tunisienne.* Tunis: Maison Tunisienne de l'édition.

Fontaine, J. (1990). *La littérature tunisienne contemporaine.* Paris: Éditions du CNRS.

Frémont, A. (1976). *La région, espace vécu.* Paris: Presses universitaires de France.

Gilbert, E. W. (1972). British regional novelists and geography. In E. W. Gilbert (Ed.), *British pioneers in geography* (pp. 116–127). New York: Barnes & Noble.

Gilbert, E. W. (1994). Transgressing boundaries: Isable Allende's Santiago de Chile. In P. Preston & P. Simpson-Housley (Eds.), *Writing the city: Eden, Babylon and the New Jerusalem* (pp. 306–330). London: Routledge.

Gilbert, E. W., & Simpson-Housley, P. (1997). Places and spaces of dislocation: *Lady Oracles*'s Toronto. *Canadian Geographer, 41*(3), 235–248.

Harel, S. (2002). *Un boitier d'écriture: Les lieux dits de Michel Leiris.* Montréal: Trait d'Union.

Khadhar, H. (1987). La littérature tunisienne de langue française. *Europe, 712,* 11–14.

Lafaille, R. (1989). Départ: Géographie et poésie. *Le géographe canadien, 33*(2), 118–130.

McKittrick, K. (2000). Black and 'cause I'm black I'm blue: Tranverse racial geographies in Toni Morrison's *The bluest eye. Gender, Place, and Culture, 7*(2), 125–142.

Mernissi, F. (1985). *Beyond the veil: Male–female dynamics in Muslim society.* London: Al Saqi Books.

Monk, J., & Norwood, V. (1990). (Re)membering the Australian city: Urban landscapes in women's fiction. in L. Zonn (Ed.), *Place images in media* (pp. 105–119). Lanham, MD: Rowman & Littlefield.

Pocock, D. C. D. (Ed.). (1981). *Humanistic geography and literature: Essays on the experience of place.* London: Croom Helm.

Porteous, D. J. (1985). Literature and humanistic geography. *Area, 17*(2), 117–122.

Porteous, D. J. (1990). *Landscapes of the mind: Worlds of sense and metaphor.* Toronto: University of Toronto Press.

Preston, P., & Simpson-Housley, P. (Eds.). (1994). *Writing the city: Eden, Babylon and the New Jerusalem.* London: Routledge.

Robinson, B. (1977). Some fragmented forms of space. *Annals of the Association of American Geographers, 67*(4), 549–563.

Segarra, M. (1997). *Leur pesant en poudre: Romancières francophones du Maghreb.* Paris: L'Harmattan.

Shurmer-Smith, P. (Ed.). (2002). *Doing cultural geography.* London: Sage.

Silk, C. P., & Silk, J. (1985). Racism, nationalism and the creation of a regional myth: The southern states after the American Civil War. In J. Burgess & J. Gold (Eds.), *Geography, the media and the popular culture* (pp. 165–191). Beckenham, UK: Croom-Helm.

Teather, E. K. (1991). Visions and realities: Images of early post-war Australia. *Transactions of the Institute of British Geographers, n.s., 16,* 470–483.

Tuan, Y. (1978). Literature and geography: Implications for geographical research. In D. Ley & M. S. Samuels (Eds.), *Humanistic geography: Prospects and problems* (pp. 194–206). Chicago: Maaroufa Press.

Zouari, F. (1996). *Pour en finir avec Shahrazad.* Tunis: Cérès Éditions.

Zouari, F. (2002). *La retournée.* Paris: Ramsay.

Novels

Bel Haj Yahia, E. (1991). *Chronique frontalière.* Tunis: Cérès Productions.

Béji, H. (1993). *L'oeil du jour.* Tunis: Cérès Productions.

Bensaad, N. (2002). *L'immeuble de la rue du Caire.* Paris: L'Harmattan.

Guellouz, S. (1982). *Les jardins du nord.* Tunis: Éditions Salammbo.

Hafsia, J. (1975). *Cendre à l'aube.* Tunis: Maison Tunisienne de l'Édition.

12 The Visual Representation of Muslim/Arab Women in Daily Newspapers in the United States

GHAZI-WALID FALAH

This chapter examines the ways in which Muslim women and their roles in society have been narrowly construed and projected though the print media in the United States. This analysis connects with and builds upon recent scholarship on the stereotyping of Muslim women in the mainstream press. Zurbrigg (1995), for instance, has found that Saudi women tend to be portrayed as an exotic, erotic, and oppressed "other" in both academic and popular literature. Wilkins (1997) similarly shows in her analysis of 230 press photos that mainstream reportage is rife with orientalized stereotypes of Muslim women as the passive emblems of "collectivistic" traditional society, and hence as the antithesis of Western individualism. Finally, Bullock (1999) challenges the tendency in the popular press to treat the headscarf (or *hijab*) as a symbol of oppression, arguing that journalistic analysis ignores the diversity of reasons why Muslim women cover themselves.

The analysis in this chapter focuses on press reports dealing with the Muslim world published in U.S. newspapers between the tragic events of September 11, 2001, and the eve of the invasion of Iraq in March 2003. I focus specifically on four key areas of reportage: the aftermath of 9/11, U.S. military intervention in Afghanistan, the lead-up to the war on Iraq, and the ongoing Palestinian Intifada. I am especially interested in the visual representation of women in this reportage and how this representation relates to wider geopolitical discourses. Following Wilkins (1997), I argue that the use of particular images of women reflects the operational practices of editors, who assign "news value" to photographs based on ideological meanings associated with certain images, thereby reinforcing these meanings. I argue that in the period covered by my study, pictures of Muslim and Arab women were selected for print with the aim of supplementing and augmenting the persuasive power of the written text. The practice of injecting political viewpoints into supposedly "objective" reportage through the use of images, also known as *editorial offerings*, is named as one of the five sources of political power of the media by Arthur Siegel (1983, pp. 14–15). The visual representations of Muslim/Arab women, in conjunction with captions, I wish to suggest, typically have served to reinforce images of Muslim society as the cultural, political, and moral "other" of the West. In this way, however consciously or unconsciously, newspaper editors have served the interests of the U.S. government by justifying U.S. involvement (or, in some cases, lack of involvement) in the Muslim world.

DATA COLLECTION AND METHODOLOGY

This analysis is based on a body of over 500 pieces of newspaper material, including reports, editorials, commentaries, and cartoons, that appeared in four American daily newspapers: the *Columbus Dispatch* (Columbus, Ohio), the *Chicago Tribune*, the *Plain Dealer* (Cleveland, Ohio), and the *Los Angles Times*. The study also includes other relevant material from major "national" newspapers, such as the *Washington Post*, the *New York Times*, and *USA Today*. It should be noted that this survey was not meant to serve as the basis for quantitative "content analysis." Nor was it intended to prove something that already has been well established, namely, that images of Arabs and Islam in the Western media are overwhelmingly negative (see Damon & Michalak, 1983; Jafri, 1998; Stockton, 1994). Instead, my objective has been to understand how negative meanings are attached to images of Muslims and Arabs and how such meanings are produced and reproduced. Again, this analysis is concerned with the ways in which editorial decisions regarding the arrangement and presentation of images and other materials relating to Muslims and Arabs impart certain meanings to newspaper readers and, by doing so, lend support to specific geopolitical discourses. The frequency or the number of articles or pieces printed in a newspaper during the period under investigation, in this regard, is not as important as the placement of the article, say, on the front page, or the selection of "attractive" headlines and large photographs to accompany the reportage.

In my examination of reportage on Arab/Muslim topics, I looked at headlines, photos, and captions, all of which directly reflect editorial decisions. *Headlines* do much more than summarize the story. According to Russell (1994 p. 160), "they . . . dress up a page visually . . . ; they titillate readers, to encourage them to try this particular item; and they help guide readers round the page, showing the comparative importance of each story." In a similar vein, van Dijk (1991, p. 51) notes that "headlines often have ideological implications. Since they express the most important information about a news event, they may bias the understanding process: they summarize what, according to the journalist, is the most important aspect, and such a summary necessarily implies an opinion or a specific perspective on the event." Such decisions, of course, are not always consciously made, and an editor's sense of what jibes with his or her paper's policy may be more implicit than explicit. This is why understanding the tacit message conveyed by visuals—uncovered through the systematic analysis of the ways particular types of images are used—is especially important.

Photographs attached to reportage play a significant role in enhancing the report and capturing the attention of the reader's eye. Readers may forget much of the content of an article shortly after reading it, but pictures can be recalled sometimes for years. Visuals are, in a sense, part of what Edward Hall (1990) has called the "hidden dimension" of culture, forming part of the powerful contextualization for the verbal message conveyed by newspaper text. The use of visual imagery, in this respect, can be problematic. As Russell (1996, p. 37) indicates, "Photographers have known for years that the camera can lie and have been perfectly comfortable with such image-altering techniques as 'pushing' film, using telescopic lenses, 'dodging' prints in the darkroom, retouching, masking and cropping." Another risk involved with the use of photography relates to what Mignault (1996, p. 134) calls a "melt-down" technique: "Under specific agreements, media are allowed to use each other's material—whether they be pictures, interview clips or news report—and to 'melt them down' into one single report narrated by their own reporter." In this process, editors of newspapers may take full liberty in selecting a single paid-for photograph that is in keeping with the editor's policy or simply his or her "gut feeling" about the appropriateness of a photo. So pictures linked to reportages function in diverse and subtle ways, far more than just "break[ing] up the monotony of grey type" (Russell, 1994, p. 159).

The *caption* is another area where the value judgment of a newspaper's editor can be easily transmitted. The words selected for captions are not simply descriptions of pictures, but instead are specific interpretations of visual representations. A given image can be interpreted in any number of ways (see Tomlinson, 1991, p. 1), so the particular caption assigned to a picture exerts a great deal of power in influencing our understanding, or "reading," of that picture.

These insights into editorial decisions, as I will show in the remainder of this chapter, are especially relevant to our understandings of newspaper reportage between September 11, 2001, and the invasion of Iraq in 2003.

STEREOTYPING ISLAM
AND THE ROLE OF "ELITE RACISM"

This section explores the production and reproduction of stereotypes of Islam and seeks to explain how these stereotypes play into editorial decision making. I draw on van Dijk's (1991) concept of "elite racism" to explain the pervasiveness of certain racial stereotypes in key societal institutions, including the press and the government.

In *Covering Islam: How the Media and Experts Determine How We See the Rest of the World*, Edward Said (1981) argued that "the canonical, orthodox coverage of Islam that we find in the academy, in the government, and in the media is all interrelated and has been *more* diffused, has seemed *more* persuasive and influential, in the West than any other 'coverage' or interpretation" (p. 169). Said's main point was that this coverage is rarely interested in "truth" or accuracy, and that it has served purposes "only tangentially related to actual knowledge of Islam itself" (p. 169). What has emerged from this coverage is a particular interpretation of Islam and a particular way of *knowing* the Islamic world.

In the decades since the publication of *Covering Islam*, several authors have examined the relentless demonization of Islam in the U.S. media. Jack Shaheen (2001), for instance, has documented thousands of examples of stereotyping of Arabs and Muslims in films and television, noting that Arabs and Muslims today are portrayed much in the same way that Jews were portrayed by the Nazis in the pre-World War II period (see also Afridi, 2001). Karen Armstrong (2000, pp. 179–180) traces the roots of this negative imagery to the time of the medieval Christian Crusades, when Islam was depicted as "the enemy of civilization." Ghareeb (1983, p. 5) has argued that the prevalence of hostile and distorted imagery, both historically and in the present day, means that "most Americans have had only the most fleeting and superficial exposure to Middle East history and culture in their educational experience. And too often this brief glimpse is distorted and confirms inaccurate stereotypes of the Arabs." Chami (2003, p. 1) similarly argues that "the average American knows very little about Islam and this is due to the selective information the American media feeds the general public."

Van Dijk's (1991) concept of "elite racism" sheds some light on the persistence of negative stereotypes concerning Muslims and Arabs. Van Dijk (1991, p. 48) argues that "the role of the Press as a corporate, social, and cultural institution needs to be analysed in relation to other institutions, such as those of the polity or the economy," and he suggests that there is a direct link between societal racism, elite ideology, and the production of news by journalists. In other words, the microlevel process of producing news is informed by, and, to a certain extent, is the manifestation of racism at the macrolevel of society and the state. "Structures of headlines, leads, thematic organization, the presence of explanatory background information, style, and especially the overall selection of newsworthy topics," van Dijk argues, are "indirectly controlled by the societal context of power relations" (p. 41). He points to powerful elite groups and institutions, especially in the corporate and political domains, who are able partially to control access to the media, and hence the portrayal of themselves and others in the media. Consequently, according to van Dijk, the "elite versions of the 'facts,' their definitions of reality, will tend to prevail over those of other, non-dominant groups" (p. 41).

Van Dijk's (1991) study, which focuses on ethnic relations and media at the state level, can be applied to the international arena, where the power exercised by corporations based in the United States over an increasingly globalized media industry becomes relevant. As A. S. Ahmed (1992, p. 241) notes, "It is the American mass media that have achieved what American political might could not: the attainment for America of world domination." The scope of this study does not allow detailed discussion of how media corporations control the news, but Lee and Soloman's (1992, p. 92) arguments are instructive:

> As with any profit-making enterprise, the media industry's chain of command runs from top down, with beat reports on the bottom of the pecking order. At the apex of the media pyramid are the owners who wield authority by assuming top executive posts or by hiring and firing those who hold these positions. Their power to replace management if it does not perform as they wish gives them control over policy and editorial direction. Ultimately, it is the media owners and managers who determine which ideas and which version of the facts shall reach the public. They have virtually unlimited power to suggest or veto stories.

Following both van Dijk (1991) and Lee and Soloman (1992), it becomes important to understand how powerful actors in the United States define America's "national interest" and foreign policy in the Middle East (or the Muslim world at large), and how the objectives of governing elites are supported, projected, and elaborated, however indirectly, by the corporate media. Up until the early 1990s, as described by Haddad (1991, pp. 223–224), "American strategic goals in the Middle East [were] generally listed as maintaining access to Middle East oil, preserving the state of Israel, perpetuating good relations with pro-Western Arab nations, maintaining peace and stability, and preventing Communist penetration of the area." After the

Cold War, of course, communism no longer was regarded as playing any role in U.S. foreign policy in the region. Consequently, many Muslims (and others) have come to feel that with communism gone, Western governments and the Western media have increasingly targeted Islam and what many commentators and government officials refer to vaguely as "Islamism." In A. S. Ahmed's (1992, p. 223) words,

> Nothing in history has threatened Muslims like the Western media; neither gunpowder in the Middle Ages, . . . nor trains and the telephone, which helped colonize them in the last century, nor even planes which they mastered for their national airlines earlier this century. The Western media are ever present and ubiquitous; never resting and never allowing respite. They probe and attack ceaselessly, showing no mercy for weakness or frailty.

THE MUSLIN/ARAB WOMEN
IN AMERICAN NEWSPAPERS

Western discourse about Muslim/Arab societies, as Leila Ahmed (1992) notes, is highly gendered, and images of Muslim/Arab women and girls feature prominently in media reports about events in the Middle East. My survey of reportage on current events in Palestine, Iraq, Afghanistan, and other Muslim countries reveals the ubiquity of female images in the U.S. press. Significantly, the survey also reveals that pictures of Muslim women rarely relate directly to the subject matter in the text, suggesting that the images serve some other purpose than elucidating Muslim women's experiences to a Western audience. I wish to suggest that these images are *insinuated* into the text, where they serve to project cultural judgments about Islam and Muslim societies and to convey the political viewpoints of editors.

The images of Muslim women found in U.S. newspapers are quite varied, but two dominant and seemingly contradictory themes or motifs emerge: first, women as passive victims, and second, women as active political agents. Within each theme there are numerous subtexts which, rather than evoking the empathy or sympathy of the viewer, call forth feelings of self-righteousness and/or moral revulsion. For instance, where women are shown as passive victims, as has often been the case with pictures from Afghanistan and Iraq, the underlying message (typically conveyed in the caption) is that their victimization is being alleviated by Western intervention and "liberation." Palestinian women are also depicted as victims, though captions and text (often using the passive voice to describe the killings of family members) tend to suggest that their own people are to blame for their victimization.

Where women are shown as active political agents, photographs are intended to be jarring and to shatter stereotypes about secluded, subordinate Muslim women. Yet the subtexts of these images project meanings that reinforce rather than challenge such stereotypes. Pictures of women wielding guns during demonstrations and preparing themselves for suicide bombing missions, for instance, do not speak to Muslim women's political consciousness and agency as much as they point to the alleged irrationality of Muslim societies and to Muslims' presumed penchant for violence. The remainder of this section explains the subtexts of these images in greater detail.

Women as Passive Victims

Arab and Muslim women are rarely portrayed as having "normal" lives by U.S. standards—that is, as simply going to work or to school, having fun or enjoying their lives and their families. Instead, images of Muslim women are used almost exclusively to communicate the abnormality of life in Muslim societies marked by violence, religious fanaticism, and political turmoil. Thus, Muslim women are often depicted as situated in landscapes of agony and despair, and the pictures of Arab and Muslim women selected by editors show sad, crying faces full of anguish. In some instances, these photographs are intended to elicit the reader's sympathy for the horrors that

FIGURE 12.1. Bosnian Muslim women mourn and place flowers at Muslim men and boys' graveyard in Srebrenica. From *The Plain Dealer,* July 12, 2002. Reproduced with permission of the Associated Press/Wide World Photos.

many Muslim women have endured. Figure 12.1, for instance, is taken from Bosnia. The headline of the picture is "Tears for Srebrenica" and its caption text reads "Bosnian Muslim women mourn anew and place flowers at a memorial yesterday during a ceremony for the 8,000 Muslim men and boys killed in the town of Srebrenica seven years ago by Bosnian Serb soldiers. It was the worst civilian massacre in Europe since the Nazi atrocities of World War II" (*Plain Dealer*, July 12, 2002). Other photographs seem to be intended to humanize Muslim women and Arab women who might otherwise be viewed as "foreign" and "different." Several U.S. newspapers, for instance, have shown faces of American Arab and Muslim women who have been saddened by the events of September 11, 2001, and who have paid respect to the victims' families and the American people (see *Chicago Tribune*, September 11, 2002, and September 12, 2002; *Los Angeles Times*, September 10, 2002, and September 27, 2002; *New York Times*, September 30, 2002; *Miami Herald*, September 12, 2002).

Yet photographs of despairing, anguished Muslim women are, in many ways, problematic. The fact that Western audiences so infrequently see Muslim women doing anything other than crying passively as they are victimized denies Muslim women as a group any kind of normal existence, and the image of the veiled woman beating her breast after the loss of a child or husband becomes almost a stylization (see, e.g., *Chicago Tribune*, December 4, 2002, and February 4, 2003; *Plain Dealer*, October 18, 2002; *Columbus Dispatch*, March 7, 2003; *Akron Beacon Journal*, October 8, 2002; *Washington Post*, October 14, 2002, and October 19, 2002).

Even more problematic than the narrow conception of Muslim women's lives that these photographs convey is the way in which they are used to support mainstream political positions that are only tangentially concerned with women's suffering and oppression. During the recent military action in Iraq, for instance, photographs of female Kurdish refugees were often used to highlight the evils of Saddam's (Arab) Baathist regime. Illustrating this is a report in the *Los Angeles Times* (December 3, 2002) with a large headline stating " 'Arabization' Forces Iraqi Kurds into Camps." Two color photos accompany the report. One shows two women and a little girl with a caption reading "Displaced: Iraqi Kurd women stand by their hut in a camp about 20 miles east of Kirkuk province in northern Iraq." The other photo has a caption that says: "Refugees: A women holds her child while walking in Iraq's north, where Kurds have fled in massive ethnic upheaval." Other photos show the miserable shelters that Kurdish refugee women and children have been forced to use as dwelling places since the renewal of open conflict in Iraq. Likewise, a *New York Times* photo published on December 11, 2002, shows a Kurdish woman lying on a hospital bed, with the caption "Hamida Hassan, 32, in a hospital bed, is still suffering from burns and disfigurement she incurred when struck during the attack by what was believed to be mustard gas."

I do not wish to dispute the reality that Kurdish women (and men) suffered heavily under Baathist rule in Iraq. Instead, I am emphasizing that the prevalence of such pictures before and during U.S. military intervention in the region have served to support and to justify this intervention. The photos, in a sense, reinforce the rhetoric coming from the Bush administration, which has consistently asserted that U.S. actions are not, as some critics claim, "anti-Muslim," because they are being undertaken to liberate vulnerable Muslim peoples—and especially Muslim women—from their oppression.

The same can be said for images of Afghan women under the Taliban. As the "Other of the Others," they, like Kurdish women, were portrayed in a sympathetic light, and their images were used to provide moral justification for military involvement in Afghanistan. Pictures from Afghanistan following the "overthrow" of the Taliban (which has proven to be, at best, a partial success) commonly make reference to the liberation of women and to the expansion of women's opportunities to learn and to work. A syndicated article entitled "Afghan Women Hope to Erase Illiteracy" that appeared in the Columbus Dispatch (September 22, 2002), for instance, is accompanied by a photo of a group of women, beneath which is the caption "An older women seeks help from a classmate as they practice writing during an adult literacy course offered in a home in northern Afghanistan's Mazar-e-Sharif. An estimated 85 percent of Afghan women are illiterate." This same article appeared in the Plain Dealer on the same day with a different headline: "Afghan Women Hunger for Literacy." In this newspaper, the article was shown with a picture of a young woman in a university lecture room freely speaking with her male professor. The caption reads "Nasreen Ahmad Zai asks Aziz Ahmed Rahmand, a history professor, for clarification on a question in the entrance exam at Kabul University."

Newspaper photographs have made much of Afghan women's ability to show their faces and to mix with men following the overthrow of the Taliban. The Plain Dealer (August 17, 2002), to illustrate, published a photograph of a young Afghan female refugee with her face and ears exposed and sitting among men of various ages. According to the caption, the people in the photograph are listening to a lecture on mine safety, reinforcing the message that the outcome of military action has been largely positive. The Los Angeles Times (September 12, 2002) published a photograph of an attractive Afghan journalist with a caption reading "The Taliban's ouster has meant the freedom to walk the streets of Kabul without having to don a burka." The Plain Dealer (August 20, 2002) used a photograph depicting the joyous celebration of women's new freedoms in Afghanistan. The caption reads: "Uniformed girls marched alongside male classmates as hundreds of spectators—men in turbans and women with their burqas thrown back—cheered them on yesterday." Finally, a photo of a group of Afghan women (one of them pregnant) undergoing training in health education was published in the *Chicago Tribune* (October 14, 2002). The photo caption states: "In a sign of Afghanistan's evolution, female medical personnel discuss a pregnancy case at a women's hospital in Kabul. Under the Taliban regime, women's health was neglected." It should be noted that the article itself, entitled "Afghan Rebuilding Plan Earns Donors' Respect," does not directly touch on any issue related to women. Instead, images of women are used to symbolize a return to a relatively "normal" existence in Afghanistan following U.S. military intervention.

Photographs published in newspapers, then, serve as photographic "evidence" of the "victory" of Western liberal values over Islamic extremism. The Taliban, to be sure, do represent an extreme interpretation of Islam that has created many hardships for women. This is not being denied. But I do wish to suggest that images of Afghan women (as with images of Kurdish women) have been used to provide unequivocal affirmation of U.S. intervention in the region. Such images continuously reproduce facile equations between U.S. involvement and liberation, when, historically, U.S. involvement in the region has not been undertaken with the well-being of "ordinary people"—much less ordinary women—as a primary aim. To equate the Taliban or Saddam Hussein exclusively with tyranny and oppression belies the complex social, political, and economic forces shaping men's and women's lives, while denying the extent to which the exercise of Western power has acted to the detriment of those living in Muslim regions.

The more positive, sympathetic depictions of Afghan and Kurdish women and girls can be contrasted with images of Iraqi Arab women and children. Iraqi Arab women *are* depicted as victims, though differently than Afghan and Kurdish women. While in some instances portrayed in agony and anguish, Iraqi Arab women and children have also been commonly portrayed as brainwashed by Saddam Hussein's regime, and images of women and schoolgirls going about their daily lives in the shadow of Saddam Hussein's ubiquitous image has brought a sense of urgency to U.S. intervention in the country.

In the *Los Angeles Times* (October 28, 2002), for instance, a full-page article about schools in Baghdad includes a picture of three girls standing under a picture of Saddam Hussein. The caption reads: "State of education: The image of President Saddam Hussein hangs in a fourth-grade classroom where students are learning math. Iraq's school system has collapsed." Another article appearing in the *Los Angeles Times* (November 11, 2002) includes a photo of a group of Iraqi girls in uniform performing, again, under the image of Saddam Hussein (see Figure 12.2). The caption reads simply: "Conspicuous effort: Traditional dancers at opening of Baghdad International Fair . . . ," but the imposing picture of Saddam Hussein quite obviously detracts from the innocence of the scene. In a similar vein, a commentary by Steve Chapman in the *Chicago Tribune* (October 3, 2002), en-

FIGURE 12.2. Iraqi girls perform a traditional dance at the opening of Baghdad International Fair held in November 2002. From *The Los Angeles Times*, November 11, 2002. Reproduced with permission of the Associated Press/Wide World Photos.

titled "Is Hussein Too Crazy for Us to Control?" includes a photo of a dozen Iraqi children in school uniforms holding pictures of Saddam Hussein, suggesting that his "craziness" has been imparted on the Iraqi people as well. Shortly after this article was published, the *Chicago Tribune* (October 14, 2002) ran a picture of children (girls and boys) yet again under the image of the Iraqi president. The caption reads: "Baghdad children mark Iraqi Child Day on Sunday with pictures of Saddam Hussein. Television clips and posters of the Iraqi leader can be seen nationwide." Again, the main message is not that children are celebrating a day set aside for them, but that their lives are being monitored and controlled by Saddam Hussein.

For U.S. viewers, the ever-present image of Saddam Hussein undoubtedly is menacing and symbolic of his iron grip over Iraqi society, though the display of pictures of the president in public places is a phenomenon common in many countries around the world. That his picture is repeatedly juxtaposed with images of children, and especially young girls, speaks very directly to U.S. rhetoric about the wickedness of Saddam Hussein. So evil is his regime that it is willing to manipulate young boys and girls and to use children as puppets. Such photographs thus act to persuade readers that military action is justified and that it will liberate the Iraqi people from tyrannical rule, seemingly in spite of themselves.

The photographs discussed thus far indicate that while such images appear, at one level, to be objective accounts of people's lives in Afghanistan and Iraq, at another level they serve a broader geopolitical agenda sanctioned by the Bush administration. The role of journalistic images in affirming particular political interests is further highlighted in the subtle messages conveyed by photographs of Muslim women in Palestine, where the Bush administration has chosen not to intervene. Palestinian women, like Kurdish and Bosnian women, are often portrayed as enduring great hardships, including the violent deaths of family members. But the captions and text that accompany such images rarely attribute blame for these women's suffering to the Israeli leadership. Consider the picture appearing in the *Los Angeles Times* (December 10, 2002) of a Palestinian girl (see Figure 12.3) whose mother was killed in the Gaza Strip. The caption for this picture reads: "Mother killed: A daughter of Palestinian Nahla Aqel stands before a bullet-scarred wall where her mother was killed in the Gaza Strip. Three

FIGURE 12.3. A crying Palestinian girl stands before a bullet-scarred wall, where Israeli soldiers in the Gaza Strip killed her mother. From *The Los Angeles Times*, December 10, 2002. Reproduced with permission of Mohammed Abed/AFP/Getty Images.

of Aqel's children were wounded in the incident." The scene is certainly a tragic one—with the tragedy amplified by the victim's femininity and the fact that she was a little girl—but nowhere does the text make specific mention of who killed the mother, and the headline for story, which reads: "Israeli Advice to Arafat Sparks Ire," seems to suggest that Yassir Arafat and the Palestinians bear responsibility for this and other tragedies (though the *Washington Post*'s [December 10, 2002] report on this incident does attribute Aqel's death directly to Israeli machine-gun fire). Indeed, the text of this article mentions the killing of another Palestinian woman when an Israeli tank crew opened fire on a taxi. But the report also defuses blame on the Israeli army with the qualifying statement, "A military official said the incident was under investigation." In a final example, the *Chicago Tribune* (December 6, 2002) used a photograph of two women and a man standing next to a grave. The caption reads: "Family members in Gaza Strip visit the grave Thursday of a Palestinian who was killed in a clash with Israeli troops." This quote is not an inaccurate description, but the use of the passive voice to describe the killing, common in articles about killings of Palestinians, needs to be questioned.

For Palestinians, tragedy appears to be a chronic condition, but who is responsible for the killing of Palestinians is seldom made explicit in newspaper reportage. The impression given by these and other photographs, reports, and captions is that the killing might have happened as an inevitable result of crossfire between two hostile parties. Such reportage does not exactly exonerate the Israeli army, but it spreads the blame for the killing of Palestinians to Palestinians themselves. Such is not the case when Israelis are victimized by Palestinians (see, e.g. *Plain Dealer*, October 22, 2002; *Columbus Dispatch*, October 11, 2002, October 22, 2002, and January 7, 2003; *Chicago Tribune*, November 7, 2002, and November 12, 2002; see also Falah, 2004). So while pictures such as the one appearing in the *Columbus Dispatch* on January 9, 2003, depicting three adult women and a young girl in tears upon learning of the shooting of a Palestinian man who had been watching Israeli tanks move into the Gaza Strip (again, the identity of the shooter is not given), elicit feelings of sympathy, they do not rally U.S. public sentiment behind Palestinians or serve to encourage U.S. intervention in the Palestinian–Israeli conflict.

Muslim/Arab Women as Misguided Political Actors

The previous examples show Muslim women as passive victims of religious extremism and dictatorship, and deserving to a greater or lesser degree of Western liberation. But not all Muslim women are portrayed as trapped in tragic circumstances. Some are shown to be politically active and to be involved in political causes and political violence. Such images shatter stereotypes of Muslim women as cloistered passive beings, and present to the

West an alternative understanding of these women as having political consciousness and voice. But in other respects, the images of politically active Muslim women and the text accompanying these images simultaneously reinforce notions of Muslims as politically misguided and as prone to extremism and fanaticism.

One photograph, for instance, published in the *Los Angles Times* near the anniversary of the September 11 attacks (September 1, 2002), depicts a group of Jordanian women at the U.S. embassy in Amman. The beginning of the caption states: "Women in Amman, Jordan, make contributions to a book of condolences outside the U.S. Embassy shortly after the Sept. 11 attacks." The photograph, along with the first sentence of the caption, presents a positive image of Muslim women expressing solidarity with Americans. But this positive image is then compromised by the remainder of the caption, which reads: "Though many Arabs were upset by the number of civilian casualties, there is a widespread belief that the United States had it coming." This statement, at the very least, suggests that their views are marginal to Arab/Muslim societies, and at worst, casts doubt on these women's sincerity. In either case, the U.S. reader is undoubtedly left with feelings of outrage and disgust at the insensitivity of Arabs to U.S. suffering—exactly the opposite reaction that the women in the photograph are presumably trying to elicit.

The political consciousness of Muslim women has been especially scrutinized in the case of Palestinian female suicide bombers. Suicide missions carried about by Palestinian women have been given a great deal of coverage, presumably because such actions defy Western preconceptions about Muslim and Arab women (though it should be noted that many suicide bombers in Chechnya are women, as are many soldiers involved in antigovernment action by Muslims in the Philippines). Photos of Wafa Idris, the first female Palestinian suicide bomber, and of Darin Abu Eisheh were published in the *New York Times* (January 31, 2002, and March 1, 2002, respectively). Seemingly not content to accept that a Muslim woman's political convictions might lead her to a suicide mission, reporters have probed family members in an attempt to understand these women's motivation for committing, what is by U.S. standards, an act of complete irrationality. A full report on female suicide bombers that appeared in the *Plain Dealer* (July 14, 2002) includes a picture of an attractive woman with a sorrowful face, under which is the caption: "Amal Siyam, research director at the Palestinian Women's Affairs Center in Gaza, listens to participants in a discussion on female suicide bombers. Women at her workshop seemed to support the action." Suicide missions carried out by two Iraqi women during the recent war have also been covered by the U.S. press (*Chicago Tribune*, April 5, 2003).

That young women seem to be supporting female suicide bombers is something that many U.S. readers undoubtedly find incomprehensible and troubling—indeed, this is why the item is newsworthy. Such stories, while appealing to Western audiences because of the exotic quality of female "terrorists," also reinforce the incomprehensibility of Muslim societies, and, more specifically, the Palestinian–Israeli conflict. The phenomenon of female suicide bombers becomes part what McClure (1994, p. 121) calls a

> resurgent Orientalist narrative [that] casts Muslims in general and Arabs of all persuasions as the Others to democratic, open, and peace-loving Westerners. It defines a zone which runs from North Africa across the Middle East into Asia as an Elsewhere inhabited by dangerous barbarians committed to a fanatical faith.

Other depictions of politically active Muslim women reinforce the idea of Muslim societies as fanatical and irredeemably foreign. Photographs of women involved in mass demonstrations are especially powerful in conveying a geopolitical image of the Muslim world as diametrically opposed to U.S. interests and well-being. An image of four Pakistani women holding toy guns (Figure 12.4), for instance, was used in a *Los Angeles Times* report (December 5, 2002) that was headlined "U.S. Losing Popularity in World." The caption of the photo reads: "In Pakistan: Women in Karachi hold toy guns and shout slogans against the U.S. and Israel at a demonstra-

FIGURE 12.4. Pakistani women hold toy guns and shout at a demonstration in Karachi. From *The Los Angeles Times*, December 5, 2002. Reproduced with permission of AFP/Getty Images.

tion during Ramadan." The *Chicago Tribune* published a similar report on the same day (December 5, 2002) with the headline: "U.S. Image Waning Despite 9/11 Sympathies, Poll Finds," and the subheadline: "Views Fall in West and Muslim Nations." Here again a photo of Muslim women in Egypt (in this case unarmed) highlights the report. The caption beneath the photo says: "Anti-U.S. slogans fill a recent demonstration at Cairo's Al-Azhar mosque. In Egypt, 69 percent of respondents to a Pew Global Attitudes Project study viewed the U.S. unfavorably." And a report on United States–Egypt relations published by the *Los Angeles Times* (October 29, 2002), under the headline, "Anti-U.S. Feelings Bubble Up in Egypt," contains a photograph of a group of young women (one of them fully veiled) shouting and holding a large poster with the words, "HEY AMERICANS, YOUR GOVT. SELLS WEAPONS TO ISRAEL TO KILL OUR CHILDREN." These reports are undoubtedly accurate, in that there is a great deal of hostility toward U.S. foreign policy in Arab and Muslim countries. But I wish to suggest that the particular gendered images selected to accompany these reports, more than simply capturing popular sentiment, convey a view that Muslim societies are adversarial to their very core and that their anti-Americanism is somehow irrational and unjustified.

Photographs of Iraqi and Palestinian women participating in marches and demonstrations, more than others, seem to communicate a sense of the political abnormality of Muslim societies, and women (yet again) appear to be brainwashed to support evil regimes. Armed Iraqi women, marching and shouting, feature in the reports of at least three newspapers surveyed for this study. In the *Plain Dealer* (August 9, 2002) a photograph appears with the caption: "Women militia members parade through Baghdad yesterday as part of a celebration of the 14th anniversary of the end of the 1980–88 Iraq–Iran war." A photograph published by the *Chicago Tribune* (January 23, 2003) shows an Iraqi woman holding a gun, with the caption: "A gun-toting Iraqi woman takes part in an anti-United States demonstration in Baghdad on Wednesday"—the expression "gun-toting" here adding a touch of disparagement to this woman's militarized demeanor. In another *Chicago Tribune* report (February 5, 2003), a photo of a group of armed women appears with the caption: "Iraqi women participate in a civilian military parade Tuesday in Mosul, where thousands marched in support of the regime."

Palestinian women are also depicted as misguided political actors, unswervingly supporting their widely discredited leader, Yasser Arafat. *USA Today* (April 5, 2002), for instance, published a photograph of an armed woman standing next to a photo of Arafat and two other fully veiled women in black. The caption beneath the photo reads: "Perpetual hostilities: Assault rifle in hand, a Palestinian woman participates in a demonstration Thursday in support of Palestinian leader Yasser Arafat in the Rafah refugee camp in southern part of Gaza." The *Plain Dealer* (October 15, 2002) shows another view of Palestinian women demonstrating in support of Arafat. The caption of the photo reads: "A Palestinian woman carries an automatic weapon during a demonstration yesterday in Gaza City, where thousands of supporters of Yasser Arafat gathered for a rally." The same pattern of representation of armed Palestinian women demonstrating in support of Arafat appears in the Israeli press (see *International Jerusalem Post*, October 11, 2002). In all of these instances, the image of women, some of them veiled and/or carrying guns, projects a sense of the deep dysfunction of these societies. These women are misguided because they are demonstrating for the wrong cause (e.g., anti-United States and anti-Israel), and for the wrong leaders (e.g., pro-Saddam or pro-Arafat). Their very presence—highly unexpected from a Western perspective, which tends to view Muslim women as silent and oppressed—suggests that states like the United States (as well as Israel) face a great, but in the case of Iraq, worthwhile, challenge in addressing the hostility against them.

A final set of notable images of Muslim women's politicization relates to the Iraqi referendum for the reelection of Saddam Hussein for president held in October 2002 (e.g., *Washington Post*, October 16, 2002 and October 17, 2002). All reports justifiably painted this as a sham event, and the absurdity of the event was captured with headlines such as "Iraqi Voters' Choice: Yes or Yes" (*Chicago Tribune*, October 14, 2002). But the use of pictures of Iraqi women demonstrating in support of Saddam Hussein to illustrate these stories suggests, yet again, that Iraqis have been brainwashed and that they are in need of deprogramming, presumably by Americans who are "in the know" (the dubious circumstances of President Bush's election remaining, of course, unmentioned). The *Plain Dealer* (October 17, 2002), for instance, published a photo of a group of Iraqi women clapping hands and smiling. The caption beneath the photo says: "Iraqis, some holding portraits of Saddam Hussein, celebrate his victory in a referendum on whether he should continue as president. The official tally was 100 percent in favor of Saddam." The *Los Angeles Times*, likewise, published a photo of a woman seen kissing her son who was wearing a shirt that has Saddam's picture on it (October 15, 2002). Part of the caption beneath the photo says: "Voters are being asked to demonstrate their support for his leadership and show that their country is a democracy, not a dictatorship." The *Miami Herald* (October 15, 2002) published a report entitled, "Hussein Stands Alone on Iraqi Ballot," to which is attached a photograph of a group of young women smiling and shouting. The caption of this photo says, somewhat flippantly, "For Hussein: A cheering section gets busy at a state-sponsored celebration in Baghdad on Monday, the presidential election's eve." The *Chicago Tribune* covered the referendum extensively (October 3, 14, 16, and 17, 2002), and published photos of cheering women and men. One caption reads: "Iraqis in Baghdad celebrate Saddam Hussein's victory in a referendum extending his rule. Outside Iraq, skepticism ruled." Finally, the *Columbus Dispatch* (October 17, 2002) published a photo of Saddam's image in a heart-shaped frame of flowers being carried by a group of women.

Such photographs, verging on the ludicrous, suggest a population in the thrall of a cult leader, when, in fact, major segments of the population opposed, actively and passively, Saddam's rule. Insofar as some Iraqis did, in fact, support Saddam Hussein, such support was perhaps not entirely irrational but reflective of the stability Saddam had ensured in the country; his constant outwitting of Americans, who were widely blamed for inflicting over a decade of misery on the Iraqi people; and his ability to dole out favors to particular groups—a situation, ironically, that was much abetted by the U.N. sanctions. Such subtleties, unfortunately, are not easily captured in photographs or captions.

This discussion has attempted to show some of the ways in which the use of photographs and captions in newspaper articles, far from enhancing the supposed "objectivity" of newspaper reportage, communicates specific political meanings. Editors, by selecting certain images and captions, frame geopolitical realities in particular ways and guide readers to think about "the Other" in a rather narrow set of terms. What we see with images of current events in Palestine, Iraq, and Afghanistan is that the geopolitics of the Middle East are being viewed and interpreted through a specifically gendered lens. Images of women abound in this reportage, but seldom are the accompanying articles about women. Women, in other words, are only technically and superficially present, and they serve primarily to reinforce preexisting understandings of Muslim societies as irrational, hostile, and antithetical to the liberal West. Such images, therefore, become a form of tacit support for the U.S. government's policies in the region.

CONCLUDING REMARKS

This chapter has attempted to probe the way in which the media, and especially print journalism, help to produce and to reproduce particular ways of knowing the Arab and Muslim worlds. My systematic survey of four daily newspapers (the *Columbus Dispatch*, the *Chicago Tribune*, the *Plain Dealer*, and the *Los Angles Times*) from September 11, 2001, to the eve of the U.S. invasion of Iraq in March 2003 reveals a number of patterns in the use of photographic imagery in newspaper reports. The gendered character of these patterns is unmistakable. Editors have systematically selected images of women and girls to communicate political turmoil in Muslim societies and to convey the supposedly liberating impacts of U.S. intervention in these regions. It should be noted that conservative commentators in the

United States frequently accuse the mainstream media of harboring a "liberal bias" and of being overly critical of Republican foreign policy. Yet the visual representation of Muslim women, more often than not, has fit quite neatly into dominant geopolitical discourses. Some newspaper editors may, in fact, have reservations about U.S. actions in the Middle East and elsewhere in the Muslim world, but it seems that editorial decision making and government policy agendas are equally prone to regard Muslim societies as politically backward and dysfunctional.

Why have images of women become so important in the minds of newspaper editors? The figure of the "Muslim woman" harkens to the exoticism of distant cultures and places and suggests an irrationality that can be contrasted with the supposed order and rationality of Western liberal societies. Whether veiled or exposed, passive or wielding weapons, Muslim women are the ultimate "Other," and they serve as the main repositories of the West's sense of fear, fascination, and superiority vis-à-vis the Muslim world. Newspaper editors seem to be aware, given the actual content of newspaper reports, that the U.S. public has little interest in learning about the lives of "ordinary" Muslim women, but that they do have an insatiable desire to be reminded of the great social and cultural gulf that exists between themselves and the Muslim world.

It is not the aim of this chapter to refute the validity of the images published in newspapers. I am not denying, for instance, that many Kurdish and Afghan refugee women, as depicted in newspaper photographs, live in miserable conditions or that many Muslims, female or male, have intensely negative feelings toward the United States. But I do wish to point out that the kinds of images of Muslim women that one tends to find in newspapers project very circumscribed understandings of Muslims. The constant repetition of a limited number of images, often with little contextualization from the reports they accompany, narrows understandings of Muslim women's lives and reduces the experiences and political sentiments of Muslim women to a few stereotypes. This process is damaging not only for Muslim women, but also for those who consume these images, as they will eventually suffer the consequences of their limited geopolitical awareness.

ACKNOWLEDGMENTS

The original version of this chapter was presented at the 2nd International Congress of Geographers of the Islamic World, held in Tehran, Iran, September 16–17, 2003. I thank Caroline Nagel for her excellent comments and suggestions for revision. I also thank Bill Templer for feedback and editorial assistance at the early stages of drafting this chapter. Responsibility for the content of this work, however, is mine alone.

REFERENCES

Afridi, S. (2001). *Muslims in America: Identity, diversity and the challenge of under-standing*. New York: Carnegie Corporation of New York.

Ahmed, A. S. (1992). *Postmodernism and Islam: Predicament and promise*. London and New York: Routledge.

Ahmed, L. (1992). *Women and gender in Islam: Historical roots to a modern debate*. New Haven, CT, and London: Yale University Press.

Akron Beacon Journal. 10/8/02.

Armstrong, K. (2000). *Islam: A short history*. New York: Random House.

Bullock, K. (1999). *The politics of the veil*. Unpublished doctoral dissertation, Department of Political Science, University of Toronto.

Chami, I. (2003). Ignorance: No longer an option. *Peer Review: HFCC'S Journal of Student Writing*. Fall Issue, updated 5/6/2003. Retrieved August 25, 2003, from *acs.hfcc.net/~ikchami/*

Chicago Tribune. 9/11/02; 9/12/02; 10/3/02; 10/14/02; 10/16/02; 10/17/03;11/7/02; 11/12/02; 12/4/02; 12/5/02;12/6/02; 1/23/03; 2/4/03; 2/5/03; 4/5/03.

Columbus Dispatch. 9/22/02; 10/11/02; 10/17/02; 10/22/02; 1/7/03; 1/9/03; 3/7/03.

Damon, G. H., Jr., & Michalak, L. D. (1983). A survey of political cartoons dealing with the Middle East. In E. Ghareeb (Ed.), *Split vision: The portrayal of Arabs in the American media* pp. 143–153. Washington, DC: American-Arab Affairs Council.

Falah, G.-W. (2004, March 14–19). *The portrayal of Israeli and Palestinian suffering and mutual violence in selected daily newspapers in the United States*. Paper presented at the annual conference of the Association of American Geographers, Philadelphia, PA.

Ghareeb, E. (Ed.). (1983). *Split vision: The portrayal of Arabs in the American media*. Washington, DC: American-Arab Affairs Council.

Haddad, Y. Y. (1991). American foreign policy in the Middle East and its impact on the identity of Arab Muslims in the United States. In Y. Y. Haddad (Ed.), *The Muslims of America* (pp. 217–235). New York and Oxford, UK: Oxford University Press.

Hall, E. (1990).*The hidden dimension*. New York: Doubleday/Anchor Books.

International Jerusalem Post. 10/11/02.

Jafri, J. G. (1998). *The portrayal of Muslim women in Canadian mainstream media: A community based analysis*. Toronto: Afghan Women's organization. Retrieved August 25, 2003, from *www.fmw.org/Articles%20and%20Presentations/ muslim%20women%20&%20media%20-report.PDF*

Los Angeles Times. 9/1/02; 9/10/02; 9/12/02; 9/27/02; 10/15/02; 10/28/02; 10/29/02; 11/11/02; 12/3/02; 12/5/02.

Lee, M. A., & Solomon, N. (1992). *Unreliable sources: A guide to detecting bias in news media*. Secaucus, NJ: Carol.

McClure, J. (1994). *Late imperial romance*. London: Verso.

Miami Herald. 9/12/02; 10/15/02.

Mignault, P. (1996). Pictures, packages and public trust: The seamless byline and instant TV. In V. Alia, B. Brennan, & B. Hoffmaster (Eds.), *Deadlines and diver-*

sity: Journalism ethics in a changing world (pp. 132–139). Halifax, Nova Scotia, Canada: Fernwood Publishing.

New York Times. 1/31/02; 3/1/02; 9/30/02; 12/11/02.

Plain Dealer. 7/12/02; 7/14/02; 8/9/02; 8/17/02; 8/20/02; 10/15/02; 10/17/02; 10/18/02; 10/22/02.

Russell, N. (1996). Lies, damned lies and journalism. In V. Alia, B. Brennan, & B. Hoffmaster, (Eds.), *Deadlines and diversity: Journalism ethics in a changing world* (pp. 30–38). Halifax, Nova Scotia, Canada: Fernwood.

Russell, N. (1994). *Morals and the media: Ethics in Canadian journalism.* Vancouver, Canada: University of British Columbia Press.

Said, E. (1981). *Covering Islam: How the media and experts determine how we see the rest of the world.* New York: Pantheon Books.

Shaheen, J. (2001). *Reel cool Arabs.* Northampton, MA: Interlink.

Siegel, A. (1983). *Politics and the media in Canada.* Toronto: McGraw-Hill Ryerson.

Stockton, R. (1994). Ethnic archetypes and the Arab image. In E. McCarus (Ed.), *The development of Arab–American identity* (pp. 119–153). Ann Arbor: University of Michigan Press.

Tomlinson, J. (1991). *Cultural imperialism: A critical introduction.* London: Printer.

USA Today. 4/5/02.

van Dijk, T. A. (1991). *Racism and the press.* London and New York: Routledge.

Washington Post. 10/14/02; 10/16/02; 10/17/02; 10/19/02; 12/10/02.

Wilkins, K. G. (1997). Middle Eastern women in Western eyes: A study of U.S. press photographs of Middle Eastern women. In Y. Kamalipour (Ed.), *The U.S. media and the Middle East: Image and perception* (pp. 50–61). Westport, CT: Greenwood Press.

Zurbrigg, J. (1995). *Unveiling portrayals of Muslim women: Examining texts on Saudi women.* Unpublished master's thesis, University of Western Ontario, Canada.

Index

About the Editors

Ghazi-Walid Falah is an associate professor in the Department of Geography and Planning, University of Akron, Ohio, and is editor-in-chief of *The Arab World Geographer*. His major areas of research include the political, social, and cultural geography of the Middle East, with a special focus on Palestine. His current research centers on Arab–American bilateral relations from the perspective of media discourse. His publications include two books in Arabic—*The Forgotten Palestinians* (1989) and *Galilee and Judaization Plans* (1993)—as well as book chapters and numerous articles in such journals as the *Annals of the Association of American Geographers*, *The Canadian Geographer, Transaction, Political Geography, Progress in Human Geography, Environment and Planning A, The Professional Geographer, Area*, and *Third World Quarterly*.

Caroline Nagel is a lecturer in human geography at Loughborough University in Leicestershire, United Kingdom. She received a PhD in 1998 from the University of Colorado, where she developed an interest in Arab and Muslim immigrant communities in Western countries. She is currently researching issues relating to citizenship and cultural identity among Arab Americans and British Arabs. She has a long-standing interest in theories of immigrant settlement and has published several scholarly articles on assimilation theory and immigrant transnationalism. She also has more general interests in urban geography and qualitative research methods.

Contributors

Naheed Gina Aaftaab is a master's candidate in the Department of Geography at the University of Washington. Her chapter is based on research done toward her thesis, entitled "Education as Development: A Case Study of Afghan Women." Her projects build upon fieldwork done in Herat, Afghanistan, in the summer of 2002. Ms. Aaftaab's next project will be to examine Muslim women's education in postcolonial India. She spent the 2003–2004 academic year in Lucknow, India, as a language fellow at the American Institute of Indian Studies.

Malek Abisaab is an instructor in the history department at McGill University, Montreal, Quebec. His article " 'Unruly' Workingwomen: Contesting French Colonialism and the National State in Lebanon, 1940–1946," appeared in *Journal of Women's History* (Fall 2004), and he coauthored "A Millennium after Qasim Amin: Past and Modern Uses of *Tahrir al-Mar'a* [The Liberation of Women]" (2000). He is currently working on a book on community and labor among tobacco workingwomen in Lebanon from the 1900s to the late 20th century.

Leila Ayari is a graduate of the Department of Geography at the University of Ottawa. She pursued her studies at the Faculty of Education at the University of Ottawa, where she is currently employed.

Marc Brosseau is an associate professor in the Department of Geography at the University of Ottawa. He was coeditor of *The Canadian Geographer* from 1999 to 2002, and is currently a member of its editorial board as well as that of *Social and Cultural Geography*. Dr. Brosseau is the author of several papers, book chapters, and a book, *Des romans-géographes* (1996). His research focuses on various aspects of social and cultural geography and, more specifically, on the relationship between geography and literature.

Diana K. Davis holds a PhD in geography from the University of California, Berkeley, and a DVM from Tufts University. She has conducted research with nomads in

335

Balochistan, Pakistan, and in southern Morocco. Her research and publications have focused on gender and indigenous knowledges as well as on the political ecology of pastoral resource use and environmental history. Dr. Davis is currently an assistant professor of geography and Middle East studies at the University of Texas at Austin and is completing a book on the environmental history of North Africa during the colonial period. Her research has been published in the *Journal of Arid Environments*, *Cultural Geographies*, the *Geographical Review*, the *Journal of North African Studies*, the *World Encyclopedia of Environmental History*, and elsewhere.

Ghazi-Walid Falah (see About the Editors).

Amy Freeman recently finished her PhD in geography at the University of Washington in Seattle. Her dissertation, titled *Contingent Modernity: Moroccan Women's Narratives in Postcolonial Perspective*, examines relational concepts of modernity from the viewpoint of Moroccan women's experiences in France and Morocco. Her research has focused on North African migrants in France and, more recently, on critiques of modernity and the construction of postcolonial gender identity in Morocco.

Sarah J. Halvorson is an assistant professor of geography and an active member of the Central Asia and Caspian Basin Program at the University of Montana. Her teaching interests include world regional geography, gender and development, water resources, and environmental hazards. Her chapter in this volume is part of her ongoing research on Muslim communities in the mountainous regions of South and Central Asia.

Robina Mohammad is currently a postdoctoral fellow in the South Asian Studies Programme at the National University of Singapore. Her research interests include political transformations and their impact on women in different national contexts and the marketing and consumption of the gendered, sexed body. Dr. Mohammad's current project is on the transnationalization of Bollywood (the Hindi film industry) to and beyond the South Asian diaspora.

Caroline Nagel (see About the Editors).

Abdi Ismail Samatar is a professor of geography and global studies at the University of Minnesota and is the author of three books on the state and development in Africa, as well as numerous articles. His book *An African Miracle: State and Class Leadership and Colonial Legacy in Botswana Development* (1999) was a finalist for the Herskovitz Prize of the African Studies Association. Currently, he is working on a two-volume publication on leadership and democracy in Africa.

Anna Secor is an assistant professor of geography at the University of Kentucky. Her recent publications have focused on gender, citizenship, and urban space in Istanbul. She is currently working on a project on everyday encounters with the state and civil society in Turkey.

Rachel Silvey is an assistant professor of geography at the University of Colorado at Boulder. Her research interests include gender and feminist geography, critical migration and development studies, social activism, Indonesia, and Islam. Her work has appeared in the *Annals of the Association of American Geographers; Political Geography; Progress in Human Geography; Gender, Place and Culture;* and *World Development.* She currently serves as a member of the Social Science Research Council's Working Group on Gender and International Migration. As a Fulbright New Century Scholar for 2004–2005, Dr. Silvey is focusing her research specifically on gender and Islam among Indonesia–U.S. transnational migrants.

Susanne H. Steinmann specializes in the geographic subfields of cultural and political ecology and feminist perspectives. She combines these approaches in her research in Morocco and North Africa on the themes of gender and resources management, agricultural intensification, economic development, and international labor migration. Dr. Steinmann lived in Morocco for 4 years, where she taught in a public high school, worked as development consultant, and conducted extensive field research toward her master's and PhD degrees. Her work challenges geographers to include and empower local people in the process of research and community development. Dr. Steinmann teaches in the geography department and international studies program at Portland State University in Oregon.